EX LIBRES

Joyce Nelms-Matzke
'83

EUROPEAN COSTUME

4000 Years of Fashion

EUROPEAN COSTUME

4000 Years of Fashion

Doreen Yarwood

Bonanza Books
New York

This 1982 edition is published by Bonanza Books,
distributed by Crown Publishers, Inc., by arrangement with
Larousse & Co., Inc.

Manufactured in the United States of America

Library of Congress Cataloging in Publication Data

Yarwood, Doreen.
  European costume.

  Reprint. Originally published: New York:
Larousse, 1975.
  Bibliography: p.
  Includes index.
  1. Costume—Europe—History.   I. Title.
GT720.Y37 1982   391′.0094   82-1215
ISBN 0-517-37739-X   AACR2
h g f e d c b a

Contents

costume; England; western and central Europe; central and eastern Europe; southern Europe; northern Europe; notes to the illustrations.

Chapter Eight
The Nineteenth Century: Internationalism

Introduction; French dominance in dress; textiles; haute couture; ready-made clothes; department stores; fashion plates and journals; men's costume 1800–1850; men's dress 1850–1900; outdoor wear; hair and hats; footwear; neckwear and linen; women's dress 1800–1820; women's dress 1820–1850; women's dress 1850–1870; women's dress 1870–1890; women's dress 1890–1900; children's costume; notes to the illustrations.

Chapter Nine
The Modern World: 1900–1975

Introduction; 1900–1920; 1920–1945; 1945–1975; man-made fibres; clothes for the young, notes to the illustrations.

Preface

The aim of this book is to describe, as straight-forwardly as possible, the story of the development of fashionable dress in Europe from prehistoric times until the present day. There is no attempt to discuss regional or national costume nor to deal fully with influences which impinged upon Europe from outside, such as the Ottoman Empire or Tartar invasions.

The purpose of the text is to give a broad outline of the trends and relate these to the various historical and social developments which were mirrored in the dress of the day and nation. The illustrations have been designed pictorially and in groups to present the maximum possible number of examples in the space available and these should provide adequate detailed information to complement the text. The drawings have all been made carefully from original costume sources and students wishing to have the data on fabrics, colours, names of garments and source of the material, may consult the comprehensive notes provided at the end of each chapter.

I have travelled extensively in Europe to gather source material for the illustrations, which have been made from sketches and notes which I executed on the spot in the museums and galleries of the different countries. I am deeply grateful for the generous assistance which I received everywhere from museum and gallery staffs. In particular, I would like to express my appreciation to Mlle. Madeleine Delpierre, Conservateur of the Musée du Costume de la Ville de Paris, Mlle. Yvonne Deslandres, Directeur of the Centre d'Enseignement et de Documentation du Costume in Paris, Miss de Jong, Curator of the Kostuummuseum at the Hague, Mr. Duyvetter, Keeper of the Costume Department at the Netherlands Openluchtmuseum in Arnhem, Dr. Elisabeth Houtzager, Director of the Centraal Museum at Utrecht, Dr. Georg Himmelheber of the Bayerische Nationalmuseum, Munich, Dr. Ludwig B. Döry of the Historisches Museum at Frankfurt-am-Main, Dr. Dénes Radocsay, Director of the Museum of Decorative Arts in Budapest, Dr. F. Fülep, Director General of the National Hungarian Museum at Budapest, Miss Pilar Tomas, Director of the Rocamora Costume Museum in Barcelona, Mrs. Nieves de Hoyos Sancho, Conservadbra of the Museo del Pueblo Español in Madrid, Miss Anna-Maja Nylén, Head Keeper of Dept. 111, Textiles and Costume at the Nordiska Museet, Stockholm, Miss Gudrun Ekstrand of the Royal Armoury, Stockholm, Miss Elisabeth Munksgaard, Assistant Keeper at the National Museum, Copenhagen, Miss Gundmund Boesen from the Royal Danish Collection at Rosenborg Palace in Copenhagen, Mrs. B. M. Ginsburg of The Textiles Dept. and the library staff of the Victoria and Albert Museum, London, and Mr. J. P. Asselberghs, Keeper of Textiles at the Musées Royaux d'Art et d'Histoire in Brussels. I should also like to thank Miss Constance Waight and Mrs Elizabeth Bangham for typing the manuscript.

Doreen Yarwood

Chapter One

The Classical World:
Greece and Rome 1700 BC to AD 1300

Introduction

Why do we wear clothes? The first reaction to this question might be that the answer is obvious. We wear clothes to keep warm and for reasons of modesty. But this confines the whole subject within too narrow limits.

Costume, by which we mean fashion in dress since man first wore garments which he had made as opposed to animal skins, is a more complex matter than merely 'clothes'. The reasons behind the designs of costume worn by differing peoples in succeeding centuries are manifold and reflect the fundamental characteristics of the nature of man since, in his attire, he displays his personality: individual and collective.

Clearly, the question of climate is vital to a study of the subject. In equatorial regions man, from earliest times until the twentieth century, has worn little but a loin-cloth, or a garment discreetly but definitively described by the French as a *cache-sexe*, and for women, little more than beads. In northern Europe, on the other hand, clothes which cover the body and give extra warmth in winter have always been necessary. But, in prehistoric times, such warmth was provided by animal furs, and such attire could hardly be designated as costume. Thus, neither the need for warmth nor modesty has acted as a basis for costume in the fashion sense. For this we must look towards other, no less fundamental, needs and instincts of the human race, needs which differentiate humanity from the animal kingdom. Such needs might aptly be grouped under the headings of religious, social, political, military, professional and erotic.

Religion has always exercised a vital influence on the conduct of man, and dress reflects this. Partly it has been seen in the emulation, in dress, of the current deity and partly, and more widespread, in the taboos which constrain the dress of the individual members of the community. Examples of this are to be seen in the covering of the arms to below the wrists in Medieval attire

as well as a discreet hiding of the legs and feet. This might be accompanied paradoxically and contemporaneously by décolleté necklines as in the fifteenth and sixteenth centuries.

Socially, fashion has been of paramount importance. It has provided a demonstration in the wearing of a rich decorative dress by the outstanding members of the community. This has often created a paradox in that the wealthy, influential member of society adopts a costume which will make him stand out against the common herd. At the same time, everyone wishes to copy the fashion, whether in the fourteenth century or in the 1970s. As everyone does so, it becomes necessary for the man or woman of importance to adopt another style in order to be different. This is a common factor in all ages and the basis for the need for sumptuary laws in the Middle Ages. The factor which varies is that by which members or nations in society set the fashions. This is discussed more fully in relevant chapters.

Political influence on fashion has similar bases. The monarch or dictator must adopt a differential dress and generally one which is ostentatious and displays wealth. This is seen in innumerable European portraits. In more recent times, the revolutionary leader, on the other hand, endeavouring to display his allegiance to the proletariat, spuriously adopts the ideals in dress based on that worn by the common man. The fact that the common man, given his own desire, would wear the clothes of his social betters, is ignored or uncomprehended. Notable modern examples of this are of leaders in French, Russian and Chinese revolutionary periods.

Costume worn by professional, academic, legal and military bodies is often based on a dress of an earlier age. Examples include barristers, the Yeomen warders of the Tower of London, the Vatican Swiss Guards, the university professor. This type of dress comprises a separate subject and books devoted to it are available.

1   2   3   4

There remains the erotic characteristic in the history of dress. This is a fundamental one, its importance in costume a reflection of its vital function in the life of mankind. Sexuality has been of prime importance in the dress of all ages; illustrating the desire of the male to impress the female and vice versa. Innumerable examples can be quoted: notable are the bare breasts of Cretan dress and Elizabethan England; the accenting of male genitals in the later Middle Ages with contemporary stress on the clean-limbed form; the artificial slendering of the feminine waist in eighteenth- and nineteenth-century designs; the deliberate denuding of garments in the First Empire and Regency with the wearing of gossamer materials and revealing of the feminine form and the mini-skirts of the mid-twentieth century with the contemporary revealingly fitted trousers of the young male.

An instinctive need of mankind is for change and a new aspect. This is apparent in all the arts and current dress fashion is related to it, forming an integral creative element in the pattern of the aesthetic side of life. Dominant centres of fashion which have initiated changes have varied throughout the ages; the influence of such centres has been dependent on wealth and power at the time. In the fifteenth century such a centre was Burgundy, quickly to be displaced by Italy with its new Renaissance forms. Later, in the sixteenth century, came the German and Swiss designs followed, in the second half of the century, by the dominance of Spain. Early seventeenth century fashion centres were in the Netherlands but after 1650 the prime influence became France, a dominance which she has largely held ever since apart from the field of masculine tailoring whose centre became London. This is the simple outline of the fashion story. The more complex events behind it are described in relevant chapters. Inevitably, fashion has followed power and wealth.

Minoan and Mycenaean Dress 1700–500 BC

Western culture stems from the Aegean peoples and more specifically from the island of Crete, which was inhabited from about 6000 BC onwards, though the traces of civilisation which have been found date from the Neolithic Age at about 3400–3000 BC. Settlers came to the island from a number of areas further east, particularly from North Africa, Syria, Asia Minor and Palestine.

5   6   7   8

By the advent of the Bronze Age in the Aegean, which began about 2500 BC, the Cretan civilisation was developing and, partly due to the origins of its people and partly to extensive maritime trade, it was strongly influenced by the cultures of Egypt and Babylon.

The Cretans evolved from these an original culture of their own, their art forms displaying vitality and spontaneity and their way of life equally rich and unconventional. They became adept at producing fine quality pottery, metal work in bronze, copper and gold, jewellery and woven textiles which they exported extensively to the eastern Mediterranean. Their first period of expansion developed by 2100 BC. There was then a temporary decline which, in turn, led to the second and greatest time of prosperity and quality of work between 1750 and 1400 BC. It was in these years that Cretan civilisation rose to a high level comparable with the contemporary Egyptian and Babylonian ones. This was the time of the great palace of Minos at Knossos.

Knossos, situated near the northern coast of the island of Crete, was the site of several palaces. The first Bronze Age palace was built on an earlier neolithic settlement mound from about 1900 BC.

A new *Palace of Minos* arose there after the earlier one had been destroyed by earthquake about 1600 BC. The later palace, whose ruins were explored and excavated by Sir Arthur Evans from 1900 and are those chiefly visible today, are the remains surviving from the destruction of the palace about 1400 BC. It is from this palace that we take the name Minoan to designate the culture. Mainly from here, from the contemporary Cretan palaces at Phaistos and Mallia, from the later Mycenaean citadel-palaces of Tiryns and Mycenae in the Peloponnese and the recent excavations of the Minoan city on the Aegean island of Thera,* we can gain a clear picture of Minoan and Mycenaean dress over the centuries. Figures in costume are shown on wall frescoes, paintings on vases and other vessels and in sculptured statuettes in marble, terracotta and coloured faience. Good examples can be studied in, especially, the museums at Heraklion (near Knossos) and Athens. From these, the desire of the Minoans for richness of dress in colour,

---

* The Minoan city on the island of Thera (Santorin) was destroyed about 1500 BC by volcanic eruption. Excavation at present continuing has yielded some exceptionally fine miniature friezes of fresco paintings which vividly depict scenes from Minoan life: seascapes, ships and ports, fishing, diving and war.

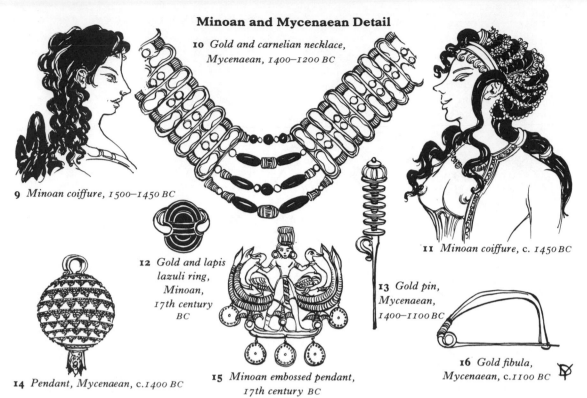

Minoan and Mycenaean Detail

9 *Minoan coiffure, 1500–1450 BC*

10 *Gold and carnelian necklace, Mycenaean, 1400–1200 BC*

11 *Minoan coiffure, c. 1450 BC*

12 *Gold and lapis lazuli ring, Minoan, 17th century BC*

13 *Gold pin, Mycenaean, 1400–1100 BC*

14 *Pendant, Mycenaean, c.1400 BC*

15 *Minoan embossed pendant, 17th century BC*

16 *Gold fibula, Mycenaean, c.1100 BC*

materials and jewelled decoration together with the tremendous variety of design in their costume, is clear. We can also see the important part played by women in the day-to-day life of Minoan society and the elegance and gaiety of their dress shown side-by-side with their menfolk, not enclosed and herded into feminine enclaves as was typical of other societies of the time.

The originality and attractiveness of Minoan dress and the high quality of their jewellery and enrichments, evidence of the wealth and sophistication of this culture, was increasingly copied elsewhere in the Aegean and even further afield by countries bordering the Black Sea and eastern Mediterranean. The Cretans conquered the Cyclades and penetrated to Greece and Cyprus, advancing as far as Syria. Their style of dress was adopted either intact or was merged with the designs currently worn in those areas. Trade and contact with countries on the eastern shores of the Mediterranean in turn influenced Cretan dress which increasingly displayed eastern features.

The Cretans had occupied the Peloponnese but here the Mycenaean civilisation evolved and, in turn, became more powerful and later destroyed centres in Crete. The Dorian invasions of about 1200–1000 BC completed the destruction in Crete and the Cretans became refugees taking their

civilisation eastwards. There was a final revival of Cretan art in the ninth to seventh centuries BC but, after this, its influence declined and was eclipsed by the rise of Hellenic Greece.

Men's Costume

Men wore few, simple garments but maintained an elegant appearance and a fastidious care of hair and bodies. All men, whether of noble or lowly birth, wore a *loin-cloth* tightly belted at the waist. The material and style of this loin-cloth varied according to the wealth of the wearer. The garment could be of harsh wool or leather but elegant men wore loin-cloths of soft linen arranged like a short skirt, formed in a point at the back (**2**), or with a point in front, weighted and finished by a triangular net of pearls or beads (**4**). The metal-decorated leather waist belt tightly constricted the waist, as in women's dress, to contrast with the broad masculine chest or full feminine breasts.

This was the Cretan style of loin-cloth; on the mainland it was more often styled like short trousers with a piece of material passed between the legs and fastened to the belt back and front. Some Cretan illustrations show longer, broad trousers, extending to the knees. The torso and legs were generally bare though, for warmth in winter, short *cloaks* of wool were worn, decorated with fringed edges or fur. They were fastened with silver or bronze pins.

Men were often bare headed but wore their *hair* very long and looped, braided and tied in varied ways on the top of the head or down the back. They shaved facial hair and bathed frequently, carefully oiling their bodies afterwards. They were conscious of the importance of maintaining a fine masculine physique, though elegant and slim. Head coverings, if worn, were wide-brimmed *hats* like the Greek petasos or, more commonly, skin caps or turbans.

Both sexes went barefoot indoors. Out-of-doors men wore *sandals* with leather thongs at the ankle, *shoes* or, in winter, calf-length *boots* in light coloured leather.

Women's dress

Before 1750 BC women also wore the loin-cloth, designed as a short skirt, with the upper part of the body unclothed. After this a longer *skirt* was usual, of ground or ankle-length and a tight-fitting jacket or *bodice* with elbow-length sleeves, still leaving the breasts bare. In the later Minoan period a metal *corset** acted as a foundation for the costume and a boned bodice on top supported and accentuated the bare breasts with lacing beneath them. The waist belt was tightly drawn, with rolled edges or in the form of a girdle wound twice round the slenderised waist. The skirt was designed in flounces which, in later years, dipped in the centre front at each level like the masculine loin-cloth (**5, 7**). These skirts were stiffened to a bell-shape by bands sewn at intervals into the garment. This resembled the sixteenth-century farthingale but it appears that the Cretan bands were inserted into the skirt itself, not an underskirt.

The whole Cretan feminine costume was characterised by vivid, rich colouring and elaborate, refined decoration, giving an impression of splendour and luxury. The skirts, in particular, presented a harmony of brilliant reds, purples, yellows and blues. Metal plates (like shingles) and embroidery were incorporated. The garments were elaborate, sewn and fitted to the figure, quite unlike either the draped classical Greek dress or the swathed eastern Mediterranean ones. Cretan costume was original, advanced, unique.

* This is the first recorded use of metal for corseting and restriction of the feminine figure.

22   23   24   25   26

All kinds of decoration were used, from fringing, ornamental aprons (back and front), embroidered banding, pleating, flouncing and inset panels (**1, 3, 5, 6, 7**).

Under the separate skirt and bodice Cretan women wore a *shift* with the corset and, probably, a simple loin cloth also. For warmth out-of-doors they wore capes or *cloaks*, the latter often having a high collar. Their footwear resembled that of the men.

The *hair* was long and carefully dressed in spiral curls and ringlets in front and falling on to the breasts and neck. The rest of the hair was often dressed high at the back, held in place by ribbons, flowers and jewels (**11**). It then hung in a pony tail from this style of coiffure (**5**). Alternatively, it hung loose or was braided. Metal hairpins were used (**3, 6, 7, 9**). *Headdresses* varied from tall, cone-shaped hats (**3, 6**) to metal fillets, turbans, caps, berets and ribbon and plume decoration (**1, 5, 7**).

Textiles had been woven and spun in Crete from early times. Spinning and weaving were family industries, undertaken in the home. Equipment used in these processes – spindles, distaffs, bobbins, carding combs etc. – have been

found in quantity, though the fabrics have not survived. Dyeing was carried out on a national scale and reached a high standard. Pigments were obtained from plant and sea life. Embroidered decoration was richly colourful and finely executed; jewels were incorporated into the designs. Motifs especially used were the spiral (as in Egypt), the trellis and the lozenge.

Cretan women, their men also, loved *jewellery* and jewelled enrichment, and indulged this desire. They wore several bracelets on each arm, necklaces in rows with pendants, finger rings, earrings, pearl ropes in the hair and decorative metal waist belts. Gold, bronze and silver were used while Mycenaean costume specialised in gold-work. The metals were set off with precious and semi-precious stones, the cutting and polishing of which was a high art in Crete. Particularly they employed amethyst, agate, cornelian, jasper, porphyry and lapis lazuli. In quality the Minoan work is the finer despite the greater use of gold by the Mycenaean peoples. Some beautiful examples of both cultures are on display in the British Museum in London and the National Museum in Athens (**10, 12, 13, 14, 15, 16**).

Greek Classical Dress. Sixth to Second Century BC

This style of Hellenic costume is in total contrast to the Minoan and Mycenaean dress just described. It is a draped costume; one in which there is little sewing, the garments for both sexes being similar and consisting of rectangular sheets of material of different fabrics and sizes which are pinned on the shoulders, draped in a myriad ways and are held to the body only by girdles. The dress is of the utmost simplicity in basis but of the greatest variety in method of wearing. There is no artificiality of silhouette in corseting or padding and no stiffening in the materials. The lines are entirely natural but sophisticated. The garments lend themselves to adaptation satisfactory to the personal taste of each individual. The only aids to draping are pins (fibula), girdles and weights for the hems and corners. There is a close affinity between the costume of the Greeks and their art and architecture. In all three modes of expression the basis is simple but the handling of the style requires precision and experience to reach perfection.

Clearly there was no sudden transition from the brightly coloured, artificially shaped and fitted erotic costume of the Minoans to the purer, natural line of Hellenic Greece. For a long time the different civilisations in mainland and island Greece, together with Asia Minor and North Africa, had co-existed, the costume of each influencing the others. Classical dress was the outcome by the sixth century BC. It had developed chiefly from the primitive Dorian styles and was then refined by Ionian influence.

The Dorians invaded the Minoan kingdoms in Crete and in the Peloponnese from about 1200 BC. They were a northern race from Illyria and a people more primitive than the Minoans whom they displaced. Our knowledge of their costume, though imperfect, shows it to be simple and crude. Garments were of woollen cloth, made from the mountain sheep of the region from which they came. These garments were pinned on the shoulder and wrapped round the body.

Later, the dress of the mainland peoples was influenced by those in Asia Minor, who lived in more extreme temperatures and who introduced cloaks with hoods, the Phrygian cap with a point on top, the wide-brimmed hat and banded leg coverings. Certain aspects of Cretan dress, which was still worn by the Cretan peoples now living further east, were also incorporated.

Later still, a new culture established itself in Greece which was called Ionian. These peoples were much less primitive than the Dorians. They developed a quality textile industry in wools and linen, making fine materials which were suited to a draped costume. In the eighth and seventh centuries BC they extended their contacts by trade and emigration all round the Mediterranean to Sicily, Egypt, Libya, Asia Minor and as far west as Gaul, slowly establishing colonies. The great period of the Greek culture was the fifth to fourth century BC, when the superb quality of their work in the arts was achieved in architecture, sculpture and literature. Naturally, this quality extended to costume, which can be studied in detail from many sources, but especially painted vases and sculpture in its varied forms. The draped modes of this period had evolved from the multiplicity of sources in the eastern Mediterranean to become one of the most elegant styles of dress of all time, at once natural, simple yet sophisticated.

The introduction of fine linens led to the pleating of material as well as simple draping. The rectangular piece of fabric was set into the required pleats, then twisted and tied at each end to maintain it in position for several hours. The use of a thin starch and then to allow the fabric to dry in the sun assisted in the longer maintenance of the pleats when the garment was worn. This treatment was most common for the feminine long tunic (**22, 28**).

Not a great deal is known about the colours of Greek dress. Neither sculpture nor vases (which are in white, black and red) give information. There are only literary references to guide us and the knowledge that buildings and ornament were originally brightly painted, so it is reasonable to believe, that in a country with brilliant Mediterranean sunlight, costume would have been coloured also. From literary sources we have references to white, yellow, red, different shades of mauve and purple, green, black, grey and golden brown. We also read of patterns and borders of flowers, stripes, circles and lozenges. Cloaks appear to have been in darker colours, tunics light.

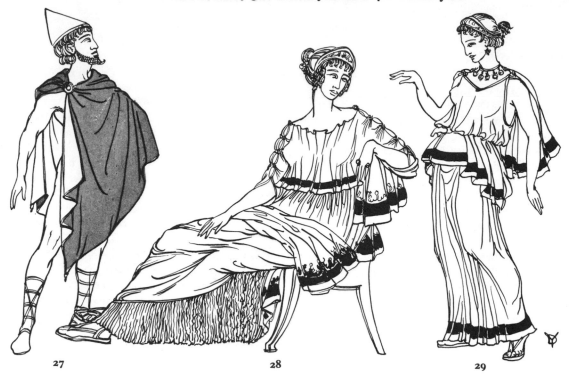

27   28   29

Men's Dress

The clothes worn by men and women were almost the same except that the masculine tunic was usually knee-length and the feminine one reached the ankles or the ground. Early garments were simple rectangles of wool, fastened on one or both shoulders by a fibula so that the material hung loose, ungirded. Sometimes the garment was sewn at one side and left open at the other. Men of action wore it pinned on one shoulder only to give freedom of movement.

There were two forms of cloak or wrap; the *chlamys*, of Dorian origin, which was of dark wool and often pinned on the right shoulder to leave the right arm free (**17, 18, 19, 23, 27**) and the *himation*, which was larger and usually worn draped over the left shoulder and round the body. In earlier days, this was the sole garment. It is also often seen in sculpture draped in this manner as the attire of the later period and for philosophers and statesmen (**20, 26**). Both cloaks were often weighted at the corners to assist draping and to hold them down in inclement weather.

Later, the usual garment was the *chiton*, of Ionian origin, first made of wool and later of thinner materials in linen and cotton. Earlier examples were sleeveless with the rectangles of material hanging back and front and simply caught on one or both shoulders, then girded. The girdle was frequently double with one belt round the waist and a lower one encircling the hips with the fabric bloused in between. For men, this garment reached the knees (**17, 18, 19, 23**); for women, it was long and generally seamed at one or both sides, below the waist (**24, 25, 29, 32**).

Later still, the chiton was adapted to provide elbow-length sleeves by the use of wider rectangles of material which were pinned with fibulae at intervals between shoulder and elbow. Men wore this style particularly for ceremonial use with an ankle-length chiton (**21, 22, 25, 26, 28, 33**).

Women's Dress

The actual garments, that is the rectangular pieces of material, were like those of the men but women wore longer garments and draped them rather differently. The feminine equivalent of the simple, loose Dorian tunic was the *peplos*. This was made of two pieces of fabric, pinned on each shoulder and hanging loose to the ankles. In later years, a ground-length chiton, like the masculine design, was worn and, on top of this, a peplos which could hang loose to just below the waist or could be longer and enclosed by the waist girdle (**24, 29, 32**). Later still, as in masculine dress, the chiton or peplos was caught by several fibulae between shoulder and elbow to form sleeves (**22, 25, 28, 33**).

Over this long tunic women wore a cloak, like the masculine himation which they draped round the body in different ways and part of it was often used to drape over the head (**22, 30, 31**). A thinner version of this, of linen, was called a *pharos*.

In the later centuries of the Hellenic age finer fabrics were introduced as a result of Alexander the Great's conquests of the late fourth century in India. To the fine linens were added cotton and silk. These delicate fabrics were excellent for pleating and draping.

Knowledge of *undergarments* worn is inadequate. Sculpture does not show these so we must rely upon literary sources which refer to a band of linen (a girdle) wound round the waist and stomach to control the figure, also a similar breast band. At the same time, a band, like a tape or ribbon, could be worn on top of the chiton to support and delineate the breasts.

Men took great care of their *hair*, dressing and decorating it. In the early years it was grown long but later, generally, hair was short; at first curled all over the head (**17**), then a band or plait encircled the head and the hair was longer but still curled (**21, 23, 36, 36, 44, 47**). The natural colour of the hair was dark but fair hair, being unusual, was admired and bleach was used to make it blond. Pomades, essences and perfume were liberally applied to give sheen and scent. Beards were common until the time of Alexander. These were carefully curled (**19, 20, 27, 36, 47**).

Greek men were usually bare-headed, *hats* being kept for use in cold, wet weather. When worn the most common designs were the *petasos*, with a brim and a ribbon to allow it to hang round the neck and down the back (**17**), the *pilos*, a brim-less cap (**19**), a helmet shape (**18**), the truncated cone of Egyptian origin (**27**) and the *Phrygian cap* (from Asia Minor) of Scythian influence (**58**). Most of these styles were made of felt, wool or fur.

Women's hair was long. It might be curled on the forehead and the sides (**24, 28, 33**) or parted in the centre and drawn back in waves to a chignon at the nape. Hair was fastened by bone, ivory or gold wire pins. Many styles were held in place by a fillet or diadem with a veil attached. The back hair was then dressed high (**24, 25, 28, 29, 33, 34**). Many women wore wigs and false pieces to alter the colour and form of their coiffure. They then added flowers, jewels, metal cauls and tiaras. Women rarely wore head covering since they were not expected to frequent public places. They generally draped the head in the cloak (**22**) and, for travelling, as in the Tanagra statuettes, wore the Boeotian straw hats perched on top (**30, 31**).

The most usual *footwear* for both sexes was the sandal. This was of leather designed with delicate straps and soles, exposing most of the foot. Many examples are to be seen in Greek sculpture (**20, 23, 38, 40, 41**). Footwear was usually removed indoors. Men also wore mid-calf buskins or longer boots. Both styles were generally laced up the front and might be fur-lined. Soles were shaped to the foot (**17, 18**).

Greek women loved *jewellery* which, in later periods especially, was worn in abundance. After 450 BC, with the defeat of the Persians, gold was available once more in quantity and filigree and enamel work of high quality was to be seen. In the later fourth century BC the work in gold was of masterly quality in items such as wreaths of leaves to wear round the brow, spiral earrings, pendants, sculptural reliefs in diadems, spectacle brooches as well as traditional fibulae, finger rings and hair-pins. Bronze mirrors were particularly intricate and decorative (**35, 37, 39, 42, 43, 45, 46, 48, 49, 50**).

Both sexes wore perfume and used body lotions, oil and cream. Perfume sprays were available. Ladies used extensive make-up to add brilliance to the eyes, lashes and cheeks.

The Etruscans: Eighth to Third Century BC

These peoples, who inhabited central Italy in the area between the Po and the Tiber from the eighth century BC, are still something of a mystery to historians. Tuscany, the centre of their culture, takes its name from them. Despite the archaeological discoveries which are being made year by year and which throw more light upon the Etruscan culture, little is known of their origins and their language has yet to be interpre-

30   31   32   33

ted. Certainly, the civilisation appears to have developed quickly and extensively so that, by about 700 BC, the Etruscans were living in fine cities, with wealthy citizens, creating buildings of high standard and displaying a mastery in the visual arts.

It appears certain that the Etruscans were not indigenous to Italy; their artistic work and dress show strong eastern Mediterranean influence. We have a clear picture of much of the pattern of their lives and what they looked like. The Etruscans constructed their burial places outside the cities and built the tombs with utmost care so that many examples have been discovered to be intact. In such a necropolis, tombs vary in size and elaboration but many display extensive wall paintings and sculpture; they are furnished with all the household equipment used in life from furniture to armour and kitchen pots and pans.

From this evidence, as well as written accounts from Roman historians, we are shown a cheerful, vigorous people with a zest for enjoyment of all that life had to offer, as well as a deep appreciation of a life after death. They loved music, dancing and athletics, feasting and banquets. They appreciated comfort, luxury and wealth; were

fine artists and artisans, creating beautiful furniture, utensils, ornaments and jewellery particularly in metal, ceramic, terracotta and ivory.

Etruscan society appears to have had much more in common with the Minoan than the Greek or the later Roman. This is particularly so in relation to the position of women and the life that they led. Greek and Roman women were expected to spend their lives in the home, ministering to the desires of their men, remaining discreetly in the background of life. Etruscan women, like the Minoan, shared all the activities of their men. In frescoes they are depicted taking full part at banquets, dances, concerts and attending racing, athletics and contests of all kinds. They were a force in Etruscan society, not overtly in their own right, but more subtly through their menfolk; they seem to have been mistresses of the concept of 'the power behind the throne'.

Etruscan dress as shown in the painted frescoes, terracotta and metal statuettes, as well as lifesize sculpture, also seems to share many features with Minoan costume, while retaining some similarities to the Greek style. We cannot be definitive about the origins of their design of dress but the influences which bore upon it were

Greek Jewellery and Detail, 700–100 BC

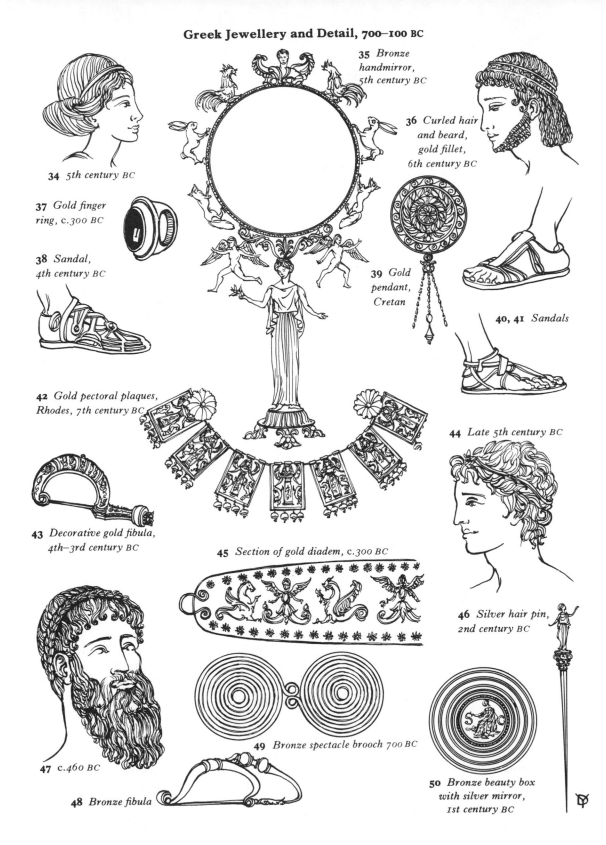

34 *5th century* BC

35 *Bronze handmirror, 5th century* BC

36 *Curled hair and beard, gold fillet, 6th century* BC

37 *Gold finger ring, c.300 BC*

38 *Sandal, 4th century* BC

39 *Gold pendant, Cretan*

40, 41 *Sandals*

42 *Gold pectoral plaques, Rhodes, 7th century* BC

43 *Decorative gold fibula, 4th–3rd century* BC

44 *Late 5th century* BC

45 *Section of gold diadem, c.300 BC*

46 *Silver hair pin, 2nd century* BC

47 *c.460 BC*

48 *Bronze fibula*

49 *Bronze spectacle brooch 700 BC*

50 *Bronze beauty box with silver mirror, 1st century* BC

51   52   53   54   55

clearly varied. Their garments are shown frequently to be sewn and fitted like Cretan ones. There are further affinities like the bright exotic colouring, rich decoration and abundance of jewellery. Again, many figures are illustrated in draped costume, pinned at the shoulders and falling in Grecian-type folds. There is also a type of toga, presaging the Roman garment and decorative collars which ante-date the Byzantine ornament of this type. Etruscan style in dress displays a marriage between eastern and western themes, blending eastern features from Egypt, Syria and Crete with a later, Ionian flavour gained possibly from the contemporary Greek colonists in southern Italy.

Men's Dress

The *tunic*, corresponding to the Greek chiton, is shown in several forms; often it is knee- or calf-length, sewn and fitted (**57, 59**). It also appears as a double-girded, knee-length garment, full, then pinned on the shoulders or sewn with sleeves (**58**). Older men are shown with an ankle-length tunic, probably finely pleated in the Greek manner, which was the usual wear for ceremonial dress (**54**). Again, a Grecian draped garment is to be seen,

pinned on one or both shoulders and falling in complex folds to the knees or calves (**55, 56**). Some men, for action or sport, are attired in a short-sleeved tunic with a loin-cloth or short trousers (**51**).

Several types of *cloak* were worn, either semi-circular or rectangular in shape. Some resembled the Greek *chlamys* (**57, 58, 59**), while others were more like the Persian *kandys*, with wide sleeves falling from the shoulder (**54**). Another, though small in the earlier period, developed into a larger garment worn rather like the Greek *himation*. The fabric, however, was more often cut as a semi-circle and the later method of draping it is similar to the Roman toga, which it ante-dates. It is usually referred to as the *tebenna* (**61**).

Women's Dress

The *gowns* or tunics were long and, especially in the earlier years, sewn and fitted to the figure. They were made in brightly coloured fabrics which were decorated by patterned borders at neck, sleeve and hem giving an oriental appearance. Sleeve styles were mostly elbow-length, either fitted or widely flaring at the bottom. The gowns usually hugged the breasts and hips but the lower part could be stiffened or flounced and was often pleated. In later years a more Grecian style of draped *chiton* was often to be seen. Sleeves were then made pinning the material with fibulae from shoulder to elbow.

The *cloak* was rectangular or semi-circular. The rectangular one was draped like a Greek himation or wound simply round the body. Sometimes it was draped over the head as well. Cloaks were of strongly-coloured fabric (red was a common shade) with richly ornamented borders with corners often weighted (**52, 53, 60, 62, 63**).

Footwear was similar for both sexes. Especially in the earlier years it was oriental in design. Shoes could be low cut or high like ankle boots and laced across the fronts. Both styles had upturned points at the toes. They were of cloth or leather, gaily coloured in red, green and brown (**52, 53, 54, 59, 60, 61, 62, 65**). Boots were also worn, reaching to mid-calf or higher. These were generally fastened by straps round the ankle or front lacing (**51, 55**). In later years, sandals made their appearance; light-weight with slender straps (**57**).

Hair styles for both sexes were complex and changing. Great care and attention was given to the coiffure which was frequently dyed. *Men* wore their hair short or long, and usually curled. Long styles were arranged to hang loosely curled or in ringlets on the shoulders. Later, a fillet was worn round the brow. Many men had curled, short beards but moustaches were rare (**51, 54, 55, 56, 57, 59, 61, 74**). *Women* dressed their hair in corkscrew curls on the forehead and temples, with the rest of the hair long, either confined in a net at the nape, hanging loose down the back or in plaits or ringlets over the shoulders and back. An alternative mode was a centre parting with hair waved back at the sides. The coiffure was controlled and ornamented by ivory or metal pins, fillets, ribbons and plumes (**52, 53, 62, 73**).

Both sexes were bare-headed most of the time. In bad weather men wore the *petasos* style of hat while women draped the cloak over the head (**60**). Both sexes also wore a conical-shaped hat with roll brim. This was an oriental style referred to as a *tutulus* (**63, 70**).

The quality of Etruscan *jewellery* is very high and it was worn in abundance. Early work is technically very fine and of great variety of design; it compares favourably with Greek workmanship of similar date. The Etruscans specialised in the decorative process known as granulation, where

56   57   58   59

Etruscan Dress, 6th–4th Century BC

60   61   62   63

gold powder is disposed in patterns on the surface of the metal. They portrayed scenes in granulated silhouettes showing figures and background; alternatively, the figures were in relief and the ground was granulated. They also developed a delicate style of filigree work in gold, using open-work patterns without a background – a superb technical achievement. Towards the end of the seventh century, they introduced inlay and enamelling, developing both techniques to a high standard. Late Etruscan jewellery, after 400 BC, is different. It is sparingly decorated and commonly sheet gold is used in convex sheets, patterns being embossed or in delicate leaf form for wreaths, necklaces and bracelets. Bronze was also worked to a high degree of perfection. All kinds of jewelled items were made and used: finger rings, earrings, bracelets, necklaces and pendants, fibulae and hand mirrors (**64, 67, 68, 69, 71, 76**). Typical of Etruscan design is the earring shown in **66**, known as a 'baule' type. This Italian word is used because it resembles a trunk or case. It is made of a strip of gold bent to a cylindrical shape and closed by a disc at either end.

Roman Dress: Second Century BC to Fifth Century AD

The Roman Republic evolved from the tribal kingdoms which were first set up in central Italy in the eighth century BC. After 500 BC the republic was established and expanded, absorbing the adjacent peoples and countryside. Area by area the country of Italy became a vassal state to the City of Rome. The Etruscans were absorbed, the Sicilians, then Carthage and North Africa and, in 146 BC Greece also became a part of the Roman Republic. This was only the beginning. In 30 BC Egypt was absorbed and soon western Europe extending to most of Britain. For 400 years after this the Romans enslaved, organised and civilised the peoples of the compass of their known world, extending all round the Mediterranean from Spain to the Black Sea and from Britain to Egypt.

The republic was severely shaken in 44 BC by the murder of Julius Caesar. The years of un-certainty and unrest were resolved when the republic developed into an empire with Augustus as its first Emperor in 27 BC. From this time, until

Etruscan Detail and Jewellery, 7th–3rd Century BC

64 *Bronze mirror, with incised decoration from Vulci, 4th–3rd century BC*

65 *Ladies shoe, 7th century BC*

66 *'Baule' type earring, Chiusi, 6th century BC*

67 *Gold earring, 4th–3rd century BC*

68 *Gold finger ring*

69 *Gold pendant necklace, 400–250 BC*

72 *Cerveteri, 6th century BC*

70

73

74 *Caere, 7th century BC*

71 *Gold ivy wreath, 3rd century BC*

75 *Ivory comb, with relief decoration, 7th century BC*

76 *Gold fibula with ducklings, 7th century BC*

15

77   78   79   80   81

AD 476 when the western empire collapsed, the Roman Empire was ruler and pace-setter to the known western world.

The story of costume under the direction of Rome is almost identical to the history of all the visual arts, architecture and crafts. The Romans inherited their designs from the Greeks. They continued in the same mode but the pattern slowly altered, becoming a mutation. The basis of design remained the same. What altered was the treatment and adaptation of the forms. In costume, as in art, the Roman version is more ornate, richly coloured, more varied and, under later Imperial Rome, most elaborate.

In dress this process was characterised by a more extensive use of ornament and jewellery, rich colours, the wearing of a greater number of garments, one on top of the others, the frequent bathing and changing of clothes during the course of the day and the introduction of richer fabrics. These materials were introduced as a result of the extension of the boundaries of empire and consequent expansion of trading relations. Cottons from India and silks from the east were freely available to the wealthy. They appeared in a wide range of colours and were then enriched further by beautiful embroidery, ornamental braid and fringing. Heliogabalus (218–222 AD) was the first Roman emperor to wear silk. Much later, looms were set up to weave silk but the raw material still had to be imported from the east. Roman ladies developed the art of embroidery to a high degree. They used coloured wools intermixed with gold thread.

Men's Dress

The most characteristic and important item of Roman clothing was the *toga*. In Republican Rome, especially in the earlier years, it was the chief garment, worn directly on top of the loincloth underwear. In Imperial Rome, emperors and other important persons wore knee-length trousers instead under their togas; these were called *femoralia*. The toga soon became the mark of the Roman citizen, who alone was permitted to wear it. A slave might not don a toga though a freed man was allowed to do so.

The toga began by having a similar function to the Greek himation in that it was a large cloak wrapped around the body in a variety of ways according to the personality and inclination of the wearer, and that it was draped, having no fastenings or pins. It differed only in that, instead of being rectangular in shape, it was a segment of a circle. It was partly this difference in shape which led to the later complex and prescribed methods of draping. It was also a much larger piece of material, being about 18 feet in length along the chord of the segment and about five and a half feet at its greatest width. Usually made of wool, it was thus a heavy, unwieldly garment to handle and, in draping, might require the assistance of another person. The most usual method of draping in general use from about the second century BC onwards is shown in **77** and **83F**. Here, some five feet of the straight edge of the fabric is placed against the centre vertical line of the front of the body, with the extreme end at the feet and the curved edge to the left, outer side. The rest of the material, some 13 feet, is thrown over the left shoulder, passed loosely round the back, under the right arm and once again partly over the left shoulder but partly also over the left arm where the second

end hangs loose. The portion of cloth on the chest from the first layer is then pulled out a little to form folds which drape over the second layer. When desired, the looser material at the back can be pulled up to give covering on the head. Draped in this and similar ways, the *toga* is depicted in innumerable figure sculptures.

The toga acted as a denoter of rank within the Roman citizenry. White was worn by tribunes – the *toga pura*; purple* was reserved for the emperor, who may also have had his decorated in gold. Those worn by magistrates and certain other ranks (*toga praetexta*) were characterised by a band of purple woven into the cloth along the chord of the material. Under the Empire the wearing of a toga was reserved more and more for ceremonial use by important personages. The garment was of fine wool and later silk and enriched with panels, bands of coloured and gold embroidery. As its general use declined, the materials became richer and the methods of draping more complex.

By the second century AD ordinary citizens had

* Purple was the symbol of power. The Latin word *purpura*, from which stems the English purple, was the name of certain molluscs from which a dye of this colour was obtained.

82 The Peristyle of a Roman House, 1st–2nd Century AD

abandoned the toga and turned to other, easier-to-handle types of cloak. In Rome, out-of-doors, it was the wearing of a cloak or mantle which distinguished a citizen from other people. There was a variety of designs to choose from. The *paludamentum* and the *sagum* were military cloaks, the former worn by officers, the latter by the ordinary soldier. Civilian cloaks were mostly similar to the Greek chlamys. One of these was the *paenula*, a heavy, cloth garment with an attached hood which was open down the front and reached to the calves. It was usually in dark shades of grey, brown, black or purple. The *abolla* and *lacerna* were also like the chlamys, and with a hood, pinned in front or on the shoulder and hanging to the knees or calves (**79, 82E, 83B**).

The *pallium* was also adopted instead of the toga. It was more like the Greek himation, being smaller and a rectangular piece of material worn draped round the body with no fastenings. It

could also be pulled up on to the head. In the later years of the Empire the material was folded lengthwise so that it resembled a long scarf; it was then draped round the shoulders, the ends hanging in front and worn on top of another cloak. In this manner its evolution can be traced through the Byzantine and later civilisations to become, eventually, a church vestment.

Indoors, the basic masculine garment was the *tunica*, made of wool or linen and almost identical with the Greek chiton. It was girded, often double-girded, at waist and hip, and reached the knees. It consisted of two rectangular pieces of material sewn at the sides and either pinned or sewn on the shoulders. Some designs were sleeveness, others had short sleeves which were cut in one with the garment, not inset (**79, 82D, 83B**). Again, colours indicated the rank and position of the wearer. Upper classes wore white, ordinary men natural or brown.

Under the Empire, especially in later years, it was customary to wear more than one tunica. Three might be worn, the one nearest to the body being of fine linen and acting as an undergarment in conjunction with the linen loin-cloth which had always been part of Roman underwear. Important citizens, especially on ceremonial occasions began, in the third century AD, to wear ankle-length tunicas on top of the shorter ones. Such a garment was called a tunica *talaris*. Also a tunica with wide sleeves appeared known as the *dalmatica*; it had been introduced about 190 AD from Dalmatia and was worn loose, without girdle, reaching to calf- or ankle-level. It was often distinguished by vertical stripes (*clavi*), which extended from shoulder to hem on each side. The tunica was worn underneath (**104, 106**).

Women's Dress

Feminine Roman costume was closely modelled on the Greek, the Roman *stola* being like the Greek chiton and the equivalent to the masculine tunica. In the Imperial period the stola was of wool, cotton or silk; it had more material in the width than the Greek prototype. Ladies of rank wore it very long, forming a train at the back. Circling under the breasts, and sometimes the hips as well, were beautiful jewelled or embroidered girdles. The garment was usually richly embroidered and sometimes fringed. Fine pleating was often employed, especially for the train. Generally the stola was sleeved, either with sewn seams or pinned at intervals in the Greek manner. Fashionable colours included yellow, greyish-blue, white, red and green.

Under the stola women wore one or more tunics. These were similar but sleeveless and often of wool. Under these, next to the skin, were worn a fitted loin-cloth, like briefs and a linen or wool breast-band, called the *mamillare*. An additional or alternative support to the breasts could be provided by the *strophium* which was a long, narrow piece of material wound round the torso on top of the underwear linen tunic. Sometimes a stomach-band or girdle was also worn to control the figure. Our information about underwear comes from written sources but mosaics, such as the example from the Piazza Armerina villa in Sicily, depict women dressed for gymnastics in a bra and briefs rather like a modern, strapless bikini (**96B**).

The feminine equivalent of the masculine toga or pallium was the *palla*, a large rectangular piece of material like the Greek prototype. This was brightly coloured and embroidered on fine wool. It could be draped or, commonly, folded lengthwise and pinned on each shoulder by a fibula. The toilette of an elegant woman was completed by a shoulder cape or scarf, a fan and a handkerchief, (**78, 80, 81, 82A, B, F, 83C, D, E, G, H**). Slaves carried long handled fans and umbrellas.

It is interesting that Roman brides wore orange-yellow veils (the *flammeum*), not white ones, but, in the later Imperial period, they carried orange blossom amongst herbal flowers; the custom, surviving today in the Christian Church, was possibly adopted in Rome after the Empire had embraced Christianity.

Children, who are depicted in both sculpture and paintings, are dressed just as adults (**82C, 83A**).

Roman *footwear* was based on Greek designs but was more varied, several styles of shoe and boot being available. Customs too differed; the Greeks generally went barefoot in the house, Romans rarely did so, regarding the wearing of footwear a mark of class distinction. In the street *men* wore the *calceus*, a shoe which was laced at the ankle (**77**). Wearing of the calceus was reserved for Roman citizens; as with other garments, its colour denoted the rank of the wearer, black or white for senators, for example. Other shoes, mainly cut away and fastened with thongs or straps were worn by the rest of the community. Some were primitive, being simply a piece of hide wrapped round the foot and laced up by thongs on the instep. In these there was no difference between left and right shoe; the calceus was shaped to the foot like the Greek models. In the later Imperial period, shoes for the wealthy were in coloured leather decorated with jewelled embroidery.

Roman men also wore *boots*. Some designs were mid-calf length, laced up the front (**79**); others, like the *cothurnes* were longer, shaped to the foot and laced all the way up. These could be fur-lined and decorated with the animals' paws or tail hanging over the top. In the house a man usually wore sandals which had leather soles and straps of leather or cord (**89, 91**).

Women wore sandals or slippers in the house. The sandal was called a *solea* and the light shoe, for indoors or out, was the *socca*. In the street, women of rank also wore the calceus. All these designs were coloured and often embroidered.

Both sexes gave great care and attention to their hair and complexion and spent a great deal of time on their toilette, bathing, perfuming their hair, bodies and attire as well as applying cosmetics to the face. The many barbers' shops did a good trade, washing, cutting and dressing the *masculine coiffure*. Hair styles in the early Imperial period were short, arranged in studied naturalness of curls brushed forward over the forehead (**84, 86**). Later, hair was worn longer in curled, artificially crimped manner (**85**). Men were mostly clean-shaven from the second century BC until about the second century AD when beards became fashionable, worn chiefly by younger men; older men, finding their beards turning grey, shaved them off. The short, trendy beard and sideboards were very much the sign of virility in Roman society. Long beards were adopted by academics and philosophers (**84, 85, 97**).

Like the men, ladies used *perfume* abundantly on their person and their clothes. They used *cosmetics* widely: powder, rouge, eye-shadow and black tints for the lashes. Veins were touched lightly in blue to emphasise them and beauty patches were applied to the face.

Under the Republic, ladies dressed their *hair* simply, in Greek styles, most commonly with a centre parting and a chignon at the nape. In Imperial Rome styles became more complex. The coiffure was dressed in a mass of curls on top in front or in rows of waves and was drawn back to ringlets and or braided plaits. After a time, noble women adopted such complicated coiffures that they required the daily attentions of several slaves and a stylist to dress it. The hair style was augmented by switches and pads, it was dyed or covered by a wig and it was held in place by nets, combs, pins and pomade. Different colours of hair were currently fashion; sometimes black was in demand, red was usually favoured, while blonde was in vogue during the Gallic and Teuton campaigns. This fashion was spread by the use of wigs made from the hair of captured slaves (**82A, B, 83G, H, 92, 93, 95, 99**).

The feminine coiffure was such a feature of the toilette that a lady needed little further head covering. In any case, like the Greeks, Roman ladies did not often go out. They enclosed part of the hair in gold or silver nets with pearls or bound it in a scarf or band. Sometimes they wore veils or draped the folds of the palla over the head (**78, 80, 81, 82B, F, 83C, D**).

Men went bareheaded for most of the time. Hoods were worn, attached to the cloak like a *cucullus* or separate. There was a hat like the Greek petasos and a close fitting cap, the *galerius* or the *pileus*, based on the Greek pilos.

Under the Republic, the wearing of *jewellery* was frowned upon and restricted. There are consequently not many examples surviving and these are based entirely on Etruscan and Greek designs. From the time of Augustus onwards, the Roman love of jewellery was permitted to have full play. Designs were still derivative, based on Hellenic Greece, and the quality of workmanship was less fine. As the Empire was extended a greater elaboration and richness became apparent; pieces were heavier, there was an abundant use of gold and precious and semi-precious stones: sapphires, emeralds, aquamarines, opals and even diamonds, though these last were not cut. A great quantity of jewellery was worn by both sexes, particularly finger rings (more than one on a finger), fibulae and bracelets. Women also adorned themselves freely with necklaces and pendants, anklets, fillets on the hair and earrings. Late Imperial jewellery presages the richness and quantity of Byzantine ornament (**87, 88, 90, 94, 96, 98, 100**).

Byzantine Dress: Fifth–Fifteenth Century

The Roman Emperor Constantine, impressed with the strategic situation of the Greek city of Byzantium, commanding the waters between east and west of the Mediterranean and the Black Sea, transferred the Imperial seat of government there in AD 330. He began the building of a great new city which he called New Rome. Later in the century, the Roman Empire was divided into two parts, eastern and western. After the fall of Rome in the fifth century, the eastern part ruled alone. Byzantium was renamed Constantinople (now Istanbul) after its first Christian Emperor and remained the capital of a vast polyglot empire till its capitulation to Mohammedanism in 1453.

Because of its geographical position between the east and the west, Byzantine culture, throughout the eleven centuries of its domination, was always a complex mixture of influences from

Roman Detail and Jewellery, 27 BC to 4th Century AD

84 *Emperor Nero, AD 54–69*

85 *Emperor Septimius Severus, AD 192–211*

86 *Emperor Augustus, 27 BC to AD 14*

89 *Leather sandal*

88 *Gold bracelet from Petrijanec, 4th century AD*

90 *Gold earring with turquoises and garnets, 3rd century AD*

87 *Gold necklace set with precious stones, 1st century AD*

91 *Sandal, Imperial Rome*

92 *Lady's coiffure, 69–96 AD*

93 *Child's coiffure, 2nd century AD*

94 *Gold ring set with beryl*

96 *Bronze fibula from Yugoslavia, 1st–3rd century AD*

95 *Coiffure, AD 217*

97 *AD 218–222*

99 *Coiffure of teen-age girl, 1st century AD*

100 *Bronze fibula from Hungary, 1st–3rd century AD*

98 *Gold fibula from Ravenna, 1st century AD*

101, 102 *10th–11th century*　　　　　　**103, 104** Temp. *Justinian* c.530–40

both sources. The results of this blending are nowhere more striking than in costume. In the first few centuries, the influence of Rome was still strong and draped styles of costume predominated in the cut of the dress. The fabrics and decoration were, from the beginning, strongly eastern and, slowly, the eastern style of costume began to assert itself in the form of trousers, footwear, headcoverings and, above all, decoration and jewellery.

During the long reign of the Byzantine Empire there were two periods of especial brilliance and prosperity when the dominance and influence of Constantinople were paramount. The first of these was under the Emperor Justinian in the sixth century AD and the second was from the ninth to the thirteenth centuries. In the former period the influence of Rome was strong, in the latter, Byzantine dress showed more features of Persian, Assyrian, Egyptian and Anatolian designs. The Byzantine Empire was immensely wealthy, due largely to its extensive commercial trade with east and west. The trade routes extended from Scandinavia and Russia to Armenia and Ethiopia. Luxury fabrics and jewels flowed into Constantinople and costume attained a

richness of colour, fabric and ornament which far exceeded that of the great days of Rome. This wealth, allied to the Oriental and Arabic craftsmanship and love of richness, produced the most dazzling attire, envied and copied by the rest of the known world.

The chief feature which characterised Byzantine dress was the beauty of the fabrics from which it was made. The development of the textile industry was responsible not only for the costly magnificence of the dress but its quality of stiffness and luminosity. These fabrics introduced into being a new kind of cut which displayed them to advantage; the draped, full attire of the Greeks and Romans, so suited to wool and linen, gave way to the simple, straight garments, without folds, giving a stiff, more formal appearance, at once hieratic and dignified. The quality of Byzantine fabrics stemmed from the beautiful woven patterns and from the extensive use of silk. The designs were floral and geometrical, the predominant motifs being circles, palmettes, all kinds of flowers and leaves, incorporating mythological, dramatic animals and birds. Imperial dress was characterised by a preponderance of purple and gold. In the ninth and tenth centuries, the garments of the well-to-do were especially vivid in reds, violets, gold, yellow and green. The influence of Saracenic, Syrian and Egyptian imported textiles spread to the Byzantine workshops, illustrated in the types of woven and embroidered patterns. Caravans from the Far East brought even more exotic, beautiful fabrics and these too were studied and copied.

The overwhelming feature which created the stiff, shimmering quality of Byzantine costume was the extensive use of silk which had been imported by both Greece and Rome at fabulous cost. Thus silk had always been a rarity, prized but reserved only for the Court and the very rich. It was the Emperor Justinian who introduced the manufacture of silk to Constantinople, thus making its use more widespread.

The silkworm was a native of China and the industry originated there in remote times. The Chinese guarded their secret of the manufacture for over 3000 years, retaining their monopoly and exporting the finished fabric as well as the raw silk to a world which prized this beautiful fabric and would pay exorbitantly for it. The Japanese finally acquired knowledge of the process via Korea in the third century AD and silk manufact-

ure became an important Japanese industry. Much earlier than this, silkworm culture and silk manufacture had been established in India in the valley of the Brahmaputra river and later, across the delta, in that of the Ganges. Knowledge of the process had spread overland from China and from India it was passed westward to Persia and central Asia.

The first mention in western literature was by Aristotle who described a great, horned worm which changed into a caterpillar and then into a chrysalis. He described the spinning of the thread and referred to the fact that it was first spun on the island of Cos. His knowledge was inaccurate but certainly raw silk was imported into Cos before Aristotle's time and woven into fabric.

The Emperor Justinian tried, in vain, to divert the silk trade from its route from Persia into eastern Europe soon after he came to the throne in 527. A greater prize than he had dreamed of came within his reach when, not long afterwards, two Persian monks, who had worked as missionaries in China and while there had studied the complete process of silkworm culture and silk weaving, came to Justinian and offered him their knowledge and some silkworm eggs in exchange

105, 106 *6th century*   **107** *13th–14th century*   **108** *6th century*

Byzantine Dress

A   B   C   D   E   F   G

for a large monetary reward. Justinian accepted. The monks returned to China and, with the eggs concealed in a hollow bamboo tube, they brought them to Justinian in 550. From these eggs were produced the strains and varieties which have yielded the quantities of silk used by Western Europe ever since.

The silkworms flourished in Constantinople. The Byzantine Empire, like China before it, kept secret the process and monopolised the silk industry in Europe. The factories there turned out some of the most magnificent silks ever produced, woven with gold and silver threads in coloured figured and plain fabrics. Branch factories were set up outside Constantinople at Athens, Corinth and Thebes but the Imperial capital retained the silkworms.

Inevitably knowledge of silkworm culture and silk manufacture percolated to Western Europe but it took many centuries before the secrets escaped from Constantinople. The Saracens learnt the process and took their knowledge eastwards and westwards. Trade and manufacture were established in the eleventh and twelfth centuries in Asia Minor and Sicily. From here it spread to the north Italian cities and in 1480 Louis XI began silk weaving at Tours, while in 1530 Francis I brought silkworm eggs from Milan and reared them in the Rhône valley. In England, silk manufacture was first introduced on a small scale in the late sixteenth century when Flemish weavers emigrated there because of the struggles with Spain. But it was the revocation of the Edict of Nantes which brought the French Huguenots flooding into Spitalfields in London to set up their silk looms as well as in Germany and Switzerland.

The dress of the Imperial Court is well documented and illustrations of it in glowing colour can be seen in numerous church mosaics. The attire of Justinian and his queen, Theodora, with their retinue, is vividly presented in the wall mosaics of the Church of S. Vitale in Ravenna in Italy. They are illustrated in **109** with a background of the contemporary nearby Church of S. Apollinare in Classe. The Emperor (**109D**) wears a straight, long-sleeved tunic, girded low in the waist and decorated with panels of embroidery. The cloak, fastened on the right shoulder by a fibula, displays the ornamental *tablion* in front. This rectangular piece of jewel-encrusted material was inset and proclaimed the wearer to be a member of the royal house or a· court dignitary. The Empress Theodora (**109E**) is similarly attired, though her tunic is long, and she wears round her shoulders the characteristic Byzantine deep collar. This, the *maniakis*, a separate collar of fabric embroidered in gold and encrusted with jewels, was of Persian derivation and also denoted the royal blood of the wearer.

The dress of these two figures, as well as their retinue (**109A, B, C, F, G**) already shows the changes in dress from the Roman model. In Byzantine costume, the limbs are always covered; sleeves extend to the wrist for both sexes. The *tunic* or stola, now made of silk-based fabrics, is loose-fitting but not draped. It hangs straight, girded only at the waist and its stiffer, plainer form admirably displays the richness of the fabric. Women's gowns were often patterned all over, though both sexes wore garments ornamented with panels and roundels of decoration applied to the material. Men's tunics were knee- or ankle-length; women's reached the ankle or below. The masculine *cloak* was generally fastened on the shoulder. Ladies wore a palla which was draped around the shoulders, and when needed, over the head also. In the fifth and sixth centuries, both men and women still wore the *dalmatica*, with loose, long sleeves and clavi decoration; a cloak was draped on top (**104, 106**).

Byzantine dress became richer and more glittering as time passed, glowing like the wall mosaics in the churches. In the second period of prosperity in the ninth to the thirteenth century, the colours were deep and strong with an extensive use of violets and reds. Materials were of silks, embroidered in gold and silver and encrusted with jewels and pearls. Imperial dress included a long panel of material, with gold, jewelled embroidery, like a scarf tied round the body, its ends hanging loose (**101, 102, 107**).

There was also a noticeable infiltration into dress of an eastern influence and the classical line had disappeared. For example, the straight loose *caftan*, an Oriental garment since ancient times and more recently, in military use in Persia, was adapted by Byzantium into a gracious, formal item of attire. The caftan form is the basis of a coat, as opposed to a tunic, in that it has a fitted back and is open all the way down the front. *Trousers* were generally worn by both sexes. They hugged the leg, like the hose of more western countries but Byzantine trousers were more elegantly cut and often had one or more jewelled, embroidered bands running vertically down the back and/or front of the limb. These trousers were then tucked into high boots or worn over shoes (**103**).

Conversely, Byzantine dress had a considerable influence upon the costume of eastern Europe. This was especially so in southern Russia and in the Balkans, where the formal, richly be-jewelled attire in stiff, encrusted silks became an integral part of the vestments of the Church as well as the lay aristocracy. The knee-length or ankle-length tunic, worn over tight trousers tucked into high boots, and covered by a fur-collared caftan, worn loose or belted, established in such countries as Bulgaria and Turkey, became the staple dress for centuries. In turn, with the westward advance of the Ottoman Empire after 1453, these styles of dress, at least for men, were brought to countries in central Europe – Hungary, Poland, Czechoslovakia – and became part of the traditional costume till the nineteenth century.

The leather boot, in black or colours was normal *footwear* for men. At court, red leather was most usual, embroidered and with pearls. Sandals were still worn but more usual for ladies and for general indoor use were the soft, ankle-clinging shoes with pointed toes. These were brightly coloured and decorated in gold and jewelled embroidery (**101, 102, 103, 104, 109D, G**).

Men were often bareheaded or wore the Phrygian cap (**103**) or a hood. *Ladies* encased their hair in a silk cap or a pearl net and this could be accompanied by a veil (**105**). Imperial headdresses, for both sexes, were heavily be-jewelled. Pendant chains hung from the royal diadem on each side of the face in Oriental fashion. The ladies' coiffure was enclosed in a jewelled silk coif with the diadem on top, decorated with aigrette or a star (**101, 102, 108, 112, 113**).

Elaborate jewellery of all kinds was worn, particularly in gold and pearls (**110, 111, 114**).

Pearls were also used in all embroideries and as edging to collars, mantles and hems. Perfumes were liberally applied and handkerchiefs were carried, as in Rome.

111 *Gold earring, 7th century*

110 *Gold earring with pearls, emeralds and sapphires,* c.600

112 *Emperor Justinian, 6th century*

114 *Gilt bronze earring, 7th–8th century*

113 *Empress Theodora, 6th century*

Byzantine Detail and Jewellery, 6th–8th Century AD

Notes on the Illustrations

1 Snake goddess from Knossos *c.*1600 BC. Faience statuette, Heraklion Museum, Crete. Jewelled turban headdress in black and white. Tight-fitting dark bodice and waist-band. Ornamental apron. Pleated, tiered skirt.

2 Fresco of the Priest-King, Knossos, *c.*1500 BC. Heraklion Museum, Crete. Crown with plumes in red and blue. White and red belt with blue roll above. Blue loin-cloth and white apron, bordered in red. Bracelet and necklace.

3 Faience figure in colour, Knossos, *c.*1600 BC. Brown headdress, fawn and brown bodice, white skirt with brown lines and border, grey apron.

4 Fresco of the vase-bearer, Knossos, *c.*1500 BC. Heraklion Museum, Crete. White loin-cloth and apron with blue bead net hanging in triangular form.

5 Fresco from the palace of Tiryns, Greece. Mycenaean. National Museum, Athens. *c.*1400 BC. Woman carrying a toilet box. Restoration. Present colours: red bodice with blue, black and gold border and belt. Orange apron. Multi-coloured skirt in white, red, orange, blue and black.

6 Goddess, marble statuette, late Minoan. Fitzwilliam Museum, Cambridge, England. Tall headdress. Fitted bodice. Patterned apron over pleated, tiered skirt.

7 Snake goddess, statuette in gold and ivory. *c.*1600 BC. Boston Museum of Fine Arts, U.S.A. Fitted bodice and tight waist belt. Tiered skirt with dipped points in front.

8 The lady of Auxerre. Limestone statue. Seventh century BC. Found in France, probably made in Crete. Louvre, Paris. Hair dressed like a wig. Narrow waist. Fringed, decorated skirt.

9 'La Parisienne'. Fresco, Knossos, 1500–1450 BC. Heraklion Museum, Crete. Black hair in ringlets. Bow to dress at the back.

10 Gold and carnelian necklace, 1400–1200 BC. Mycenaean. British Museum, London.

11 Coiffure with pearls, bands and ribbons over ringleted hair. Fresco, Knossos *c.*1450 BC. Heraklion Museum, Crete.

12 Minoan finger ring. British Museum, London.

13 Mycenaean pin in gold with blue head. About two inches long. British Museum, London.

14 Mycenaean pendant from Cyprus. Granulated pomegranate form. British Museum, London.

15 Minoan pendant illustrating the nature-god standing on a field with lotuses and holding a water bird in each hand. Egyptian influence. British Museum, London.

16 Gold fibula, Mycenaean. British Museum, London.

17 and 18 Relief sculpture, fifth century BC. Louvre, Paris. Both figures wear the double-girded chiton and the chlamys. 17 has a petasos slung at the back of his shoulders, 18 wears a pilos-shaped helmet. 17 wears boots and 18 has tall guards with boots.

19 Horseman, Parthenon frieze, c.440 BC. British Museum, London. Chiton fastened on left shoulder only, chlamys pinned in front. Leather topped boots. Cap.

20 Relief sculpture, fifth century BC Louvre, Paris. The himation and sandals.

21 The Charioteer, Delphi Museum, Greece, c.470 BC. Long chiton for ceremonial wear. Hair band.

22 Fourth century BC statue, Louvre, Paris. Pleated chiton, himation.

23 Relief sculpture, Parthenon frieze, c.440 BC. Chlamys and double-girded chiton, sandals.

24 Roman copy of Greek statue of fifth century BC. Museo Nazionale, Rome. Girded peplos.

25 Roman copy of Greek statue of fifth century BC. Museo Capitoline, Rome. Ungirded peplos.

26 Fourth century BC statue, National Museum, Athens. Man in long chiton with himation on top.

27 Statue, early fifth century BC Louvre, Paris. Chlamys, felt cap, shoes and leg bands.

28 Roman statue in Greek dress of fifth century BC. Musco Capitoline, Rome. Pleated chiton, himation.

29 Fourth century Greek vase. Ashmolean Museum, Oxford, England. Girded peplos.

30 and 31 Tanagra terracotta statuettes (from Boeotia), 300–200 BC. 30 from Louvre, Paris, 31 from British Museum, London.

32 Ungirded peplos taken from caryatid figures of south porch of the Erechtheion, Athens also statue in Museo Capitoline, Rome. Fifth century BC.

33 Statue, Temple of Artemis, Ephesos, c.340 BC. British Museum, London. Chiton and himation.

34 Greek bust, fifth century BC. Museo Nazionale, Rome.

35 Bronze hand mirror, fifth century BC. Louvre, Paris. About 21 inches high.

36 Head of Greek horseman, sixth century BC Louvre, Paris.

37 Finger ring, British Museum, London.

38, 40 and 41 Sandals from Greek statues. British Museum, London and Louvre, Paris.

39 Pendant from Crete. About two and a half inches high. British Museum, London.

42 Pectoral plaques. British Museum, London.

43 Gold fibula. Kunsthistorisches Museum, Vienna.

44 Greek head in bronze. Louvre, Paris.

45 Diadem, about 21 inches long in total. British Museum, London.

46 Silver hairpin. Louvre, Paris.

47 Bronze statue of Poseidon. Archaeological Museum, Athens.

48 Bronze fibula, Louvre, Paris.

49 Bronze spectacle brooch, British Museum, London.

50 Lid of beauty box. Louvre, Paris.

51 Mural frieze, late sixth century from Cerveteri (Caere), Louvre, Paris. In red, black and white.

52 Bronze statuette, 510–500 BC from Naples. British Museum, London.

53 As 51. Mantle, gown and pleated undergown.

54 As 51. Long, pleated tunic with cloak. Older man.

55 Male statue, late sixth century BC. Museo di Villa Giulia, Rome.

56 Female statue of goddess, late sixth century BC. Museo di Villa Giulia, Rome.

57 Wall painting from tomb of the Leopards, 470 BC in National Museum, Tarquinia. Tunic, cloak and sandals. White garments with blue and red stripes.

58 Sculpture, Vatican Museum, Rome. Chiton with long sleeves, double-girded, cloak, banded leggings, shoes, Phrygian cap.

59 Wall painting from tomb of the wishes, Tarquinia, 550–500 BC. White, long tunic, black and red cloak, black shoes.

60 Fresco, National Museum, Naples. Fifth century BC. Bordered cloak on pattern of tebenna worn over tunic.

61 Male tebenna with fringed decoration. Bronze sculpture. Private collection.

62 Terracotta statuette. Museo di Villa Giulia, Rome. In black and red on white chiton with long draped peplos.

63 Bronze statuette and bronze engraving, c.300 BC, British Museum, London.

64 Bronze mirror from the necropolis 'dell' Osterie', near Vulci, fourth to third century BC. Museo di Villa Giulia, Rome.

65 Lady's shoe from the sarcophagus 'degli Sposi', 540–30 BC, Cerveteri. Museo di Villa Giulia, Rome.

66 'Baule' earring, three-quarters of an inch in length. British Museum, London.

67 Earring, two inches deep, British Museum, London.

68 Finger ring, 400–250 BC. British Museum, London.

69 Necklace, 400–250 BC. British Museum, London.

70 Terracotta, Museo di Villa Giulia, Rome.

71 Ivy wreath, British Museum, London.

72 and 74 As 65 and in Louvre, Paris.

73 Sculpture, Vatican Museum, Rome.

75 Ivory comb, seventh century BC. Museo Archeologico, Florence.

76 Gold fibula, as 75.

77 Marble figure, second century AD. Museo Arqueologico Nacional, Madrid. Tunic and toga. Calcei.

78 Relief sculpture from Roman sarcophogus. Museo Nazionale, Rome. Long tunic, pleated, palla draped on top.

79 Wall painting from Pompeii, National Museum, Naples. Tunic and chlamys. Short boots.

80 Statue, Museo Capitoline, Rome. Palla used as a headcovering.

81 Similar example from Museo Nazionale, Rome.

82A Terracotta statuette AD 20, British Museum, London.

   B and C Mother and child statue group, Museo Nazionale, Rome.

   D and E Chlamys and Tunic, Trajan Column, Rome, AD 114.

   F Statue, mid-first century AD Louvre, Paris.

83A and B Wall painting from Pompeii, first century AD. National Museum, Naples. Chlamys and tunic.

   C and D Pompeian women from frescoes.

   E Roman empress, statue, National Museum, Naples.

   F Emperor Tiberius in toga. Statue, Louvre, Paris.

   G Statue, Museo Nazionale, Rome.

   H Livia, wife of Augustus, 56–29 BC. Statue, Louvre, Paris.

84 Bust, Emperor Nero, Museo Capitoline, Rome.

85 Bust, Emperor Septimius Severus, as 84.

86 Bronze head of Emperor Augustus. Museo Arqueologico Nacional, Madrid.

87 Necklace, British Museum, London.

88 Bracelet, Kunsthistorisches Museum, Vienna.

89 Sandal, Roman sculpture.

90 Earring, British Museum, London.

91 Sandal, Roman sculpture.

92 Sculpture, Museo Capitoline, Rome.

93 Child's head in sculpture, Museo Nazionale, Rome.

94 Finger ring, British Museum, London.
95 Bust, Museo Capitoline, Rome.

96 Fibula, Kunsthistorisches Museum, Vienna.

97 Bust, Museo Capitoline, Rome.

98 Fibula, two and three-quarters of an inch long. British Museum, London.

99 Bust, Museo Nazionale, Rome.

100 Fibula, Kunsthistorisches Museum, Vienna.

101 and 102 Emperor Romanos and his wife Eudoxia from an ivory relief on the cover of a gospel book from Besançon. National Library, Paris.

103 and 104 Nave arcade mosaics, church of S. Apollinare Nuovo, Ravenna, Italy. 103 has a red cap, tunic and shoes, a dark grey cloak with gold edge and red and gold collar and light grey patterned trousers. 104 is dressed in a white dalmatica with gold, decorated clavi and white cloak.

105 One of the procession of virgins. Mosaic of same date in the same church as 103. A richly decorated gold gown with jewelled belt and collar worn over a white undergown. White fringed palla. Red shoes.

106 Apse vault mosaic, church of S. Vitale, Ravenna, 526–47. Dalmatica with clavi and cloak.

107 Saint Eudoxia in marble with inset stones. Museum, Istanbul.

108 Empress Ariadne in ivory. Museo Nazionale, Florence.

109A, B, C, F, G From mosaic panels of retinue of Queen Theodora in the Church of S. Vitale, Ravenna.

   A Has white tunic and cloak, purple tablion and tunic decoration. Black and white shoes.

   B In dark blue gown with multi-coloured clavi, a palla in light pattern and silk coif.

   C In a palla of gold and red and a gown of white and blue. Gold headdress.

   F Has a white, patterned palla and a fawn gown with blue and gold decoration. Silk coif.

   G In a gold cloth cloak.
109D Is the Emperor Justinian in a purple cloak with gold, red and green patterned tablion. His tunic is white with gold decoration, his trousers purple and shoes red.

   E Is the Empress Theodora in a purple cloak with jewelled gold collar and gold ornament at the hem. Her gown is white with decoration in gold, green and red.

110 Earring, about four inches long. British Museum, London.

111 and 114 Earrings. British Museum, London.

112 Emperor Justinian. Mosaic. Church of S. Vitale, Ravenna.

113 Empress Theodora, Mosaic, S. Vitale.

Chapter Two

The Dress of Non-classical Europe
10,000 BC to AD 1340

Prehistoric and Primitive peoples

The picture of how these different peoples of Europe dressed and lived is still incomplete. Actual garments have only survived in a few instances. From these it is clear what certain peoples wore at a given period but it is conjectural how long such clothes were the mode and whether they were also adopted in areas distant from where they were found. Modern scientific methods of handling and analysing the fibres of surviving garments have provided extensive knowledge of the materials themselves and the method of weaving, dyeing, decoration etc.

The majority of finds from primitive Europe before the coming of Christ are of more durable materials – metals, bone, ivory, ceramics – and these are generally in the form of jewellery, decorative fastenings and arms. Often such items are found far from their place of origin since they were used for barter and exchange along the extended trade routes from the Stone Age onwards. These routes followed great distances from the Mediterranean to places as far away as Scandinavia, Britain and the north Baltic coast to the Iberian Peninsular and the Black Sea. Doubtless more perishable materials such as garments of fur or wool were traded in the same manner.

In the *Stone Age* clothing consisted largely of furs and hides, at first held in place round the body by a rough thong belt, later sewn or pinned at the shoulders and sides. Actual garments have not survived from these times but we possess necklaces, bracelets and armlets of beads, animals' teeth and fish vertebrae, amber and ivory as well as reindeer horn plaques and boxwood and bone combs. Finds from tombs and living sites of the later Stone Age show us that these peoples knew how to dress skins for clothing, weave simple garments, work leather and sew.

Dating of the advent of the *Bronze Age* varies in different parts of Europe; this indicates a state of knowledge reached rather than a general period of time. The art of bronze working spread to Italy from the near East then westwards to Britain, Scandinavia and the Iberian Peninsula. With the development of this knowledge, craftsmanship became more skilled, not only in bronze articles, but in other metals – gold and silver, for instance – as well as amber, ivory and ceramics. The arts of spinning and weaving were developed using simple warp-weighted looms and wool from sheep and goats and linen from flax. In northern Europe more wool and furs were utilised, in the south, linen. Simple, natural dyes were used and decoration was by embroidery, fringing and plaiting also cording in the weaving. Our chief knowledge of this period comes from the excavation of tombs and burial places where the dead were interred fully clothed and with their valuables beside them, also from sculptured and painted decoration on vases, jewellery and household items.

The Bronze Age period from 1500–600 BC has yielded some most interesting finds of weapons, jewellery and actual garments from the tombs and peat bogs of Denmark and northern Holland and Germany. The preservation of some of the oak coffins and their contents is remarkable, especially those from Jutland in *Denmark*. In these graves have been found four complete men's sets of garments and three women's from the earlier Bronze Age. These are now in the Danish National Museum in Copenhagen. The best of them came from the graves at Borum Esh∮j, Muldbjerg, Egtved and Skrydstrup. Fig. **118** shows a man wearing clothes like those found at *Muldbjerg* (near Ringkj∮bing) in 1883. These comprise a woollen cloak, roughly semi-circular in shape, about 91 inches by 46 inches, a round cap of a matted fibre like a coarse felt and a tunic, girded by a broad, leather belt, fastened at the back by a double, horn button. Leather bands over the shoulders held up the tunic and were fixed at the back by decorative bronze tutuli in loops. From *Trindh∮j*, near Ribe, comes a similar outfit, while the garments at *Borum Esh∮j* were

115–117 *Scythian, 4th century BC*   **118, 119** *Jutland, Denmark*

simpler; the comb in fig. **127** comes from there.

The woman's dress in fig. **119** is based on the clothes from the grave at *Egtved*, near Vejle. The woman was young, about 18–20 years old, and had long hair, worn loose and held in place by a fillet round the brow. She was wearing a short jacket with sleeves, belted at the waist. The large belt disc (**119, 133**) is of bronze, with spiral decoration in concentric circles. It has a central spike, perhaps to repel unwanted attentions? Below the jacket she wore a skirt made of looped cords, fastened at top and bottom by woven bands; it was long enough to be wrapped twice round the body and tied on by a belt below waist level. The belt is intricately woven and ends in decorative tasselling. This type of skirt is essentially a Bronze Age garment. It is thought to have been given up when later the climate became colder.

Fig. **123** shows a young woman dressed in the manner of the body found in the *Skrydstrup* grave, excavated in 1935. Her hair was covered by a horsehair and wool cord net; she wore gold thread earrings. Her skirt is a long one folded up and with a jacket on top, both held together by a belt at the waist.

These types of garments and fragments of others like them have been found in a number of graves. They are accompanied by bronze and gold necklaces, bracelets, armlets, rings also caps, hair-nets, combs and other personal items. From the peat bogs of Denmark have been recovered beautiful belt boxes and heavy necklaces and brooches as well as toilet articles such as combs and razors.

From north Germany and Holland garments on bodies found in peat bogs show a style of short breeches or longer trousers, a tunic and a cloak. The lower leg is sometimes wrapped by bindings and footwear is of simple leather shoes fastened by a lace threaded through holes on the top. Remains can be seen, for example, in the Schleswig–Holstein Prehistory Museum.

Knowledge of another style of dress from a very different people comes from the beautiful, decorative metalware of the *Scythians*. They were a nomad people, a group of tribes who wandered the steppes which extended over Europe and Asia from Hungary to Manchuria. The western flank of these nomadic tribes had established themselves by 600 BC in European Russia, round the Black Sea. By 400 BC they had moved westwards to Hungary, Bulgaria, Rumania and eastern Germany, but after 250–200 BC trace of them disappears, though their art forms lived on in Viking, Gallic and Irish design.

This nomad society, with its various groups such as the earlier Cimmerians, the later Sarmatians and the Parthians who occupied the area south-east of the Caspian Sea, travelled immense distances on horseback; they were magnificent horsemen as warriors and hunters. Our knowledge of them comes firstly from the descriptions of the Greek historian Herodotus, who was writing in the fifth century BC and from the contemporary essays of Hippocrates. From the eighteenth century onwards, and especially in the late nineteenth and twentieth centuries, excavations in Russia and Mongolia have supported the accuracy of these historic accounts. These Russian researches have taken place chiefly in the Ukraine in the Dnieper valley near Kiev and further south towards the Crimea. The chief city excavated there so far, Neapolis near Simferopol, was an important centre for the Scythians in the fourth century BC. Other Scythian burials have been found in the Balkans, Hungary, Rumania and eastern Germany.

The Scythians developed an original style of art, vigorous and related to their nomad life. Gold was used a great deal, also bronze. Animals, especially stags, horses and lions, also fish, feature often in the designs. From their vases and plaques we have a clear picture of their dress (**115, 116, 117**) which generally illustrate only men though it is thought that both sexes wore similar garments. Actual clothes found in the royal tombs in the Dnieper burials bear out the relief sculpture pictures.

The *men's clothes* have something in common with the Teutonic dress of the time. They are depicted in tunics (often one or more worn on top of each other), belted at the waist and open in front. Some tunics had short sleeves, some long. Underneath, there was a shirt. They wore trousers with short boots on top, tied at the ankle. Other illustrations show long, loose trousers to the foot, reminiscent of the 'Oxford bags' of the 1920s. They had long hair, beards and moustaches and caps of round design, often with a point in front like the Phrygians of Asia Minor. Their clothes were of wool, tanned leather or fur, simply cut and sewn but rich in colour and to a great degree decorated with embroidery and braid. From excavation of the burial chambers in Outer Mongolia (of the Asiatic Scyths), *women's clothes* were shown to be more ornate than the men's, with felt, fur-edged cloaks, decorated

120, 121 *Iron Age Celts in Britain*   **122** *North German* **123** *Bronze Age, Denmark* **124** *Spain, 4th century BC*

Bronze and Iron Age Dress

almost all over in intricate appliqué work in bright colours and with a gown underneath with fitted bodice and sleeves, also ornamented. The women dressed their hair in plaits, with a high headdress or veil over the coiffure. They wore decorated white stockings, mounted on leather soles; these might be covered by overboots, ornamented by fur strips dyed in colours.

Among the accessories necessary to the Scythian family were hand-mirrors, combs, pins, needles and jewellery which included headdresses, necklaces, belts, pendants, armlets, rings, earrings, bracelets, lockets and buckles. The Scythians loved jewellery and personal adornment. They used precious metals and stones also enamelling and cloisonné work. Their motifs, apart from animals, included geometrical and floral patterns (**131**).

The earliest phase of the Central European Iron Age was the *Halstatt Culture* in Bohemia and Bavaria, but named after the Austrian town in the Salzkammergut where a rich find was made of iron swords and daggers. In the sixth century BC further evidence of this culture was to be found at Marseilles, where Greek trading extended from here up the rivers Rhône and Saône to the Swiss Lakes and the Danube. From this Mediterranean influence stemmed the new art style of the northern Alpine area, that of *La Tène*. The composite forces which went towards influencing this style included Scythian, Greek and Etruscan. The name is taken from the site at the north-east end of Lake Neuchâtel where, when the lake level sank, it revealed a quantity of iron weapons.

The next phase, and the last, of European prehistoric cultures was embodied in the *Celts*. These tribes invaded Italy in the fourth century BC and moved westwards over Europe to Britain, Ireland and the Iberian Peninsular. Their art was of a high standard of craftsmanship and of individual character.

Iron Age finds in *Danish* peat bogs are considerable but do not yield complete costumes as in the Bronze Age. The climate had become colder and animal skins comprise the chief material. Leather shoes have been found, made in one piece with a leather thong threaded through holes on top of the foot to lace the shoe across the instep. Similar finds have been made in Austria and Spain.

In *Czechoslovakia* extensive Celtic finds have been made of ornaments and jewellery of all kinds as well as toilet articles. These reflect influence from Scythian, Greek and Etruscan sources. From *Italy* came many *fibula* designs. Based on the safety pin pattern, these comprise a pin, the spring, a catch plate and a bow; they are varied in style, presaging Roman examples. Some of the finest jewellery comes from *Spain* and *Portugal*. Mainly in gold, this is of Late Bronze Age and early Celtic design, beautifully styled and made. The chief sites are Cáceres, Jaén and Córdova in Southern Spain and Sintra near Lisbon (**125, 126, 128, 129, 130, 132, 134**). The lady in Spanish dress in fig. **124** is taken from the sculptures from southern Spain near Albacete now on display in the National Archaeological Museum in Madrid.

From *England* and *Ireland* comes also some fine Celtic jewellery and arms as well as toilet articles (**135, 136**). Dress is shown in figs. **120** and **121** comprising tunic or gown, cloak and trousers. Bright colours are usual, also striped and check patterns. Cloaks are often of wool, lined with fur, or simply fur skins turned inside or outwards. The trousers, *bracco* in Celtic, were introduced to the Celts in Britain by the incoming Belgae. Hair was long and men wore luxuriant moustaches. Women's hair was held in place by a fillet or veil. Shoes were like the ones described on page 30.

European Dress 1 – 500 AD

With the gradual conquest of much of Europe by the Romans and its absorption into the Empire, Roman influence on dress became marked amongst the wealthier and more important members of the community. This influence was to a certain extent two-way, in that the trousers and leg-banding worn by the Celts and Gauls were adopted by some Romans, particularly in the army, since these garments had obvious advantages over bare legs and short tunics in the colder, damper parts of the Empire. Climate continued to be an important factor in determining the costume of any particular region.

Evidence of dress worn in Europe outside Rome itself is chiefly from sculpture and written accounts. Of interest among the latter are the monographs of the Roman historian *Cornelius Tacitus*, born in AD 56. His *Germania*, published in AD 98, gives a picture of dress in different parts of Germany in the first century AD. He describes

125 Silver fibula, Jaén, Southern Spain, 4th century BC

126 Gold necklace. Cáceres, Spain. Celtic. 7th century BC also **128**, gold bracelet

127 Horn comb, Bronze Age, Borum Eshøj, Denmark

129 Gold pendant on chain from Cáceres, as **126**

130 Solid gold bracelet, Entremez, Portugal

131 Bronze mount, Scythian, c. 5th century BC

132 Gold collar, Sintra, Portugal, Bronze Age

133 Bronze Age bronze belt disc, Egtved, Denmark

134 Silver fibula, Cordoba, Spain, c. 4th century BC

135 Iron Age Celtic mirror, Britain

136 Celtic gold torc, Snettisham, Britain, c.50 BC

137 Bronze brooch, Bronze Age, Denmark

138, 139 *Britain, 1st and 2nd centuries AD*   **140–42** *Franks and Gauls, 2nd–5th century AD*

the fur cloak fastened with a brooch or thorn, worn often without any other garments (**146**). He also tells us that women's dress was similar to that of their menfolk but that they wore outer garments of linen, decorated with purple and that these were sleeveless and round or low-necked.

Tacitus' accounts, taken together with the famous sculptural reliefs on the columns of Trajan (AD 114) and Marcus Aurelius (AD 174) in Rome, give a fairly comprehensive picture of dress of this time. The *Trajan column* depicts incidents in the Emperor's war with the *Dacians*. These people, at a considerable level of civilisation before the Roman conquest, inhabited a part of Europe corresponding to modern Rumania. They remained unsubdued by Rome until Trajan conquered their land and made it a Roman province in the early second century AD. Privileged classes wore sleeved tunics, long trousers, a cloak often with fringed edge and had a felt cap over their shortish hair. Their loose type of trouser, tied at the ankle and worn with leather shoes, had much in common with Scythian dress. They generally wore beards and moustaches (**172**).

The *Marcus Aurelius column* illustrates his campaigns against German tribes north of the Danube. Here, as on other Roman reliefs, can be seen the fur cloak worn alone (**146**) and the fur-lined cloth cloak over a pair of loose trousers, the torso remaining bare (**145**). Figs. **143** and **144** show the stronger Roman influence on some dress in the area of Seville, as depicted in high relief sculptures from Osuna, now in the archaeological museum in Madrid.

Though the clothes of different peoples varied somewhat from area to area, depending upon climate, wealth and degree of Roman influence, barbarian dress, in general, comprised, for *men*, a cloak of fur or cloth, pinned at the chest or shoulder, a belted tunic, hip- or knee-length, bare legs or, more commonly, short or long trousers and shoes or sandals of leather, with woollen socks inside. Footwear (though not always worn) was heelless and generally held in place by leather thongs tied on the top of the instep (**140**). The legs were often bound or cross-gartered with linen or wool bands, especially in Gaul (**142**). Head coverings were not common, though round caps and hoods were worn (**141, 147**). Treatment of hair varied greatly from area to area. Tacitus describes the characteristic and unusual style of a major part of the Teutonic race who twisted and knotted their hair on top or the side of the head to make it stand erect. Side locks were grown long and the hair at the back cut short or shaved (**140**). This elaborate coiffure was apparently to give them greater height and to strike terror into the heart of their foes when they went into battle. Moustaches were worn sometimes and beards commonly. These were carefully trimmed and combed, not unkempt, and hair was, in many cases, cut into a bob. Materials were of leather, fur, felt, wool and linen. Garments found in graves and bogs in northern Germany compare with the other sources available.

Less is known about *women's dress* which is not featured as often in sculptural reliefs. There are, however, both pictorial and written records. It was more commonly of linen, a material which does not survive satisfactorily from burials in earth and bogs. Of the latter, the later account by the Roman historian *Dio Cassius Cocceianus* tells of the appearance of *Queen Boadicea* (Boudicca) arrayed for battle. She was very tall, grim in appearance, harsh-voiced and with a wealth of exceedingly yellow hair falling below her waist, wearing a great golden collar and bracelets on her arms and wrists. She was attired in a tunica of several colours, blue, red and yellow predominating, which hung in folds about her. A *sagum*

(cloak) was thrown about her, fastened by a fibula or brooch. This was her usual dress (**138**). Some women wore a shorter tunic over a long gown (**139**). Footwear, and underwear when worn, were like those of the men as was also jewellery and decoration. In general, it was single women who wore their hair loose or bound by a fillet on the brow. Married women plaited and bound the hair with ribbons and gold thread and held it up in place with combs and pins.

The years between the third and sixth centuries AD were those of the great migrations. The movements of peoples were complex and, it is presumed, due to climatic changes following the retreating ice northwards which brought an alteration to the flora and fauna of the great central regions of Asia and eastern Europe. The main trend of movement was from east to west and from north in Scandinavia southwards and westwards. The principal stream of peoples in the fourth century AD were the Huns, moving westwards from the area round the River Don to the Danube, Hungary and eventually to the Rhine, and the Goths who also moved westwards and divided into two streams. The eastern part, the Ostrogoths settled in northern Italy at the end of the fifth century while the western, the Visigoths

143, 144 *Southern Spain, 1st century*   **145-47** *Teutonic tribesmen, 1st and 2nd centuries*

Western and Northern Europe, 1st and 2nd Centuries AD

148   149   150   151

moved to Gaul and Spain. Meanwhile, the Angles, Saxons and Jutes from northern Germany and Denmark came into a Britain left open to attack after the departure of the Roman legions.

These were centuries of struggle, movement of peoples, destruction of Roman civilisation and, with it, loss of industrial development in textiles, metalwork and trade. Costume, like the other trappings of culture, remained stagnant or declined in standard. The writers of the period, such as Sidonius Apollinaris of the fifth century, paint a picture of dress which had changed little from the descriptions of Tacitus 400 years earlier. It also shows that dress did not vary greatly from one area to another: Celtic, Saxon, Gallic and Frankish dress merged to become a general style.

The *Franks* comprised a large group of Germanic peoples of central Europe covering an area extending from the Baltic Sea to the Danube and from Poland to the Rhine. In the early fifth century they moved westwards into Gaul and annexed Flanders and parts of France. They are described by Sidonius Apollinaris as having red hair, knotted in front of the top of their heads and shaved at the nape, and with long moustaches. They wore a fitting tunic, often striped, with a wide belt, decorated with metal studs and having

a dependent sword and dagger. On top was a coloured cloth cloak with different lining. Legs were bare and boots were laced to the ankles (**140**). This description was made in 470 in Lyons and is similar to those of Tacitus in the first century AD.

Agathius, writing in the sixth century, describes the linen or leather trousers which they wore, tied to the legs by thongs, like those of the Gauls of the first and second centuries.

500–800 AD

The *Merovingian* dynasty of the Franks was established under King Clovis*. The Emperor of Byzantium awarded him the title of Augustus, thus setting the seal on his conquest of Gaul. Frankish noblemen and their wives after this adopted more and more a Byzantine mode of dress, though they were generally clad in a knee-length tunic, bordered and belted and probably decorated with clavi. They kept their bracco leg-coverings with boots on top or simply bound with strips of linen and often with the toes left bare in Teutonic fashion (**148**). They were usually clean-shaven or with moustaches and had moder-

---

* German – Ludwig; French – Louis.

ate length hair or longer styles plaited on top of the head. Feminine dress was very much like that of Byzantium; a long gown with decorated neckband and clavi or a band of ornament down the centre front. They wore a veil and/or mantle, draped around the body (**149**).

The Merovingian dynasty was succeeded by the Carolingian in the eighth century. In 768 *Charlemagne* became joint King of the Franks with his brother and sole ruler from 771; in AD 800 he was crowned Holy Roman Emperor by the Pope. Charlemagne himself preferred to wear normal Frankish dress, though he appeared in full Byzantine splendour on state occasions. His usual attire, like other Frankish noblemen, and indeed those of much of Europe, comprised a linen under-tunic, bracco or braies of the same material, cross-gartered to the knee with leather thongs; these were often coloured and decorated by metal studs. His shoes were of leather. The belted over-tunic was of linen or cloth and had a coloured border. Its sleeves were wide at the top, fitting at the wrist. His cloak, pinned on the shoulder, was lined with fur or silk and bordered. He sometimes wore a sleeveless, short jacket as well, in cold weather, and a round cap. Some noblemen wore sock-like, calf-length boots or a fabric hose (chausses) pulled up over the bracco (**150**, **176**). Indeed, the masculine leg was a feature which received great attention and was covered in many different ways. This practice continued until the advent of long tunics.

Women's gowns, in the eighth century, had changed little. They were more elegant and fully cut. The gown was decorated with bands of embroidery at neck and centre front. A long, crossed scarf, like the Roman palla, was draped round the body and over one arm (**151**). Like the men, women wore *braies* under the gown and undergown. Their shoes were also like the men's styles. Their hair was dressed in nets of woven beads and precious stones, with veils worn on top.

A great deal of decorative and functional *jewellery* and *ornament* was worn by both sexes in the first eight centuries of the Christian era. A wealth of this has been discovered and is on view in the great museums of Europe. In gold, silver, bronze and iron, it is set with stones of all kinds and decorated with incised lines, embossing and enamel. Beads of amber, garnets and other stones are also common. Much of the work is characteristic of the culture from which it springs and is

readily identifiable as such. Designs take some features from Roman and Byzantine sources but, in general, it is noticeable how individual they are and how original. Visigothic work from Spain in **155**, **164**, **167**; Anglo-Saxon items from Britain **168**, **170**, **171**; Celtic from Ireland **165**; Ostrogothic work from Italy **156**, **157**; Teutonic examples from Germany and Hungary **160**, **162**; designs from Scandinavia **161**, **163**; and some work from Southern Russia **152**, **153**, **154**, **169**.

AD 800–1100

There were three centres of power which dominated the life of the peoples of Europe in these years: the Carolingian Empire, the Byzantine Empire and the Arabic world. Charlemagne and his successors ruled over the largest area, influencing the life and dress of the peoples of northern and central Europe. Italy was largely under the Byzantine imperial aegis which, though the capital was at Byzantium (Istanbul), was still strongly dominant in Venice, Ravenna and the south. Spain, Greece and Sicily were under Moorish control, though the Visigoths held out in the Asturias and, by the end of this period, the Christian tide began to push the Arabs southwards.

The dress of these different areas of Europe was affected to a certain degree by these spheres of influence, but there was an underlying basis of similarity. Carolingian costume continued much as under the Merovingian dynasty; the classical type of dress was more to be seen in Italy and Oriental shaped, three-quarter-length coats with trousers, in rich, colourful materials, were common in Spain. A valuable source material for eleventh century costume is the *Bayeux tapestry* (a linen strip about 75 yards long and nearly 20 inches wide, embroidered in coloured wools and telling the story of the Norman Conquest of England) made between 1066–77. The dress of kings and courts, soldiers and ordinary men are all shown here in considerable detail (**174**).

In general men wore shorter costume for average use but, in the eleventh century, the nobility tended to adopt longer tunics; these were always worn on formal occasions. Such longer garments were also common in areas closely influenced by Byzantine customs. The less wealthy families adhered to the short tunic styles and dressed in darker, more sombre colours and

Jewellery and Detail, 1st–8th Century AD

152 Incised silver brooch, River Dnieper, near Kiev, 7th century

153, 154 Gold ring and earring, South Russia, 3rd and 4th centuries

155 Visigothic gold, jewelled earring, Jaen, Spain

156, 157 Gold, jewelled ring and pin, Ostrogothic Italy, 5th–7th century

158, 159 German footwear, 3rd–6th century

160 Gold buckle, Hungary, 5th century

161 Brass and stone brooch, Island of Gotland, 7th–8th century

162 Gold brooch with stones and filigree work, German 7th century

163 Bronze brooch, relief decoration, Oslo, 5th century

164 Bronze fibula, Visigothic, 6th century

165 Massive bronze armlet, Ireland 2nd century

166 Silver pin, English, 7th century

167 Bronze brooch, Visigothic, 6th century

168 Anglo-Saxon, English, 7th century

169 Gold, garnet brooch, South Russia, 3rd century

170 Gold necklace with garnets, Anglo-Saxon, English, 7th century

171 Jewelled brooch, Anglo-Saxon, English, 6th–7th century

172 *Dacian king*   **173** *Anglo-Saxon,*
10th–11th century   **174** *Norman, 1070*   **175** *Czechoslovakia,*
c.1085   **176** *Carolingian nobleman*

coarser materials than the nobility.

Also in the eleventh century, the overtunic called the *bliaud* became general wear for both men and women; on men it reached knee or calf, becoming later ankle-length; on women it was three-quarter length. Called previously the *gonelle* (from which the English word gown stems), it was, by this time, more commonly referred to as a *bliaud*, from the Germanic word blialt meaning cloth. This overtunic, when worn by the wealthier classes, was in bright colours, of wool, linen and sometimes silk, girded by a jewelled, leather belt and had decorative borders at neck, sleeves, hem and, sometimes, at side slits in the skirt (**176**). Sleeves were generally three-quarter length and wide at the bottom.

Under the bliaud, also for both sexes, was worn the undertunic with long, fitted sleeves, the *chainse*, which was white or light coloured. On women it reached the ground, on men it was shorter. A chemise or shirt served as an undergarment.

Men were still clad in *braies* or breeches; the long, loose trousers of the western world (**175**). On top, they often wore *chausses*, a hose made of shaped, seamed pieces of cloth, not very well

fitting and sometimes bound with cross-gartering (**174, 177E**). It is thought that women also wore similar garments but these are not visible.

Men wore a *cloak* on top of their tunics, generally long, rectangular, circular or semi-circular in shape and still usually pinned by a brooch on the right shoulder or in the front (**174, 175, 176, 177A, E**). This might have a contrasting lining, perhaps fur, and a decorative border. *Footwear* was of leather or cloth, often ankle-length, where it was fastened by lace or buckle. Some styles were laced round the lower leg (**177A, 179, 182**). *Hair* was cut fairly short, though longer styles began to return towards 1100. The Normans (*c.* 1060) often shaved or trimmed their hair short at the back of the head and combed the remainder forward over the forehead (**174, 177C**). They were usually clean-shaven, but in the Carolingian period, trim moustaches and beards were worn while, towards 1100, longer styles accompanied longer hair (**176, 177A**). Head-covering, if worn, was a *cap* of round shape, sometimes with a point in front (**177A, E**).

Women also wore cloaks or mantles, pinned or fastened with cords in front. Some styles were circular with a hole for the head set nearer to one

39

edge. This left more material at the back, where it hung nearly to the ground (**173**). Their hair was long, plaited and bound and usually covered by a veil or the folds of the mantle (**173, 177B, D**). Their footwear was like that of the men. *Jewellery* was still fairly heavy in design, but richly engraved and embossed, also set with stones.

AD 1100–1340

Twelfth-century dress changed only slowly and the garments worn were similar to those of the previous century. In the first 20–25 years, clothes were exceptionally long and voluminous. This applied to both sexes, mantles and gowns, especially, sweeping the ground and sleeves so long as to cover the hand or else knotted to avoid this.

Tunics and gowns were loose and, when belted, pouched into many folds at the waist. Girdles became decorative, valuable articles; those worn by the nobility were of gilded and jewelled leather, often with one long end hanging from the buckle. Less costly ones were woven in bright colours. The outer garment, the bliaud, was still generally shorter than the chainse beneath and had decorative borders at hem, sleeves and neck.

The Crusades, which began in 1095 and extended through much of the thirteenth century, had a great effect on the quality and type of textiles becoming available to Europe. Whether this movement effected the pious detachment from worldly affairs, as is sometimes claimed, is doubtful. The Crusaders, or at least a number of them, evinced an appetite more towards material enjoyment and luxury as was evidenced in the desecration and pillage of Santa Sophia in Constantinople.

The influence of these events on costume was more in the field of textiles than design of dress. Fabrics such as silks, damasks, thin cottons and other soft, pliable materials were introduced to the West from the Middle East and the Orient. These, in turn, affected styles, leading to garments which could be finely pleated and gathered and, consequently, delineated the figure more closely.

By the middle of the twelfth century garments had returned to more normal lengths; *masculine tunics* reached to the knees, when in common use for all in everyday life, and to the ankles when for the formal dress of noblemen (**190**). *Women's gowns* just cleared the floor. Made of the thinner fabrics, they were full-skirted and wide-sleeved yet, due to the fine pleating, clung more to the line of the breasts and hips, falling in elegant, narrow folds to the ground. The *double girdle* became fashionable, wherein the broad, flat, decorative band was passed round the waist from front to back, then fastened in front at hip level. Made of leather or woven braid, it was tied or buckled and long silken, tasselled threads hung nearly to the floor. A classic instance of this style of gown is depicted in the formality of the draped figures on the west front of Chartres Cathedral (**188**).

As can also be seen in other French and English ecclesiastical sculptures of the time, women grew their *hair* as long as possible and – adding false hair if their own was not adequate – plaited it in two braids on each side of the head, then bound the braids with silk and encased the ends in decorative, metal cylinders which hung to below the knees (**188**). Men's hair was very long while the fashion for lengthy garments persisted; their moustaches and beards were also long and flowing, the latter carefully arranged in two or three straggly points. By 1130–40 much of this excess hair was trimmed back till, by 1170, the coiffure was a neat bob and men were clean-shaven or had small pointed beards and moustaches.

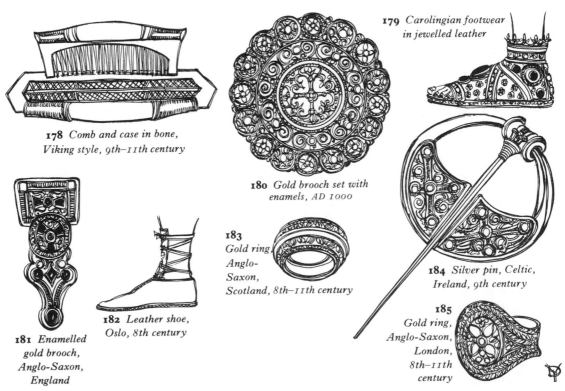

178 *Comb and case in bone, Viking style, 9th–11th century*

179 *Carolingian footwear in jewelled leather*

180 *Gold brooch set with enamels, AD 1000*

181 *Enamelled gold brooch, Anglo-Saxon, England*

182 *Leather shoe, Oslo, 8th century*

183 *Gold ring, Anglo-Saxon, Scotland, 8th–11th century*

184 *Silver pin, Celtic, Ireland, 9th century*

185 *Gold ring, Anglo-Saxon, London, 8th–11th century*

Jewellery and Detail, 8th–11th Century AD

186, 187 *12th century Spanish*   **188** *French, c.1150*   **189** *Later 12th century, Swiss*   **190** *Danish, c.1200*

By the twelfth century *Spanish dress* had begun to reflect the richness of the decorative arts in the Iberian Peninsula, which stemmed from the merging of the Celtic, Visigothic and Moorish influences of this new mixed population. *Southern Italy* and *Sicily* showed a similar Saracenic quality and the Sicilian textiles became famous for their richness. In costume, this could be seen in the vivid colouring and patterning of fabrics, the greater frequency and luxury of ornamental bordering and the decoration of all garments, including footwear, hose and girdles. Motifs, vigorous and lively, influenced from Saracenic sources, were similar in Spain and Italy. This reflected the extensive trade in textiles which had developed between Moorish Spain and the Italian Peninsula. The Byzantine form of deep, decorative collars was common in Spain especially (**186, 187**).

By the end of the twelfth century fashions which became universal later were beginning to make their appearance in certain areas. *Dagged edges*, that is, hems of garments cut into decorative shapes, were to be seen in Switzerland and Germany (**189**); *parti-colouring* was in use in Spain and, in Scandinavia and France, the tabard-

like *surcoat* was being worn. The tabard had been introduced as a covering to his armour for the Crusading knight as a practical measure to conceal the sun's glare upon the metal in hot countries. It was then slowly adapted for civilian use though, at this stage, it was yet little more than a loose, rectangular tunic, hanging back and front over the bliaud (**190**).

By 1200 trade routes for *textiles* were altering as a result of the Crusades and the consequent expansion of international contacts. Materials were manufactured and developed more in France, Flanders and Italy and the Mediterranean regained its former position as the centre of this world, lost when the western part of the Roman Empire had collapsed in the fifth century. Bruges, London, Antwerp and Hanseatic western cities took over the influential position held for 800 years by the eastern sector of Europe in the Baltic and Dnieper valley.

Thirteenth-century dress for men and women is characterised by its simplicity. Garments were loosely fitting, almost unornamented and made of heavy, sometimes costly materials, which fell in deep, graceful folds. This type of costume was prevalent until about 1330–40, when the transformation from these loose, draped garments to tailored, fitting ones took place.

In general, in the years 1200–1340, the wealthy and middle classes wore long garments and the less well-to-do shorter ones. It is not easy to follow the nomenclature of the different items of dress in these years, as the names varied from country to country and overlapped one another. *Men* continued to wear the tunic or bliaud (**191**) but, more commonly now, this was covered by a *surcoat* (surcote). Originating from the knight's tabard by 1220 it was a loose, sleeveless garment with large armholes; it was generally of three-quarter length, showing the bliaud below (**193, 196B, C, 203**). For both men and women, indeed, the thirteenth century was a time of ungirded clothes and, though these might fall straight from shoulder to hem or be waisted, they were never tight fitting.

Later in the century, the surcoat developed sleeves (**207**). These were usually loose and long and had a slit in front at elbow-level. The arm was passed through this slit and the surcoat sleeve hung down behind (**195**). Purses were often attached to belts which were worn on the bliaud. Slits, called *fitchets* were then made in the sur-

coat, over the hip bone, so that the wearer had access to his money or keys while still keeping them hidden. The word 'mugging' had not been coined in the Middle Ages but the action was more prevalent than today. In the early fourteenth century the belt was often once more worn on the outside garment, but more commonly round the hips than the waist (**197, 201, 204**). Also, at this time, the surcoat became more fitted than previously and was appropriately called a *garde-corps* or corset. This developed by mid-century into the *cotehardie*. Due to the wearing of the surcoat, mantles and cloaks became superfluous in the thirteenth century, their use being reserved for travelling and cold weather.

For undergarments men still wore breeches or *braies* and *hose* (chausses). As time passed the hose, which were still tailored and seamed, were cut to fit the limbs more accurately. Simultaneously they became longer, reaching to mid-thigh, where they were attached by lacing to the lower edge of an undertunic. The braies had now become underwear, generally knee-length, and tied at the waist by a draw-string. The hose were then pulled up over the leg portion of the braies.

The *chainse*, the earlier undertunic, had also

191, 192 *Spain*   193 *France*   194 *Germany*   195 *France*

13th Century Dress

196 13th Century Dress in England

now become underwear, in the form of a chemise or shirt. It was white or saffron colour and made of thin material. In the thirteenth century this was often batiste, which was a finely woven fabric named after Batiste Chambray who developed it. Unlike the modern material of that name, it was of linen thread, not cotton. The garment was visible only at neck and wrists.

Women's clothes were also very simple and plain and generally ungirded. A ground-length bliaud (**194, 196A**) was worn frequently with a surcoat on top. The feminine version of this, more commonly called the *cyclas*, was at first sleeveless with wide armholes (**202, 205, 206**), but later had half or three-quarter sleeves which, like the men's, often hung down behind the arm (**192, 196D**). In the early fourteenth century this garment was more waisted (**198**). In some countries, notably Italy, the gown was sometimes girded at a high waistline and the hem material caught up underneath nearly to knee-level (**199**). Alternatively, at this time, the cyclas developed into the beginnings of the fashion for the *sideless surcoat* or sideless gown; one which lasted well into the fifteenth century. At this stage it had very deep armholes,

extending down to the hips, which were edged with embroidery or fur. The more fitting gown beneath could be seen at the sleeves and sides (**200**). Feminine underwear and hose were much like the men's.

There was, by this time, a greater choice of *fabrics* for the well-to-do. Beautiful silks and cottons were imported from the Orient and the Middle East, while silk and velvet were being made in Italy; Germany was noted for its fustian (a cotton material woven with linen) and England manufactured some good quality woollen cloth. One rich version of this was called scarlet (escarlate), derived from the Persian *saqalãt*. Because it was so often made and used in a brilliant red hue, the name became associated more with the colour than the material. It was used especially for making hose. Fine quality decorative leatherwork came from Spain and Germany.

Footwear, for both sexes, was simple and fitting to the foot. Shoes had a roll top and were laced or had a button or buckle fastening. They were made in leather, silk and velvet often embroidered and even jewelled (**193, 195, 196C, 197, 201, 204, 207, 210, 213**). Footwear made in costly materials was protected out-of-doors by wooden pattens, with cork soles and heels, worn on top and fastened by leather straps over the instep and toes. In the fourteenth century soled hose began to be worn. Short, lightweight boots were alternatives (**191**).

Men usually wore their *hair* in a bob. They were often clean-shaven or had small beards and moustaches. A common thirteenth-century style was to wear the back hair dressed in a long, horizontal curl (**193, 203, 204, 207, 208**). The most usual head covering was the *hood*. This had now been separated from the cloak and was attached to a cape covering the shoulders only. In the fourteenth century the point on top began to lengthen into a padded sausage which hung down the wearer's back. This was called the *liripipe* and grew to fantastic lengths later in the century (**197**). Indoors, and also out-of-doors under other headcovering, men frequently wore a linen cap which could be tied under the chin (**196C, 203, 208**). It was known by various names, most usually a *coif* (coiffe) or cale. Different designs of outdoor caps made in felt or wool were worn instead of a hood. Some were round like a

skull cap, others were pill-box shaped (**191, 195, 201, 204**).

Women wore a variety of *headcovering* and the names of the different styles can be confusing to the costume historian as the same word signified different styles in various countries. At the end of the twelfth century appeared the *wimple*, as it was called in England or, more commonly in France, the *guimp*. At first it was only a simple square of white linen or silk draped over the head. Then it was tucked into the neckline of the gown and, from this, developed the *barbette* or wimple which was pinned to the hair above the ears and then draped round the throat; it could hang loose or be tucked in the gown neckline. It might be worn alone or with a veil or couvrechef on top as well (**192, 196D, 198, 200, 205**). In the thirteenth century, a band of white linen was often bound round the head and under the chin, pinned in place on top. It was frequently surmounted by the *fillet* which had now evolved into a pill-box shape, stiffened and covered in white linen, often pleated or fluted; this was sometimes called a *touret*. It could have a flat top or be

197 *Germany, c.1310*   **198** *Spain, 1300–40*   **199** *Italy, c.1305–15*   **200** *Danish queen, 1319*   **201** *Spain, 1300–40*

Early 14th Century Dress

45

open, showing the hair and chinbard inside (**194, 196A, 202, 209, 214, 215**). A veil could be draped over it.

The *hair*, still long, was parted in the centre and plaited. It could then be drawn into a chignon at the back or coiled on each side over the ears. Usually it was confined in a net. This might be of wool or velvet or a metal mesh, sometimes shaped like a box. Such nets were referred to as *cauls*, crespinettes, crispines etc. (**209, 211, 215**). In Italy, the hair was most often simply braided with the plaits pinned up and decorated by a jewel or fillet round the brow and left uncovered (**199, 206**).

Costume accessories were now becoming more numerous and elegantly designed. Crusaders returning from the wars in the thirteenth century brought back examples of decorative work in the form of footwear, purses and bags, girdles, gloves and handkerchiefs which were then copied. They were elaborately embroidered with jewels or appliqué on leather and silk. Italy, especially Venice, was the meeting place between east and west and from here the luxury goods flowed westwards. It is in Venice and Genoa, therefore, that we find the nobility first wearing and using such items as *perfumed gloves* and *handkerchiefs*. The latter were still such a costly rarity in the west that a wealthy nobleman only possessed one, albeit, a work of art in itself. *Fans* also came in from the Orient, made of ostrich or peacock plumes or painted silk set into elegant handles of jewelled gold or ivory.

By the fourteenth century Venice was the leader of European fashion. It reached the height of its prosperity soon after this. One result was that it became one of the first places in Europe where attempts were made, by means of sumptuary laws, to limit the natural instinct of mankind to express his wealth and status in luxury apparel. Further attempts, throughout the Middle Ages, were made all over Europe, to contain and restrict extravagance and to preserve this privilege for the wealthy nobility. It goes without saying that, despite heavy penalties, all such attempts failed.

202, 203 *Italian, 1305–6*   **204, 205** *German, 1310–30*   **206** *Italian, 1305–6*   **207** *German, 1310–30*

208 *White coif, Denmark*

209 *White linen headdress and net, England, mid-13th century*

210 *Leather shoe, Sweden*

211 *White linen headdress and metal caul, Denmark, c.1300*

212 *Gold, jewelled brooch, England*

214 *Linen headdress, c.1250*

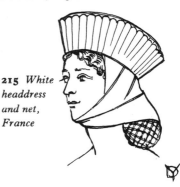

215 *White headdress and net, France*

213 *Felt shoe, Sweden*

Notes on the Illustrations

115, 116 and 117 Scythian dress from metal plaques and vases from Kul-Oba. In Hermitage Museum, Leningrad, copy in Victoria and Albert Museum, London. The men are wearing woollen tunics and trousers with decorative banding. Felt caps and boots. Leather belts.

118 Clothes from Muldbjerg burial, Denmark. National Museum, Copenhagen. Man in woollen tunic and cloak. Leather belt. Matted curly fibre cap.

119 Clothes from Egtved burial, Denmark. National Museum, Copenhagen. Woman in corded skirt and wool jacket. Longer skirt below presumed. Bronze belt disc, arm ring and necklace.

120 Based on description. British Celtic woman. Woollen striped gown over plain wool undergown. Leather shoes.

121 Based on description. British Celtic man. Dark wool cloak with contrasting wool lining, fastened with bronze brooch. Check wool tunic and trousers (braccae). Leather shoes. Leather belt with bronze buckle.

122 Based on burial finds in northern Germany. Wool cloak, tunic and short trousers. Bronze armlet. Leather shoes.

123 Clothes from Skrydstrup burial, Denmark. National Museum, Copenhagen. Reconstruction in Copenhagen. Wool dress.

124 Sculptured figures from Baza and Albacete in southern Spain in the Museo Arqueologico, Madrid.

125 Fibula, Jaén.

126 Gold necklace, Cáceres, both in Museo Arqueologico, Madrid.

127 Horn comb from burial at Borum Eshøj, Denmark. National Museum, Copenhagen.

128 and 129 Bracelet and pendant on chain, Cáceres, Spain. In Museo Arqueologico, Madrid.

130 Bracelet, Entremez, Portugal. Museo Arqueologico, Madrid.

131 Bronze mount, Scythian.

132 Gold collar, Sintra, Portugal, both in British Museum, London.

133 Bronze belt disc from Egtved burial, Denmark. National Museum, Copenhagen.

134 Fibula, Córdoba, Spain. Museo Arqueologico, Madrid.

135 Celtic mirror, Desborough, Britain.

136 Gold torc, Snettisham, Britain, both in British Museum, London.

137 Bronze brooch, Denmark. British Museum, London.

138 Based on description. British woman in dark cloak fastened with bronze brooch and lined with black fur. Gown of red, yellow and blue checks in wool. Leather belt with bronze ornaments. Gold necklace and bracelet. Leather shoes.

139 Based on description. British woman in outer and under gown of plain wool. Wool braid belt. Leather shoes.

140 Based on description. Frankish man in wool tunic with fur over-tunic. Wool mantle fastened with bronze brooch. Bare legs; leather boots. Leather belt, bronze buckle and armlets.

141 Based on description. Gallic man in woollen hood, tunic and trousers.

142 Based on description. Gallic man in woollen cloak. Tunic with belt and decorative border. Braccae or braies crossgartered with linen bands. Leather shoes.

143 and 144 Southern Spanish dress influenced by Roman modes. From relief sculptures from Osuna (near Seville) c.50 BC. Museo Arqueologico, Madrid.

145, 146 and 147 Teutonic dress from the Trajan Column, Rome. AD 114.

148 and 149 Bible of Charles the Bald, National Library, Paris. Byzantine influence on dress in embroidered panels and borders and thinner fabrics. Legs covered by braies and cross-banding.

150 Book cover design, Carolingian King. Boots over cross-banding.

151 Frankish aristocratic dress. Byzantine influence very strong.

152, 153 and 154 Brooch, ring and earring, British Museum, London.

155 Earring. Museo Arqueologico, Madrid.

156 and 157 Ring and pin. British Museum, London.

158 and 159 Leather shoes found in peat bogs, northern Germany.

160 Brooch, British Museum, London.

161, 162 and 163 Brooches, British Museum, London.

164 Fibula. Museo Arqueologico, Madrid.

165 and 166 Armlet and pin. British Museum, London.

167 Brooch. Museo Arqueologico, Madrid.

168, 169, 170 and 171 Clasp, brooches and necklace. British Museum, London.

172 Dacian King from classical sculpture in Rome.

173 Anglo-Saxon lady, based on descriptions. Circular cloak and veil. Three-quarter gown over long under-gown.

174 Norman from Bayeux Tapestry in Bayeux, Normandy.

175 Bohemian King from the Vyšehrad Gospels, University Library, Prague. Cloak and tunic over trousers and shoes. Byzantine influence.

176 Carolingian king from a miniature. Byzantine dress of dalmatica over undertunic. Cloak on top. Ankle boots.

177 Norman dress from the Bayeux tapestry in Bayeux, Normandy and from cathedral sculpture in England and northern France.

178 Comb and case, British Museum, London.

179 Carolingian style shoe in jewelled leather. A later reliquiary in jewelled gold and silver in Landesmuseum, Zürich, from Basle Minster treasure.

180 and 181 Brooches. British Museum, London.

182 Leather shoe, Oslo Museum.

183, 184 and 185 Rings and pin. British Museum, London.

186 Pantocrator, S. Clemente of Tahull. Fresco from apse of church. Museum of Catalan Art, Barcelona. Bordered cloak and over-tunic with belt. Undertunic.

187 Foolish Virgin from Church of S. Pedret. Fresco in apse. Museum of Catalan Art, Barcelona. Byzantine dress. Influence especially in headdress and decorative collar.

188 Sculpture from Royal Portal, Chartres Cathedral, France and from church in the Louvre, Paris. Pleated gown with double girdle and hanging ends. Braided hair encased in long metal cylinders. Veil. Mantle.

189 Dagged tunic, Swiss. Manuscript showing St. George. Morgan Library.

190 Bronze relief, Copenhagen National Museum. Tabard over tunic. Cloak. Braies and boots. Hat.

191 Spain c.1210. Short bliaud, waisted. Woollen mantle, different coloured lining and deep dagged hem. Hose and boots. Cap. Altar-painting, Museum of Catalan Art, Barcelona.

192 Gown and veil, mid-thirteenth century, Spain. Museum of Catalan Art, Barcelona. Altar-painting.

193 Surcote and undertunic. French. Sculpture, Amiens Cathedral.

194 Germany. After sculptures in choir of Naumburg Cathedral.

195 France. Surcote or garde-corps with hanging sleeves. Hood, cap, hose and shoes. Sculptural statue, Reims Cathedral.

196 Group taken from English sources in sculpture and memorial brasses. Men's dress shows the surcote over the tunic and coif on the head. Women's dress shows the surcote or cyclas over an undergown and the wimple and barbette.

197 German costume from the Minnesinger manuscript, library, Heidelberg University. Hood, with liripipe. Belted tunic with purse, Hose, shoes.

198 Spanish painting, altar-piece. Museum of Catalan Art, Barcelona. White veil and wimple. Green gown in cyclas style. Dark blue mantle.

199 Italian. Fresco by Giotto in the Cappella degli Scrovegni at Padua. Hair uncovered, wimple tucked into gown neckline (gorget). Gown (white). Skirt turned up to show grey undergown. Mantle over arm.

200 Danish queen, 1319. From brass rubbing.

201 Painting, altar-piece. Museum of Catalan Art, Barcelona. Green tunic with high neckline. Undertunic red, shows at sleeve. Brown mantle. Red hose and gold decorated shoes. Cap.

202 Italian fresco by Taddeo Gaddi in Church of S. Croce, Florence. Headdress of barbette and bag in white linen. Patterned gown, plain undergown.

203 and 206 Italian frescoes by Giotto in the Cappella degli Scrovegni at Padua. 203, White coif and band. Grey-mauve surcote, darker undertunic. 206. Hair uncovered. Surcote or cyclas and undergown in plain white.

204, 205 and 207 German. From the Minnesänger Manesse manuscript in the library of Heidelberg University. 204. Parti-coloured surcote, deep pink on right side, alternate stripes of ultramarine blue and yellow on the left. White hood and gloves. Pink hat with turquoise brim. Dark green hose, black shoes. 205. White wimple and veil. Cyclas of pink, undergown of spotted blue. 207. Horizontally striped surcote in strawberry pink and blue-purple, white lining. Purple undertunic. Yellow hose, shoes yellow with black cross-hatch pattern.

208 Based on description.

209 Church sculptural effigy.

210 and 213 Swedish from Lund and Uppsala museums.

211 Danish manuscript.

212 Brooch, British Museum, London.

214 Church sculpture.

215 Reims Cathedral sculpture.

Chapter Three

The Later Middle Ages and the Début of the Renaissance 1340–1465

The first half of the fourteenth century had been transitional years for fashion. Between 1340 and 1350 the great change came, sweeping over Western Europe first and establishing the basis of modern dress. For the first time clothes were tailored to fit and display the human figure, male and female. Before this, all European costume had been draped and loose, held to the body only by a girdle or bands and ties and, for many costumes, long and voluminous.

The change, like most fundamental, far-reaching events in human history, occurred for several reasons and, at this particular time, because society was then in a condition ready to receive it. It was comparatively sudden, though the alterations evolved over a decade or two, not a few months as with modern fashion. It was, considering the slowness and inadequacy of communications of the day, a rapid and comprehensive change. The basic reason for the desire for the new mode stems from the ideas of the Renaissance. The fact that it appeared at this time rather than – as with architecture and sculpture – many years later, was partly due to the new-found ability to tailor clothes accurately, partly due to the availability of rich new fabrics and textile patterning and, thirdly, because the early Renaissance was expressed in ideas and ideals rather than arts.

The Renaissance began in Italy, almost a century before the movement stirred elsewhere. Its theme was expressed in words – in literature, poetry and prose. It was, in the second stage, then interpreted in painting and drawing. The early ideas were put forward by men such as Petrarch, Dante, Boccaccio, moving on to Cimabue and Giotto. In words and pictures the pent-up spring flooded out, expressing man's curiosity about his life, origins, purpose; he was no longer satisfied by the Medieval answers to these questions which had been accepted, both on religious and secular planes, for so long.

The first questioning came in Italy since here was the centre of the Ancient Roman classical world. Scholars began to study the literature of Greece and Rome and they seized upon the classical concept of man as an individual human being, important in his own right. This conflicted with the established theological ruling that man's life on earth should be subjugated to his future life after death. There evolved a new spirit, a desire to find the ideal forms of beauty. The human body was studied and admired and became the essential factor in man's search for the aesthetic ideal. The doctrine of Humanism was established and things secular acquired a value and standing which they had not had in Medieval life. As literature and painting accepted and glorified the human figure, so fashion became one of the prime exponents of the theme. Under the Church's influence, from the early days of Byzantium and the conversion of the Roman Empire, the idea of showing off and displaying the human form was frowned upon. Now, this was cast aside and, though arms were still covered to the wrists, clothes were revealingly tight and necklines often décolleté.

Although Italy was the source of the Renaissance, it was not the only country dominant in fashion influence in these years. England, Spain and, later, especially Burgundy, contributed greatly. Costume became national again. The long, loose styles had tended to surpass frontiers and create a European mode. Now, with widely differing political and social structures governing the different states of Europe which were advancing at varied speeds of development, such distinctions manifested themselves in dress. The fundamental style was general but there were noticeable variations in fabrics, motifs, style and choice of garments.

In some countries, notably *England*, the feudal system was breaking up and the aristocracy losing some of its power to the emergent merchant classes. Here, also, a nation was being forged and this was reflected in a national rather than local style of dress. *Italy*, in contrast, advanced artistically but backward politically, was still essentially a land of city states, wealthy, competi-

216, 217 *1365*   **218** *1360*   **219** *1365*   **220** *1370*

tive and reflecting this in the variations of fashion style. The mode worn by a Venetian was far removed from that of a Florentine. The rivalry, which existed between these rich, independent states, stimulated design, not only in the arts, but in fashion also. From here came many of the new, imaginative ideas which transformed costume in these years.

A sumptuously rich and elegant costume was worn also in *Flanders* and *Burgundy*. Here, where the court still set the pattern, there was wealth to support such dress. In the later fourteenth century and for much of the fifteenth, it was Burgundy which became the dominant influence in western countries of Europe. The Burgundians were people of Germanic origin who first settled in what is now East Germany. Under the later Roman Empire they established themselves in Gaul in present day France. It was after 1360 that the Dukes of Burgundy succeeded in expanding their kingdom dramatically to take over Flanders, Lorraine and areas of France. This rich, powerful state became the pace-setter for much of European costume. In *Spain* also, the aristocracy retained their power and court costume displayed sumptuous luxury.

Although a time of war and struggle, this was also one of developing commercial stability. The Turks were moving westwards in the Mediterranean so western trade interests developed a sea route, from the luxury textile producing countries such as Italy and Spain, through the Mediterranean, round the Iberian Peninsula to Flanders and the German coastal towns. The Hanseatic League, dominant in this latter area, maintained a safe trade route from Flanders and Britain to Russia.

An important feature of fourteenth- and fifteenth-century dress was the richness of the materials from which it was made and with which it was ornamented. All through these years, a great expansion took place in the manufacture, importation and spread of such fabrics. In the west, Italy was the chief source. Especially in the northern half of the country, in centres such as Lucca and Venice, luxury materials like silk, satin, velvet and taffeta were made in quantity and exported all over Europe. Spain also developed a silk industry under Moorish initiative. Both countries were extensive users themselves of these materials, rich in colour and pattern.

Woollen and linen fabrics were manufactured in even greater quantity, for only the wealthy could afford luxury materials. Flanders, England and Germany produced most of these goods.

These years are noted for fabrics patterned with large motifs of which heraldic forms were paramount. Designs were, above all, of counterchange type, used on hoods, mantles, tunics, gowns and hose. These were either in plain bright colours worn parti-coloured, half or quarterly, or in designs counterchanged on the other half of the garment (**259, 278E**). One half or quarter would be emblazoned with an enormous heraldic lion while the other part(s) might have smaller heraldic insignia in different colours; alternatively, the same design would be counterchanged (**280**). Many varieties of geometrical and floral designs, patterned all over the material, were fashionable; these too were often counterchanged or were used on only part of the garment (**225, 226G, 231, 240, 247, 253, 261, 273, 281, 283, 286**). Brilliant colours and jewelled embroideries were all the rage.

Despite the growth of the luxury textile industry in the west, Oriental fabrics were still imported in quantity for those who could afford them. They came from China, Persia and Middle Eastern areas such as Egypt and Damascus. Some were plain, others richly patterned in floral or abstract motifs. Such fabrics were largely copied and redesigned in the west for the home market.

The fourteenth century was the era when decoration by *dagged edges* ran riot. This strange method of decorating a garment by cutting its edges into diverse, jagged shapes had begun earlier, but, from 1360 onwards, became one of the major features of masculine attire especially in Germany and England. Except for hose, no external garment escaped the dagges. The shoulder cape, hood, tunic, hem, tippets and mantle edge all received attention, varying from simple V-shaped cuts to complex leaf shapes and imitation of torn leather. The practice continued well into the fifteenth century. (**224, 234, 242, 246, 248–9, 257, 278A, D**).

In women's dress, dagges were rare in the fourteenth century, their gown styles not being suited to such ornamentation, but with the introduction of the *houppelande* late in the century, the

221 *1380*

222 *1377*

223 *1380*

224 *1380*

225 *1380*

Italy

wide sleeves of this garment were often treated in this manner (**223, 226A, 268, 278D, 286**).

The most popular decoration for the edges of garments in the fifteenth century was by *fur* trimming. Garments were also often lined throughout with fur. This was evidence of wealth and sumptuary laws were passed in most countries enumerating precisely which furs were permitted to be worn by diverse classes of society. Furs allowed for use by royalty and the wealthy aristocracy included marten, vair* and ermine†. Descending the social scale, one comes to otter, fox, beaver, lamb, goat and wolf. The most common use for decorative fur edging was round

the large armholes of the sideless surcoat or the plastron down its front (**229, 233, 238, 243, 250, 263, 264, 279, 287, 291**), as edging to tunic and houppelande sleeves and hem (**226E, G, 227B, D, F, 231, 235, 237, 240, 245, 246, 247, 252B, C, 255, 258, 261, 262, 265, 269, 270, 272, 274, 284**), and, in the later fifteenth century, for women's gown low necklines (**226E, 232, 252A, 271, 273**).

Men's Costume

By 1340 the surcoat had disappeared for normal wear. The principal garments were a tight-fitting tunic and under-tunic covering the torso, hose similarly close-fitting on the nether part of the body, the hood in varied guise for the head and,

---

* A squirrel with grey fur on its back and a white stomach.
† This is the white winter coat of an animal of the weasel tribe. The black markings are the tips of the tails.

where needed, a cloak. The looser tunic, belted at the waist, seen in the first half of the century, became tighter and shorter. A design like that in fig. **242** was still seen in 1340–50, with wide dagged-edged sleeves but, more typical from this time, was the garment made in four fitted sections, seamed vertically at the sides and back and buttoned the full length of the centre front. It barely covered the buttocks and a heavy, jewelled plaque leather belt encircled the hips rather than the waist. The neckline, generally hidden under the shoulder cape, was round and not too high. The four sections of the tunic, known by various names such as *pourpoint* or *gipon*, could be of different materials and colours, plain or patterned, counterchanged or all of one material (**220, 253, 265, 278E, 280, 281**). The *undertunic* was of similar style but with a higher neckline, generally open

in the centre front. The sleeves of both garments were narrow. At first, the outer tunic sleeve was so tight fitting that it had a row of buttons to close it from elbow to wrist, along the outer edge of the arm. Soon, the sleeve of the outer tunic finished above the elbow in a band and hung down as a streamer, often dagged, some two to three feet long, called a *tippet*. The under tunic sleeve then displayed the row of buttons and was long enough to extend over the hand to the first row of knuckles (**280, 281**).

As time passed, the *pourpoint* became shorter and shorter. Its hemline rose above the hips, making the wearing of a hip belt over it impossible, so a waist belt was resumed, leaving a short frill skirt below. The garment was padded on the chest and shoulders and the belt pulled tight to accentuate the contrastingly small waistline. The shoulder

227 Italian Dress in Venice, 1450–65

228   229   230   231   232

cape had been abandoned so either the pourpoint neckline was very high, under the ears, with frilled or fur edge (**221, 224, 244, 246, 259, 278B, E, 288, 289**) or it was round and lower, with the undertunic showing above at a high level (**226B, G, 227B, D, F, 230, 231, 241, 252B, C, 260, 276, 283**). From about 1380, several varieties of sleeve style were worn. Some were very wide at the wrist and turned back to show the fur or contrasting silk lining, the latter often dagged (**246, 258**). Others were very full in the lower part but gathered tightly in to the wrist where they were usually finished with a fur band (**228, 231**). By about 1420–25, the chest was padded more fully as were also the upper sleeves and the tunic pleated with the almost vertical pleats set at a slight angle to radiate outward from waist to shoulder on each side above the belt, and waist to hip below it. The sleeve here was very full and padded at the shoulder and tapered to a tight wristband (**226G, 227B, D, F, 228, 231, 235, 252B, C, 260**).

The most characteristic feature of male dress in the later Middle Ages was the *hose*. This garment was now expertly cut, generally in four sections, and tailored to fit the leg tightly from foot to crotch. With the ability of tailors to excel at such a high standard of fitting, men were able to display their virility to the utmost. The fourteenth and, even more the fifteenth century, were exceptional years for this expression of the peacock idiosyncrasy, with males always the more gloriously apparelled and sexually paramount. Women were elegantly and richly dressed but their femininity was discreetly shown.

Hose were made of velvet, silk or cloth; in winter they could be fur-lined. Often the foot portion was soled so that shoes were unnecessary. The garment evolved slowly. In the earlier Middle Ages it had begun as chausses or stockings, pulled up to the knee over the braies. Gradually, the hose became longer and the braies shorter. In 1340 the two legs of the hose were still separate, but, by 1360, were long enough to reach the hips and fit closely into the fork. They were kept up by being laced through eyelet holes all round the outer leg to the lower edge of the undertunic. These lacings were known as *points*.

By 1370–80, the legs of the hose had joined to become 'tights' and soon extended nearly to waist level, where they were attached to the shorter undertunic by laces and eyelet holes all round the body. With the metamorphosis of the hose into tights, the *cod-piece* (in French, *braguette*) became necessary. In these years it was a small bag of matching or parti-coloured material attached to the hose by points and covering the genitals.

Shoes and *boots* became superfluous indoors with the advent of soled hose. The most usual foot-covering for outdoors were *pattens* of wood, often with cork soles and heels. These were attached by a leather strap over the instep and toes (**228, 235, 260, 305, 313, 314**). Shoes, if worn, were of rich materials, embroidered and jewelled and had straps or turned down tops (**218, 221, 224, 230, 253, 255, 262, 283, 304, 306**). Boots were only worn for travelling (**307**). In the fourteenth century the fashion for extended toes was introduced. First popular in Poland and Italy, the trend spread westwards, being especially exaggerated about 1380. Some toe points were so extreme – up to two feet in length – that it became

difficult to walk and the point had to be stuffed, or stiffened with whalebone, alternatively attached by a metal chain to a garter at the knee. The style was known as a *poulaine* or, sometimes, a *crackow*, after the Polish town of that name, where the fashion was popular.

Masculine *underwear* was not now dissimilar from the modern design. It consisted of a chemise or long-sleeved shirt and the braies, which were now so abbreviated as to be trunks or pants. Both were of light-coloured silk or linen and were not visible when a man was fully dressed.

From about 1360–65, a new garment appeared: the *houppelande*. It was popular and the fashion lasted a long time. In the fourteenth century, it was very long and full, sweeping the ground. It could be buttoned full length down the centre front, like the pourpoint, alternatively it was not open but the skirt was slit at one or both sides up to the knee. Its neckline was very high, up to the ears, and its sleeves generally excessively wide at the wrist, falling in folds to the ground and generally dagged. Commonly a *baldric* was worn on top, round the torso; this was a wide band of ribbon or other material, embroidered and often

233 *c.1465*   234 *1455*   235 *c.1450*   236 *Early 15th century*

The Low Countries

237 *1434*   238 c.*1465*   239 *1445*   240, 241 c.*1459*

edged with small bells. The houppelande was generally belted at the waist and the fullness of the material created numerous folds which fell voluminously to the ground. It provided an alternative style to the pourpoint and was in total contrast to it, the pourpoint being tight, short and figure-displaying, the houppelande full, draped and figure-obscuring. It was made from rich fabrics and lined with a contrasting one, often fur. In general, as with the modern mini-skirt, it was the young who liked to display their legs and the older people who thankfully took to the houppelande (**234, 248, 249, 257, 278A**).

The houppelande continued to be worn through most of the fifteenth century though the style changed and it was given other names. Firstly diverse lengths were introduced so that it could vary from ground to calf-length (**237**). Then it began to acquire the same characteristics as the contemporary pourpoint. The neckline was lowered to a round or boat-shape and generally fur-edged, the undertunic neckline showing above. The chest and upper sleeves were heavily padded and pleated. Sleeve styles varied as in the case of the short tunics. The hem, whatever its level, was then usually fur-edged also (**240, 251, 255, 262, 269, 270, 272, 274, 284**).

The wearing of the houppelande made a cloak unnecessary. Earlier, however, with the shorter tunic, cloaks were still worn, especially for travelling. (**216, 224, 226B, 246, 265, 267**).

The chief headcovering for men during these years remained the *hood*, but it changed its form more than once in this time. At first, the shoulder cape was still often attached. This had dagged edges and a three to four feet liripipe, extending from the top of the head (**218, 242, 248, 253, 296, 312**). Soon, the shoulder cape was separated and worn over the shoulders by itself (**220**). Meanwhile, new ways of wearing the hood, plus the shoulder cape, were experimented with. A common method was to place the face opening of the hood upon the head itself and arrange the folds of the shoulder cape over the edge to drape down the back, front or sides, as the wearer wished. The liripipe, now some five to six feet long, could be held in the hand, hang loose or draped round the body (**246, 255, 278A, 280, 281, 298, 311**).

By the 1420s, the *hood* with attached shoulder

58

cape, had been worn for so long that further change was desired. A last, and more formal version of the chaperon was designed which obviated the need to re-drape the material every time it was donned. Now part of the *chaperon*, where the part set upon the head was made up into a padded tyre, called the roundlet. The shoulder cape was then sewn to the inside of the roundlet on one side and the liripipe to the other. The new style lasted for many years. A jewelled brooch often decorated one side of the roundlet which was usually of velvet or other rich fabric (**227F, 228, 234, 235, 240, 252B, C, 258, 260, 272, 283, 284, 294, 301**).

Hats were worn in the fourteenth century instead of or on top of the hood. They were of a low, round shape, with turned-up brim (**242, 249, 251, 257, 265, 278B, 289, 297**). They did not rival the hood in popularity until after about 1430. Then a tall, sugar loaf style hat became fashionable, especially for young men. It could be decorated with a jewel, brooch or plume. From 1440–65 more varied styles of hat were worn; these were made of felt, beaver, fur or velvet (**226B, G, 227B, D, 237, 262, 270, 299, 310**).

Men wore their *hair* short for most of this period and were generally clean-shaven. Four-

teenth-century styles had a centre parting, with the hair curled loosely at sides and back (**216, 218, 220, 224, 244, 258–60, 274, 276, 281**). From about 1390–1415 a very short style was favoured. It had no parting but the hair was combed in a bowl crop, radiating outwards all round from the crown of the head and turned under all round high up the head; by our standards not very attractive (**221**). After this, the hair was grown a little longer and fashionable young men in the 1450s and 1460s wore their hair very bushy at the sides and back. It was fluffed out and a tall sugar loaf hat perched on top (**230, 231, 241**).

Women's Costume

The clothes worn by women shared many of the same characteristics as those worn by men. They were made of the same type of fabrics, in the same colours, with the same type of heraldic, floral and geometric patterns; they were particoloured and counterchanged just the same, the edges of sleeves and hems were dagged and, especially in the fifteenth century, fur trimmings, edgings and linings were general. In cut also there were similarities. The *gown*, from 1340, was, like the man's pourpoint, fitting on the torso. Generally, it had a low, wide neckline and clung

242 *14th century*   **243** *1390*   **244** *14th century*   **245** *c.1420*   **246** *1450*

France

| 247 | 248 | 249 | 250 | 251 |

tightly to the body as far as the hips where a jewelled, heavy plaque leather belt was often worn. Sleeves too were exactly like the men's at this time, tight-fitting, reaching to the first row of knuckles on the hand and with buttons all along the outer arm from elbow to wrist. Also, like the masculine version, the gown sleeves often ended at the elbow in a band, with tippet dangling and the undergown sleeve continued tight and buttoned to the hand. Only the skirt was different. Instead of tight hose was a very full long skirt with train (**217, 219, 225, 226D, 278C**).

Although this gown was worn alone, more popular in the years from 1340–1460 was the *sideless surcoat* worn on top. With the same almost off-the-shoulder wide neckline, this had immensely large armholes reaching to the hips. The neck and armhole edge were usually fur-edged and, in addition, down the front was a fur plastron set with jewelled buttons down the centre, which usually attached it, for support, to the gown underneath. Sometimes the central fur strip was very narrow and needed such assistance to take the weight of the immensely full, long skirt and train, gathered into the armholes at hip level (**243, 250, 254, 263, 264, 266, 279, 290, 292**).

In some designs, the plastron was very wide and had deep fur-edging to both armholes and below, round the hips. Some surcoats had deep fur hems also (**233, 238, 287**).

Towards the end of the fourteenth century, women began to wear the *houppelande*, which was very similar to that worn then by the men. It had a high waist girded by a deep belt, a high or wide collar at the neck and immensely wide sleeves, generally with dagged edges. The garment itself was very long and full (**223, 226A, 236, 239, 245, 247, 256, 268, 271, 275, 278D, 282, 285, 286**). Towards 1460, the feminine gown returned to a less full style. Sleeves were long and narrow, the bodice fitting and the neckline in a low V or U, with an inserted ornamental plastron to fill the space. These gowns were usually fur-trimmed at neck, wrists and hem and were often fur-lined also. The skirt was usually held up to show the kirtle or undergown (**226E, 227A, C, E, 229, 232, 252A, 261, 273, 277**).

Mantles and cloaks were worn for travelling during these years, but the sideless surcoat and the voluminous houppelande rendered them unnecessary for ordinary outdoor wear.

Feminine *underwear* comprised similar items

to that of the men. Ladies wore a similar full chemise and braies. In addition, the more fitting gowns required some figure control, especially to maintain a slender waist which would contrast attractively with the delineated breast and hip line. So, underneath the chemise, ladies began to wear a stiffened linen underbodice. The stiffening was provided by paste inserted between two layers of linen in the bodice. Generally referred to as the cotte, it is the earliest form of corset known in the Medieval period. It seems likely that the ladies of the fourteenth century would have been horrified if they had realised where these modest beginnings, in women's search for the ideal figure,

would lead in the sixteenth, eighteenth and nineteenth centuries.

Women wore hose and their *footwear* was also similar to the men's but never attained the excessive length of toe to the masculine counterpart. They also wore soft leather shoes in bright colours, jewelled and embroidered, generally fastened by a strap on the instep.

Women wore their *hair* long all this period, with a centre parting and dressed in long plaits coiled or arranged on each side of the head over the ears. In the *fourteenth century*, the most usual *headdress* was the metal caul. By mid-century this was generally in the form of a mesh cylinder worn

253 c.1375   254 1380   255 c.1400   256 c.1425–50   257 1413

one on each side of the head. Each cylinder had a jewelled, metal band top and bottom, though the ends were open to tuck the plaits inside. The two cylinders were attached to a metal fillet round the brow. This could be worn alone or in conjunction with a veil, crown or wimple (**243, 266, 278C, D, 279, 293**).

The varied selection of incredible headdresses worn by ladies in the *fifteenth century* have been the target for the wit, sarcasm and approbation of writers then and now. It seemed as if the desire to express individuality and personality which was displayed by the men in their tight hose and tunics was given rein by the women in their headdresses. This was also the feature which varied most between one country and another, expressing not only individual personality but national character also.

Although the diversity was almost limitless, there were four chief categories of headdress: the caul, the turban, the heart-shaped headdress and the steeple or cone. In the first quarter of the fifteenth century the *caul* was now a different shape from previously. Still in boxes over the ears, the cylindrical form had changed to a wide shape, rising to a point or horn above and on each side of the head. A wired veil was then draped over this so that it hung in graceful folds on

either side and dipped over the forehead in front. This headdress is characterised by its extreme width (**238, 275, 282, 285, 300**).

The *turban* was of Oriental influence and worn for much of the first half of the century. Some examples, especially Burgundian and Flemish ones, were very deep padded rolls, draped with beads and pearls and decorated with jewels. They were worn with or without a veil (**226A, C, E, 227E, 236, 239, 247, 268, 273, 277, 308**). The *heart-shaped headdress* developed from the turban. It also was a padded roll, covered in fine material, jewelled and with bead ropes, but it was curved in shape, dipping in the centre of the forehead and rising at each side. It was frequently worn over side cauls of a softer nature than before, not set in a metal framework. Sometimes a veil accompanied the headdress, sometimes a liripipe was added to hang down some four or five feet (**227A, 233, 245, 261, 286, 287, 302**).

In the second half of the century, headdresses became tall rather than wide. Towards 1460 a tall version of the heart-shaped headdress developed, still dipping in the centre front but rising higher and narrower at the sides. This had deeper flanking cauls and material draped at the back (**226F, 232, 252A**).

The *steeple headdress* like a dunce's cap, sometimes truncated to half its length, developed after 1430 and was especially to be seen in the second half of the century. In this style the hair was barely visible. It was drawn tightly back and covered by the cap headdress which was set on the back of the head just behind the ears. Any hair that showed on temples and nape was plucked out. The cap was of luxurious material, most often favoured was gold or silver cloth which would glisten through the transparent white wired veil worn on top of it (**229, 295**).

The chief *accessories* worn and carried by men and women were gold and silver neck- or hip-chains, sometimes with a small dagger attached, a purse, again hung from the belt, the baldric and, occasionally, gloves.

Jewellery was more delicate and intricate in design now. Jewelled articles especially prized were necklaces and heavy neckchains; brooches – worn especially in the hat or hood; crowns, fillets and cauls.

There was, as yet, little contemporary evidence of *children's clothes*. Where they are illustrated in manuscripts, tapestries and paintings, they are dressed as facsimiles of their parents (**222, 249**). Babies of both sexes were swaddled, that is,

wrapped in bandages from neck to toe, arms and legs bound tightly to the body, since it was feared that in extreme youth these appendages might fall off. Little girls were often bareheaded and did not wear such elaborate headdresses as their mothers, though they might be seen in a small turban or coif with veil.

Italy

Though divided into city states, each wealthy and powerful, distinguished by its individual version of the current fashion, Italian dress overall throughout the Middle Ages differed from that worn elsewhere in Europe. It is characterised on the one hand by the luxurious beauty of the fabrics, their colours and enrichment and, on the other, by a national elegance of cut which, allied to the equally natural dignified deportment of the wearers, gave to the Italians the reputation of the best dressed country of Europe. The years from the mid-fourteenth to the late fifteenth century were a time of economic prosperity for these city states. Italy herself produced a wealth of those wonderful fabrics in silks, brocades, damasks, velvets, woven in rich and delicate colours as well

258 *1413*   **259** *1425–50*   **260** *1450*   **261** *1455*   **262** *1460*

Spain

263 *Austrian, c.1410* **264** *German, 1350–60* **265** *German, c.1420* **266, 267** *Austrian, 1350–1400*

as gold and silver materials. Gold cloth was especially favoured as were outfits designed in one or more shades of a single colour. Some fabrics were plain but were more often patterned in stripes, heraldic and floral motifs and embroidered with colour, gold, pearls and jewels.

In the fourteenth century and the early years of the fifteenth the Italians enthusiastically adopted *dagged* edges. These were employed especially on cloaks and mantles, shoulder capes, houppelande sleeves and tippets. They could be simple shapes or cut into complex oak leaf patterns (**216, 218, 223, 224, 226A, D**). *Parti-colouring* was especially popular in Italy (**226B**) and *fur* was widely used in the fifteenth century as a trimming to hems and sleeves, also as a lining (**226A, E, F, 227B, D, F**).

Renaissance ideals were particularly evidenced in Italy, the source of the movement. The masculine figure was shown to advantage, as elsewhere, but in Italy this was noticeable earlier in the fourteenth century and the stress was always on the natural figure, not an artificially constricted one. Thus, men's dress closely followed the lines of the male form, displaying it and delineating its features on torso and limbs but not exaggerating the broad chest or narrow waist and hips as, in

Burgundy, for instance. The natural form was especially in evidence in the fourteenth century (**216, 218, 220, 221, 224, 226B**). In the mid-fifteenth century padding was used extensively in the great variety of sleeve styles. Sometimes these hung behind the arm in padded, pleated capes (**227B, D**), sometimes they were padded into a huge bag which was pleated into a fur-edged cuff. This sleeve could be worn normally or hang behind the arm (**226G, 227F**).

Most men wore their *hair* short in the fourteenth century in a neat bang (**216, 218, 220, 221, 311**). After 1420, longer, curled and bushy styles were popular and, by 1450–60, hair was loose and long (**226B, G, 227B, F, 310**). It was always well groomed and most Italian males shaved facial hair. Variety in headcovering was tremendous. The *hood* was normal wear for much of the fourteenth century, with shoulder cape attached; the hood portion often being pushed back partly or wholly from the head (**216, 218, 220, 312**). As elsewhere, the hood from then changed its form by stages (**301, 311**), when it could be worn with a hat on top (**227F**). Fifteenth-century *hat* styles were most varied, from high soft crowns, with or without a point (**226B, 227D**) and hats with high or low crowns, but a long, forward peak (**226G, 310**) to early instances of the velvet beret so characteristic everywhere later in the century (**227B**). Many men went bareheaded.

Footwear reflected the general European modes but delicately patterned, coloured leather *boots* were always fashionable in Italy (**216, 226G, 307**). *Shoes*, in the current styles, were also brightly coloured and finely made (**221, 224**), while soled hose were worn indoors with wood and cork *pattens* outdoors. The excessively long-toed styles were less extravagant in Italy than in Burgundy or Flanders.

It was a feature of Renaissance Italy that the dress of the *Italian female* was as rich and elegant as that of her man. The cult of humanism gave a greater freedom and importance to the position of women in society than Christian Medieval life had done. The well-to-do, fashionable Italian lady took every advantage of this and dressed with taste and elegance, wealth and luxury, in the most glorious fabrics, cut to show off her figure in its natural lines. Décolleté necklines were in vogue

in square, V or boat-shape (**217, 219, 225, 227A, C, E**). Higher necklines were also worn but usually with a houppelande style of dress (**223, 226A**). The gown was closely fitting to the bust and waist and the skirt very full, gathered or belted at a high waistline or slinkily following a princess line over waist and hips. The former style was usual wear after 1380 (**223, 226C, D, E, 227A, C, E**), while the latter was seen in the fourteenth century especially, when the hips might be encircled by a girdle (**217, 219, 225**). Throughout this period ladies pinned or held their skirts up to show the beautiful fabric of the undergown and their sleeves were designed in complex styles, slit and puffed also to display their under-sleeves (**225, 226E, 227C**).

It continued to be a characteristic of Italy that ladies often wore their *hair* uncovered, though an astonishing variety of headdresses were available, especially in the fifteenth century. Veils were much less common than in other countries. In the fourteenth century the Italian lady's coiffure was dressed in plaits or braids which were tightly bound round the back of her head and dressed

268, 269 *Swiss, 1430–40*   **270** *Austrian, 1440*   **271, 272** *Swiss, 1430–40*

Switzerland and Austria

273, 274 *Swiss, 1460–70*   **275** *German, 1460*   **276** *German, c.1465*   **277** *Swiss, c.1460*

there with a pearl and jewelled net or with ribbons and a small plume. Only occasionally were the plaits worn at the sides and the cylindrical cauls fashionable elsewhere were rarely to be seen. It was the coiffure which was decorated not a headdress (**217, 223, 225, 226D, 303, 309**). The *heart-shaped headdress* of the mid-fifteenth century appeared in Italy in differing forms, generally with a liripipe attached (**226F, 227A, C, 302**). By far the most popular and characteristic Italian feminine headdress of this time was the *turban*, made of beautiful fabrics, jewelled and embroidered and worn soft (**226A, 308**) or padded to huge dimensions (**226C, E, 227E**).

Burgundy

France had been one of the leaders of Medieval fashion until the fourteenth century but, during the years 1340–65, was too weakened by the Hundred Years' War (1377–1453) with England to develop to the full her textile industries. The country was impoverished and luxury in costume

only manifested itself in two short periods during this time: the late fourteenth and early fifteenth century and in the 1450s.

The pace-setter in fashion in this part of Europe was the Duchy of Burgundy which possessed the most beautiful fabrics of wealth and design, rich colours with gold and silver cloth and jewelled embroideries. Especially in the first two-thirds of the fifteenth century, was Burgundian dress admired, copied and envied by the whole western world. It was noted not only for the richness of its fabrics and jewels but for its extremes as well as elegance of style. In men's dress, the tight tunics were more fitting, padding and pleats more excessive, skirts shorter showing a larger area of hose whose toes extended in ridiculous points. Young men wore tall hats at a rakish angle over fluffy, bushy hair. Ladies' gowns had more fitting bodices delineating the breast line, higher waist belts, lower necklines and tall, be-jewelled headdresses with complex wired veils. Both sexes wore their clothes with an air of elegance and insouciance, the men displaying their mascu-

66

linity by gesture and stance, the ladies their feminine attractions in a coyly lifted skirt and tilt to the head (**228, 229, 230, 231, 232, 294**).

The Burgundian domination of Flanders had a strong influence on dress there. Here also were rich fabrics, elegant headdresses, tight, short tunics, tall hats and long, pointed toes. Older men and women also displayed elegance though in a more formal, dignified manner (**233, 234, 235, 236, 237, 238, 239, 240, 241, 295, 299**).

Costume in *France* was therefore influenced from outside during these years, first from Italy, then from Burgundy and England. It followed the pattern as described and illustrated in this chapter and fig. **293** show its traditional interpretations.

Spain

Moorish power was now limited to the southern half of the peninsula but its influence was felt strongly all over the country in textile design, the fabrics used and the richness of the colours. The materials made in the south were used all over the peninsula and exported overseas.

While the decorative motifs and embroidery were predominantly Moorish, Spain followed western fashion in style. Fabrics were patterned all over more than elsewhere and fur trimming was used less than embroidered edging. The fitting gown and the houppelande were, in general, more favoured than the sideless surcoat **297**).

Costume in *Germany* and *England* had much in common. In Germany less decoration was used in embroidery and woven textiles also less richness in jewelled decoration and in the use of cosmetics. Brilliant colours were in demand in both countries also dagged edging to garments, parti-colouring and counterchange patterns. Indeed, the dagges were sometimes referred to as

279 *1360*   280 *1350*   281 *1365*   282 *1415*   283 *1455*

the 'German mode'. In Germany, printed textiles, in imitation of the Italian brocades, were popular due to their economic price, (**263, 264, 265, 275, 276, 305, 306, 314**). English dress was more modish than German at this time and, for much of the period, strongly influenced French designs (**298**).

Swiss dress was more elegant than the German and was closer to English modes. This can be seen in the extensive use of fur for linings and hems and the prevalence of pleated, padded tunics and gowns (**269, 271, 272, 274**). Dagged edges were worn to excess (**268**). Italian and Oriental influence is shown in the popularity in Switzerland for large turbans, worn by men as well as women. These were draped and swathed and had liripipes attached which were plain or dagged (**268, 269, 273, 277, 304, 313**).

Costume in *northern Europe* followed the general mode but lagged behind so that each style was later in coming into fashion. In the Middle Ages this applied to all the arts here as a simple result of the geographical isolation of areas such as Scandinavia. In general, dress was plainer, less extreme and with a smaller quantity of decoration

than elsewhere page 70 and (**296**).

Central and Eastern Europe

The influences here were strongly Asiatic. Under Genghis Khan the Mongolian Empire had been extended in the thirteenth century as far west as the Danube delta in the south and Cracow further north. In the following century the Turks advanced to establish the Ottoman Empire over this area taking Constantinople in 1453. For *eastern Europe*, in countries like Greece, Bulgaria, Russia and Poland, the *caftan* style of coat was worn. This was buttoned up to the neck in front and had long, full sleeves. Under it was worn a shirt and trousers.

In *central Europe*, in Czechoslovakia, Hungary and Austria this influence was also felt but to a lesser extent. Western influence on dress was fairly strong in Austria and Czechoslovakia (**263, 266, 267, 270**) and also in Hungary during the fourteenth century, when the Magyars enjoyed economic prosperity and evinced a high standard of art and culture. During the fifteenth century Hungary continued to prosper but Turkish pressure on her boundaries increased steadily and a Turkish influence on dress became apparent from the close military contact between the races. This had little effect on women's dress, which followed Italian lines, but more so on men's, where the dolman coat and trousers began to be worn.

Notes on the Illustrations

216 Painting by Giovanni da Milano, 1365. Red cloak with white lining and gold border. Red tunic, patterned in gold. Dark purple and blue dagges. Blue and gold undertunic. Deep blue hose, black boots. Blue hood.

217 Fresco, Cappella Rinunccini in the Church of S. Croce, Florence, 1365. White dress with gold banding. Crimson centre panel.

218 Painting by Tommaso da Modena in Museo Civico, Treviso.

219 Painting by Giovanni da Milano, 1365. Deep blue gown with gold, jewelled girdle and neckband. Jewelled hair-band.

220 Illuminated MS of Lancelot du lac. Bibliotèque Nationale, Paris.

221 Illuminated MS, 1380. Biblioteca Casantense, Rome.

222 Fresco, Oratorio di San Giorgio, Padua, 1377.

Child in striped gown.

223 Painting by Andrea di Bartolo in the Metropolitan Museum of Art, New York. c.1380.

224 Illuminated MS, 1380. Bibliotèque Nationale, Paris.

225 Illuminated MS, 1380. Bibliotèque Nationale, Paris. Pink gown with white lining and gold neckband. Dark blue undergown.

226A Painting by Gentile da Fabriano, Louvre, Paris, 1423. Deep crimson velvet houppelande with white fur lining and dagged sleeves. Gold caul and turban of dark green leaves and gold, red and white flowers.

B Painting by Maestro del Cassone Adimari, Accademia, Florence, mid-fifteenth century. Red cloak with white border, and same coloured tunic. Sleeve in gold and black. Hose, one leg plain black, the other black and white. Black hat.

C Fresco. Palazzo della Ragione, Padua. c.1430. Light grey-blue patterned gown. Magenta sleeves with gold and white design. Blue belt with gold medallions. Gold necklace. Pink turban with embroidered ribbon bands.

D Florentine School of Painting. Bargello Palace and Museum, Florence, 1445. Purple gown with gold jewelled neckband and hem. Sleeves red with gold cuffs and double dagges, two to each sleeve, in gold. Gold tiara.

E Illuminated MS from Mantua. Now in Vatican

284 c.1450   **285** c.1435   **286** 1445   **287** 1458

England   69

Library, Rome. 1435. Pearl coloured gown lined and decorated with grey fur. Deep red belt and turban.

F Painting by Maestro del Cassone Adimari, Accademia, Florence, mid-fifteenth century. Black gown with gold pattern. Gold and white sleeves. Headdress in black and gold.

G Painting by Domenico di Bartolo 'Banchetto dei Poveri'. Spedale di Santa Maria della Scala, Siena, 1440–4. Patterned tunic and sleeves with dark fur. White shirt. Fur hat with gold tassels. Black boots.

227A Tapestry 27 scenes from the 'Life of S. John the Baptist' designed by Antonio del Pollaiolo. Completed 1469. Museo dell' Opera del Duomo, Florence. Red dress, gold belt, hem and neckband. Gold decorative undersleeves. Red headdress and liripipe over gold cauls.

B Venetian painting by Francesco dei Francesci 'The Martyrdom of S. Momente'. Museo Correr, Venice, 1450–60. Blue pleated tunic, brown fur, gold belt. Red undertunic and hat. Dark green hose, white shoes.

C Tapestry as in 'A'. Yellow gown with gold hem border, belt and neckband. Crimson undergown shows through lacings. Gold headdress.

D Venetian painting by Maestro dei Cassoni Jarves. Museo Correr, Venice, 1450–60. Deep red tunic and hat. Grey fur on tunic, brown on hat. Gold, jewelled belt. Sleeves pleated of gold frabric patterned in black line. Gold undertunic. Scarlet hose.

E Painting as 'D'. Gold cloth gown and turban with brown pattern. Plain brown lining. Jewelled belt and neckline. Pearls on turban.

F Painting by Antonio Vivarini 'Wedding of Santa Monica'. Accademia Galley, Venice, c.1465. Blue tunic, pleated and padded. Brown fur. Green hose and hood. Gold undertunic.

228 Duke Philip of Burgundy. Chronicles of Hainault. MS. Bibliotèque Royale, Brussels. c.1447. Plain, dark costume, fur trimmed and with gold chain. Wood pattens.

229 and 232 Burgundian coronation ceremony from Jean Mansel's 'Fleur des Histoires', painted c.1425–35. Book miniature. The lady in 229 has a fur plastron and heavily brocaded gown with fringed hem held up over a light undergown. Steeple headdress with stiffened veil. In 232 the lady wears a tall, padded headdress in dark velvet and fur trimmed gown over a striped inset.

230 and 231 MS c.1450 Bibliotèque Nationale,

288 *Sweden, 1440*   **289** *Denmark, 1410*   **290** *Poland, 1361*   **291, 292** *Denmark, 1350*

Northern Europe

294 *Chaperon and liripipe in velvet, Burgundy, mid 15th century*

293 *Caul headdress, France, 14th century*

295 *Flemish Burgundian hennin and veil, c.1435*

297 *Felt hat, Spain, c.1430*

296 *Cloth hood, Greenland*

299 *Young man, Flemish Burgundian, c.1456*

298 *Hood, English, c.1400*

300 *Horned headdress, Flemish Burgundian, 1420–30*

Paris. The young man in 230 wears a blue padded and pleated tunic with brown hose and black shoes. Red hat. In 231, the tunic is loose and short, of gold cloth, patterned in red and edged with grey fur. Black hat with gold ornaments. Black hose.

233 Painting 'The Virgin and Child with Saints' by Hans Memlinc, National Gallery, London. c.1465. Gold and black pomegrante patterned sideless gown with white fur plastron and edging. Deep red undergown. Dark blue mantle with gold cord and jewelled fastening. Headdress of gold, jewelled black velvet. White veil.

234 Carved wood statuette from grave of Graf van Isabella Bourbon, South Brabant. Rijksmuseum, Amsterdam, 1476. Houppelande with dagged sleeves. Jewelled hip-belt. Chaperon.

235 Painting, triptych, by Roger van der Weyden, c.1450. Musé des Beaux Arts, Antwerp. Red tunic with brown fur trimming. Brown chaperon slung over shoulder by liripipe. Red hose. Black shoes, wood pattens. Brown undertunic.

236 Statuette as '234'. Turban with jewel and pearl ropes and veil. High belted gown with full skirt and sleeves over fringed-hemmed undergown.

237 Painting 'Marriage of Giovanni Arnolfini' by Jan van Eyck, National Gallery, London. c.1434. Brown velvet and fur houppelande over black tunic and hose. Black hat.

238 Painting, Musée Communal des Beaux Arts, Bruges. c.1465. Navy velvet sideless surcoat with ermine plastron and trimming. Pale blue undergown. Wired veil headdress over gold cauls.

239 Statuette as '234'. Padded turban with lace-edged tabs hung over it. Mantle fastened with cords over a high-waisted gown.

240 and 241 Court of Burgundy, Chronicles of Hainault c.1447–50. MS. Bibliotèque Royale, Brussels. In 240 the gentleman wears a pleated, patterned houppelande with fur trimming. Chaperon with liripipe. Long-toed hose. The young man in 241 has a short pleated tunic with waistbelt and full, padded sleeves. Tall hat.

242 Stone statue, Cathedral of S. Denis. Tunic with long, dagged sleeves. Dagged shoulder cape and hood with hat on top. Boots over hose.

243 Stone statue of Jeanne de Bourbon, Louvre, Paris. Sideless surcoat with jewelled plastron and fur edging. Jewelled hip belt over undergown.

244 Stone statue, Cathedral of S. Denis. Tunic with high neckline and chain necklace. Wide bag sleeves.

245 Harley MS. British Museum, London. Blue houppelande with grey fur lining. Red, jewelled belt. Heart-shaped headdress in black and gold over gold caul.

246 Tapestry, Musée de Cluny, Paris. Deep red cloak and tunic, grey fur edging and lining. Grey hose. Blue hood.

247 Tapestry, Musée des Arts Decoratifs, Paris.

Light coloured fur-lined houppelande with floral design. Jewelled baldric, belt and neckchain. Jewelled turban and white veil. Red undergown shows at sleeves.

248 MS. Grandes Heures de Duc du Berry. Pink houppelande, white lining, dagged edges. Blue tunic. Black hose. Scarlet hood.

249 Tapestry, Musée des Arts Decoratifs, Paris. Boy in floral patterned houppelande with dagged sleeves. Jewelled turban and veil.

250 MS. White linen wired headdress. Surcoat with fur edging.

251 Tapestry, Musée des Arts Decoratifs, Paris. Shorter houppelande with gold pattern all over and gold belt. Embroidered baldric. Jewelled hood.

252 Tapestry, Musée des Arts Decoratifs, Paris.

A Plain dress with decorative border, fur neckline and jewelled belt. Striped plastron. Gold necklace. Striped headdress over black, jewelled cap.

B Plain tunic with fur hem and leather belt. Brown Chaperon with dagged liripipe. Plain hose, brown boots. Patterned undertunic.

C Padded, pleated, fur trimmed tunic with jewelled leather belt. Patterned undertunic. Chaperon. Hose.

253 Altar painting. Museum of Catalan Art, Barcelona. Fitted, patterned tunic with jewelled, plaque hip-belt. Hood with liripipe and dagged cape. Hose with legs in different colours. Black shoes.

254 Altar painting, Museum of Catalan Art, Barcelona. Surcote with gold decorated neckband and plastron. Jewelled hip-belt on undergown. White chemise.

255 Altar painting, Museum of Catalan Art, Barcelona. Purple velvet gown with grey fur, leather belt and gold decorated purse. Light blue undertunic. Dark blue chaperon. Red hose. Black shoes.

256 Painting, Prado, Madrid. Green houppelande with all over pattern of gold bells. Brown fur trimming. Gold neckchain and belt. Brown hat.

257 Altar piece of S. Peter by Lluis Borrasá, Santa Maria d'Egara, Terrassa. Houppelande with dagged sleeves and patterned baldric. Striped headdress.

258 Altarpiece as '257'. Pink tunic with brown fur trimming and jewelled leather and metal hip-belt. Dark green chaperon and liripipe.

259 Painting, Prado, Madrid. Parti-coloured tunic, one half purple, one grey. Parti-coloured hose, one leg red, one white.

260 Altar painting, Museum of Catalan Art, Barcelona. Purple, pleated tunic with black jewelled belt, purse and hem. Dark green undertunic. Boots and pattens.

261 Painting, Catalan School 'Banquet of Herod'. Metropolitan Museum, New York. Patterned houppelande with ermine trimming. White chemise. Red heart-shaped headdress, jewelled, over gold caul.

262 Altar painting, Museum of Catalan Art, Barcelona. Brown, fur-trimmed gown. Fur hat and plume.

Headdresses and Footwear, 1340–1465

301 *Chaperon, Italian, 1449*

302 *Black velvet and gold, jewelled headdress, Italian, c.1450–60*

303 *White silk, jewelled, pearl headdress, Italian, c.1450*

304 *Leather shoe, Swiss*

305 *Wooden patten, German*

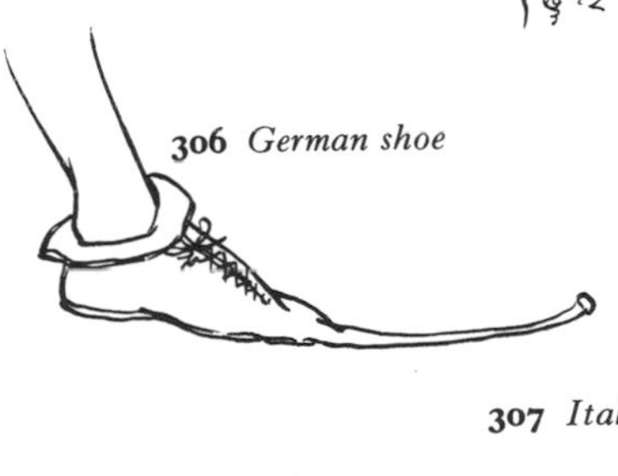

306 *German shoe*

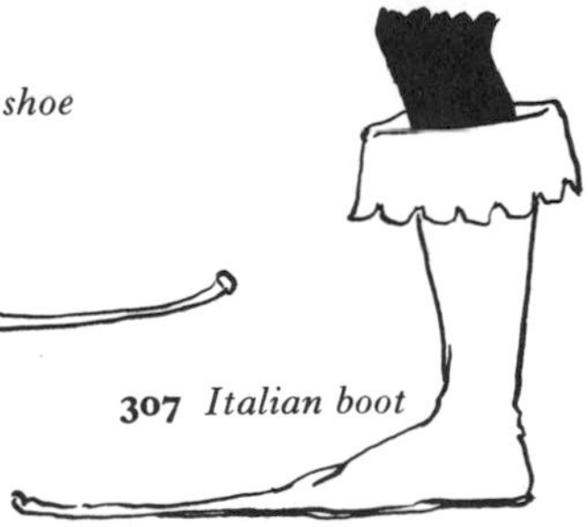

307 *Italian boot*

308 *Silk, soft turban and jewelled bands, Italian c.1450*

309 *Florentine white headdress with pearl decoration, c.1460*

310 *Italian hat, 1400*

311 *Italian hood, 1363*

312 *Parti-coloured hood, Italian, 1355*

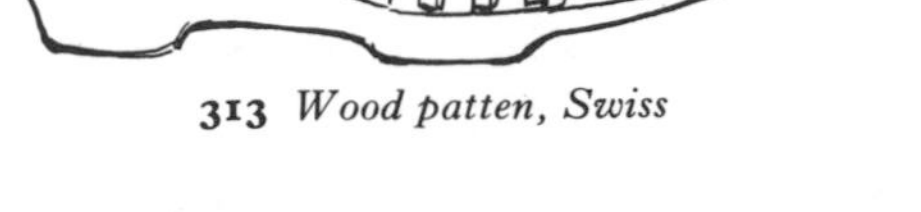

313 *Wood patten, Swiss*

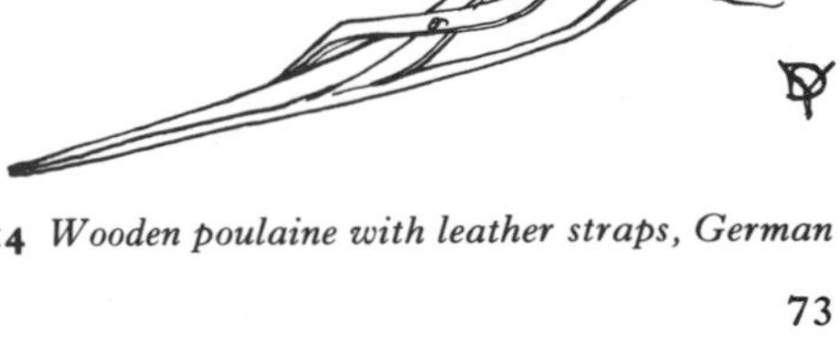

314 *Wooden poulaine with leather straps, German*

Red hose. Black shoes.

263 German altar-painting, Kunsthistorisches Museum, Vienna. Red sideless surcoat with white fur plastron and edging. White fur lining. Blue undergown with jewelled hip-belt. Gold fillet, white veil.

264 German painting from Kloster Langheim bei Lichtenfels at the Bayerische Nationalmuseum, Munich. Silver-grey sideless surcoat with ermine trimming. Red undergown with gold design. Gold fillet.

265 Crossing altar painting from Furstätt, in the Bayerische Nationalmuseum, Munich. Red tunic with brown fur hem and gold belt. Green cloak with gold edge and ermine lining. Red cap with white brim and gold band.

266 and 267 Stone statues from the west façade of S. Stephen's Cathedral, Vienna in the Historisches Museum der Stadt Wien. Duke Rudolf and his wife.

268 Tapestry, Historisches Museum, Basle. Houppelande with sleeves with double dagged edges in red and blue. Turban with dagged tabs and liripipe.

269 Painting 'the Three Kings' from west Switzerland in the Bayerische Nationalmuseum, Munich. Deep blue and grey tunic. Scarlet hose. Crimson overtunic with light brown fur. Brown boots with grey lining. White turban.

270 Painting, Unteres Belvedere, Vienna. Dull green houppelande with brown fur and black and gold belt. Green cap.

271 Tapestry, Historisches Museum, Basle. Blue gown with white fur trimming and red belt with gold plaque decoration. Floral hair-band. Red undersleeves.

272 Tapestry, Historisches Museum, Basle. Blue houppelande with fur trimming and jewelled belt. Chaperon. Black boots, blue hose.

273 Tapestry, Historisches Museum, Basle. Blue and fawn patterned dress with white fur. White undergown with white fur hem. White turban and liripipe.

274 Tapestry, Historisches Museum, Basle. Red, patterned gown with fur trimming. Blue undertunic. Blue hose, boots.

275 Painting of S. Katharine from Kloster Ottobeuren at the Bayerische Nationalmuseum, Munich. Scarlet dress and cloak. Ermine lining to cloak. Black and gold belt. Pale pink headdress.

276 Wall painting from 'Altenhof' in Munich at the Bayerische Nationalmuseum, Munich. Red tunic and hose. Gold bells on chains hang from gold belt. Gold neckchain.

277 Painting by Basle painter, Kunstmuseum, Basle. Blue gown with pink cuffs and neckband. Brown undergown. White turban with gold and black decoration.

278A Gold cloth houppelande with white fur lining and trimming. Fawn baldric with gold bells. Red hose. White hood. Gold chain necklace, 1390.

B Patterned blue tunic with bag sleeves. Parti-coloured hose in green and grey. Fur brimmed velvet cap, 1385.

C Plain gown with tippets at elbow. Gold fillet on head, 1340.

D Pale blue houppelande with dagged sleeves. Jewelled belt. Gold cylindrical cauls and veil, 1380.

E Patterned tunic with jewelled plaque hip-belt. Parti-coloured hose in red, green and white, 1377.

279 Crimson velvet sideless surcoat with white fur trimming and jewelled buttons on front of plastron. Grey undergown with jewelled hip-belt. Gold cylindrical cauls.

280 Heraldic counterchange design to tunic with dagged hem. Dark hood with liripipe. Parti-coloured hose.

281 Tunic with floral pattern and jewelled, plaque hip-belt. Tippets at elbow. Shoulder cape parti-coloured, hood thrown back. Parti-coloured hose.

282 Plain, high-belted houppelande with double collar. Gold cauls with wired white veil.

283 Grey and red patterned tunic. Blue hose, black shoes. Blue chaperon with brooch.

284 Patterned gold and blue pleated houppelande with fur trimming. Dark velvet chaperon with liripipe. Leather belt and purse.

285 Dark red houppelande with white collar and jewelled belt. Gold, jewelled headdress and veil.

286 Gold and red houppelande with white collar, high, jewelled, black belt and dagged sleeves. Dark red velvet heart-shaped headdress with liripipe, decorated with brooch and pearls. Worn over gold cauls.

287 Grey sideless surcoat with white plastron and edges over pink spotted undergown with jewelled hip-belt. Dark blue mantle with light edge and cord fastening. Dark velvet heart-shaped headdress with veil over gold cauls.

English examples from church brasses all over the country, MS in British Museum and paintings, tapestries and sculpture in Victoria and Albert Museum, London.

288 Church wall painting, Sweden. Plain buttoned tunic with hip-belt and purse. Dark cap and plain hose.

289 Church wall painting, Denmark. Fur-edged short tunic. Gold neckchain with bells on chains. Plumed hat.

290 Church brass, Poland. Sideless surcoat with embroidered edges. No hip-belt. Mantle, Decorative headdress over striped silk cap.

291 Church wall painting, Denmark. Fur-edged sideless surcoat. Ungirded undergown. Crown and veil.

292 Wall painting, Denmark. Dagged, decorative shoulder cape. Plain tunic with hip-belt. Ornamental sleeve tippets.

293 Sculpture, Poitiers, France. Gold fillet and cauls.

294 Tapestry, Victoria and Albert Museum, London. Red chaperon and liripipe. Blue tunic with brown fur collar. Black undertunic.

295 Portrait by Roger van der Weyden. National

Gallery, London. White veil over gold headdress. Dark red gown with black velvet edge over red plastron and white linen.

296 Actual hood from Greenland. Copenhagen National Museum.

297 Altar painting, Spain. Hat with brooch.

298 Portrait of King Henry IV of England. National Portrait Gallery, London. Red hood with gold border and jewel. Gold neckchain. Blue tunic with gold decorative border.

299 Portrait of a young man. Grey, tall hat. Black tunic with gold neckchain.

300 Portrait of the painter's wife by Jan van Eyck. Musée des Beaux Arts, Bruges. White pleated, stiffened headdress over brown check cauls. Deep red dress with grey fur collar and green belt.

301 Medallion by Pisanello, Berlin Museum.

302 Painting, Galleria Nazionale di Sicilia, Palermo.

303 Portrait by Paolo Uccello, Metropolitan Museum of Art, New York.

304 to 307 Bally Shoe Museum, Schönenwerd, Switzerland.

308 Fresco, 'Trionfo della Morte', Galleria Nazionale di Sicilia, Palermo.

309 Florentine painting, National Galley, London.

310 Portrait, Pisa.

311 Fresco, Camposanto, Pisa, Piazza dei Miracoli.

312 Fresco, cloisters, S. Maria Novella, Florence.

313 Bally Shoe Museum.

314 Bayerische Nationalmuseum, Munich.

Chapter Four

Spread of the Renaissance 1465–1540

The later fifteenth century saw a Europe divided into larger units than in the earlier Middle Ages; only Italy, with its small but rich and powerful city states, was the exception. Dominant European kingdoms included Spain, England, France, in the west, the Scandinavian countries, Russia and Poland in the north, with the Holy Roman Empire still of importance in central Europe and the Ottoman Empire establishing itself further west than before. Europe was also looking outside the continent. From Portugal, Spain and Italy especially, men sailed on voyages of discovery to the East and across the Atlantic to the far West. Both the grouping by means of warfare and inter-marriage in the European states and the exploration overseas had an effect on costume. The larger units created stronger influences over a larger area and population; the overseas discoveries led to the introduction of new materials, metals and jewels.

In Europe itself, the effects of two great movements were reflected in people's dress: they were the Renaissance and the Reformation. The former affected most closely the southern and Latin peoples, firstly Italy, from where it had sprung, but also Spain, Portugal, much of France and Burgundy. The Reformation dominated chiefly the northern lands – Germany, Switzerland, Holland, England, Scandinavia. In Bohemia, the Hussite Movement, called after Jan Hus, was strongest a century earlier. These two movements had opposite effects. The Italian Renaissance, with its Humanist outlook and idealisation of the human body, encouraged elegant, rich dress, natural in line, but often extravagant in fabric, decoration and form. The protagonists of the Reformation frowned upon richness of dress, décolleté necklines and other indications of coquetry and display. In countries where the movement was strongest, people were exhorted to wear dull colours, plain clothes and eschew all ornament and permissive ostentation.

The picture thus conjured up of a northern Europe attired in sombre, reticent garments and a southern Europe in gay exuberance, is too facile. The reality was more complex, for human needs, frailties and desires more often prevailed against the political and authoritarian forces. For two hundred years, sumptuary laws had been passed with increasing severity and frequency in an attempt to restrain people from aping their betters and wearing clothes of a richness and ornamentation which compared with the royal courts of the continent. This method always failed. The aristocracy just had to find something new, more ostentatious and luxurious in order to maintain their distinction. So the pattern continued. Dress was the outward, visible symbol of position and importance. In the Middle Ages it had the same status effect as has the automobile in the twentieth century. Because of this, although it is true to say that the Reformation curbed some of the excesses and luxury of dress in northern Europe and the Renaissance encouraged the display and enhancement of the human figure in the south, the pattern is not too different in various countries. The wealthy and the powerful often succeeded in dressing in a rich and elaborate manner wherever they lived, though materials used and silhouette differed to a greater extent.

The arbiters of fashion in the years 1465–1540 were, successively, *Burgundy, Italy, Germany, Spain*. Until the defeat of Charles the Bold, Duke of Burgundy, at Nancy in 1477, the *Court of Burgundy* remained the leader of European fashion. Both in France and Flanders, Burgundian dress was of rich, patterned fabrics, generously edged and lined with furs. These were a necessity for comfort in the chill draughts of castle living. Young *men* wore tight, abbreviated tunics, tall hats perched rakishly over long bushy or flowing hair and displayed their hips and legs in meticulously fitting hose. The long toes to the foot portion of these reached their most excessive about 1470 (**347, 352, 371**). Alternative wear for both young and older men was the contrastingly

315 *1470–90* 316 *1470–5* 317 *1470–5* 318 *1470–5* 319 *1470–80*

voluminous gowns, with enormous leg-of-mutton sleeves; the skirts of these gowns swept the ground, the edges and linings were of fur or silk and the garment was held in place by a belt or the hands clasped round the body (**349, 350, 354**).

Ladies wore richly ornamented, deep, high belts, fur-edged necklines, plunging to the belt-level in front and only saved from complete exposure of the breasts by a plastron – a small piece of rich fabric – inserted inside. The skirts were immensely full and long, fur-edged and often lined. They were generally held up by the hand or under the arm to display the beautiful under-skirt below. The back of the bodice was also often open to the waist and laced across an insert of different material. Steeple headdresses and rich, bejewelled turbans, with flowing or stiffened, transparent veils provided an extravagant, dramatic finish to the costume (**348, 351, 353, 363, 366, 367, 370**).

In the late fifteenth century *Italian influence* was universal. The beautiful fabrics produced in the city states, richly patterned silks and velvets,

ornamented with gold and silver embroidery and sparkling with jewels, were coveted by all of Europe. The styles of dress were elegant, the colours clear and gay, the human figure, whether male or female, displayed to greatest advantage. Men wore tight hose, often striped to emphasise the shape of the leg, long, flowing hair half-way to the waist at the back and surmounted by caps of various styles, ornamented by jewels and plumes. Tunics were either so short as to reveal the buttocks or longer and loose with flaring collars and hanging sleeves (**316, 317, 320, 321**). Sleeves, for both sexes, other than the hanging styles, were in two or more sections, attached to one another by points and displaying the white undergarment in puffs between. Ladies wore their hair uncovered, braided and long, or with delicate, small, jewelled caps perched on the very back of the head. Dresses were high waisted and very long and full, especially at the back (**324, 326, 361**).

The early years of the *sixteenth century* were a time of transition in style. Italian modes continued to dominate and the men's tight hose and short tunics or alternative gowns became more extreme as did the long hair, but signs of the sixteenth century fuller, squarer form began to appear in wide shoulders and collars, large sleeves and slashed decoration (**328, 358, 364, 378, 390, 393, 402**). In feminine dress, the wide, square neckline replaced the deep V, the waistline returned to normal level and skirts were pinned or held up at side or back (**355, 361, 376, 379, 382, 384C, 403**). Completely different are the headdresses of these years. For men, the velvet bonnet or circular beaver hat replaces the tall fifteenth-century hats (**325, 344, 350, 358, 374, 377, 384A**), while women took to wearing a white coif and over it a velvet cap or hood (**357, 365, 376, 379, 382, 384C, 401**).

The years from *1520–40* were strongly influenced by the strange fashion for *puffs* and *slashes*. The idea came from the Swiss and Bavarian mercenaries, the *lansquenets* (*landsknecht*). Several different explanations exist, putting forward reasons for the origins of this type of decoration. One tells of how, after the battle of 1477, when the Swiss mercenaries had defeated the Burgund-ians, they mended their tattered uniforms with strips of banners and hangings from the tents of the vanquished enemy, producing a multi-coloured attire slashed and showing different materials through the slits. Another states that the clothes of the lansquenets were too tight and that they slashed them to make them more comfortable, thus displaying the undertunic or shirt beneath. Whatever the reason for the beginnings of this custom, by 1520 the fashion had spread over Europe. All garments, for men and women, received this treatment, from tunics, hose and gowns to hats, boots and shoes. The undergarment or white shirt or chemise was pulled through the slits to form a puff of material. The edges of the slash were embroidered or braided and its ends held by points or a jewel clasp (**395, 398**).

As clothes became richer in the 1530s, slashes were extended into patterns of stars or diamonds and garments padded on the shoulders and chest to give a squarer silhouette. This was especially the mode for men who wore a knee-length gown, very full and with an enormous collar and padded

320, 321 *1490–5*   322 *1490–1500*   323 c.*1496*   324 *1485–90*

Italy

79

325 *1502–7*　　　326 *1495–1500*　　　327 *1502–7*　　　328 *1512*　　　329 *1525–30*

sleeves. The chest was padded as was also the cod-piece which now protruded predominantly between the open slit in the skirt which now usually covered the hose to the knees (**362, 384D, 387, 405A**).

In women's dress, the Spanish style of framework skirt began to take over in Europe. The long, full skirt of the early sixteenth century now covered a frame of hoops, which held it out away from the body in a cone-shape from waist to ground and the fullness of the material was concentrated in folds falling to a train. The gown skirts were often open in front, in an inverted V, to show the contrasting, but also rich material of the underskirt. An ornate girdle encircled the waist and sometimes hung down the centre front with a pendant jewel or pomander. In Spain, the framework skirt, the *vertugado*, had been worn since 1470, but generally with the hoops visible (**407, 408**). When adopted in other countries in the 1520s, the framework was made as an underskirt, then covered by further skirts, the bands not being shown on the outside. The name, taken from the Spanish, differed from country to country. It was a farthingale in England, a

vertugale in France. It was accompanied by a stiffened bodice or corset to provide a slender waist to show off the skirt. Other characteristic features of this gown in the 1530s were the square neckline and full, padded and slashed sleeves (**333, 362C, 389, 396, 405B, C, 416A, C**). The hair was worn coiled up on the head and covered by a jewelled cap or hood. The style of these varied greatly from country to country. In general, the costume of the 1530s (a mixture of influence from Germany and Spain), for both sexes, was rich, of superb fabrics, heavily ornamented, jewelled, padded and restricted. It was also most impressive and brilliantly coloured.

Italy

Italian cultural influence in Europe had been a vigorous force since the thirteenth century. The Renaissance movement, developing steadily, established new concepts which led to a complete reappraisal in all the arts, altering the attitude and thoughts of everyone. Not surprisingly costume reflected this new mode of life, as did also general behaviour and manners. The Italians led Europe for over 200 years in their cultural standards and, in the fifteenth century, were the most elegant, best dressed and finely mannered Europeans. Their standards were a model, in this period, of cleanliness and etiquette.

Italy was still a country divided into city states, several of which were wealthy and powerful, ruled by families or the Church. Costume and customs differed from one region to another and there was, as yet, no national style. In the second half of the fifteenth century, when Italian fashion was still so influential, the Venetians were the leaders in the mode and, though many centres were famous for their materials, Venice was especially noted for its damasks, velvets and brocades. Italian fabrics were, by this time, prized and exported all over Europe. Beautiful materials had been woven and embroidered since the twelfth century in Sicily and southern Italy, under the guidance of Byzantine craftsmen and following Oriental designs. In the thirteenth century silkworm culture was established in Tuscany in the region of Lucca and Florence and, a 100 years later, the most superb brocades of silk and velvet, gold and silver cloth and ornately embroidered fabrics were also being manufactured in Genoa, Milan, Bologna and Venice. The second half of the fifteenth century saw the zenith of this achievement, after which Italian weavers moved further afield to set up workshops in France and Flanders.

The sophistication of the Italian civilisation was apparent at this time in the *accessories* and adjuncts to dress as well as in the style itself. Jewellery was ornate and of superb design. It was in the form of belts and girdles, earrings and rings, buttons and brooches. Pearls, jewels and gold were used extravagantly in embroidery on clothes and accessories which was richer than elsewhere. It decorated gloves, purses, hats and caps, shoes and all garments. Lace began to be made. Venetian ladies were noted for their elegant, Oriental style fans and tiny muffs of brocade or velvet. From Italy stemmed the manufacture of perfume, knowledge which had come to the Veneto from the Orient. The handkerchief also appeared here in the fifteenth century, then called a hand-couvrechef or napkin. These early handkerchiefs were large and made of linen or cambric. They were lavishly embroidered and

330 *c.1535*   **331** *1535–40*   **332** *1536–7*   **333** *1535–40*

Italy

Details, 1465–1540

334 *Italian girl, 1515–20*

335 *Pearl-decorated velvet hat, Hungarian, 1525*

336 *Gold turban, German, 1510–12*

337 *Polish nobleman, 1532*

338 *Duke William IV of Bavaria*

339 *Venetian zoccolo*

340 *Italian turban, 1505*

341 *Pantoffle*

342 *Venetian zoccolo*

343 *Velvet shoe*

344 *Francesco Maria della Rovere*

345 *Italian gentleman*

346 *Duchess of Bavaria, 1531*

edged with lace or fringe – it goes without saying that they were costly!

In general, Venice and the eastern part of Italy led the fashion and were affected by Oriental motifs and designs in dress, while the north-western cities such as Genoa had more in common with Burgundian modes. The Spanish influence predominated in Milan, Naples and Florence. Above all, however, Italians loved clear, gay colours and display in their dress. Renaissance ideals demanded the glorification of the human figure and, in men's dress especially, this was revealed and accentuated. The Italians used fewer artificial aids than other nations, rarely employing padding or corsetry to the same extent. They relied for their beautification of the body upon designs which emphasised its natural line. In Burgundy, Spain and even France, the effect was achieved more by constriction and bombast, giving a stiffer appearance. The Italian was able to move freely with grace and elegance.

Men's clothes were more affected by the Renaissance than women's. Virility and masculinity were displayed, in an especially refined, not brutish manner. Particularly Italian were the abbreviated tunics which often did not even extend as far down as the waist. A slender torso was the vogue and this short tunic, often open in front, belted if long enough, or hanging loose if too short, left the lower part of the body below the waist to be tightly encased in *hose*. These were frequently striped vertically so that the form of the limbs was delineated. A popular fashion was to have one leg plain and the other striped. The cod-piece, necessary with tight hose, was often made a focal feature by gold or coloured points fastenings (**316, 317, 320, 321, 322**).

One or two tunics were worn. If two, the outer one, the *jerkin*, would have a lower neckline than the under one, the *doublet*. In both cases, Italian necklines were not as high as Burgundian ones; they were round, boat-shaped or square. The square pattern became more usual at the end of the fifteenth century. Under these tunics was worn a *shirt*. Italian styles were full, gathered or pleated at neck and wrists and embroidered in gold or black silk. By the end of the century the doublet was often cut open at back and front and laced across, showing the shirt beneath. Likewise, Italian sleeve styles, when tight-fitting, were in two or three parts, laced together and fastened by points but leaving full puffs of the shirt fabric between the sections (**317, 321, 328**).

347, 348 *1470*   **349** *1475*   **350** *1500*   **351** *1480*

Burgundy

352, 353 *1475–85*   **354** *1465–70*   **355, 356** c.*1490*

The fitting doublet and hose were not suited to the older and fatter figure. Alternatives were available in the loose, full *gown*. In length this varied from a hem-line six inches above the knee to the ground. The style was similar whatever the length. The garment had a wide collar and revers turned back all down the front to show the contrasting lining material. Sleeves differed. The most common style was a full, long one, slashed in front so that the arm could be put through the opening, leaving the sleeve hanging down behind the elbow, often nearly to the ground. These gowns could be belted at the waist or tied with a sash or they hung loose like a dressing gown, which could be open showing doublet and hose or held to the body as desired. The style was most fashionable in the years 1490–1505 (**318, 325**).

Italian men, in the fifteenth century, were generally clean-shaven and wore their *hair* loose and long. Young men of fashion wore it flowing on the shoulders and down the back to below the shoulder blades. Heads were often uncovered. *Hats*, if worn, were most often the beret or cap style, which originated in Italy then spread to the rest of Europe. This was made of felt, velvet or silk. Sometimes it had a turned-up brim and

generally was drawn up to fit the head with lacing and points and was jewelled for decoration. In the last decade of the century, the wide brimmed beaver hat with plumes was seen, but it was less popular here than elsewhere (**317, 318, 320, 321, 322, 325, 329, 344, 345**).

Soled hose with wooden *pattens* on top were worn till the end of the century, but soft *boots* were also fashionable from 1485. These were mid-calf length or extended to just below the knee. They had a roll top or turned down cuff.

Though Italian Renaissance *feminine dress* was less strikingly different than that of the men, it is characteristic that the *robe à l'italienne* made its appearance not only in France but in Flanders and Poland. The Italian gown of the later fifteenth century is noted for the brilliance of colour and richness of the fabric from which it was made. Frequently patterned, it was of silk brocade, velvet, gold or silver cloth, with large floral or geometrical motifs, formal and often Oriental in origin. Fur trimming and lining was often used. The bodice was fitting and the waistline high. A heavy linen bodice was worn underneath to preserve the silhouette. The neckline was round, V-shaped and, later, square. It was fairly décolleté but not so long as contemporary designs in Flanders or Burgundy. This gown or overgown, called the *cioppa* or *gamurra*, had wide loose sleeves, often hung down behind the arm. The skirt was full, usually open in front and looped or brooched back. It was very full, gathered or pleated in at the waist, the fullness chiefly arranged at the back, where it fell to a train. Waistline girdles were richly jewelled (**324, 326**).

The *undergown*, of darker shade in equally rich but different material, showed in front at the skirt where the overgown was looped back. Generally, the sleeves which belonged to this undergown were fitting and, like those of the men's doublet, were made in sections, laced together with points fastenings and showing the puffs of the white chemise at shoulder, elbow and wrist. This garment was also visible above the gown neckline.

Ladies' underwear and hose or stockings were like those of the men. They often wore high pattens, when they went out-of-doors, to keep their skirts from the dirt of the streets (**339**).

The *coiffure* of Italian ladies continued to differ from that of the rest of Western Europe. Not for them the complex steeple, horned or reticulated headdresses; their hair was worn long, loose or braided. These tresses or braids might hang down the back or be looped up at the back of the head and neck (**324, 326, 327**). False hair and wigs were often worn. The head might be uncovered with only ribbons or jewels for decoration. A favourite was a fine chain round the head in which was set a single jewel on the forehead. Headdresses, if worn, were usually in the form of jewelled turbans or caps and cauls. The latter were perched at the very back of the head and the hair was drawn back fairly tightly from the forehead. Veils were much less common than in other countries. Pearl ropes were wound round both headdress and hair. The hair was always dressed to show to advantage and given precedence over the headdress (**334, 340**). Cosmetics were used extensively and hair could be dyed. Colour was added to face, neck and bosom and patches were added for effect.

Italian fifteenth-century styles in dress presaged the *sixteenth century* mode elsewhere. This could be seen in the square necklines for both sexes, the elegant frilled and pleated shirts, the laced in sleeves and the loose, wide-collared gown. With the advent of the sixteenth century, Italian pre-eminence in dress was overtaken by foreign fashions and the German modes of padding and puffs, and slashed all-over garments affected

357 *c.1500* **358** *1505–10* **359** *c.1500* **360** *1505–10* **361** *c.1500*

France

85

Italian dress also. Slashes were fashionable as were the fuller cone-shaped skirts for women, based on the Spanish *vertugado*. The stiffened bodice, now called a 'body' or a 'pair of bodys', was generally worn to keep the waist slender and the torso rigid. The fuller skirts were worn over several layers of material. The under one of these, by 1535–40, was stiffened with hoops like the Spanish prototype. In general, figure shape, for both sexes, was chunkier, more solid, richly decorated but less graceful in line and movement.

Children's clothes were much like those of their elders. Young boys wore an unbelted, loose gown; older boys dressed like their fathers. Head-dresses were simpler and girls wore their hair loose (**323, 381, 388, 399C, 417C**).

Burgundy

The sumptuous, luxurious costume of the Burgundian Court retained its influence on European dress till nearly 1480. The costly fabrics were strongly coloured and heavy, velvets and brocades, patterned in large motif, all-over designs and with gold and silver embroidery. Ornate jewellery was added to the costume, especially in the form of neckchains, jewelled belts and girdles and brooches.

In style, the dress was still exaggerated and extreme, though graceful and impressive. Men wore very short tunics or pourpoints, tightly waisted, still padded on the chest and shoulders and pleated. The round or V neckline revealed the undertunic collar above. Hose were fitting, often striped or parti-coloured, cod-pieces padded and protruding. Shoes, boots and hose retained their exaggeratedly elongated toes, though the peak of this fashion had passed by 1470. Hair was long, faces clean-shaven, hats tall or of velvet bonnet style. Fur trimmings and linings were still much in vogue (**347, 349, 352, 354, 371**).

The *ladies' gowns* were décolleté, dipping into a low V or U shape front and back, finished with fur or silk collar and with plastron tucked inside. The deep belt tightly encircled the body just below the breasts. The skirt fell full and long to the ground, usually held up to show a richly patterned underskirt. Steeple headdresses of tall or half-height design, covered with flowing or stiffened, transparent veils were still *de rigueur* (**348, 351, 353, 363, 366, 367, 370, 429**).

France and Flanders

Both countries followed *Burgundian fashion* in the first decade of this period. French dress was less luxurious, the fabrics less costly and the colours more sombre and subtle (**352, 353, 354**). Flemish clothes were more closely modelled on the Court of Burgundy and rivalled it in design and luxury (**363, 366, 367, 370, 371, 426, 431**).

After 1475–80, *Italian styles* dominated the fashion of both countries. Again, the *French version* of these was less colourful and the fabrics less costly than the prototype but the style of garments was similar. The French enthusiastically adopted Italian Renaissance ideals and their fifteenth- and early sixteenth-century dress was closely modelled on the Italian designs of two or three decades earlier. The differences between the French Renaissance style and the Italian were parallel to those in the architecture of the two countries. The French approach was always more classically pure, sober and restrained in its ornamentation.

Men wore the elegant, full, white shirt, gathered and embroidered at the neck and wrists and, over it, the short tunic or doublet. The hose were fitting, like the Italian, often striped on one leg to show off its contours, and with braguette (codpiece), striped also. Later, the waist-length doublet was sometimes accompanied by a pleated or gored skirt, which was generally ornamented with horizontal banding (**356**). The full gown with silk or fur revers was worn also, in two lengths,

363 *1470–80*   364 *1500*   365 *1480–90*   366 *1473*   367 *1475–85*

Flemish

368 *1470*   **369** *1480–90*   **370, 371** *1465–75*   **372** *1480–90*

to the knee or to the ground, and this generally had the slit, hanging sleeve. Slashes were beginning to appear on doublet and sleeves, with the shirt puffed through the slits (**358, 360**).

Women's gowns were usually in one of two styles. The dress *à la française* had a long skirt with a train, which was often held or pinned up at sides and back, displaying the lining and the underskirt, both of different fabrics. The sleeves were wide and full, with turned back cuffs. An ornate girdle encircled the waist and sometimes hung down in front (**355, 357, 359**). The other style, the *robe à l'italienne*, also had a square neckline but showed the elegant chemise gathered or pleated above it. The belt was more frequently on the hips and the dress pinned up at side or front to display the underskirt. The sleeves, like their Italian prototypes, were made in two fitting sections, laced together, and revealing the full puffs of the white chemise between (**361**). In both instances the bodice was fitting over a heavy linen underbodice. The skirt was worn over a taffeta and canvas petticoat to preserve the line of the gown.

Flemish dress for this period also closely fol-lowed the Italian. Fabrics were richer than the French and, in men's clothes especially, gayer and more affected. The long hair and large hats, boots with turned down cuffs and swashbuckling shoes or long full gowns were much in evidence (**364, 374, 377**). At the same time, Flemish young men liked to wear the fitting, waist-length doublets, displaying their hose with its padded cod-piece. The hose which closely hugged the figure, were striped and decorated with fringe or ribbon points. The fine white, frilled shirt was revealed at neck and wrists (**375**). The ladies' gowns were made of magnificent fabrics, patterned, embroidered, the skirt lifted to show another costly material underneath. Sleeves were fitting or bag-shaped but less often in the Italian style (**365, 369, 376, 379, 382**).

Francis I, King of France (*1515–47*), strongly encouraged Renaissance culture and ideals. He employed Italian artisans and artists, built in Renaissance style and established a brilliant Court based on the vitality and richness of Italian counterparts. In costume particularly the Venetian origins were most clearly marked in the luxurious fabrics – brocaded silks and patterned velvets ornamented with jewels, embroideries and fur – but earlier fashions from Florence, Genoa and Milan could also be seen. Costume became, for both sexes, magnificent and costly.

After *about 1525* the emphasis changed. Dress, materials and decoration were richer than ever but the stylistic influence had passed from Italian elegance to German padding and slashes. The silhouette widened at the shoulder and sleeves of both sexes were heavily bombasted; the men presented a square shape in padded gown and doublet, the women a bell formation in farthingale skirts. Fig. **362** illustrates the change. In *male costume* **D** shows the transitional mode. The new style gown with its immensely broad fur collar and padded puff sleeves to the elbow displays the puffed and slashed sleeves of the doublet on the forearm. The shirt is seen as a frill at neck and wrists also through the slashed pattern on the doublet bodice, which only extends as far as the waist. Below this are striped trunk hose, padded cod-piece and striped lower hose. **A** and **B** show the later, fully fledged style where a skirt to match the doublet hangs in tubular gores to the knee, but open in front like a coat for the excessively padded cod-piece to protrude. The

shoulders are now very wide and bombasted and the whole costume is slashed and jewelled. Shoes, by this time, with excessively wide toes, are slashed also.

The *female silhouette* (**362**) was, after 1530, dictated by the corset (**969**) and farthingale. The bodice (*basquine*) was rigid and fitting over its stiffened lining. It had a wide, square neck, fairly low and arched upwards in the centre front. It was edged with jewelled embroidery and often just displayed the frilled chemise edge above. This could also be discerned at the wrists. Beautiful pendants and neck collars adorned the bare neck and bosom. Sleeves were full, padded and slashed and frequently had false or hanging cuffs in fur or alternative material.

The skirt was maintained in a cone shape, creaseless at sides and front and gathered at the waist in the rear to fall into a train. The framework which retained this form came to France from Spain via Italy. It was later popularised in 1530 by Eleanor of Castile, second queen of Francis I. In France called the *vertugade* (*vertugale*) or, later, *la mode vertugadin*, it was the first of the hooped skirts which have recurred since in the history of feminine dress in Europe. The

373 *1495*   **374** *1500*   **375, 376, 377** *1490*

Flemish

378 *1522*   **379** *1515*   **380** *1530*   **381** *1520*   **382** *1515–20*

vertugale was a canvas skirt, of the requisite shape, tied on at the waist. It was inset at intervals with circular hoops of wicker and was covered by taffeta (**970**). The gown skirt worn over it was usually open in front in an inverted V shape to display the underskirt. The pendant and jewelled girdle often hung nearly to the ground in the centre of this, terminating in a jewel or pomander (**362**). The French skirt silhouette of this period was less rigidly cone-shaped than the English one and nearer to the bell form of the Spanish prototype.

Flemish dress of the second quarter of the sixteenth century followed similar lines but was less rich and impressive. With the ending of the close ties with Burgundy and the movement away from the influence of Italy, Flemish styles followed the German pattern in padding and slashes. The needs of a northern climate were re-acknowledged with the wearing of warmer materials and less décolleté styles. The Reformation also began to affect modes of dress, discouraging the wearing of gay colours and over-ornamentation (**378, 379, 380, 381, 382**).

The clean-shaven, long-haired man of the years 1465–1520 (**352, 354, 356, 358, 360, 374,**

375, 377), gave place to men with short hair and small beards and moustaches in the middle years of Francis I's reign (**362A, B, D, 380, 428**). At the same time, the tall *hats* (**352, 371**) were replaced by firstly, a large beaver or fur hat style, worn with scarf, cap or net and multi-coloured plumes (**360, 364, 374, 377**) and, later, by the velvet bonnet or beret laced with points and decorated by brooch, jewels and plumes (**356, 358, 380, 428**). The typical bonnet or cap of the years 1530–40 was dark velvet, flat-crowned and small-brimmed, worn at a rakish angle and decorated with jewels and a plume (**362A, B, D**).

Women in both Flanders and France still wore the *steeple headdress* in the years 1465–80. These were long and pointed, like a dunce's cap, or truncated into a tall pill-box shape. They were made of stiffened velvet or brocade or, often, gold or silver cloth which scintillated through the transparent vëil which draped over them. This was sometimes long and softly falling or was wired and stiffened. The *hair* was pulled back tightly behind the ears so that it hardly showed. Offending stray hairs on the temples and nape were meticulously plucked out (**353, 363, 366, 367, 370, 429, 431**).

After this the *hair* was dressed more loosely. Parted in the centre, it was drawn back softly, Italian fashion, and coiled, in braids or tresses in a chignon at the back. *Headdresses* were either, like the Italian, jewelled cauls and caps of gauze and gold thread, worn on the back of the head (**426**) or richly bejewelled turbans, with or without veils (**359, 361, 369, 373**). Some ladies followed Italian custom and wore a delicate chain round the head with a jewel on the forehead. In France, this was called *la ferronière* after Francis' beautiful mistress.

From the late fifteenth century, the *hood* evolved. This was an important sixteenth-century headdress. At first it was simple, a velvet cap with hanging ends and back worn over a white coif. The sides were flaps falling on to the shoulders, called *lappets* and the back was a semi-circular piece of material, hanging in folds and termed the *fall*. Most hoods were of black velvet lined with colour (**355, 376**). The hood then evolved into the curving form usually known as a *French hood*, in distinction to the more typically English gable pattern. There were different variations on the theme. The most usual had a metal, jewelled framework of horseshoe shape which edged the hood and framed the face. Sometimes there were two of these frontlets with satin or silk bands between. The coif was still worn underneath and showed in front of the metal band. The velvet hood then hung in folds or a tube behind the head. Different typical designs are shown in **357, 365, 372, 382, 436**.

In *footwear*, as in Italy, the shape slowly changed from long, slender toes to broad square ones between 1465–1540. The very long toes, *poulaines*, were excessive in the years 1465–70, with equally long, wooden pattens underneath.

383 German Dress, 1470–1500

After this they shortened to a normal length by 1480. *Soled hose* with pattens were commonly worn till then, after which, *boots* were also popular. Shoes were of short or knee-length styles, with roll tops or turned-down cuffs. Later they were appropriately slashed (**352, 364, 378**). The broad, square toes were fashionable from about 1515–20 onwards. Shoes had low fronts and, sometimes, a strap over the instep. They were made of leather, silk or velvet, were slashed and often jewelled and embroidered. Men's and women's styles were similar to one another (**356, 358, 362A, B, 380**).

Germany and England

In the second half of the fifteenth century costume in these countries followed mainly the lines of Burgundian and Italian dress. *English styles* closely resembled the French, though gayer and nearer to Italian modes in the years 1490–1510 (**399, 400, 401, 402, 403, 404**). *German clothes* were made of heavier, costly fabrics, the figure was stouter, the dress more padded and slashed at an earlier date than elsewhere (**383, 384A, E**). The feminine silhouette, at the end of the century, was exaggeratedly full over the stomach below a tight waistline. The underskirt was of a heavy contrasting fabric and, under this, were worn a number of linen petticoats.

Women drew their *hair* back tightly from their faces and wore it in a caul or cap (**336, 383D, 389**). By the end of the century, men dressed their longish hair in curls and ringlets and, on top, wore a cap and then a large *hat* (**383A, E, F, 384A**). Women wore similar hats over the caul (**346, 384E**). The hats were ornamented with jewels and plumes, also slashed and tied with points. Some designs had a chin-strap to keep

them in place. Alternatively, ladies wore large *turbans* or *hoods*. Headcoverings were retained at all times, even in church and at table (**385**).

From about 1520, the *English Court*, under King Henry VIII, followed a similar pattern to that of Francis I in France. Clothes were of most costly fabrics, jewelled, embroidered and with fur trimmings. Henry also tried to introduce Renaissance artists and culture into England. Though this attempt was curtailed because of his breach with the Catholic Church in Rome, the costume followed the same pattern as in France. Enormous sums of money were spent on the royal and court wardrobes and the upper and merchant classes in England naturally emulated such a glittering monarch. Typical of the age in these two countries was that parade of fashion and display called '*The Field of the Cloth of Gold*', held near Ardres in Normandy in 1520, when Henry and Francis met and set up their respective courts. We can gain an idea of the splendour displayed there from contemporary paintings of the scene.

English dress in the 1530s was strongly influen-

385 *1535–40*   **386** *c.1530*   **387** *1524–5*   **388** *1531*   **389** *1530–40*

Germany   93

390 *1516*   **391** *c.1510*   **392** *1514*   **393** *1475–95*   **394** *1514*

ced by the German mode. The male silhouette was even wider and squarer than in France as can be seen by the portraits of the time by Holbein and Eworth. Also, the garments were even more richly slashed, embroidered and jewelled all over than the French (**405A**). The effect of the Reformation, in this respect, was much less marked in England than in Germany.

After 1530, *women's gowns,* like French ones, were defined by the restrictive bodice and the *farthingale* – the English name for the hooped skirt. The English silhouette was more cone-shaped, that is straight-sided, than the French or Spanish, but otherwise the style was similar (**405B, C**). English girdles, unlike Spanish ones, nearly always hung in one or two pendant ends down the centre front of the inverted V of the gown. On the end depended a jewel or, more generally, a *pomander* (**438**). This was a hollow gold or silver sphere, chased or incised and jewelled, about one and a half to two inches in diameter. It was hinged in order to open and insert the solid perfume which it usually contained. Italian perfumes were, by this time, influencing the rest of Europe. Francis I was

responsible for helping to establish the perfume industry in France.

There were two distinctive features of dress in Germany and England in these years. *German ladies* wore lower necklines than in other countries and only rarely was the chemise neck frill to be seen above them. More commonly, an embroidered plastron was retained inside from Medieval fashion. A heavy, jewelled collar then encircled the neck. The bodice was sometimes open down the front to the waist and laced across the chemise underneath. This fashion, also to be seen in central and eastern Europe, is often depicted in the portraits by Lucas Cranach (the Elder) (**336**). In the years 1530–40, German garments were particularly heavily padded and slashed. This is seen especially in sleeve styles worn by both sexes. (**338, 346, 385, 386, 387, 388, 389**).

In England, a characteristic feature in feminine attire in the first part of the sixteenth century was the *gable hood.* This developed at the same time as the French hood, which was worn in many other countries besides France (**436**). The English version was similar in construction, being worn over a white coif, having a metal, jewelled frontlet to keep the shape and a velvet hood hanging behind. Embroidered velvet lappets hung on the shoulders in front. The difference lay in the shape. The French hood had a curved or horse-shoe form, the English style was a pyramid. It was called a gable or kennel or pyramid hood. It remained in fashion from the early years of the sixteenth century (**401, 403**) till about 1535–40, when it was replaced by the French style (**427**). The lappets were often pinned up at one or both sides after about 1520 (**405, 425, 430**). In front the hair was usually covered by a striped silk padded roll which filled in the gable shape on the forehead.

Though influenced by similar sources as the German, *Swiss dress* displayed greater elegance and sensitivity. In the later fifteenth century it showed clear affinities with Italian modes and something of this was noticeable until about 1520 though, blended with it, was the prevalent desire for padded sleeves and slashes all over the garments (**390, 392**). Ladies' gowns of this date were also elegant, with slender, natural waistlines, low,

decorative necklines and extensive use of contrasting materials in soft colours and rich patterns (**384B, C, 391, 394**). Italian-style turbans, cauls and German-patterned hoods were equally fashionable (**384B, C, 391**).

From 1525–40 the vogue for puffs and slashes, deriving from the lansquenet dress, became irresistible. The men were attired in fine shirts, beautifully embroidered and gathered at the round necklines, and fitting doublets and hose, slashed all over in the most complex designs, the slits being clasped at intervals by jewels and ribbon bows. Wide sashes were tied at the knee. The hair was curled and fairly short; moustaches and beards had a swashbuckling air. A jaunty, wide-brimmed hat, worn at an angle, was often held in place by ribbons tied over it and under the chin. The hat was slashed, be-ribboned and partially hidden by sweeping plumes. A full gown completed the costume; this had immense, puffed upper sleeves, displaying the full white shirt ruffles at the wrists (**384D, 395, 398**). Ladies' dress also had a flamboyant air, with be-plumed

395 c.*1525*   **396** c.*1530*   **397** *1530*   **398** *1520–30*

Switzerland

399 *Dress in England, 1465–85*

hats set jauntily over cauls and ringlets, low, square necklines with necklaces and pendants. Sleeves were also full and slashed like those of their husbands. Only the skirt, falling from a high waist-belt and held up to show the rich underskirt beneath, was simpler, though even this was full and fur-trimmed and/or lined (**396, 397**).

Spain and Portugal

Like the other countries of western Europe, Spanish dress in the years 1465–75 was dominated by the Court of Burgundy (**410**) and, from then until about 1500, by Italy (**406, 409, 413, 415**). But, unlike the other countries, it was masculine dress which was so determined. Women's attire remained under national influence in the earlier part of this period and was original and quite different from the rest of Europe. Until about 1470, gowns were formally pleated as in mid-century designs. After this the *verdugado* was introduced and totally altered the

silhouette. This was the skirt reinforced with *aros*, the hoops of wood which were called *verdugos*. They were inserted at regular intervals into the skirt.

The *gowns* which were worn in Spain in the 1470s on this pattern differed from the later styles introduced into France and England in that the hoops were sewn into the gown itself and were visible on the exterior (**407, 408**). As can be seen in these illustrations, the skirt has a bell-shape not cone-shape as in foreign and later versions. The bodice and sleeves are fitting. The former is left open in the front and laced across the chemise, which is also revealed at the neckline and in the sleeve openings, as in some German fashions. The sleeves have similarities with some contemporary Italian designs.

The *verdugado* first appeared in Castile about 1470. The dress hung over it in a creaseless flat manner in the skirt, which was sometimes opened in front in an inverted V shape to display the underskirt (**407**). Many stories have been related to explain why this hooped skirt was first introduced and they nearly all attribute it to different female members of various royal houses who wished to conceal an unwanted, embarrassing pregnancy. Possibly all such stories are apocryphal, though understandable. The farthingale was suited to such concealment but it is doubtful if the accompanying boned bodice was of equal benefit to the mother-to-be. In the 1480s the fashion waned in Spain but, by the end of the century, spread to Venice and the rest of Italy and was adopted in France and England by the 1520s. Spanish feminine dress in the years 1485–1515 were based more on Italian styles (**412, 414**).

With the coming of the *sixteenth century* Spain also felt the German influence of padding and slashes. Both men's and women's dress of the years 1520–40 followed the pattern of the rest of Western Europe (**411, 416**). There were, however, certain differences. The Spanish cape styles were always more popular in Spain than the full padded gowns with fur collars, though the latter were worn extensively in the 1530s (**416B**). These capes and cloaks, like some of the hood styles, were of Moorish origin. There were many ways of wearing

and draping them round the person. The style came into its own in the second half of the century when the fashion spread to the rest of Europe. Moorish influence could also be seen in the continuing popularity of the profusely decorated turbans and veils. Spanish dress was rich in jewelled embroidery and ornament. The wealth of Spain was growing apace with the extension of her territories in the Indies and central and north America. This ornamentation could be seen on all garments for both sexes. It was especially characteristic in the black silk embroidery on chemise and shirt, known as Spanish blackwork. It was accentuated with gold and red stitching and was of Persian origin (**424, 435, 439**).

Central and Northern Europe

The Hussite Movement in *Bohemia* (Czechoslovakia) still acted as a damper on fashionable dress in the fifteenth century. Like the later Reformation, the movement disapproved strongly of the display of the Roman Catholic Church in Italy and its followers attempted to dissuade the wealthy and the bourgeoisie from wearing osten-

400 *1475*   **401** *1500*   **402** *1520*   **403** c.*1495*   **404** *Young man of fashion, 1505*

England

tatious clothes. By mid-century, reaction set in and elegant, costly garments were being worn once more in Burgundian and then Italian fashion. Attempts were made by authority to curtail this display but were unsuccessful.

By 1500 Bohemia had developed as an important cultural centre influencing neighbouring countries. Renaissance forms of art appeared early here and fashion was no exception. The Italian Renaissance styles were adopted with enthusiasm (**417A, B, 437**). Only in one or two respects did Czech dress differ from the prototype. The feminine coiffure was dressed slightly differently and there was a strong vogue for richly ornamented turban headdresses as well as Italian-style gold and jewelled cauls. German influence later became apparent, puffs and slashes making their appearance (**417C, D**) and, by 1540, the Spanish farthingale also.

Austrian dress followed the international pattern, influenced especially by Italy and Germany. The figures shown in **418** show an English

derivation also, though the styles are being worn about twenty years later than in the fashion centres of western Europe.

Styles in *Hungary* were more strongly influenced from the east, the masculine dress being especially Turkish in character. Hungary had fallen to the Turks in 1526, who ruled over the larger part of the country for over 150 years. *Men* wore the dolman tunic with fitted hose or trousers (both of which are referred to as hose), boots, and a cape or mantle on top. Caps of fur or with fur trimming completed the costume. Materials were richly embroidered, the decoration often covering the whole garment. Fur trimmings and linings were extensively worn. From the latter part of the fifteenth century the cape was replaced by a loose, sleeveless, ground-length coat. This, the origin of the *mente*, was open in front, showing the dolman. A hanging sleeve was fashionable, falling behind the arm (**417E**).

In the later fifteenth century the Hungarian

aristocracy had begun to adopt Italian Renaissance dress. In men's attire this movement was soon superseded by the Turkish style but *women's clothes* continued to show Italian cut, elegance and beauty of fabrics. The design of their clothes changed remarkably little between 1465 and 1540. They wore fitted bodices, often laced across in front over a white chemise which had richly embroidered cuffs and neck-edge. Sleeves of the gown were very long and full at the bottom. The separate skirts were long, with a train, and very full. Hems and bodices were embroidered. Cauls were worn over the hair, Italian style, with jewelled caps and hats on top (**335, 417F**).

In the north in the sixteenth century, *Scandinavia* was following German styles of dress (**421, 423**), while *Poland* was adopting Renaissance modes with Italian long gowns with hanging sleeves for men (**420**), and Spanish farthingale skirts for ladies (**419**). A fashionable style of ladies' sleeve was a very full chemise ending in a frill at the wrist and confined at intervals by gold embroidered bands (**419, 422**). Turban head-

dresses were popular, richly ornamented and jewelled (**422**), while the French hood was early adopted as fashionable wear (**419**). Men's hair and hat styles followed the prevailing western modes (**337**).

Notes on the Illustrations

315 Painting by Sandro Botticelli 'Adoration of the Magi', Uffizi Gallery, Florence. Crimson velvet tunic with gold embroidery and grey-blue fringing. Sash of yellow silk. Blue undertunic. Gold necklace. Grey hose, brown boots.

316 Painting by Francesco del Cossa. Vatican Picture Gallery, Rome. Yellow tunic and hose. Red undertunic. Black shoes and hat, green hat ribbon.

317 Painting as 316. Black tunic, slit to show white shirt. Red hose, black shoes. Red hat with white plume.

318 Painting by Melozzo da Forli 'Pope Sixtus IV with Platina'. Vatican Picture Gallery, Rome. Purple-blue gown, with black cuffs and gold chain necklace. White undertunic with brown fur edging.

319 Painting by Il Vecchietta. The Louvre, Paris.

406 *1490*   **407** *Vertugado, 1477*   **408** *Vertugado, 1470–80*   **409** *1490*   **410** *1465–70*

411 *Fashionable young man,* c.*1530*   **412** *1510*   **413** *1500*   **414** *1515*   **415** *1500*

Pale pink tunic edged in white with dark green lining to loose, hanging sleeves. Red undertunic. Green hose.

320 and 321 Painting by Luca Signorelli. Uffizi Gallery, Florence. 320 has a sleeveless tunic striped in dark green, red and orange. Undertunic has dark green upper sleeves and orange on the forearm. Hose are dark green on the buttocks then left leg is striped like the bodice and the right is striped white and dark green on the inside but is red on the outside. Fawn shoes. Dark green cap with coloured plumes. Black and red purse and belt. 321 has a dark green tunic and undertunic with red sleeves. The latter are slashed to show the white shirt which is also visible on the chest where it is laced across with red ties. The belt and purse are red and the points black. The hose are striped and patterned in white, dark green, red and black. Shoes are white. The hat is scarlet with black ribbons and coloured plumes.

322 Painting by Pintoricchio 'Return of Odysseus'. National Gallery, London. Green tunic decorated in gold, white sash. Red and grey hat. Hose checked in red and grey at the top, decorated in gold bands then striped in red and grey. Blue boots.

323 Maximilian Sforza as a boy. MS Biblioteca Trivalziana, Milan. Tunic with gold bodice and skirt panelled in white and white ornamented in gold. Dark red upper sleeves slashed to show shirt, blue on fore-

arm. Dark red hat with gold ornament and white aigrette. Red hose, black shoes with gold edge.

324 Painting by Crivelli. National Gallery, London. Crimson dress decorated in gold on the bodice and skirt. White chemise. Cloak in green with gold edge and hem. Belt of gold, decorated leather. Jewelled hair band. Red shoes.

325 Painting by Vittore Carpaccio 'The Miracle of S. Trifone'. La Scuola Dalmata, Venice. Dark green gown with red lining. Red sleeves in two parts, white shirt between. Red hose, black shoes and hat.

326 Painting of S. Catherine. Galleria Nazionale, Rome. Deep red gown with black hem and edging. Black lacing on bodice over gold and black fabric in pomegranate pattern. White revers. Sleeves to match bodice. Headdress of gold and pearls.

327 Painting by Vittore Carpaccio 'The Triumph of S. George'. La Scuola Dalmata, Venice. Gown of blue and gold patterned. Sleeves striped brown and blue. Undergown red with gold stripes. Red shoes and hat, gold decoration.

328 Painting by Raphael 'Mass at Bolsena'. Vatican Rooms, Rome. Dark green tunic with gold stripes. Red sleeves. White shirt and hose. Black shoes.

329 Painting by Raphael. Vatican Rooms, Rome.

Doublet and skirt black with gold bands. Sleeves to match, puffed. Under-sleeves pale grey with yellow material pulled through the slashes. Black points. Dove grey cloak. Grey hose. Black shoes. Black hat with ribbon threaded through. Gold brooch, white plume.

330 Painting of a lady by Moretto da Brescia. Kunsthistorisches Museum, Vienna. Red satin gown with black banding on bodice and sleeves. Dark green under-sleeves slashed to show white chemise. Fox fur. Pearl necklace and pendant. Gold belt.

331 Portrait of the Duke of Ferrara by Titian. Pitti Palace, Florence. Doublet and skirt in purple velvet. Black belt. Gown of red brocade with brown fur collar and gold neckchain and pendant. Gold brocade under-sleeves.

332 Portrait of the Duchess of Urbino by Titian. Uffizi Gallery, Florence. Black gown with brown decoration and girdle. White ruched neck partlet, ruffles at neck and wrists and jewelled edging. Headdress

to match gown. Chain necklace and pendant.

333 Portrait of a woman by Titian. Pitti Palace, Florence. Blue-green dress decorated in gold line. White chemise ruffle at neck and wrists. Gold girdle. Upper sleeves puffed, of purple and green-blue with gold decoration. Lower sleeves of purple with white puffs through the slashes. Gold ornament. Chain necklace. Bead hair ornament.

334 Portrait by Jacopo Pontorno. Uffizi Gallery, Florence. Patterned dress in two shades of red. White, finely pleated chemise. White straw halo hat with gold banding.

335 Portrait. Velvet hat with pearl decoration worn over a net.

336 Painting of Salome by Lucas Cranach the Elder. Bayerische Nationalmuseum, Munich. Gold headdress. Gold neckchain and jewelled collar. Black neck cord. Bottle green gown. White chemise in front of bodice,

416 Spanish Dress, 1530–40. Courtyard and Staircase, Hospital of Santa Cruz, Toledo

under lacing, and in puffs on sleeves covered by bottle green straps.

337 Medallion portrait of Sigismund. Narodowe Museum, Cracow. Hat with plumes. Embroidered and finely gathered shirt. Fur-collared gown. Neckchain. Bordered doublet.

338 Duke William IV of Bavaria. Portrait by Hans Wertinger. Bayerische Nationalmuseum, Munich. Gown and doublet of brown material striped with gold decoration. Brown fur collar. Gold, jewelled neck collar. Sleeves brown with gold decoration. White chemise, finely pleated, with gold embroidery and necklace. Dark brown hat with gold ornament.

339 Venetian zoccolo. Later sixteenth century. Bayerische Nationalmuseum, Munich.

340 Portrait of a girl by Andrea Solario. Galleria Nazionale, Rome. Brown turban. Bead necklace. White

chemise with black decoration. Green gown.

341 German pantoffle of leather with cork insole. About 1530. Bayerische Nationalmuseum, Munich.

342 Venetian zoccolo. About two feet high. Late sixteenth century. Bayerische Nationalmuseum, Munich.

343 German shoe. About 1540. Bally Shoe Museum, Switzerland.

344 Portrait of Francesco Maria della Rovere by Raphael. Uffizi Gallery, Florence. Gold gown with red lines. Deep red sleeves. Brown fur collar. White shirt. Red hat.

345 Portrait of a gentleman by Baldassare Estense. Museo Correr, Venice. Red hat.

346 Portrait of the Duchess of Bavaria by Peter Gärtner. Bayerische Nationalmuseum, Munich. Gown of patterned material in black and blue. Deep neckband patterned in gold. Sleeves alternate deep bands of blue-grey and gold design. Slashed and with white material pulled through slashes. Gold wristbands. Double white wrist ruffles. White chemise, finely pleated with black and gold neckband. Gold necklace. Red hat over gold and white cap and looped plaits. Gold patterned leather girdle.

347 and 348   Court of the Duke of Burgundy. Flemish book illustration. Painted at Bruges, 1470, by Loyset Liédet. 347 wears a pleated tunic with padded sleeves, fitted hose, long-toed shoes and a tall hat. 348 wears a high waisted gown with deep ornamented belt. Very low fur-edged neckline with plastron. Steeple headdress with veil. The gown is fur-edged and lined.

349, 350 and 351   Burgundian court dress. The men wear long houppelandes, open in front and fur-edged and lined. 349 wears the tall hat, 350 the later velvet hat of Italian design. The lady has a similar gown to 348 but this is laced across the back of the bodice. The transparent white veil is draped over the steeple headdress.

352, 353 and 354   Froissart's Chronicle, Harley MS British Museum, London. 352 wears tall boots with turned-down cuffs over striped hose. The tunic is belted at the waist and has heavily padded sleeves. 353 wears a deep blue gown with red collar, waistbelt and hem. The steeple headdress, with dangling liripipe, is black. 354 has fuzzed, bushy hair, the black hat perched jauntily on top. The pleated houppelande is deep blue with gold neck chains. The tunic, showing at the neck, is scarlet.

355   Tapestry. Musée de Cluny, Paris. A plain gown pinned up at the back to show the lining of contrasting colour. The patterned undergown has a black hem edging. The belt is jewelled. The bodice is laced across the deep V at the back and displays the chemise. Black velvet hood.

356   Tapestry. Musée de Cluny, Paris. Sleeveless tunic with skirt banded in black decorative strips. Sleeves of different colour with fur cuffs. White pleated shirt. Hose, one leg striped, one plain. White beaver

A   B   C   D   E

418 Austrian Dress in Salzburg Castle, 1510–20

419 *Poland, 1535*   **420** *Poland, 1506*   **421** *Sweden, 1530*   **422** *Poland, 1532*   **423** *Sweden/Finland, 1530*

hat with ribbon decoration.

357 Tapestry. Musée de Cluny, Paris. Velvet gown with fur cuffs and lining. Girdle of two cords and central decorative pendant end. Jewelled neckchain and pendant. Blue neckband. White chemise. Gold turban over white frontlet and hood behind.

358 Portrait Charles d'Amboise and Paris tapestry. Square-necked doublet slashed to show white shirt. Striped hose in red, yellow and blue. Three-quarter length gown, belted, with purse, and with fur collar and lining. Velvet hat and coloured plumes. The gown has hanging sleeves to display doublet sleeves which are slashed to show shirt.

359 Wood sculpture. Musée des Arts Decoratifs, Paris. Flemish style of gown with full sleeves and skirt. Padded, draped turban.

360 Tapestry, Paris. Long gown with fur collar and lining, leather belt and hanging sleeves. Fur hat.

361 Tapestry, Paris. Robe à l'Italienne. Blue gown with silver ornamentation. Undergown and sleeves of red, embroidered in gold. Gold bows on sleeves with white chemise sleeve puffs and wrist frills. White pleated chemise at neck. Red velvet hood with gold frontlet.

362A Portrait of Francis I by Clouet. Louvre, Paris, combined with portrait of Jean de Dinteville by Hol-

bein. National Gallery, London. Doublet, skirt and gown of white silk striped vertically in black and gold embroidered white. Slashed to show white chemise. Black-edged wrist ruffles, and neckline. Chain and pendant. Black, jewelled hat with white plume. Black hose and shoes. *c.*1525.

B Portrait of Francis I by Titian. Louvre, Paris. Dark red-brown velvet gown with fur collar and edging and puffed, slashed, fur-trimmed sleeves. Doublet of red silk, slashed on chest and sleeves to show white chemise. Gold chain and locket. Black hat with jewel and white plume. *c.*1538.

C Portrait of Eleanor of Austria, Francis I's second queen. Dark dress with fur cuffs and hanging sleeves. Gold edging. Undergown of light-coloured fabric lined in black. Slashed sleeves. Jewelled girdle with pendant. Jewelled turban. 1540–7.

D Portrait of Duc de Guise *c.*1530. Doublet and hose all slashed and gathered. Sleeves padded and slashed. Short gown with wide collar and puffed upper sleeves. Jewelled hat and plume.

363 Portrait of Mary, Duchess of Burgundy. Stained glass life-size figure from Chapel of the Holy Blood, Bruges. Victoria and Albert Museum, London. White gown delicately patterned in gold. Black bands across bodice over gold. Undergown dark green. Steeple headdress.

424 *Flat velvet cap, Spain, 1525–30*

425 *Catherine of Aragon, Henry VIII of England's first queen*

426 *Gold caul and ear-plate. White veil, Flemish, 1505–10*

427 *Anne Boleyn, Henry VIII's second queen, c.1535*

428 *Velvet cap, gold points, Flemish, c.1530–5*

429 *White, double, stiff veil. Steeple cap. French, 1470*

430 *Jane Seymour, Henry VIII's third queen, 1536*

431 *Transparent veil over green headdress, Flemish, 1478*

432 *Leather shoe, Spain, 1465–75*

433 *Gold, jewelled ring, English*

434 *English shoe*

435 *Jewelled cap and net, Spain 1515*

436 *Flemish hood, c.1530*

437 *Young man, Czechoslovakia, c.1500*

438 *Silver gilt pomander, English, 1490–5*

439 *Silk turban, Spain, c.1530*

364 Tapestry. Rijksmuseum, Amsterdam. Gown of gold damask with red design, sleeves in grey blue. Red hose. White boots. Red fur hat.

365 Painting, Musée d'Art Ancien, Brussels. Red dress, green undergown. Blue hood, jewelled frontlets and white coif.

366 Triptych by Jan de Witte of Bruges. Musée des Beaux-Arts, Brussels. Black velvet dress with red waist-belt and white fur edging to hem and neckline. Red and gold plastron. Gold, jewelled necklace. Black and gold headdress with white, transparent veil.

367 Brussels tapestry. Musée des Arts Decoratifs, Paris. Dress of blue with gold pattern. Deep hem and neckband in red and gold. Plastron fawn and gold. Red steeple headdress with black borders. White veil and neckcovering. Jewelled necklace.

368 Wood statuette, Rijksmuseum, Amsterdam. Pleated, three-quarter length houppelande. Slit, bag sleeves. Chain necklace.

369 Painting. Musée d'Art Ancien, Brussels. Red dress with gold, jewelled hip-belt and gold chain girdle and ornament. Black collar. Undergown of gold, patterned in black. Black shoes. Black turban with jewelled ornament. White veil also wrapped round turban in swathes.

370 and 371 Painting 'Judgement of the Emperor Othon' by Dirk Bouts. Musée des Beaux Arts, Brussels. 370 wears a red gown with black collar and gold hem. Steeple headdress in check light and dark browns. Black velvet lappets and white veil. 371 has a dark green velvet tunic with brown fur at neck, cuffs and hem. The undertunic is brown, also the hat and the hose red and shoes black.

372 Painting on wood of Jeanne la Folle by a master of the Abbey of Affighem. Musée des Beaux Arts, Brussels. White fur plastron with gold, jewelled neckband and centre band. Dress of red with pattern in gold and black and white edging. Hood of black velvet with gold, jewelled frontlets and red velvet between. Necklace and pendant.

373 Wood statuette from Brussels. Victoria and Albert Museum, London. Gown with ermine neckline and plastron. Cloak with patterned edge. Turban.

374 Portrait of Philippe le Beau in stained glass from the Chapel of the Holy Blood, Bruges. Victoria and Albert Museum, London. Fawn houppelande with light green lining, fur collar and jewelled leather belt and tasselled leather purse. Blue tunic. Brown beaver hat.

375, 376 and 377 Roman de la Rose. Harley MS British Museum, London. 375 wears a waist-length pourpoint and striped trunk hose above two coloured nether hose. Gold belt and fringed purse. Beaver hat slung behind from the shoulder. 376 wears a gown with bodice laced across the chemise and low, square neck. Decorative girdle with pendant. Velvet hood with jewelled frontlet. 377 has a knee-length gown with hanging sleeves. Collar and revers turned back to show lining. Gold neckchain. Embroidered leather belt and purse. Beaver hat, tied under chin with scarf, plumes.

378 MS 'The Adoration of the Magi', Sforza Book of Hours. British Museum, London. Doublet and skirt of alternate stripes of gold and white material, the white being decorated in gold pattern. Red hose, brown boots. Black hat over coif, plumes and jewels.

379 Painting by J. Provost. Mauritshuis, The Hague. White gown with black velvet lining and edging. Red velvet belt with gold centre fastening. Gold undergown. Red velvet headdress with gold, jewelled frontlet.

380 Early sixteenth century Flemish Calendar. British Museum, London. Red gown, brown fur. Blue doublet, white shirt. Black hose, shoes and bonnet.

381 Flemish calendar. British Museum, London. Young girl in a blue, patterned dress with black cuffs, neckline and hem banding. French hood.

382 Tapestry. Musée de Cluny, Paris. Italian style gown, patterned, with plain underskirt. White chemise seen gathered at neck and puffed on the sleeves. French hood.

383 *Germany. The Old Town Hall, Brunswick.*

A German engraving. Waist-length tunic, slashed on chest to show gathered shirt. Points at waist. Fitted hose. Slashed shoes. Beaver hat with plumes. Late fifteenth century.

B German wood engraving. 1465–75. High-waisted gown with collar and plastron. Steeple headdress with frontlet and long, transparent veil.

C German wood engraving. 1465–75. Short tunic, open in front in deep V to show undertunic, slashed to display shirt. Fitted hose.

D German MS 1480. Gown open on bodice and sleeves to show chemise. Held up to display undergown. Fur muff with ribbon sash and plumes. Padded turban and coif. Wood pattens and hose.

E German MS. Short tunic open in front and held by sash tie at neck. Gathered shirt. Fitted hose and shoes. 1480.

F German MS. Tunic with waist belt, open in front and laced across undertunic. Embroidered edged double collar. Velvet, jewelled bonnet. Shoes and wooden pattens. 1480.

384 *Germany. Town gateway (Holstentor) Lübeck.*

A German. Painting from Kloster Weltenhausen. Bayerische Nationalmuseum, Munich. Dark green, three-quarter length gown with black band decoration. Hanging sleeves. Red tunic. Hose striped red and white. Black shoes. Red bonnet with coloured plumes. *c*.1515.

B and C Swiss. Drawing by Niklaus Manuel Deutsch. Kunstmuseum, Basle. B. Jewelled, silk headdress with plumes. Gown with slashed and hanging sleeves, *c*.1520. C wears a gown striped in broad horizontal bands of yellow, pink, blue and red with a white patterned hem and gold patterned neckband. Chemise frill above this. Sleeves in Italian style with white chemise puffs at shoulder, elbow and wrists. Gown sleeves attached by points. Sash tied round hips. Blue hood with brown and white turban.

D Swiss. Drawing by Niklaus Manuel Deutsch. Kunstmuseum, Basle. Richly clad young man in full cloak with padded, puffed sleeves and slashed doublet and hose. Embroidered, finely patterned shirt. Velvet hat with ribbon tie and plumes. c.1520.

E German engraving. Simple dress with Italian style sleeves. Velvet, jewelled hat worn over caul.

385 Painting by Barthel Beham 'Story of S. Helena'. Alte Pinakothek, Munich. Scarlet gown over farthingale with brown turned back wide cuffs. Undersleeves crimson with white puffs. Bodice ornamented by rows of pearls. White chemise frill at neck. Gable hood of black velvet with red and gold frontlet over white coif. Padded silk underneath striped in gold and silver.

386 Stained glass by Jörg Breu the Elder from Augsburg. Bayerische Nationalmuseum, Munich. Gown with coloured border and fur collar. Gold chain necklace. White shirt. Tunic with black hem.

387 Portrait of a gentleman by Amberger. Kunsthistorisches Museum, Vienna. Three-quarter length gown of black silk with black velvet banding. Brown fur collar and lining. Inner sleeves red. White, pleated shirt and wrist frills. Hose striped in white, grey and red. Upper part puffed and slashed. Black shoes.

388 Little boy in child's chair. Painting of the family of Duke Wilhelm of Bavaria by Peter Gärtner. Bayerische Nationalmuseum, Munich. Red velvet dress with banding of darker red. Gold bands at neck and forearms. White puffs between. Two necklaces and several finger rings. White apron, finely pleated and banded in gold. Red velvet hat over gold edged cap. Hair in thin, looped-up plaits.

389 Painting by Hans Schöpfer 'Geschichte der Verginia'. Alte Pinakothek, Munich. Plain pink gown with dark hem bands. Dark green undergown. Neckband in brown and lemon, jewelled. Sleeves puffed and slashed in brown and lemon. White puffs on forearms. Turban headdress in red and gold with pearls.

390 Painting for school signboard by Hans Holbein. Kunstmuseum, Basle. Pink waist-length tunic slashed to show white shirt. Hose striped in yellow and red. Red hat with red tie under chin. Shirt embroidered in black at neckline. Black shoes.

391 Painting by Ratgels. Kunstmuseum, Basle. Gown banded horizontally. Bodice gold, decorated in black, then deep band of white patterned, then plain crimson and hem of ermine. Gold girdle. Hanging sleeves in crimson with gold decoration and fringe. Pleated white band at neck and upper sleeve. Neckband in white decorated in gold. Lower sleeves red. Hat in gold and black.

392 Painting by Hans Fries. Kunstmuseum, Basle. Short red tunic, open, with holes in bottom edge to attach to points at waist. White shirt. Hose striped on one leg, in green and gold, the other plain, in red. Deeper red knee sashes. Black shoes.

393 Tapestry. Historisches Museum, Basle. Tunic of brocade with fur trimming and hanging sleeves. Jewelled, velvet bonnet.

394 Painting by Hans Fries. Kunstmuseum, Basle. Pale blue dress with yellow bands at hem, neck and sleeves. Deep red lining. White, pleated chemise. Pearl decorated headband.

395 Drawing of landsknecht by Hans Holbein. Kunstmuseum, Basle. Doublet and hose puffed and slashed. White chemise. Lower hose, one leg striped, one plain. Hat tied under chin with sash. Coloured plumes.

396 Basle costume. Engraving by Hans Holbein. Print Room, Art Collection, Basle. Banded and jewelled bodice. Fur hem and lining. Padded sleeves with ribbon bows. Hat with plumes worn over net and cap.

397 Drawing by Hans Holbein. Kunstmuseum, Basle. Bodice open in front and laced across chemise. Gold chain necklace. Sleeves Italian style in white puffs and flounces banded at intervals. Veil headdress.

398 Drawing of landsknecht. Historisches Museum, Basle. White shirt with collar. White shirt shows through slashes on chest and sleeves. Slashes caught at intervals by ribbon bows.

399A MS British Museum, London. Patterned gown with fur collar and hem. Brocade plastron. Deep waistbelt. Steeple headdress with black velvet frontlet and white veil. c.1470.

B MS British Museum. Pleated tunic with padded sleeves and fur edging. Hose. Tall hat. c.1470.

C Small boy. Short patterned tunic and hose.

D Painting. c.1465. Cambridge University. Steeple headdress with butterfly wing veil. Fur trimmed gown with patterned belt. Plastron.

400 MS British Museum, London. Patterned houppelande with fur trimming and hanging sleeves. Hat worn but chaperon hung over shoulder by liripipe held in hand.

401 Portrait. Elizabeth of York, queen of Henry VII. Ermine trimmed gown. Dark undergown. Gable hood of black velvet with pearl encrusted lappets.

402 Painting. Young man in light green cloth doublet with black velvet trimming. White shirt. Grey hose. Black shoes.

403 Painting. Fur lined gown buttoned up to waist at rear. Bodice laced across silk undergown at the back. Black velvet hood lined with silk and edged with gold embroidery.

404 Painting. Fashionable young man in short gown of grey lined with pink. Hanging sleeves. Red velvet doublet over white shirt. Pink hose. Black shoes. Fawn beaver hat with plumes over gold net.

405 Abbot's Room. Thame Park.

A Portrait of Henry VIII by Hans Eworth. c. 1539. Chatsworth. Red velvet gown decorated in gold with brown fur collar. Grey-blue doublet, jerkin and skirt also gold ornamented and slashed to show white shirt. Gold, jewelled collar. White hose and shoes. Black hat, jewelled, white plume.

B and C Portrait of Jane Seymour, Henry VIII's third queen by Hans Holbein. 1536. Kunsthistorisches

Museum, Vienna. Red velvet gown with gold and jewelled edging worn over farthingale. Sleeves turned back to show lining of gold crosshatch on red. False, padded sleeves of grey-blue brocade match undergown skirt. Jewelled girdle. Gold, jewelled necklaces and pendant. Gable hood of black velvet with gold jewelled frontlet and lappets. One side of hood and one lappet pinned up. Striped gold, pad beneath frontlet.

406 Painting. Long velvet gown with hanging sleeves and ermine lining and edging. Velvet turban hat and plumes.

407 Painting. Museum of Catalan Art, Barcelona. Vertugado skirt. Separate bodice laced across chemise. Halo headdress.

408 Painting 'Banquet of Herodias'. Museum of Catalan Art, Barcelona. Vertugado. Gown of floral pattern of gold on black, bands visible on top. White puffs of chemise all along underside of arm culminating in a pleated cuff. Ornamented turban. Hair bound.

409 Painting. Museum of Catalan Art, Barcelona. Red tunic, pleated and belted. Dark undertunic shows at neck and through slashes. Dark hose. Shoes. Black felt hat, plume.

410 Painting. Prado, Madrid. Green waist-length tunic. Black belt and purse. Red cords and tassels. Grey hose. Black hat and shoes.

411 Painting. Young man in patterned doublet and skirt. Puffed and slashed sleeves. White gathered shirt. Hose, black boots. Hat with chin strap over coif.

412 Painting in Museo de Santa Cruz, Toledo combined with painting in the Prado, Madrid. Gold cloth gown with black line decoration. Brown sleeves with gold edging and red undersleeves. White chemise. Gold net over hair.

413 Painting. Long, loose gown with wide collar. Gold chain collar. Striped tunic. Cap.

414 Painting. Museo de Santa Cruz, Toledo. Gold dress with self colour pattern. Black banding at neck and hem. Pink lining shows in turned back cuffs. Blue undergown. Gold necklaces. Black hood with gold, jewelled frontlet.

415 Painting. Three-quarter length gown with hanging sleeves. Dark tunic. Gold chain collar. Hose. Black shoes. Beaver hat with brooch and plumes.

416A Portrait of Empress Isabella. Dark velvet gown over a farthingale. Jewelled embroidery at neck, sleeves and skirt. Silver brocade underskirt. Puffed, slashed and jewelled sleeves. Embroidered chemise and high small ruff. Jewelled girdle. No headdress. 1530–9.

B Portrait of Emperor Charles V, c.1535. All black costume except for ermine collar to the gown and gold embroidery on gown and skirt.

C Sculptured statue of 1564 representing Empress Isabella in costume of c.1535. Prado, Madrid. No headdress.

417A Czech Renaissance painting, 1525. Loose full gown patterned all over and edged and lined with fur.

Patterned gown underneath. Gold, jewelled collar and necklaces. Pearl encrusted hair-net.

B Czech altarpiece painting. Italian style gown with low neck and brocade plastron. Gold collar. Jewelled hair-net. c.1520.

C Portrait of Ferdinand I as a boy, c.1540. Czech. Full gown with puff sleeves and embroidered collar and hem. Plainer tunic. White shirt. Black hat, shoes and gloves.

D Painting by W. Krodel, 1525–30. Kunsthistorisches Museum, Vienna. Dark velvet dress with gold embroidered banding. Gold leather girdle. Bodice laced across in front. Gold chain necklace and collar. Jewelled, pearl decorated turban.

E and F Actual costumes. Hungarian National Museum, Budapest. E shows the sleeveless mente with hanging sleeves. At the neck and sleeve are the white shirt. 1522. F shows the wedding dress of Queen Maria, made in Florence in 1500. It is of green silk while the bodice is open in front to the waist to display the silver embroidered white chemise.

418A Altar painting, Unteres Belvedere, Vienna. c.1520. Blue gown with white hem, hanging sleeves and neckband. Striped turban in blue and gold with jewelled band and white veil. Underdress in grey, striped in red.

B Altar painting, Unteres Belvedere, Vienna. c.1510. Gold gown patterned in red. Gold jewelled belt. White lining to turned back sleeve. Tunic red, white shirt. Black hat and shoes.

C Carved wood relief. Kunsthistorisches Museum, Vienna. From Salzburg c.1520. Long gown with wide collar and turned back revers. Bonnet with points.

D Altar piece. Unteres Belvedere, Vienna. Red gown with black banding and gold embroidered neckline. Jewelled headdress.

E Painting 'Susanna Legend'. Unteres Belvedere, Vienna, c.1520. Grey-green gown with fur hem. Italian style sleeves. Gold neckband decoration. White turban and veil.

419 Portrait, Narodowe Museum, Cracow. Patterned gown over farthingale, jewelled and knotted girdle. Sleeves turned back to show black lining. Lower sleeves white with gold embroidered bands. French hood.

420 Woodcarving, Narodowe Museum, Cracow. Long gown with turned back collar and revers.

421 Painting. Doublet and skirt of striped fabric. White shirt. Black shoes, light hose. Black hat.

422 Portrait of Anne Tenczynska. Narodowe Museum, Cracow. Patterned gown with dark overgown and hanging sleeves. Italian style sleeves with gold embroidered bands alternating with white puffed chemise sleeve. Three-roll turban decorated in gold with white coif.

423 Drawing. Dark doublet and skirt with light undersleeves, slashed. Velvet bonnet.

424 Painting. White shirt embroidered in black silk. Gold neckchain. Fur collar.

425 Painting. Queen Catherine of Aragon. National Portrait Gallery, London. Gable headdress with striped silk underpad, gold, jewelled frontlet, gold lappets (one pinned up) and black velvet hood.

426 Painting. Musée d'Art Ancien, Brussels.

427 Painting, Queen Anne Boleyn. National Portrait Gallery, London. French hood in black velvet edged with pearls.

428 Painting by J. Gossaert. Mauritshuis, The Hague. Black velvet hat with gold points. Pink doublet slashed to show white shirt. Fur collar to gown.

429 French MS.

430 Queen Jane Seymour. Painting by Hans Holbein. Mauritshuis, The Hague. Gable hood of black velvet, pinned up on one side. Gold and pearl lappets, jewelled frontlet, gold striped pad.

431 Painting of Barbara van Vlaenderbergh by Hans Memlinc. Musée des Beaux-Arts, Brussels. Steeple headdress in grey-green with white veil. Black edging.

432 Spanish shoe.

433 Gold, jewelled ring. Victoria and Albert Museum, London.

434 English shoe.

435 Painting. Hat over jewelled net.

436 Painting by Van Orley. Musée d'Art Ancien, Brussels. French hood over white coif. Gold, jewelled frontlet, pink satin band, and black velvet hood.

437 Italian Renaissance mode. Sculpture. Czechoslovakia.

438 Pomander. Victoria and Albert Museum, London.

439 Painting. Jewelled, silk turban.

Chapter Five

The Dominance of Spain 1540–1620

The costume worn in these years in western Europe was the richest ever seen in the history of the subject. There were several reasons for this. Quality of materials, cut of garments, enrichment, decoration and patterning of fabrics had been improving and evolving since the early Middle Ages. *Quattrocento*, Renaissance Italy had introduced beautiful fabrics, jewelled embroideries, glorious colours and elegant modes to the rest of Europe. By the mid-sixteenth century there were fewer small courts to support and encourage luxury and dress but the larger ones were flourishing and were powerful and wealthy. A larger proportion of the population in western countries now enjoyed a higher standard of living and desired to emulate the fashions of the wealthy.

The explorations to the New World and to the East had begun to tap vast resources in precious metals, jewels and beautiful fabrics. The Spaniards and Portuguese controlled this lucrative trade, reaping the reward for their initiative in discovery. It had become clear that the potential of such trade was too extensive for two countries to handle in isolation. The commercial expertise of other nations, notably Germany, Flanders and France, was employed in building up centres in Europe to handle this trade and exploit the material wealth. In the chief centres in western Europe cities expanded, land was developed and plant assembled for raising sheep for wool, the culture of the silkworm, for the processes of spinning, dyeing, fulling and weaving of fabrics of all kinds from plain woollen cloth to the most exotic of patterned velvets and silks. Italy, which had long been the centre of production for such fabrics, joined in vigorously to protect her interests. Her cities of Venice, Florence, Milan and Genoa became richer than ever in competition with the newer centres of Lyons, Paris, Rouen, London, Antwerp, Ypres, Munich and Augsburg.

Luxurious fabrics were adorned by jewelled embroideries, fine lacework and further elaborated with glittering jewellery of all kinds from pendants and heavy necklaces to bracelets, rings, earrings, brooches and hat ornaments. In the succeeding centuries, costume has often been superb, elegant, of luxury fabrics and with magnificent distortion of line and form. Never has the sixteenth century been surpassed for its glittering panoply of jewelled splendour.

The colonisation of the New World had given great wealth and power to Spain and Portugal. It was, therefore, the designs of dress established in the Iberian peninsula which influenced the whole of Europe (not under Turkish subjugation) during this century. The Spanish influence only began to decline after 1600 when, first Holland, then France, gained supremacy.

Initially, there was strong resistance to Spanish dominance in dress from the areas of northern Europe under the influence of the Reformation. In Scandinavia, Holland, Germany and Czechoslovakia this was notable. Catholic countries quickly followed the Spanish line, with adaptations. Countries such as England, with a Spanish consort to the Queen, did likewise. Even when Elizabeth succeeded her sister and engaged in the protracted struggle against the might of Spain, Spanish fashions remained paramount. It was Germany* who resisted Spanish styles longest and, in the end, only capitulated when the Catholic south of the country had adopted the more elegant, luxury modes. Countries such as Italy and France, whose garments had long displayed harmony and beauty, embraced the Spanish styles but adapted them to their own tastes, modifying the rigidity of the prototype with a softer line and introducing lighter colours into the predominance of black in the Spanish wardrobe.

The influence of military dress upon the civil, seen so clearly in the early sixteenth century in the German styles of puffed and

---

* There were many in the Church, and outside it, who railed against the wickedness of wearing Spanish dress. Typical is the sermon preached by the Professor in the Holy Scriptures at Frankfurt University in 1555, which condemned trunk hose as being possessed of the Devil; he described these garments as *Hosenteufel*.

440 *1550*   **441** *1564*   **442** *1560–70*   **443** *Philip II, 1553*

slashed garments, was still effective, though now in a more moderate form. The later sixteenth century characteristics stemming from military costume, include the excessive padding to shoulder and chest, also the peasecod-belly protuberance reminiscent of the shape of the cuirass and the shell contour of the still projecting cod-piece. In military attire these features were all means of protection for vulnerable parts of the body.

Spain

Spanish dress was characterised by its elegance, austerity, rigidity and superb decoration. Black was the dominant colour for normal wear; gayer colours were for special, festive occasions. Fabrics were rich and heavy; decoration was in gold and silver thread, with jewels and pearls. These qualities typified the Spanish way of life. By the mid-century Charles V, the Hapsburg German Emperor, ruled (apart from Spain) over peoples in Austria, Burgundy, Holland and Italy, as well as the immense new lands in north and south America and Africa.

Spanish rule was essentially that of the Roman Catholic Church which in a restrictive, rigid manner, prescribed and opposed reform or change. The insistence on traditional ceremonial at court, the limitations on the life of the people were epitomised in the elegant but profoundly uncomfortable constriction of the whaleboned and bombasted costume. These modes were beautiful works of art in themselves but artificial in form and far from the natural elegances of fifteenth-century Italy which preceded them.

The Moorish inheritance was still apparent, especially in the textiles, the rich embroideries, the use of jewels and jewelled buttons, points and ornaments as well as heavy girdles and collars. The jewelled buttons attached down the centre front of the ladies' gowns stemmed from the Moorish styles of coat dresses. This was a characteristic Spanish fashion, unlike the long girdle chains terminating in pendant or pomander, usual in France or England. The leather styles of shoe and chopine were decorated on Moorish motifs in silver or gold ornament and had slightly upturned, pointed toes.

The Spanish contributed a number of innovations to sixteenth-century costume. These included the cape, in all its varied forms, the corset and farthingale, the high neckline supporting a ruff and the bombasted doublet and trunk hose. During the century other nations took these up and extended and adapted them. Spain's use of these features was always restrained and austere. It was in Holland and England, for example, that were seen the massive cartwheel ruffs, in Germany and Holland the excessive bombast and in France the largest farthingales, developing the theme from cone to cartwheel form. Spanish dress continued, until 1620, to be austere and tasteful, not in excess except, perhaps, in the decoration of the fabric themselves.

Men's dress from 1540–1620 comprised a shirt, doublet and undertunic or jubon, upper and lower stocks or hose, cape or cloak, hat, gloves and shoes.

The *shirt* was white, silk or cambric, full and decorated with black silk embroidery – Spanish blackwork – often intertwined with gold or silver thread. This decoration was employed especially at the edges of the elegant wrist ruffles and neck ruffle or collar. The Spanish were the first to take to the high neckline. The square or boat-shaped line of the 1540s became a high collar to the doublet. Over this, the shirt ended in the 1550s

and 1560s in a neat ruffle or ruffle-edged collar (**440, 443, 445**).

As time passed, these ruffles became full scale *ruffs* which were termed *bands*. They were then separate items of wear, not attached to the shirt, made from linen, lawn or Holland cambric. They consisted of a long strip of fabric, pleated and set into a neckband. They became larger after the introduction of starch to stiffen them. They required frequent and expert laundering. They were washed, starched, then set, while damp, into form and goffered (gauffered) by inserting heated metal setting or poking sticks into the individual folds (**461, 462**). When dry the ruff was then placed in a low, wide *band-box*. The fashionable ruff increased gradually in size until 1580–85, when it might extend nine inches on either side of the neck and consist of eighteen yards of material. It would be starched, often in colour, and require a wire frame (*rebato* or *supportasse*) underneath to support it. The edge of the ruff was also often wired. Lace edging, or even a ruff entirely of lace, was particularly to be desired. Wrist ruffles were in matching sets with the ruff. These sets might be embroidered in black, gold or silver thread with tiny jewels sewn

444 *c.1560–5*   **445** *Sebastian of* **446** *Infante Don Carlos, 1559*   **447** *1565–70*
Portugal, 1570–3

Spain

into the pattern. Spanish styles of ruff, though decorative, were not generally of excessive width and larger ones were circular and not often open in front (**446, 448A, 449B, D, 465**).

From about 1550 the Spanish *doublet* generally accentuated a slim waist. It was pointed in front and finished with narrow basques. The garment was buttoned down the centre front from high neck to waist. It had short sleeves or was finished by wings or picadils at the shoulder. It was slashed on the chest and back but Spanish slashing was always restrained and narrow, the undergarment barely showing through the slits. The undertunic or jubon had long, fitting sleeves with decorative, horizontal banding, of slashes or embroidery. Longitudinal slashes were held together at intervals by points. Typical doublet styles of 1550–70 are shown in **440, 443, 446**. Later in the century the doublet was padded on the chest and lower in front, giving an artificial

paunch called a *peasecod-belly*. Whalebone was also inserted in the seams to maintain the desired shape. Sleeves were often excessively padded on the upper arm but less so in Spain than in northern countries. Later doublet styles were sometimes left unbuttoned to show the undertunic (**445, 448A, 449B, D**).

In Spain, the fashion for upper stocks – the part of the hose covering the buttocks and upper thigh – in full, slashed style was introduced before elsewhere. These stocks, usually described as *trunk hose*, were like full knickerbockers. They had a fitting waistband and thigh bands. The fullness of the material draped over the latter, often hiding the bands from view. Trunk hose were slashed to display an undergarment of similar form but of different colour and material. The strips of the outer garment were known as *panes* and were usually richly embroidered, even jewelled. This style of hose, worn with fitting stockings on the lower leg, was in general use during these years though its length varied. Trunk hose were shorter in the 1580s and 1590s and padded to give a wide, stiff silhouette at buttock level. The exaggeratedly prominent cod-piece continued in fashion (**440, 443, 445, 446, 448A, 449B, D**).

Capes and *cloaks* had long been traditional Spanish garments. In the sixteenth century they came into their own and the fashion spread all over Europe. Spanish modes were greatly varied, in length, in fullness, the addition of hanging or open sleeves, the use of a wide collar or small turn-back one or none. The method of wearing differed also. The garment could be worn round both shoulders or only one or might be simply draped over an arm or slung round the body by its fastening cords. Materials used in the capes were rich and heavy; linings contrasted and edges and collars especially were luxuriously decorated. Earlier styles tended to be larger, later ones very short (**445, 446, 448A, 449B**). The German and English style of shaped coat or gown of the mid-century was adopted in Spain after 1550 (**443**), but never ousted the cape from favour.

Men wore their *hair* trimmed neatly and short, sometimes curling at the ears and on top. They were cleanshaven or wore moustaches and dainty, pointed beards. *Hats* were mainly of velvet or satin. Earlier styles had soft crowns and small, soft brims. Later in the century, taller hats were fashionable with waved or turned-up brims.

449 Spanish Dress 1590–1620. (Background: Plaza Mayor, Madrid)

115

Details, 1540–1620

450 *Leather chopine*

451 *Velvet brocade chopine*

Spanish footwear, 16th century

452 *Red velvet boot*

453 *Princess Mary of England, 1544*

454 *Charles IX of France, c.1560*

455 *Queen Mary I of England, 1554*

456 *French, c.1550*

457 *Queen Elizabeth I of England, 1589–90*

458 *Dutch, c.1554*

459 *Gold, jewelled pendant, Spanish, 1550–1600*

460 *Swedish princess, c.1590*

461 *Ruff hanging on wall peg*

462 *Goffering irons for setting starched ruffs*

463 *Spanish princess, c.1584*

464 *English, 1577*

465 *Spanish prince, c.1565*

466 *Dutch, 1619*

467 *c.1545–50*   **468** *1545*   **469** *c.1550*   **470** *1555*

There was usually a jewelled hat band and decoration consisted of ostrich tips and aigrettes with a jewelled brooch pinned at the side (**440, 445, 446, 448A, 465**).

Stockings or hose were fitting; silk knitted ones appeared in Spain from the 1560s. They were costly and of fine quality, much prized and envied by the rest of Europe.

The wide-toed *shoes* of the 1530s and 1540s had given way by 1550 to a natural shape, still slashed, pierced and embroidered with jewels. Differing fabrics were used for shoes, most generally, velvet, satin or leather. For street wear they were covered by *chopines* which had deep cork soles. *Boots* were sometimes worn (**440, 443, 445, 446, 448A, D, 449B**).

Masculine dress in Spain in this period was noted for its elegance and subtlety. Black was predominant, even more for men than for women. Often the whole costume (except for the ruff) was in black, in different materials, with each garment embroidered and decorated in silver or gold thread with jewels. Colours, when introduced, were in muted tones or in small quantity, as in the slashed openings of the trunk hose or doublet, the lining of a cape, sleeves of the undertunic, for

instance. There was a quality of serious dignity and quiet autocratic splendour about the slender men's attire in sixteenth century Spain.

The *feminine silhouette* in the years 1540–1620 was created by the corset and the farthingale, which ensured an unnatural, though elegant, but rigid form, on which could be displayed to advantage the most beautiful fabrics, enriched and jewelled over almost the entire receptive surface. The woman thus became a display model. Beautiful the ensemble certainly was but no less uncomfortable. Spain was the instigator and leader of these styles and maintained them, with variations, well into the seventeenth century, far longer than other countries which abandoned them for more natural forms after 1620. The rigid figure, encased in this way, made any movement which was not stately, difficult. It expressed clearly the Spanish preoccupation with autocratic dignity and chastity; gaiety and frivolity were incongruous intrusions in such costume which, even children in aristocratic families, had to wear. Such constriction was not endured by the common people.

The fitting bodice and full skirt styles based upon early forms of *corset* were described in

chapter 4. In the second half of the sixteenth century the linen corset was shaped to keep a slender waist and flatten and raise the breasts to give a concave cone shape to the upper torso. This form was maintained by the insertion of strips of wood, horn or whalebone in the seams, down the front, sides and back. The garment was laced up centre back or front. Since it was not shaped to cup the breasts, as in a modern corselette, shoulder straps were necessary to hold it in place and give an upwards thrust or lift, rather than the less attractive downward flattening, to the breasts. In the final gown bodice form the outline of the breasts was not discernible as such but their forward prominence was not obliterated as in the flattening process of other periods, the 1920s for example.

The *gown bodice*, worn over the corset or body, was of heavy, rich material. Some styles, particularly until 1570, retained the wide, square neckline, arched in front. In these instances, the shoulders above this neckline were covered by a transparent fabric, jewelled and embroidered, which supported the traditional high collar or ruffle (**441, 448B**). In Spanish dress, the shoulders and neck were always covered; the décolleté, square necklines of England and France were not seen in Spain. The majority of gown necklines were high and all of one material, surmounted by the lace and embroidered edged ruffle or ruff; as with the men, ruffs tended to increase in size in the 1580s. There were few examples of open ruffs or collars worn in Spain. Heavy, jewelled pendants and necklaces, as well as rows of jewelled buttons decorated such bodices (**442, 444, 447, 448C, F, G, 449A, C, E, 463**).

Sleeves were generally in two parts. The inner sleeve was long and fairly fitting, though later styles were padded and slashed. They were of contrasting fabric to the gown and were often banded horizontally and embroidered in gold or silver. At the shoulder was a puff or padded roll, sometimes cut into picadils. From this hung a detachable outer sleeve which matched the gown, though it had a contrasting lining. Sometimes this hung simply behind the arm (**442, 444, 448F, G, 449A, C, E**); in other styles it was very wide at the lower edge and was held at intervals by jewelled clasps (**447, 448B, C**). At the wrist, ruffles or cuffs matched the neckwear.

While the upper torso was confined and its shape determined by the corset, so the lower part of the body was encased in the *farthingale*. The introduction of this verdugado in fifteenth century Spain was described in chapter 4. This underskirt of linen or canvas, with hoops of cane inserted horizontally at regular intervals from waist to ground, continued to be worn throughout this period in Spain. Here, the bell shape was retained in these years; the variations of wheel and padded roll seen elsewhere were never worn in Spain. As time passed, the skirt became wider at the base and, from 1570 onwards, the sides were flatter and straighter, making the bell nearer to a cone in form. Under the farthingale was worn a black skirt called a *basquina*. On top could be worn as many as three skirts, the inner one ground length and the outer ones slightly shorter in front but long at the back.

All skirts were cut to hang flat at front and sides, with the fullness concentrated at the rear. In some designs the overskirt was open in front to display the underskirt of contrasting but equally richly patterned fabric (**441, 444, 449A**), in others, the sides of the front opening were held together by jewelled brooches, buttons or points, all the way down (**442, 447, 448B, C, F, G, 449E**). Although the entire costume was heavily encrusted with jewels and embroidery, it was the skirt which displayed the large motif, formal designs to best advantage. The creaseless form gave no interruption to these superb patterns.

Ladies wore *stockings* and *footwear* like those of the men. They frequently wore chopines or pantoffles on top of their shoes (**450, 451**). This gave them extra height and resulted in an apparently mechanical form of motion when combined with the constriction engendered by the corset and farthingale; their progression resembled a glide or slide rather than a walk.

Spanish ladies, like the Italians, did not favour the wearing of hoods, as in northern Europe. Their *hair* was dressed in curls or loose pompadour style in front then braided at the back. It was then enclosed in gold, jewelled cauls or pearl string nets with decorative little caps perched on the

472, 473 *1581–2*   **474** *1595–1600*   **475** *1580–2*

476 *1610*   477 *1615*   478, 479 *1610*

back of the head (**441, 444, 447, 448F**). Sometimes the hair was uncovered, decorated only by
jewels and pearls (**448B, 449A, C, E**). *Hats*, in
similar modes to the masculine designs, were often
worn on top of the cauls (**442, 448C, G, 463**).

Fabrics worn by women were rich and heavy,
patterned, embroidered and jewelled. Black was
especially to be seen, generally in velvet or satin
and enriched with gold or silver threadwork. Rich
colours were also worn, especially for festive
occasions; women's costume displayed a greater
variety in light colours than men's attire.

Among important *accessories* was the *fan*.
Feather fans, with ivory handles, were in use, but
the folding fan, of Oriental origin, was first used
in Spain and became popular in the sixteenth
century. This was made of vellum or perfumed
leather. Both sexes carried large lace-edged
handkerchiefs, perfumed *gloves* of Spanish leather
and sunshades.

France

Like all the nations of western Europe, the French
based their modes on Spanish pattern. This was

particularly the case until 1575–80, after which
they introduced a number of variations in both
men's and women's dress, all of which were
exaggerations of a Spanish prototype. Most
notable examples were the effeminate silhouettes
in masculine dress in the reign of Henry III – the
abbreviated trunk hose and the cartwheel ruffs,
for instance – and the immense wheel farthingale
skirts worn by ladies from the *fin de siècle*.

During the years *1540–75*, *men's dress* was
closely modelled on that of the Spanish. Colours
were darker than previously, black was worn a
great deal, decoration tended to be in gold or
silver embroidery or passementerie. The French
produced at home most of their own needs in the
rich fabrics so popular at this time – silks, velvets,
satins – in the weaving centres at such towns as
Lyons, Tours, Nîmes and Orléans. It was also in
those years that the French seriously developed
their system of state restrictions against the
competitive importation of such fabrics. This
has been a bulwark of the French economy ever
since.

Masculine *doublets, trunk hose*, shirts and high
collars or *ruffs* were all like those worn in Spain.

Knitted silk *hose*, instead of tailored cloth styles were introduced from Spain and worn for the first time by Henry II. Frenchmen adopted the Spanish *cape* in its varied styles (**469, 471A, D, 473**), but, for some years yet, also continued to wear, as an alternative, the open gown or coat called the *chamarre*, which had been fashionable under Francis I (chapter 4). In the 1550s it was not padded as before but had loose, puff sleeves to the elbow and hung open and full all round to the knees (**467**). The Spanish style of soft black velvet *hat,* with jewelled band, narrow brim and ostrich plume trimming was worn. Hair was short and beards and moustaches neat and pointed (**454, 467, 469, 471A, D, 473**).

The reign of Henry III, *1574–89*, was noted for the effeminacy and degeneracy of *men's fashions*. The characteristics of these styles were also to be seen in some other countries, notably England, though not in Spain. In France they were more extreme than elsewhere. The *doublet* was padded to the peasecod-belly silhouette in front and whaleboned in the seams to keep the shape; it was buttoned full length and dipped to a low V in the centre front, sloping upwards to hip-bone level at the sides. The basques were small, mere tabs, and the *trunk hose* padded and abbreviated. The cod-piece had now disappeared.

Below the trunk hose were fitting breeches, called *canions*, which were slashed and puffed in rows. *Stockings* were fastened at the knee with ribbon decorated garters and rose above these by a few inches. The doublet had a high neck covered by a large cartwheel *ruff*. Undertunic sleeves were also puffed and slashed, visible full length as the doublet terminated in wings or picadils at the shoulder. Sleeve wrists were fitting and ended in a lace cuff or ruffle. Very short *capes* were slung round the shoulders.

Gentlemen took immense care of their complexions, using cosmetics and perfume and wearing gloves and masks to protect the skin. Their

480 The Villa Giulia, Rome. Italian Dress, 1550–65

481, 482, 483 *1581*   484 *1575*   485 c.*1585*

hair was carefully curled, their beards elegantly pointed, moustaches plucked to give a fine line. They wore tall crowned *hats*, piled high with plumes, also jewellery of all kinds, especially earrings. *Shoes* were slashed and jewelled; pantoffles and chopines were worn on top for out of doors (**473**).

In the years *1595–1620*, **men's fashions** returned to a more masculine line. The same garments were worn but their design altered subtly. *Doublets* were less padded, the peasecod-belly had disappeared, the waistline was gently rounded or pointed; the decoration was still by slashes and larger wings finished the armhole. Longer trunk hose were worn once more and with less bombast. An alternative mode was the *Venetians*, a longer, loose type of breeches, which were tied at the knee with ribbon sashes. The cartwheel ruff had gone also, replaced by a smaller collar or ruff or, alternatively, a stiff collar held up by a frame beneath. In France this was called the *col rotonde*; a larger open version was worn by ladies – the

collet monte (**470, 471C, 472, 477, 478**). A third type of neckwear presaged the falling band of the next generation. This was the *falling ruff,* which was unstiffened and draped softly from the neck over the shoulders.

From 1600, *shoes* had heels and on the instep were ribbon roses. *Boots* were becoming fashionable again; these were of soft leather from Spain or Russia (**476**).

Ladies' gowns also closely followed the Spanish pattern from *1540* until *1575*. The fitting corset, boned and laced, was worn, giving the concave chest and upward bosom line with a slender waist. The gown bodice had a low, wide, square neckline, inside which was sometimes seen the white chemise. Necklaces enhanced the bare neck (**468, 470, 471C**). Many ladies followed the Spanish prototype more closely and wore a high-necked bodice and ruff (**471B, E**). Sleeves were tight fitting with a broad, turned-back cuff, often of fur, which displayed the undergown sleeve to the wrist, with finishing ruffle (**468, 470, 471C**).

It was Catherine de' Medici, queen of Henry II, who was reputed to have introduced the metal *corset* into France from Italy. This was in the form of a stomacher, which was a bodice, stiffened with strips of metal and covered with rich fabric, heavily embroidered and jewelled. Under this was the stiff linen bodice as before. This garment produced an artificially slender waist, low and deeply pointed in front (**470, 471C, 472**).

The Spanish *farthingale* was worn during the entire sixteenth century but soon the French began to wear extra padding in the form of a circular roll tied round the waist so that, when the very full, gathered skirt was arranged over it, the material fell in a bell shape rather than the straighter cone-sided Spanish form (**470, 471C, 472, 972**). The linen corset was then finished with stiffened picadils at the waist to support this roll.

A popular garment in these years was the loose surcote or mantle, which had puff sleeves and often hanging ones also. It was brooched at the neck and generally had an upstanding small collar under the small, high ruff. It then hung straight and open in front to the ground. It was based on the *ropa*, a garment which originated in the Iberian Peninsular and became popular in the period 1555–75 in other countries also, especially England and Holland (**471B**).

The *coiffure* was simply dressed, parted in the centre and drawn back softly to a chignon at the back. Sometimes it was dressed over pads on the temples to add width to the style. The *French hood* continued to be worn for some years though, as the ruff grew larger, the fall was omitted (**456, 468, 470, 471B, E**).

By the 1570s French women had, in general, abandoned the Spanish farthingale and exchanged the rigid canvas skirt for a fat *bolster roll* tied round the waist (**972**), over which the full skirt fell in many folds into a wide, bell shape. The waist was slenderer still and more pointed in front. Sleeves were full and padded and an over-sleeve, generally loose and clasped only at intervals, was worn over it. By this time also a jewelled cap had replaced the French hood and, either the ruff was very large with a high neckline or, more

486 c.1590   **487** 1607   **488** 1620   **489** 1581

Italy

usually in France, the neckline was décolleté and a standing collar (the *collet monté*), lace-edged and wired, framed the head; it had a framework support behind to raise it at the back (**470, 471C, 472, 474**). This is sometimes referred to as the Medici collar. Large, open ruffs were similarly supported (**475**).

Later in the century, even larger skirts were desired and the bolster roll became inadequate to create this shape so the wheel or drum farthingale was evolved; this is generally known as the *French farthingale*. Like its Spanish predecessor, it was a canvas or linen petticoat with circular hoops of cane or whalebone set at regular intervals from waist to ground. In this type the hoops were of equal diameter and the flat top of the cartwheel was also of canvas, pleated and with a hole for the waist, where it could be drawn tightly and affixed with tapes (**971**).

The *corset*, by this time, had a long, central busk of metal or bone which extended almost to the pubis. The stiff picadil trimming was still attached to the lower edge of the corset bodice round the waist, which was now excessively slender and low-pointed in front. When worn with the wheel farthingale, the busk point rested upon the edge of the front frame of the drum, providing the fashionable tilt to the dress (**971**).

Gowns worn on top of this style of farthingale and corset were elaborately and artificially shaped; they contained an immense quantity of material. Typical designs are shown in **474, 475,** and **479**. Fig **475** shows a fashionable mode of the latter part of the sixteenth century with a high standing, wired ruff or collar, excessively padded sleeves and a full skirt gathered at the slender waist over the framework structure and two or three underskirts. Usually, as in this illustration, the gown skirt is held or pinned up to show the underskirt. In figs. **474** and **479**, the sleeves are also in a popular style in padded rolls, the neckline is very low, lace-edged and with high

Details 1540–1620

491 *Duke Karl of Austria,* c.*1610*

492 *German portrait*

493 *Italian young man,* 1590

494 *Italian gentleman,* c.*1590*

495 *Polish queen,* c.*1610*

496 *Czech portrait,* 1578

497 *Hungarian boot,* 1602

498 *German shoes,* 1570–90

499 *Gold, jewelled pendant, Italian*

500 *Eleanor of Toledo,* 1545

501 *Italian girl*

502 *Lady's chopine,* c.*1610*

503 *White leather glove*

collet monté. Ropes of pearls and jewels decorate the bodice and the form of the long, boned busk is visible in front. This descends on to the drum ruffle which, in general, was less commonly to be seen in France than in England.

Coiffures were dressed higher in this period and headdresses rarely worn. Jewels and pearl ropes were the usual decoration and cosmetics and perfumes were widely used. Gloves and handkerchiefs were carried. Shoes were like the men's, heels being added in the second half of the sixteenth century.

Italy

The Italian peninsula continued to be divided into small states ruled by different factions. This meant that there was still no national fashion in dress. Spanish influence had been strong since the Pope and the head of the Hapsburg Empire, Charles V, came to terms in 1529. In that year Charles received the Imperial Crown from Pope Clement VII at Bologna. As a result of the agreement, the Papacy held the largest Italian state, around Rome, and much of the north was still controlled by the Italian princes. However, in 1559, Philip II the new Spanish King, ruled over the larger part of Italy, the whole of the south and Sicily, including Naples, and much of the north, including Milan, as well. Only Venice, under its old republican government, Genoa and Corsica under the Dorias and the small republics of Lucca and San Martino, together with the Papal State were free of Spain.

In these Spanish dominions, Spanish dress was, of course, worn. In the north, centred on Milan, it was a reflection of fashion in Madrid (**480A, E, 484, 485, 488**). In the south, it took its cue from Naples, and this was a glittering, sumptuous interpretation of Spanish dress. Rich and bright colours, silks and satins in luxurious Italian fabrics presented a glowing Neapolitan version of Spain, full of life, gaiety, insouciance and completely lacking the austere dignity of the Spanish prototype.

Outside the range of Spanish influence, the Italian characteristics of fashion continued to assert themselves. Italians, especially since the Renaissance, had always liked comfortable clothes, light, gay colours, silk fabrics and a natural, elegant line which brought out the most attractive features of the human figure, whether male or female. They, therefore, adopted Spanish dress within the framework of their natural bent. In *men's dress*, ruffs were small, padding and whalebone in the seams non-existent or kept to a minimum, trunk hose easily fitting and of medium length, doublet naturally waisted and sleeves fitting. The masculine silhouette was slender and elegant (**480A, B, 484, 489, 490A, D**).

Women wore a corset in the form of a reinforced, brocaded stomacher, not too tightly adjusted. The gown bodice on top was laced across this. They preferred several petticoats to a farthingale and liked fullness in their gown skirts. They eschewed cartwheel ruffs and wore gowns with low necklines and standing collars or higher necklines with dainty, lace ruffs.

The *fabrics* from which garments were made, for both sexes, were sumptuous, but almost always of silks, light coloured and embroidered but with much less jewelled enrichment than in Spain. The smaller quantity of jewellery was unostentatious but finely wrought and of high quality. It was displayed to greater advantage since it was sparingly worn.

Men's hair and hat styles were simple versions of the Spanish (**480A, B, 484, 489, 494**). Ladies wore their hair loose or bound and braided in gold cauls and caps with pearl ropes wound overall, as they had for generations (**480C, D, E, 482, 483, 486, 488, 500, 501**). Turbans were still in evidence.

There were noticeable differences in costume between these non-Spanish, Italian dominions. The intrepid travellers in the sixteenth century who include such voyagers as Fynes Moryson (see bibliography), describe the dress of Ferrara and Mantua (1591–93) as fashionable and elegant, of Genoa like the French and with a fondness for

505 *Lady Jane Grey, c.1547* **506** *Princess Mary, c.1545*   **507** *c.1580*   **508** *Queen Elizabeth I, c.1590*

England

black velvet and gold chain decoration, the Florentines as being modestly dressed.

It was Venice, always a law unto itself, which showed the greatest variations from elsewhere. The Venetians had strict sumptuary laws still and Moryson tells us that gentlemen wore their rich apparel underneath plainer garments only when going out at night to visit their mistresses. Venetians were also noted for the extreme height of their chopines (*zoccolo*) which made them very tall and also unable to walk steadily in the street without assistance (**339, 342**). Wealthy ladies required a woman servant to lean upon and to hold up their skirt trains which were exceptionally long. Venetian feminine dress was also remarkable for its décolleté necklines and for the red and white cosmetics applied to both face and bosom. The neckline, in many instances, was so low as to display the nipples, which were appropriately painted. An elegant, lace white collar framed the back of the head and a transparent veil was draped over the shoulders and down the back (**480D, 482, 486**).

England

The styles of the *1540s* were still based on German modes, with the square silhouette for men formed by the excessively padded shoulders and gowns; the costume of both sexes was slashed to show the fabrics beneath (**504, 505, 506**).

The marriage of Queen Mary I in 1554 to Philip II of Spain accelerated the trend towards the adoption of Spanish fashions; a movement which was already perceptible, as elsewhere in western Europe. The Spanish mode had been worn by English women for some time. The corset, creating a rigid bodice with the farthingale creaseless skirt, had been fashionable since 1530. But, until the 1550s, the feminine neckline had been a wide square, arched in front, with bare neck above decorated by a jewelled necklace and pendant. From 1535, the French hood was the usual headcovering (**453, 504A, E, 505, 506**).

From the 1550s, the Spanish high neckline was adopted, with an open collar and small open ruff or, later, a circular small ruff (**455, 509A**). In the

1560s, the French hood was replaced by the Spanish caul with pearl decoration and the surcote, based on the *ropa*, was much in evidence (**509E**).

Though, after Mary's death in 1558, England reverted to Protestantism under Elizabeth I and increasingly pursued a policy determined to resist Spanish domination of the country, there was no diminution in the popularity of Spanish dress. Until 1580, men's and women's fashions closely paralleled those of the Spanish, though fewer people wore black than in Spain; rich, gay colours and costly fabrics were usual (**464, 509**).

In the 1580s, English dress, for both sexes, became extravagantly costly and exaggerated in form but it always remained elegant and less effeminate than the French modes of the period. *Men* wore gigantic cartwheel ruffs, doublets padded in sleeves and into peasecod-belly shape in front, with whalebone inserted in the seams. The doublet waist dipped excessively in front and up at the sides; it was finished by small basques, resting on the bombasted, abbreviated trunk hose. Hats were tall and be-plumed, beards pointed and capes, short or long, slung carelessly round the body. Hose could be in one section (**507**) or pulled up over the knee, gartered, and dis-

playing a decorated upper hose or canion beneath on the thigh (**510C, H**).

Women continued to wear the Spanish farthingale or the French bolster roll. In both cases, the skirt silhouette had widened and the skirt was gathered in at the waist at sides and back, and fell fully to the ground. It was still usually open in front to display the embroidered, jewelled underskirt. Sleeves were heavily padded and matched the undergown. The bodice, over a rigid, constricting corset, was pointed in front and matched the overskirt. There was a greater variation in ruff and collar styles in England than anywhere else. Ladies often wore two ruffs, a small one hugging the neck and a larger one outside it. Lace edging was popular and the cartwheel ruffs and wired collars were supported on a framework, especially at the back (**510E**).

In the later years of the *sixteenth century, men's dress* returned to a less padded and extreme silhouette. Doublets were longer and so also were trunk hose. Cartwheel ruffs gave place to smaller designs, whisks or soft, falling ruffs. In contrast, *ladies* adopted the French wheel farthingale and, with it, the necessary accompaniment, the long, bone-busked corset. Almost always in England the gown had a drum flounce. The skirt was now

510 Costume in England. Queen Elizabeth I in Procession, 1585–1610
(Background: English flagship)

511, 512 *1550–5*   **513** *1575*   **514** *c.1560*

shorter, clearing the ground by a few inches. The bodice was long, narrow and excessively pointed in front. Sleeves were padded into leg-of-mutton shape and hanging sleeves depended behind the arm from the shoulder. The neckline of these gowns was usually very low displaying, as in Venice, most of the bosom. The neck was then framed behind by an open ruff or collar, like the French *collet monté*. An especially English fashion was the butterfly wing ornamentation which could accompany either the open or closed ruff. This was in the form of two wired, circular wings, one on each side of the back of the head; these were filled with white gauze or silk and edged with pearls and jewels. Accompanying this was a white, transparent veil which draped over the shoulders and fell to the ground. Costumes of this period were most ornate, in the richest of fabrics, most brilliant of colours and elaborately jewelled and embroidered all over. Queen Elizabeth herself set the pattern for this and possessed an immense wardrobe (**457, 508, 510B, F, I**).

England imported her costly fabrics but was renowned for the quality of her own woollen cloth which was the staple material for the use of

the bulk of the population. The country was self sufficient in this, from the flocks of sheep pastured and through all the processes of dyeing, spinning and weaving. Large quantities of this cloth were exported all over Europe and this amply paid for the import of luxury silks and velvets.

Northern and Eastern Europe

The northern Baltic area, from Holland in the west to beyond Danzig (Gdansk) in the east, showed similar elements in dress. These countries of Holland and Germany, together with Scandinavia, had shared a common development and interests through the Middle Ages under Hanseatic control. Their climate, their way of life, their religion and their architecture had much in common; so also did their costume.

In the earlier part of the sixteenth century the German influence had been strongest. In the years from 1530–75, as elsewhere in western Europe, these lands also began to fall under the sway of Spanish fashions. Protestantism, especially strong in Germany and Scandinavia, was unsympathetic towards the adoption of Spanish dress but even

Germany finally came under the influence of its own southern kingdoms and followed the general line.

In the last quarter of the sixteenth century, the struggles of the Netherlands to break away from Spanish domination and their final success brought a divergence in costume. At the end of the century, the Dutch developed their own style of dress, different from the Spanish and more in tune with Reformation ideals and way of life. The Dutch pattern was followed by the other Baltic countries so that, after 1620, Holland led the fashions of the second quarter of the seventeenth century.

Unlike Spain, England or France, the immense area of northern and eastern Europe was divided into many states and kingdoms. Costume followed geographical contours rather than national boundaries. The dress for the middle classes differed greatly from one region to another, even from one town to the next. These differences were much more marked in bourgeois dress; the styles of the upper classes followed first on Spanish lines then on Dutch.

Flanders and Holland

Until about *1570–80*, the Spanish style of dress was generally followed. *Men* wore doublet and trunk hose. The doublet was high-necked, with a small, neat collar or ruff above. It was buttoned down the centre front and belted at a natural waistline, pointed in front. Trunk hose were loose and of medium length; cod-pieces were prominent. The doublet sleeve ended in a short, slashed puff or a roll or picadils. Hats, hair, shoes and hose were like the Spanish. In general, materials were heavier than in Spain to suit a colder climate, cloth was worn more and there was less decorative embroidery and jewellery (**511, 514**). In the 1570s and 1580s bombast was introduced into the upper sleeves and to form a peasecod-belly shape. Trunk hose were shorter and padded also. Capes were slung round the body. Ruffs became larger but these were always plain. Styles were never extreme (**516, 519**).

With the division of the country, the southern part remained with the Hapsburg Empire while Holland became independent. From this time Dutch trade developed quickly and the country

515 *1590–90*   **516** *1575*   **517, 518** *1590–1600*

519 *1580–5*   **520** *1610*   **521, 522** *1615–20*

became wealthier and began to lead fashion with its own styles. *Men's wear* in the years *1600–20* abandoned the Spanish austere and rigid line. Doublets were slim fitting and neither corseted nor padded; waistlines were natural. Loose, knee-length breeches replaced the trunk hose and finished with silk, fringed sashes tied at the knee. Shoes had ribbon rosettes on the instep and were designed with low heels. The ruff was still large, white and plain, supported on a framework at the back. Hair was looser and longer and large-brimmed hats, with long ostrich plumes curling about the round crown, were worn at a jaunty angle (**521**).

Women's dress passed through similar phases. From 1540–70, the fashions were Spanish but the skirt was fuller and wider, more bell-shaped than cone. It was worn over a farthingale (*fardegalijn* in Dutch) and with a corset. A long girdle generally hung down the centre front. The loose surcote, the *ropa*, was very popular in Holland, where it was termed the *vlieger*. It generally had puff sleeves and often hanging ones as well. Ruffs and collars were small. White linen caps were worn on the head. Ornament was very restrained.

The most usual decoration was banding of a different material, such as velvet (**512**).

From 1570 to the early seventeenth century the ruffs became larger, though they were plain white linen or cambric, not lace-edged. The gown bodice terminated in a padded roll at the shoulders and the sleeves, of a different material, were more padded as time passed; hanging sleeves were added behind the shoulder. At the same time the skirt became very wide and bell-shaped, its form being given by a thick bolster roll worn under it round the waist. The skirt was often open in front to show the underskirt (**513**). By 1580, the bodice had developed a characteristically Dutch form, quite different from the contemporary Spanish one. It was of a contrasting fabric to the rest of the gown, very rich and embroidered – the focal centre of decoration of the costume. The breasts were full and accentuated by the concave curve under them which then bowed out forwards to the low, broad point in front where it was finished by basques. A heavy, padded roll was worn on the shoulders. Ruffs were very large (**515, 518**).

The variety of Dutch *caps* is immense. They

were normal headcovering for all women and were seen in heart-shaped designs, simple small caps on the back of the head and complex patterns of layers of starched and wired linen or cambric. All were white, with simple or no decoration (**458, 512, 513, 517, 518**).

In the seventeenth century, the feminine silhouette changed after 1615. It became much slimmer and more elegant. As with the men's styles, Spanish influences disappeared and, with them, the stiffened skirt. The overgown was often pinned or held up to show the underskirt. Ruffs were still very large and tall hats with plumes were placed on top of the cambric caps (**466, 520, 522**).

A characteristically Dutch garment, also seen in Flanders and northern Germany, was the heuke (huik, hoyke). This was a voluminous veil or cape which was affixed to a wired framing worn over the head, above it. The material then fell, flowing to the ground. Alternatively it could be attached to the cap instead of a framework. The design varied from region to region; often it was finely pleated.

Northern Germany

Until after 1550, the broad masculine silhouette, with puffed sleeves and doublet slashed for decoration, was fashionable. Ladies' gowns were full-skirted with outer skirts held up to show the underskirt. In the second half of the sixteenth century, Spanish styles were followed but materials were heavier and ornamentation restrained. Velvet and brocade were worn by the wealthy. Styles were similar to those of the Dutch.

Fynes Moryson comments, from his travels from 1591, that 'the Germans spend least of other nations on their clothes. They take care that the material is good and hard-wearing. Their linen is thick and coarse in Prussia and ruffs are very large and supported on wire frames. They carry large handkerchiefs.' Moryson also thought that the German styles were old-fashioned compared to those he had left behind in England. There is no doubt, however, that the costume of the German nobility was lavish and luxurious.

One of the richest cities in northern Germany in the sixteenth and early seventeenth century was Danzig. The city functioned as a great merchant

523 *16th century Russian*　　**524** *Danzig, c.1600*　　**525** *Russia, 1560–1600*　　**526** *Polish, c.1600*

Baltic Europe　　133

A   B   C   D   E

port between east and west Baltic, dealing with trade all along the coastline from Russia to Holland. Fashions here were richer than elsewhere in northern Germany. Ruffs were immense. Velvet and silk was to be seen rather than cloth; the costume was enriched with pearl ropes, lace edging, satin-lined, coloured cloaks and fur-lined caps. Stomachers were of brocade or fur. Jewellery was rarely worn in northern Germany but was to be seen more widely in Danzig (524).

As in Holland, white linen and cambric starched caps were worn a great deal in northern Germany. Some designs were made into decorative headdresses by gold embroidery and pearls. Some were based on Spanish styles of caul.

Poland

The Hanseatic and Dutch styles predominated here except that figure silhouettes for men and women were more elegant and slim. Fur linings and trimmings were ubiquitous, especially in winter. Fur was used particularly for caps, coat collars and linings and for stomachers. As in Hungary, the eastern influence led to men wearing two coats, one on top of the other. The outer coat had sleeves and was longer than the under, sleeveless one, which was generally girded. Boots were often worn rather than shoes. Hose and breeches were of cloth material to match the undercoat. Men's hair was cut fairly short, moustaches were worn and hats were decorated with feathers (**495, 526**). *Russian costume* was not dissimilar but hair and beards were longer (**523, 525**). Women's dress was very like a slimmer version of the Dutch. White starched caps were general wear. Ruffs were not often seen; instead, the gown collar was fur-lined or richly embroidered while ropes of pearls encircled the neck.

Scandinavia

Danish costume was based on Dutch styles, while their unostentatious colours and restrained ornamentation were similar to those of German dress. Black, with gold decoration, was worn a great deal by the aristocracy, especially the men: a reflection of the dominant Spanish mode behind all fashion of the years 1540–90.

Whereas Danish fashions were taken from the prevailing Dutch styles, Swedish ones were from Germany. Until the sixteenth century, *Sweden*, and *Finland* which was a duchy of Sweden, were, due to their geographical position, on the fringe of European development. Fashions were indigenous, apart from the nobility, whose garments were moulded on foreign styles many years after the inception of these modes.

The Court of the Vasas was the first in Sweden to bring fashions there up to date. Under the founder of the dynasty, Gustav Vasa, 1523–60, German tailors were brought to Stockholm and German garments imported from Lübeck. Fabrics of all kinds were also imported; woollen cloth from England, Holland and Germany, fine linen from Holland and rich fabrics such as silks, velvets, brocades, came from Italy, Spain and the East. The nobility and gentry wore imported fabrics chiefly. Plain linen was made in Sweden and a wide variety of furs were home produced.

Until after 1580, *men's dress* was based on the German pattern. The short gown with wide, padded shoulders and puff and hanging sleeves was of this design. With it were worn German slops called *pluderhosen*. These were loose breeches, nearly knee-length and unpadded. A prominent cod-piece was usual (**527C**). In the last quarter of the sixteenth century, Spanish styles reached Sweden in the form of padded trunk hose, high-collared doublets and ruffs and Spanish

528 *Swiss, 1552*   **529** *German, 1540*   **530** *Charles V, 1555*   **531** *German, 1540–50*

Germany and Switzerland   135

capes (**527A, E**). Trunk hose were never very popular here. They were considered to be uncomfortable and, at the end of the century, Venetians were adopted as a looser, more commodious style.

The *long gown*, which had been worn in Sweden in the Middle Ages, continued to be seen during the sixteenth century, for colder weather and for wear by older men. It was particularly suited to the climate of the Finnish and Swedish winter months. It had much in common with the Russian coat, the *caftan* (**523**), in its braid decoration and fastenings on the chest. It was fur-lined, the fabric patterned in floral designs, and had long hanging sleeves.

Women's dresses followed a simpler form than

fashionable design. The bodice, often separate and sleeveless, was laced up the back, and whaleboned in the seams to give a rigid, slim torso. Separate sleeves were richly embroidered or brocaded. Two skirts were worn; a luxuriously patterned underskirt and an overskirt open in front to display the other. Petticoats and bolster were preferred to a farthingale though, at the end of the century, the French wheel farthingale was adopted, worn with drum frill, low, open neck and wired, stand-up collar (**527B**). The *ropa* style of surcote was popular here, accompanied by a small, high ruff and a hood or heart-shaped cap (**527D**). Hair and headdress styles in general followed the fashion line (**460**).

Central Europe

The costume of *Germany* south of the Baltic coastal area more closely followed Spanish lines in the years *1540–90*. In the most southerly parts of the region, in particular, the Spanish influence was especially strong. This was to be seen in the cut of the garments and the fabrics and patterns used; ornamentation was less rich and jewelled embroideries rarer than in Spain. Decoration was predominantly by fur trimmings, braid, passementerie and velvet banding. This band enrichment could be embroidered and gold and silver thread were used in this work (**492, 498, 529, 530, 531, 532B**). Towards the *end of the century* German styles followed more nearly the Dutch pattern. These were modes more attractive to the Germans, more comfortable to wear with the less restrictive boning and padding. Gay hats with plumes worn jauntily on one side of head were adopted by the men who continued to wear large ruffs but exchanged trunk hose for looser breeches fastened at the knee, often with a ribbon sash. Cloaks and capes were slung with apparent

533 Making Music. German Costume, 1611

534, 535 *1570*   **536, 537** c.*1560*   **538** *1600–5*

carelessness round the body (**532A, 533A, C, D, E**). Ladies also followed the Dutch mode in the early years of the seventeenth century. The large ruff was supported at the back to frame the head. Gowns were looser and less constricted at the waist. They had padded sleeves. The skirt was full and long (**533B**).

The costume of *Switzerland* was similar to that of central/southern Germany but, especially in masculine dress, was characterised by a more swashbuckling air. The figure illustrated in **532C** is typical of the turn of the century attire. Ladies' dress was more sober. Styles of the years 1540–60 had changed little from earlier in the century (**532D, E**). Still fashionable were the central European mode of full, white sleeves, banded tightly at intervals by decorative embroidered strips. Long, beautifully ornamented aprons were worn (**528**).

In *Austria*, the Spanish influence was paramount (**491**). *Czechoslovakia*, that is, Bohemia and Moravia, were governed by a branch of the Hapsburg family and so followed closely on Spanish fashions. This pattern was adhered to here, as in Austria, until 1620, with Spanish colours, materials, decoration and silhouette form employed as in the master design (**496, 534, 535, 536, 537, 538, 540, 542**).

Costume in *Hungary* was different. Here the chief influence was from Turkey, which was strong because of the nearness of their forces and constant contact with them. This especially affected *men's dress*, which from the early sixteenth until the early nineteenth century was dominated by Ottoman fashion. The basic dress during those years comprised two coats, hose or trousers and boots. The coats were the *dolman* and the *mente*. The dolman was cut to fit closely to the body. It was waisted, made in light, richly coloured materials, often embroidered all over in gold or silver, and had a flared skirt nearly to the knee. The mente was worn on top of the dolman. It was wider and about twelve inches longer, with longer sleeves and a wide collar spread over the shoulders. Both coats were buttoned down the centre front. Under the coats was worn a finely embroidered white shirt. On the legs were hose which resembled tight-fitting trousers. Boots, over these, were more common than shoes. Hats were often of fur and trimmed with plumes (**497, 541**).

Women's styles of dress changed more than the men's and followed the international line more closely. Rich and costly materials were worn, embroidered and jewelled. By the mid-sixteenth century, Hungarian women were dressing in Spanish style with constricted bodice, tiny waist, farthingale, hanging sleeves and ruff. Spanish style hats were perched on the coiffure and short, fur-trimmed capes were fashionable. The only

central European note was a long, lace-trimmed apron (**539**). In the early years of the seventeenth century hanging sleeves were especially fashionable and the skirt was open in front to show the elaborate underskirt. Falling ruffs began to replace the upstanding ones (**543**).

Children's dress continued to be a miniature version of adult attire. Little boys of up to five or six years were dressed in skirts, like little girls and this included the farthingale whether of Spanish or French version. Children's dress is illustrated in figs. **448D, E, 478, 480A, C, F, 481, 483, 487, 504D, 510A, 517, 532D, 533D, 535, 540, 542.**

Hungary and Czechoslovakia

539 *Hungarian. Late 16th century*

540 *Czech, 1605*

541 *Hungarian, 1594*

542 *Czech, c.1580* **543** *Hungarian, 1618*

Notes on the Illustrations

440 Portrait of Emperor Maximilian II by Antonio Moro. Prado, Madrid. Leather jerkin over doublet of white striped in gold. White trunk hose, gold decorated panes. White satin hose and shoes. Black velvet hat, white plume. Black, gold embroidered purse.

441 Portrait by Sanchez-Coello. Imperial Museum, Vienna. Patterned velvet gown over farthingale. Jewelled neckband and collar and jewelled partlet. White satin sleeves slashed and clasped with points. Jewelled girdle. Brocade underskirt. Jewelled caul.

442 Portrait of Queen Isabella by Pantoja de la Cruz. Prado, Madrid. Black velvet gown. Brocade undersleeves. Gold fastenings to centre skirt opening. Jewelled buttons on bodice. Jewelled girdle and neckchains. Ruff embroidered in black silk. Hat decorated with pearl ropes, ostrich tips and aigrette.

443 King Philip II. Portrait by Titian. Naples Museum. Doublet, trunk hose, hose and shoes of yellow embroidered in silver. Gown of brown satin with sable fur.

444 Portrait by Antonio Moro. Prado, Madrid. Black figured silk gown. Silver brocade underskirt. Lace-edged cap with pearls. Pearl necklaces. Jewelled girdle and gold buttons. Sleeves white with gold bands.

445 King Sebastien of Portugal. Portrait by Cristoforo Morales, Monasterio de las Descalzas Reales, Madrid. White and gold embroidered doublet and trunk hose. Red velvet cape ornamented in gold. Red velvet lining. White hose and shoes. Black hat, white plume, gold decoration.

446 Portrait of Infante Don Carlos by Coello. Prado, Madrid. Black velvet cloak with ermine collar. Doublet and trunk hose red with gold stripes. Gold hose and shoes. Black velvet hat, white plume, jewelled band.

447 Queen Isabella. Portrait, Prado, Madrid. Black velvet gown lined with white satin. Heavy jewelled girdle. Gold and pearl clasps and collar. White sleeves with gold banding. Gold, jewelled caul.

448A Portrait of Don Fernando d'Aragon by Pantoja de la Cruz, 1575–80. Nelahozeves Castle, Czechoslovakia. Black hat with coloured plumes and jewelled band. Lace-edged ruff. Dark velvet cape. White doublet and hose, silver decoration. White shoes.

B Portrait by Antonio Moro, 1575. Prado, Madrid. Black velvet gown with white puffs and gold tags and buckles. Jewelled, gold girdle and neckband. Transparent, white neck frill. Gold, jewelled cap. Fawn gloves.

C Portrait of Infanta Isabella Clara by de Llano, 1584. Prado, Madrid. White gown and undergown with gold pattern. White satin lining. Gold, jewelled collar and girdle. Lace-edged ruff. Black hat with pearls, plumes and jewelled aigrette.

D Portrait of Infante Don Fernando by Coello, 1577. Monasterio de las Descalzas Reales, Madrid. Brown jerkin with gold banding. Gold doublet sleeves,

trunk hose and upper stocks. White stockings and shoes. Lace-edged ruff.

E Portrait of Infante Don Diego, as a little boy, by Coello, 1577. Private collection, London.

F Portrait of Infanta, daughter of Philip II, by Coello. Prado, Madrid. Gold and black gown. White satin sleeves, striped in gold. Pearl ropes round neck and coiffure.

G Portrait of Infanta Isabella by Coello, 1579. Prado, Madrid. Pale gold gown with red-banded sleeves. Lace-edged ruff. White handkerchief. Jewelled, gold girdle, buttons and necklace. Pearl decorated caul and white silk hat with plumes and aigrette.

449A Portrait of Queen Isabella by Pourbus, 1615–20. Uffizi, Florence. Brocade gown over richly embroidered underskirt. Lace-edged ruff and handkerchief.

B Portrait by Coello, 1590–1600. Brown and gold doublet, jerkin and trunk hose. Dark cape. Purple hose, white shoes.

C Portrait by Coello, 1590–1600. Paris. Dark gown with gold design. Lighter, patterned undergown and sleeves. Lace ruff. White handkerchief.

D Portrait of Archduke Alberto, the head by Rubens, c.1600–5. Monasterio de las Descalzas Reales, Madrid. Buff jerkin. White doublet sleeves with gold banding. Trunk hose of gold and fawn. White stockings and shoes. Lace-edged ruff.

E Portrait of a Spanish princess by Coello, c.1600. George Mercer College, New York. Wired, lace-edged collar and cuffs.

450, 451 and 452 Actual shoes, Rocamora Museum, Barcelona.

453 Painting by unknown artist. National Portrait Gallery, London. French hood with jewelled frontlets, red velvet between, and black velvet fall. Pearl and bead necklace and neckband. Gold jewelled pendant and brooch. White neck-edging. Gown of gold and red.

454 Portrait by Francois Clouet. Kunsthistorisches Museum, Vienna. Black velvet hat and doublet, both gold embroidered. Fur trimming. Ostrich plume.

455 Portrait by Hans Eworth. National Portrait Gallery, London. French hood with jewelled frontlet, of white satin and black velvet. Purple velvet gown with white collar lining and edging. Gold, jewelled necklace and pendant.

456 Portrait of Claude de Beaune from studio of Clouet. Louvre, Paris. Black hood with white lining. Black gown with white banding. Partlet of white studded with pearls.

457 Portrait by unknown artist. National Portrait Gallery, London. Lace-edged wired collar. Pearl necklaces and hair ornaments. Dark gown decorated with pearls and bows. Sleeves light and jewelled.

458 Portrait by Moro. Prado, Madrid. Two white caps, one over the other. White collar with ruffle edge. Black gown.

459 Pendant. Victoria and Albert Museum, London.

460 Portrait of Elizabeth, Swedish princess. Gripsholm Castle, Sweden. Gold, pearled cap. Plain ruff. Black and white gown with gold chains.

461 and 462 Anonymous caricature engraving.

463 Portrait of Infanta Isabella Clara by Pantoja de la Cruz. Château de Villandry, France. Black hat with jewelled band and plume. Ropa with high collar and puffed, short sleeves.

464 Portrait of Sir Edward Hoby by unknown artist. Ipswich Museum. Black hat and plume with jewelled band. White ruff embroidered in black.

465 Portrait of Infante Don Carlos by Coello. Kunsthistorisches Museum, Vienna. Jewelled black cap with white plumes. Dark cape. Light doublet with jewelled buttons and horizontal stripes.

466 Portrait by Salomon Mesdach. Rijksmuseum, Amsterdam. Dark hat over cap. Lace-edged ruff and neckline. Dark, figured gown.

467 Portrait. Black velvet chamarre with white fur trimming and lining. Black velvet hat with white plume and jewelled band. Pale grey silk doublet and trunk hose decorated in silver. Grey hose and shoes.

468 Portrait. Purple gown with brown fur lining and cuffs. Brocaded stomacher. Gold cloth underskirt. Gold neckband. Black velvet French hood. White silk frontlet and jewelled band.

469 Portrait of Henry II, probably by Clouet. Louvre, Paris. Black cape, jerkin and doublet with gold stripe decoration. Gold patterned panes over white trunk hose. White stockings and shoes, also gloves. Black hat with jewelled bands and white plume.

470 Portrait of Catherine de' Medici by unknown artist. Uffizi Gallery, Florence. Black velvet gown embroidered in gold and pearls and sapphires. Pink satin undergown. Fur cuffs. Wired, lace-edged collar. French hood.

471A Portrait of King Charles IX, 1560–74. White doublet and trunk hose decorated in gold edging. White hose and shoes. Black and gold cape and hat. White plume.

   B Painting, 1560–5. Dark blue velvet ropa with fur edging and lining. Brocade gown. Lace cap.

   C Portrait of Henry III's queen, c.1575. Deep rose velvet gown with fur edging and cuffs. White satin undergown embroidered in colour. Jewelled girdle with pendant. Pearl ropes on bodice. Lace-edged handkerchief, collet monté and cap.

   D Portrait of Charles IX by François Clouet. Kunsthistorisches Museum, Vienna, c.1565. Black velvet cape and jerkin with gold embroidered decoration. White doublet sleeves, trunk hose and hose with shoes. Black velvet hat with white plume and jewelled band.

   E Sculpture, Louvre, Paris. 1575–80. Hood with fall. Bodice and sleeves with braid and button trimming. Patterned skirt.

472, 473, 475 Painting 'Ball for the Wedding of the Duc de Joyeuse' by unknown artist. Louvre, Paris. 472 wears a white silk gown with gold undersleeves, an open, lace-edged collar, a ribbon decorated cap. 473 has a dark doublet and upper hose with dark red lower hose and black shoes. He wear a grey, gold-edged cape with crimson lining, a large ruff and plumed hat. The lady in 475 has a light satin gown with gold hem and a red undergown. White shows through the sleeve slashes. The ruff is supported at the back by a framework.

474 Portrait of a lady c.1595–1600. She wears the French wheel farthingale under her gown like 475, but in 474 the circular drum ruffle covers the top of the wheel. This is an English custom more commonly than a French one. Dark velvet gown with gold banding at the hem. Puffed and slashed sleeves. Lace-edged cuffs and collet monté. Fan.

476 Painting of Henry IV. Louvre, Paris. Gold, jewelled jerkin and trunk hose panes. White satin doublet and cloak. Leather boots. White hose.

477 Painting of Marie de' Medici, Louvre, Paris. Ice-blue satin dress with gold bands. Jewelled, gold decoration. Undersleeve of gold brocade. Lace-edged collet monté.

478, 479 Painting of Marie de' Medici and the Dauphin by Rubens. Louvre, Paris. 478 shows the Dauphin in a white satin doublet with blue baldric, gold-edged basques and red ribbon points. Red breeches have gold side stripes. Red hose and sashes, gold tassels. Gold shoes with red ribbon rosettes. The queen in 479 wears a deep purple satin gown over a wheel farthingale. Decoration by pearls. Lace-edged collet monté.

480A Portrait of a boy by Francesco Salviati, c.1550. National Gallery, London. Dark velvet gown with gold banding and fur lining. Black hat with plume and brooch. Light, slashed doublet and upper hose.

   B Portrait by Giovanni Battista Moroni, 1554. Pinacoteca Ambrosiana, Milan. Light green jerkin with black velvet banding, short puff sleeves. Doublet sleeves black. Black upper and lower hose, shoes and hat. Black velvet cape lined with lynx fur.

   C Portrait of Anna Eleonora Sanvitali, aged 4, 1562, by Girolamo Mazzola-Bedoli. Pinacoteca, Parma. Dress with jewelled waist-belt and banding decoration. White double lace-edged collar. Jewelled cap.

   D Painting by Paolo Veronese, 1560. Dresden State Gallery. Dark velvet gown with gold banding. White chemise and partlet.

   E Portrait of Lucrezia or Maria Borgia by Bronzino, 1550–62. Kunsthistorisches Museum, Vienna. Blue silk gown with blue and gold embroidered borders. Undergown of white with gold stripes. Jewelled necklace. Jewelled lace collar and cap.

   F Portrait of small boy by Paolo Veronese, 1560. Dresden State Gallery. Suit of striped material. Dark hose.

481 and 483 Portraits of two children in the Colonna family by Scipione Pulzone. Galleria Colonna, Rome.

481 shows prince Giulio Cesare in a jerkin of two shades of pink. The doublet is white with gold decoration and the trunk hose gold. He wears brown gloves, a ruff and white hose and shoes. His sister, princess Vittoria, in 483, wears a gold cloth dress with undersleeves of white, banded in gold. The banding on the dress is in a deeper shade of gold. She has a high ruff, ribbons and feathers in her hair and a heavy, jewelled necklace.

482 Engraving of a lady of the court by Abraham de Bruyn. She appears unusually tall because, under her gold cloth gown, she is wearing tall chopines. She also wears a jewelled cap and carries a fan of colourful plumes.

484 Portrait of Bernardo Spini by Giovanni Battista Moroni. Galleria dell' Accademia Carrara, Bergamo. Dressed entirely in black except for white ruff and fawn gloves.

485 Portrait by Scipione Pulzone. Galleria Doria, Rome. Black dress with white collar. Undergown white with black threaded decoration. Brown satin sash. Brown velvet hat, brown plume.

486 Venetian dress. Portrait. State Gallery, Dresden. Gown with large floral all-over pattern. Jewelled bands over partlet. Lace-edged collar. Pearl ropes and jewelled girdle. White, lace-edged handkerchief.

487 Portrait of little boy, Federico d'Urbino by Barocci. Pinacoteca, Siena. Red dress with gold buttons and decoration. Red sash with gold lace edging. White satin sleeves. White, lace-edged collar. White stockings and shoes.

488 Portrait of Margherita de' Medici by Giusto Sustermans. Palazzo Vecchio, Florence. Dark gown with light floral pattern and braid decoration. Lace ruff and lace-edged handkerchief. Plumes and jewels in coiffure.

489 Venetian dress. Engraving by Giacomo Franco.

490 Painting by Ludovico Pozzoserrato. Museo Civico, Treviso. The young man, A, plays a lute. He wears red doublet and breeches, red stockings and white shoes. His hat is black. The gentleman, D, plays a flute. He is dressed in two shades of green. The gentleman, C, playing a viola and the other gentleman, E, holding the music for singing, are both in black. The seated lady, F, plays the cembalo. She wears a yellow gown with white neck ruffles.

491 Miniature painting. Bayerische Nationalmuseum, Munich. Black hat, white plume.

492 Painting by Lucas Cranach, Bayerische National-museum, Munich. Black, jewelled hat over jewelled cap. Black ropa decorated with jewelled buttons and gold bands. Red dress with horizontal gold lines. Jewelled necklace, girdle and bracelets.

493 Painting 'the fortune-teller' by Caravaggio. Louvre, Paris. Black hat with black and white plumes. Golden brown doublet with black banding. Brown gloves. Black cape.

494 Portrait by Bartolomeo Passarotti. Musei Capitoline, Rome. Purple velvet hat. Black jerkin, white doublet sleeves.

495 Miniature painting of the queen of Sigismund III of Poland. Bayerische Nationalmuseum, Munich. Green dress with jewelled neckchains and girdle. White under-sleeves with gold embroidered bands. Jewelled hair band.

496 Portrait showing a black hat with jewelled band worn over a gold, jewelled cap.

497 Actual boot. Hungarian Museum of Decorative Arts, Budapest.

498 Actual shoes. The upper drawing shows a woman's figured velvet shoe of 1592 from the Bayerische Nationalmuseum, Munich. The lower drawing is a man's shoe from the Bally Shoe Museum in Switzerland.

499 Gold pendant, enamelled, with gems and pearls. Later sixteenth century. Museo Poldi Pezzoli, Milan.

500 Portrait of Eleanor of Toledo by Arnoldo Bronzino. Uffizi Gallery, Florence. Richly patterned gown in black and brown on pale blue background. Grey cord decoration. Partlet of gold cord and pearls. Pearl necklaces. Pearl and net cap.

501 Portrait by Alessandro Allori. Uffizi Gallery, Florence. Red velvet dress with gold chain necklace and gold clasps. White puffs on sleeves. White open ruff. Jewelled cap with silver bows.

502 German chopine, in leather, decorated with lace and fringe. Dresden State Museum.

503 Glove with green velvet cuffs and silver fringe. Early seventeenth century. Dresden State Msueum.

504A Queen Mary I. Portrait by Hans Eworth, 1554. National Portrait Gallery, London. Black velvet French hood, jewelled frontlet. Purple velvet gown.

B Painting of young man, 1545. Black velvet doublet, gold banded and slashed to show white shirt. Gold cape with patterned lining. Black velvet hat with white plume and jewelled band. Grey stockings, yellow shoes.

C Portrait 'A gentleman in red', c.1548, at Hampton Court Palace. Gown, doublet, breeches and hose all in scarlet with gold borders. White shirt embroidered in black silk thread. Red shoes and cap, white plume.

D Little boy in gown, doublet and hose.

E Princess Mary. Portrait, 1544, in National Portrait Gallery, London. Red gown with jewelled neckband and girdle. Pale blue undergown. White chemise. French hood.

505 Portrait. Lady Jane Grey, National Portrait Gallery, London. Grey brocade gown with white fur sleeves. Undergown and false sleeves of red and gold fabric. Jewelled neckband and girdle. French hood of jewelled frontlets and red velvet. Black velvet fall.

506 Portrait Princess Mary by Hans Eworth. Fitz-william Museum, Cambridge. Black silk gown with black velvet yoke and cuffs. Red satin false sleeves and underskirt. Gold edged collar and wrist ruffles. Gold girdle. Gold embroidered neck ruffle. French hood of gold, jewelled frontlets and red velvet with black velvet fall.

507 Miniature painting of gentleman by Nicholas Hilliard. Victoria and Albert Museum. London. White doublet with black embroidered decoration, peasecod-belly shape. Trunk hose to match. Black cape. Cartwheel ruff. White hose and shoes.

508 Queen Elizabeth I. Drawing by Isaac Oliver. Victoria and Albert Museum, London. Richly embroidered gown over wheel farthingale. Lace-edged open ruff. Butterfly wings with veil. Decoration by pearl ropes and jewels.

509A Queen Elizabeth I. Portrait by Nicholas Hilliard, c.1575–80. National Portrait Gallery, London. Black velvet gown with gold embroidery, leaf pattern in diamond frames. White puffs at shoulders. Jewelled and pearled partlet and neckband. Pearl girdle. Silver brocade underskirt. Lace-edged ruff. Jewelled cap, gauze veil.

B Sir Christopher Hatton. Portrait c.1575. Dark patterned cape. Gold and white striped jerkin. Dark, embroidered trunk hose. Patterned canions. White stockings, black shoes. Black hat with jewels and plume.

C, D 1565.

E Portrait 1560 5. Black velvet ropa with gold edging. White satin gown, jewelled girdle and pendant. Black velvet cap with pearl ropes.

F Portrait of the Earl of Leicester, artist unknown, c.1560–70. National Portrait Gallery, London. Red doublet, jerkin and trunk hose, ornamented in gold. Black velvet hat with jewelled band and red plume.

510A Child in wheel farthingale gown and cartwheel ruff.

B Queen Elizabeth I. Portrait 1592–4. Hardwick Hall. Wheel farthingale. Gown with drum ruffle and heavily padded sleeves. Richly embroidered all over the fabric. Open, lace ruff. Butterfly wings and veil. Coiffure piled high with jewels and pearls.

C Painting. Gentleman, 1590. Gold decorated, white satin doublet, peasecod-belly shape. Cartwheel ruff. Patterned canions. White netherstocks. Black shoes, hat and cape.

D Painting. Gentleman, 1600. Normal waisted doublet and unpadded trunk hose.

E Painting. Patterned gown worn over bolster roll. Contrasting, padded sleeves. Wired, lace collar. Feather fan.

F Portrait. Queen Elizabeth I. c.1592–3. National Portrait Gallery, London. White satin gown worn over wheel farthingale. Embroidered in gold, colours and jewels. Lace-edged, open ruff. Gauze butterfly wings and veil. Decoration by pearl ropes. Jewelled necklace and coiffure. Folding fan and gloves.

G Similar to C.

H Portrait Earl of Essex, c.1595, by Gheeraedts. Light coloured costume. Upper and lower stocks. Black shoes.

I Portrait of Anne Vavasour, c.1610. White gown with embroidered sprig pattern in colour worn over

wheel farthingale. Open, lace-edged ruff. Padded sleeves.

511 Painting. Musée des Beaux Arts, Antwerp. Costume all in black except for trunk hose which are red and black and white lace ruff.

512 Portrait by Van der Mast. Rijksmuseum, Amsterdam. Vlieger (ropa) of plain dark fabric worn over light-coloured gown with black banding. Gold chain girdle and pendant. Double white cap.

513 Painting by de Oude. Musée d'Art Ancien, Brussels. Dark brown dress with black velvet bands. Red sleeves with horizontal gold stripes. Gold chain girdle. White ruff and pearl-edged cap.

514 Painting by Moro. National Gallery, Washington.

515 Painting. Musée des Beaux Arts, Antwerp. Black vlieger over black silk skirt, underskirt red with black bands. Bodice gold and black patterned. Plain ruff. Lace-edged cuffs.

516 Painting by de Oude Musée d'Art Ancien, Brussels. Costume entirely in black. Doublet padded and ruched in horizontal bands.

517 Painting by Moreelse. Musée d'Art Ancien, Brussels. Very small child in a grey dress banded in black braid, worn over a wheel farthingale. Underskirt and sleeves of cream satin with black braiding. Plain, double ruff. White embroidered cap.

518 Painting by Franz Hals. Mauritshuis, The Hague. Vlieger in figured black with black velvet edging. Pink taffeta skirt. Gold and black decorated bodice. Gold sleeves with black bands. Plain white ruff. White lawn cap with lace edging.

519 Painting by Francken. Musée d'Art Ancien, Brussels. Gold cape, doublet and trunk hose. Red sleeves and draped sash. Pink hose with gold knee sashes. Brown shoes.

520 Isabella Brandt, portrait by Rubens. Alte Pinakothek, Munich. Black overgown. Red skirt with gold banding. White satin bodice with gold floral pattern. Lace-edged ruff and cap. Straw hat with black silk lining.

521 and 522 Painting 'Banquet out of doors' by Van der Velde. Rijksmuseum, Amsterdam. 521 wears a white doublet and red, loose breeches, tied with gold knee sashes. White stockings, and shoes. Red rosettes. Gold cloak and hat. White plumes and ruff. 522 wears a gold dress pinned up to show red underskirt banded in silver. Sleeves to match. Brown hat with red plume. Large ruff.

523 Russian nobleman. Dark cloth caftan with braid fastenings, fur trimming and lining. Fur edged cap. Leather boots.

524 Drawing by Hollar. Patterned velvet gown. Pale satin slashed sleeves. Large ruff. Jewelled cap. Gold, jewelled girdle and pendant.

525 Actual kaftan, Kremlin, Moscow. Light coloured floral pattern on dark ground.

526 Fur lined and edged coat. Fur cap. Leather boots.

527A Portrait of Erik XIV, 1561. Gripsholm Castle, Sweden. Black cape. Doublet and trunk hose of black, embroidered in gold. Gold neckchain. Black hose and shoes.

B Finnish sculptural relief, *c.*1613. Lady in wheel farthingale.

C Portrait of Gustav Vasa, *c.*1550. Swedish. Gown, doublet and hose in black, embroidered in gold. Leather boots. Black hose.

D Finnish/Swedish sculptural relief, 1575. Ropa worn over patterned gown. Hood on top of cap.

E Portrait of Sigismund, 1584–5. Costume all in black with silver embroidered decoration.

528 Portrait of Barbara Meuer by Hans Hug Kluber. Kunstmuseum, Basle. White gown with black collar and bodice. Gold, embroidered sleeve bands. White chemise and apron with black embroidery. Red cap with gold design on top of white pleated cap.

529 Painting by Hans Schöpfer. Alte Pinakothek, Munich. Crimson gown with hanging sleeves and brown fur collar and lining. Grey hose, black shoes. White shirt. Black hat, white plumes. Brown gloves.

530 Wood engraving by Christoph Schwyzer. Kupferstichsammlung, Vienna. Patterned gown with fur lining and trimming. Plain doublet and trunk hose with gold neckchains and leather belt. High boots.

531 Actual costume which belonged to a Prince of Saxony. Historiches Museum, Dresden. Doublet and hose in yellow satin, black velvet bands. Outer gown in yellow silk damask.

532 Landhaus courtyard, Graz.

A Actual costume, *c.*1600. Niedersächsische Landesgalerie, Hanover Museum. Red suit with black all-over design and gold braid trimming.

B Actual costume which belonged to Princess Dorothea Sabina, *c.*1590. Bayerische Nationalmuseum, Munich. Brown velvet gown with embroidered bands. Sleeves of white silk banded in gold.

C Coloured glass painting by Josias Murer of Lucerne, 1608. Schweizerisches Landesmuseum, Zürich. Grey doublet with yellow fabric showing through slashes. Deep crimson sleeves with white shirt visible through slashes. White panes over pale blue slops on left leg, deep blue over pale blue on right leg. Hose deep blue on right leg, white on left leg. Deep blue knee sashes. Black shoes. Black hat with jewelled band, gold cord and white and blue plumes.

D, E Little girl and her mother. Painting by Martin Moser, 1557. Kunstmuseum, Lucerne. The child wears a blue dress banded in black, a white chemise and gold neckchain. The cap is of white material, gathered in rows. The mother wears a red skirt with black banding and a bodice of gold fabric patterned in brown. The full sleeves are black. A hat is worn on top of a white cap banded in black.

533 Copper engraving by Von de Bry, Frankfurt-am-Main, 1611. The lady playing a spinet (B) wears a patterned dress with hanging fur sleeves. Her large ruff has a framework support as does also that of the small boy (D).

534 Portrait of Czech nobleman. Dark cloak with white satin lining. Light doublet and trunk hose.

535 Little girl, painting.

536 Young lady, portrait. Spanish farthingale. Patterned gown with jewelled girdle and neckbands. Jewelled necklace over embroidered partlet. Jewelled cap.

537 Portrait. Costume in black with silver embroidery and dark fur.

538 Portrait. Black velvet dress over Spanish farthingale. Gold and silver ornamentation. White silk ties down skirt front. Undersleeves of white with gold banding. Lace-edged ruff. Jewelled cap.

539 Portrait. Lace-edged long apron, over dark gown. Fur edged cape. Plain ruff. Hat and gloves.

540 Small boy, portrait, in dress over farthingale skirt.

541 Portrait of Duke Ferenc Nádasdy. Dark mente worn over light coloured silk dolman. Light brown leather boots and gloves.

542 Young boy, portrait. Dark green jerkin decorated in silver. White doublet sleeves. Rust brown trunk hose. Red hose, white shoes. Lace-edged ruff.

543 Portrait. Dark figured velvet gown. Light coloured silk, striped undergown. Falling ruff. Jewelled cap.

Chapter Six

Baroque Elegance 1620–1700

Seventeenth century dress, after 1620, contrasted in every way with the glitter and luxury of that of the sixteenth. The power of Spain had ebbed and, in consequence, Spanish fashions disappeared from the European scene; with them vanished the stiff, corseted and padded silhouette and the rich be-jewelled fabrics.

The dominant influence of the years 1620–45 was the freer, more comfortable attire worn by the Dutch; a reaction from the hierarchy and rigidity of Spanish dress. Freed from Spanish control, Holland blossomed in these years, becoming wealthy in commerce and extending her trade far overseas. The characteristically Dutch line (**545, 549, 552, 554, 555**), described under Dutch costume, was closely adhered to in northern Protestant countries – northern Germany, England, Scandinavia – but its influence in a more slender, elegant guise was extensive elsewhere. In the Baroque areas of southern Germany and Switzerland, for example, Baroque characteristics were notable in costume in the free, flowing lines. Only the Iberian Peninsula and, to a lesser extent, Italy, continued in the Spanish pattern. Everywhere else clothes were looser, less richly ornamented and much more comfortable. This applied equally to men and women. The styles of these years were aptly described, many years ago, by Kelly and Schwabe as the time of 'long locks, lace and leather'.*

Men, freed from the constriction of large ruff and stand-up collar, grew their hair long, as long as it would grow. It was worn naturally, unpowdered and uncurled so that some men dressed it straight, others curly and wavy. A longer lock was encouraged, often tied in a ribbon bow: the love-lock. This was trained elegantly forward over the lace-edged collar, which in the thirties, draped over the shoulders. Waistlines for both sexes were a little higher than natural. They were not constricted and below were large

tassets. The men's doublet soon developed into a shorter jacket, loose and displaying the white shirt. Linen, for both men and women, became an important part of their attire. It was white, silk if possible and lace-edged. It showed at the collar, matching cuffs and at waist. Men completed their cavalier-style dress with a sweeping large-brimmed hat, decked with ostrich plumes, loose breeches tied at the knee with ribbon sashes and elegant lace-fringed boots. The cape was slung round the body rather than worn (**566, 569, 592**). Women's dress was on similar lines, high-waisted, uncorseted with lace collar and softly flowing skirt. Pearl ropes replaced gold necklaces (**570, 573**).

The 'leather' of Kelly and Schwabe's epigram stems from the influence of military dress worn in the Thirty Years' War (1618–48). Particularly from Holland and Sweden this is seen in men's dress in the leather jackets held at the waist by vast sashes and in the boot styles (**555, 556**).

From mid-century, French influence, under Louis XIV, became paramount. This, France's 'Grand Règne', established the country in Europe as a great power and, in fashion, set her up as a leader whose pre-eminence has yet to be seriously challenged. From 1650 onwards indeed, apart from some divergencies in England, the Baltic coastal area and eastern Europe, the history of French costume is equally that of Europe.

In the second half of the seventeenth century there were two distinct styles of dress, especially in masculine wear. Those seen from 1650–70 were, by today's standards, effeminate. Men wore long wigs or long natural hair; their entire costume was bedecked by lace, ribbon loops and bows from their hats to their shoes. Then, final indignity, they wore, not breeches, but skirts. These, commonly known as petticoat breeches, but like skirts or full shorts, were profusely decorated by ribbon loops (**614A**).

It is interesting to consider the appearance of these men of 1650–70, also that of the cavalier of 1630–45, all with very long hair and compare

---

* *Historic Costume*, p. 121, by Kelly and Schwabe. First published 1925 by B. T. Batsford.

544, 545 *Huygens and his clerk, 1627*   **546, 547, 548, 549** *Family, 1621*

them with the long hair styles of the twentieth century. In the 1960s long hair was a prerogative of the young and often the extrovert youth. In the 1970s long hair has become respectable and is, in many instances, very long, elegantly curled and beautifully coiffured. Yet these styles have limited affinity with those in seventeenth century portraits. It is difficult to be objective, since men had worn short hair from 1820–1960 and no-one living in the twentieth century is, therefore, conditioned to seeing long hair on men. It is likely, though, that the reason for a certain feeling of incongruity about the very long hair styles – that is, those worn below shoulderblade level – on modern men, is due to their being accompanied by modern dress. Such garments as a suit, informal jacket, pullover or jeans, with their severe lines and lack of softening decoration seems out of tune with long hair. The cavalier hat and boots, jacket and lace collar or the mid-century petticoat breeches and ribbon loops were more suitable. It is notable that today, when men wear, especially in the evening, velvet jackets, silk cravats, and decorative trousers, the ensemble is sympathetic.

The second style of the seventeenth century, from 1670 onwards, introduced for men the classic garment grouping of coat, waistcoat and breeches, which was to last throughout the eighteenth century. A French innovation, it was a suit, the coat and breeches often of the same material while the vest or waistcoat was generally brocaded. Worn with stockings and shoes, a voluminous wig and tricorne hat, the costume set the pattern for the eighteenth century. Only minor alterations to proportion, line and fabrics were made in a hundred years.

An important characteristic of the last years of the century, from 1685–1700, was the height of the costume. In men's dress this was shown in the wig which ascended to twin peaks of curls on either side of a centre parting. In feminine attire the height was attained in the coiffure surmounted by a headdress of lace and ribbons (**579, 584, 605**). It is interesting that the furniture of the time, especially chair and settee backs, also showed this characteristic and were exceptionally tall for a decade. In this same period, the line of women's gowns changed. There was a return to corseting, slender long waists, dipping to a point in front and much fuller skirts, the overskirt swept up and back to a bustle form thence falling to a train. Necklines were décolleté and bodices rigid and stiff. The years of ease and simple elegance were over.

Children's Clothes

There was still no special style for children: they wore a smaller version of adult dress. Swaddling was now only carried out for young babies. At about six weeks the baby was unbound and dressed in a gown reaching to its feet with a long apron, a bib and a cap. Little boys were still dressed as girls till they were about five or six years old, then they wore clothes like those of their fathers. In the second half of the century, boys of the age of eight or nine began to wear the large periwigs. Little girls were dressed from two years onwards like their mothers. Illustrations of children at different ages are shown in figs. **546, 548, 553, 561, 562, 563, 565, 572, 581, 591C, E, 596, 598E, 601, 603, 608A, C, D, G, 611, 613, 619, 651**.

Textiles

The industrial revolution and, in consequence, the textile industry, developed earlier in England than elsewhere. Together with Holland, England produced vast quantities of broadcloth which, due to maritime supremacy, were exported widely.

Broadcloth was the material most used by the mass of the population. Silk remained the fabric of the wealthy. Italy and Spain were the two main sources of this. By 1640 cotton began to be imported into Europe from India via Asia Minor. These painted cottons were popular. Supplies were limited so the fabrics acquired a scarcity value and became the 'in' mode with the well-to-do. Elegant society with a sense of inverted snobbery prized such cottons more than silk, and used them especially for dressing gowns which became known as 'indiennes'. The most fashionable material in the seventeenth century was lace which was used to edge collars and cuffs and as decoration to many garments (**580, 590**). Italy was the main source of lace where Venice was an important centre for lacemaking. Flanders also produced a quantity of fine lace. Later France began to make her own lace and set up manufactories using a nucleus of Venetian workers to get them established. Valenciennes, also Normandy and Burgundy, were centres.

Towards the end of the seventeenth century the textile industry in England was greatly assisted by the influx of emigré workers from

550, 551 *1625–30*   552 c.*1630*   553 c.*1625*   554 c.*1630*

Holland   147

555, 556 *1637–40*   557 *1649–50*   558 *1669–70*

Flanders and then from France. Traditionally England had always been a refuge for people fleeing from the Continent in search of political and religious freedom. The flood of Huguenot refugees improved the quality and standard of English textiles enormously. But, where England gained from the tolerance of her people and government, she lost by her inability to recognise the potential value of the inventiveness of her peoples. Traditionally also the English monarchy and government has failed on many occasions to profit from inventions which were later marketed by other nations whom the spurned English inventor approached with his ideas. The textile industry of the seventeenth century was no exception to this.

In mid-seventeenth century Louis XIV looked with interest and some envy at the flourishing textile industries of England and Holland. Through his chief minister, Jean-Baptiste Colbert, the classic French approach to the problem of establishing France as an equally great or greater textile source, was made. The importation of foreign fabrics such as lace, silks and cotton was restricted or forbidden and those which were

permitted entry carried a heavy duty. Manufactories were set up in France based on numbers of foreign craftsmen and these were given all the financial assistance needed to establish them. With foreign competition stifled, France quickly became a producer in quality and quantity of lace, silks and other fabrics. One famous manufactory which was set up at this time was that of Gobelins, making tapestry.

Colbert also encouraged the textile trade with India, exporting France's goods in exchange for Indian cottons. Soon these became so popular that French weavers begged for protection and imports from India were stopped. In the 1680s, for the same reason, imitation Indian cottons, made in France, were also forbidden. This, together with the revocation of the Edict of Nantes, caused the flood of French textile workers to emigrate to England and, in smaller numbers, to Switzerland and Holland, where they set up factories to produce fine quality cottons to export all over Europe. Due to French prohibition, a smuggling trade arose to supply the French aristocracy with the cottons they desired even more strongly when they became unobtainable. For many years cotton was the chief luxury black-market commodity in France as cognac and silks became in England during the Napoleonic wars. The Indian cottons had been painted in floral designs based on Indian and Chinese motifs. The European versions were printed copies. Their quality was excellent and they wore well.

Costume Plates

The fashion plate and magazine were still creations of the future but there were a number of artists working in the seventeenth century who produced costume plates. These were engravings illustrating what fashionable people were wearing in their individual countries at a given date. Unlike the fashion plate, which depicted a design for costume, the costume plates were only a record, but they are a valuable source material for the student of historic and fashionable costume. Early examples, showing especially regional and national dress, were drawn by such artists as Albrecht Dürer in 1494 and Giacomo Franco in

1610. Romeyn de Hoaghe produced a set of drawings in Amsterdam soon afterwards.

The best known seventeenth century artist to draw accurately and well the costumes of the people he saw was the Bohemian artist Václav (Wenceslaus) Hollar, born in Prague in 1607. He fled from the city where he was practising law because of the Thirty Years' War and worked as an engraver in Frankfurt, Strasbourg and Cologne, before living for many years in Antwerp and later London. From 1640 he made many plates in England showing individual costumes and details of accessories as well as figures set in a background of famous and typical London scenes which form invaluable, interesting records. With the advent of the Puritan régime in England he went back to Holland but later returned to England where he produced 2740 plates working at the rate of 4d an hour, timing his work by an hour glass on his desk. He died in poverty in London in 1677.

Other artists followed Hollar producing interesting, useful costume plates. Of note is Jean Dieu de Saint Jean whose work covers the years

Flemish family, _c._1655–60

566, 567 *1635*   **568, 569, 570** *1637*

1678–95, also N. Bonnart and, in the last years of the century, Antoine Trouvain and Nicholas Arnoult. Actual fabrics are often glued to the engraving like a type of collage.

The Low Countries

The Dutch set the pattern for costume in the years 1620–35. *Men* continued to wear a *doublet* but this had now become high waisted though still buttoned centre front and dipping to a point at the centre waist. Large tassets all round formed a short skirt. The garment was still slashed on the torso and upper sleeves and had shoulder wings. The Spanish style trunk hose had disappeared and men wore loose, full *breeches* which reached to, or just below, the knee. These were finished there with ribbon tags or a sash tie. Below this were stockings and shoes which now had low heels, an upstanding tongue and a button or ribbon tie. The large ruff was not often worn by men after 1620; it was replaced by a *falling ruff*, that is, an unstarched or unstiffened one which

fell softly in layers over the shoulders. An alternative still was the lace-edged, stand-up collar (**547**). Cuffs were in matching sets. *Hair* was fairly short and many men wore elegant, upturned moustaches and Van Dyck beards. The *hat* had a wide, curling brim and sweeping ostrich plumes. A cloak was draped round the shoulders or under one arm (**545, 551, 554**).

In the 1630s Dutchmen dressed, as in France and England, in the romantic, swashbuckling Cavalier style. The paintings of Frans Hals – for example, his 'Laughing Cavalier' – vividly depict this type of dress (**555, 556**). The doublet slowly becomes a hip-length *jacket* and, in Holland, the military style of broad sash is bound round the waist and hangs bunched at back or side, its ends trimmed with lace or fringe. The ruff has been superseded by the *falling band*, the white collar with lace-edging which covers the shoulders and is tied at the throat with cords and tassels.* The *breeches* are now more fitting but the stockings are

* These valuable items of wear were carefully stored in band boxes, a name still in use in the English language.

covered by soft leather *boots*. These often have wide bucket tops (**557**) and inside are boot hose decorated with lace. The butterfly flap covers the instep and the boots have heels and spurs. The cavalier wears his *hair* loose and long. His moustache curls upwards and his beard is pointed. The costume is completed by a broad-brimmed hat.

By mid-century Dutch costume was following French fashions (see France) and developed on the same lines till 1700 (**557, 559, 640**).

The dress of *Dutch women* until 1630 was especially characteristic and, though copied in other countries, was never quite the same elsewhere. Only in Holland were worn the plain, enormously wide, white *ruffs*. They were rarely lace-trimmed but nearly always deep with narrow gauge goffering and so large a diameter that they swayed and dipped over the shoulders. Holland was also noted for the infinite variety of white plain or decorative *caps*. Still sometimes worn one on top of another, lace-edged or jewelled, the tendency was more and more to set them further back on the head and to display the hair in front

drawn tightly back from the face. The classic style of Dutch *gown* had a jacket form of bodice, open in front to show the stomacher, and with shoulder wings and sleeves ending in tiered, lace-edged cuffs. This stomacher was a characteristic feature. It was a vest, round ended below the waist in front and edged with scallops or tassets. It was richly patterned in gold and vivid colours, often being the only point of colour in the whole costume, standing out like a jewel against the plain or figured black of the gown and the startlingly white ruff. The sleeves matched the undergown not the stomacher. The gown skirt was still held up to display the patterned under-skirt (**549, 550**).

In the 1630s, Dutch gown styles followed those of France and England with high waists marked by a sash with stomacher beneath. The neckline was low and framed by a lace-edged, wide collar. Sleeves were full, slashed and puffed with decoration by ribbon bows. They were finished by lace-edged cuffs (**552, 635**). French fashions dominated Dutch dress from mid-century as can be seen in **558, 560** and **564**.

571 *Duke of Lorraine, c.1630*   **572** c.*1645* **573** *1634*   **574, 575** c.*1635*

A B C D

France

Until about 1635 French styles were either still modelled on the Spanish, with rich embroidery and be-jewelled fabrics, corseting and padding giving a rigid silhouette or they followed the Dutch line. Between 1625 and 1635 several governmental edicts were issued to try to curtail the extravagant use of imported fabrics, chiefly Italian, such as gold and silver cloth, velvet brocades and gold and silver lace and embroidery. The import of such rich materials was to be restricted and the French were instructed to wear clothes made of fabrics manufactured in France. This led to a simpler style of dress for both sexes, made from plain or less extravagantly patterned velvets, silks and satins. The most usual trimmings for these styles were lace and ribbon. The

lace was used to edge the falling bands and matching cuffs, boot hose and for applying as garniture to any part of the garments. Ribbon, now made as we know it, with a selvedge edge on each side, was then a novelty. Soon it was used all over the costume, in bows, rosettes, loops and streamers. By 1660, men's dress, in particular, was a riot of ribbon decoration.

With these simpler modes France began to acquire a reputation as a leader of fashion. The Cavalier style of dress was worn by nearly all European countries but that worn in France was more elegant and stylish than elsewhere, except for England, where the Royalists were outstanding patrons of this type of dress. The French flair for elegance can be seen by comparing the Dutch attire, described earlier, with figs. **566–75**.

In *men's dress* from *1630–40*, the *doublet* was higher-waisted and often was only buttoned on the chest, being open lower down to display the fine white shirt. Tassets were large. Their junction with the waistline was covered by ribbon bows (**566, 568, 571**). The doublet soon developed into a *jacket*, open from chest downwards. The sleeves were full and slit in one longitudinal slash, showing the white shirt sleeve beneath. The jacket sleeve was only three-quarter length and ended in a lace-edged cuff (**569, 575**). These cuffs were matched by the *falling band* on the shoulders.

Breeches were loose and generally buttoned full length down the outer seams. They had fly fastenings. They were finished at the knee by a sash tie or ribbon bows and loops. Silk stockings were worn in all colours. To protect these valuable items of dress, cloth *boot hose* were worn on top. Some of these had feet, some only straps under the instep to hold them in place. They flared out at the upper end and were finished with elegant lace tops so that only the lace was visible above the bucket-topped soft boots (**566, 568, 569, 571, 575**).

Women's dress underwent a similar transformation. The rigid, corseted appearance vanished; materials were plain or lightly figured, though still heavy and rich, and a softer, more comfor-

A   B   C   D   E

577 The Grand Trianon, Versailles, French Dress, 1680–1700   153

Details, 1620–1700

578 *Louis XIV, c.1680*

579 *Lady of the French Court, temp. Louis XIV*

580 *French lace*

582 *Swedish, 1640*

581 *Spanish Infanta, c.1657*

583 *Spanish men's shoes*

585 *Lady's shoe, Spain*

584 *Italian, 1690–5*

586 *German glove*

587 *German, 1630*

588 *Swedish, 1640*

589 *Spanish shoe*

590 *Italian lace*

table silhouette emerged. Like masculine dress, it was an elegant mode but, at this stage, the male was the more lavishly apparelled. Ladies' fashions were attractive but subdued.

The new silhouette had broad shoulders and bosom, a high, unconstricted waist and a full skirt. The bodice had some bones inserted and in front was formed into a shaped plastron or stomacher which dipped in front to a rounded end which extended down over the skirt. Sleeves were full and padded with lace-edged cuffs. On top of this gown, which was generally of a light coloured material, was a darker overgown, slashed on the sleeves to show the undergown and open in front in the skirt from waist to ground. The skirt was then held up to display the undergown. Generally, three skirts were worn: the outer – *la modeste* –, the under – *la friponne** – and the inner one – *la secrète*. The neckline was décolleté and finished either with a lace-edged collar, framing the head, or partly covered by a lace-trimmed falling band (**567, 570, 573, 574**).

Underwear had altered little. The chemise was tucked into drawers which were held up by a waist drawstring. Stockings were fastened to the lower edge of these.

Louis XIV

This, the *Grand Règne*, lasted from 1643–1715. In these years *Louis le Grand* established France as a great power in Europe and, as a natural corollary, all Europe modelled its dress upon French fashions. France was confirmed as the arbiter in dress, a process which had tentatively begun about 1635. From the 1660s Paris published her fashions and each month sent life-size dolls dressed *à la mode* to the capitals of Europe.

There were two distinct styles of dress for *men* in these years. The first lasted from the beginning of the reign until about 1665–70 then was superseded by a completely new mode. The years 1643–70 were a time of transition between the garments worn in the sixteenth century, then slowly adapted through the early decades of the seventeenth and this metamorphosis in the 1670s into an almost modern grouping of garments based on coat, waistcoat and breeches.

The years of transition – 1643–70 – illustrated

the final phase of the garments worn since 1530–40. They comprised doublet or jacket, trunk hose or breeches and cloak. The mid-seventeenth century form of these was so blurred by the excessive decorative use of ribbon and lace that they were barely recognisable as the last phase of the styling of the garments. It was, above all, a time for elaboration and effeminacy.

This type of costume ornamentation, by ribbons and lace, was a direct result of the sumptuary decrees which continued to come from succeeding administrations in an attempt to curtail the extravagant use of foreign fabrics and decoration. This practice had continued despite the decrees of the 1630s. Mazarin made further attempts in the 1650s, making the edicts stricter and banning the import of Venetian and Flemish lace and Italian gold and silver materials. It was after Mazrin's death in 1661 that Louis XIV was advised by his chief Minister Colbert to bring some Venetian lace-makers to France to set up the craft there. The king helped to popularise the new lace made in France at his Court (**580**). From this time onward, French fabrics were worn and the main possibilities for decoration were yards of silk and velvet ribbon and lace so these finally replaced the imported jewelled embroideries and brocades of the sixteenth century. The dress (indeed, mostly of the men) of the 1660s was the most be-ribboned ever seen.

Typical of masculine dress at this time is that illustrated in fig. **576**. The *jacket* was now short, worn open and ending above the waist. The full, white *shirt* was displayed here and on the sleeve where it ended in lace and silk flounces, falling over the hand. The linen, made in lawn or silk, was finished at the neck by an elegant lace ruffle, replacing the falling band of Cavalier dress. On top of the now abbreviated jacket could be worn a cloak slung round the body (**576D**) or a longer coat which had short sleeves with turned-back cuffs (**576B**).

Full *breeches* to the knee and tied there with a sash could be worn (**576B**), but the most fashionable wear were *petticoat breeches*; a style typical of the mid-century and never, so far, revived. A strange masculine fashion, they were either in the form of a knee-length skirt, like a Scottish kilt or, more usually, resembled full, knee-length shorts having the appearance of a skirt. The garment was bedecked almost all over by ribbon loops and bows, sometimes with the addition of lace ruffles.

---

* hussy, minx.

A small apron of ribbon loops covered the front closing. There are many suggestions regarding the origins of this style of breeches. It seems certain that they came from the Rhineland since the proper name for them was *rhinegraves* or *rhinegrave breeches*. This is a translation of the German *rheingrafhose* which derives from the Rhineland count – Rheingrafen Karl – who wore the costume and from where it was taken up with enthusiasm by Louis XIV and his Court. The fashion lasted in France from about 1652–75.

It is interesting to compare the new, gay, be-ribboned, effeminate elegance of the French court as depicted in 1660 in the tapestry showing Louis XIV receiving Philip IV of Spain with the old-fashioned corseted rigidity of the Spanish courtiers and their ladies.* The other characteristic feature of masculine dress at this time is, of course, the great periwig.

It was about 1665–70 that the coat being worn over the short jacket began to develop into the new form. This was a French style, called the *justaucorps* and, at first, was fairly long, reaching to between hip and knee level and was worn flared, open and loose, its front edges turned back and decorated. It had short sleeves ending in deep cuffs. There was no collar because of the mass of wig curls draped over the shoulders. This coat was worn with full, baggy breeches (**576B**). By 1680 the breeches (*culottes*) became more fitting and at the end of the century were very tight and fastened by buttons or a buckle at the outside of the knee.

The *justaucorps* was by now nearly knee-length and was buttoned at the waist and part way above and below. Above it was displayed the cravat and, below, the waistcoat. The buttons extended the full length of the still collarless coat and these and the buttonholes were generally decorated by gold, silver or coloured braid† and embroidery. The coat had immense turned-back cuffs with buttons and ornamentation, also decorative pocket-flaps, in which horizontal slit openings had replaced the earlier vertical ones. The rich baldric was still slung round the body and, in the 1680s, waist sashes were also fashionable. The *justaucorps* became more waisted towards the end of the century. At the same time its skirt was made fuller and was slit at each hip and pleated there in fan shape. A button was sewn at the head of the pleat, a fashion which still survives in the tail coat.

* Gobelins Tapestry designed by Le Brun. National Museum, Versailles.

† These braid decorations or frogging were called brandenburgs, after the Electors of Brandenburg. The fashion originated with German and Polish military coats.

Under the *justaucorps*, which had evolved from the jerkin, the doublet had become the *veste* or vest (waistcoat). This garment had long, narrow sleeves, otherwise it was similar in form to the *justaucorps*, though a little shorter. The *veste* could be worn indoors without the *justaucorps* on top.

Towards the last decades of the century men's garments became plainer. Broadcloth was often used for the *justaucorps* and was plain except for the braiding, embroidery and buttons. Breeches were of matching material or black. The waistcoat was, in contrast, usually patterned all over in brocade or embroidered silk. The white shirt had full sleeves which were gathered in at the wrist above the ruffles which draped over the hand. The neck cravat was fringed or lace-trimmed (**577A, C, E**).

Women's Dress

Until the end of the century, in ostentation, gaiety and ornamentation, women took a back seat to their men. They were attractively and femininely dressed but their qualities were muted. The styles of their garments changed much more slowly and less outrageously than the men's fashions. In feminine dress, as in the male, the mode was set by Paris, especially after 1660. The Court of Versailles was the arbiter of the fashion world and because of this the French attitude to the relative status of women in court life was paramount. It was not the queen and the wives of court gentlemen who led the vogue but the mistresses of the king and his gentlemen. The French aristocracy's view of marital fidelity was that this was suitable for the bourgeoisie, not for them. The king's mistress was undisputed leader of feminine fashion and every nuance of her toilette was carefully studied and copied.

From 1645–1700 the *gown* styles and silhouette slowly, almost imperceptibly, altered from the high-waisted, unconstricted fashions of the 1630s with the falling band over the shoulders to a return to corseting, small waists and extended skirts. By 1670 the neckline had become low, almost horizontal across and slightly off the shoulders. It was finished, no longer by a collar

592 *1630–5*   **593** *1645*   **594** *Charles I, 1638–40*   **595** *Queen Henrietta Maria, 1635–45*   **596** *Prince Charles, c.1636*

England   157

but by a broad band of lace covering the actual gown neckline. The bodice became tighter. It was stiff and boned to give a slenderised waist, round at the back and pointed in front (**974**). It was laced up the back and opened in front over a centre panel or stomacher of richly decorated material, sometimes with a row of ribbon bows. A corset began to be worn underneath. This came up high in front, supporting and constricting the breasts. Sleeves were at first three-quarter length but gradually shortened to above the elbow and often terminated in a deep cuff, decorated by a ribbon bow. Below this were layers of lace ruffles. The skirt was very full and long. The overskirt was looped back on each side and fell to a train at the back; the higher the rank of the wearer, the longer the train. The underskirt became more important. It was of richer fabric and was decorated by flouncing and ruching (**576C, 577B**).

In the last decade of the century, the neckline changed its shape slightly to a rounder or squarer form, not now off the shoulders but still décolleté and edged with a frill. The corset was now longer, descending to a lower, more pointed centre front and was gored and boned. Below the waist-line it ended in a row of tabs which were worn under the underskirt waistband. The boned centre front extended down over this waistband and was often reinforced by a metal strip. The overskirt was bunched further back in a bustle form. The skirt silhouette was a bell shape and petticoats alone were no longer adequate to maintain this desired contour. Once again, as in the sixteenth century, a framework was needed to support the weight of layers of skirts; this time it took the form of *paniers* or basket frames on the hips, tied on at the waist. The fashion was not fully established in France before the eighteenth century though it was common in some other countries, notably England.

In this decade (1690–1700), while masculine dress had become plainer and less effeminate, female attire had become more richly decorated and more feminine. The whole costume was ornamented with ribbon bows and loops, lace ruffles and flounces. The centre front of the bodice was decorated by the *échelle*, the ladder of diminishing ribbon bows, and the underskirt was particularly ornamented by lace, gold embroidery, fringe and tassels (**577D**). Out-of-doors women wore capes and long cloaks. Winter fabrics were heavily lined.

Hair and Headdresses

From 1630 onwards *men* wore their *hair* long, either naturally or as a wig. The natural hair was dressed in a soft, flowing style from the 1630s. By about 1640 it was worn very long, hanging down the back, over the falling band, to the shoulder blades. A love-lock, that is, a lock of hair grown longer than the rest, was carefully dressed forwards over the shoulder and often tied with a ribbon bow. This style of coiffure was accompanied by elegant moustaches, the ends upturned, and small beards at the point or centre of the chin. The sweeping Cavalier *hat** was of soft material, with round crown and very large brim, usually rolling or turned up at one side. It was ornamented with several long, coloured ostrich plumes (**566, 568, 569, 571, 575, 576A**).

In the second half of the century the *wig* slowly took over from natural hair styles. In 1633 King Louis XIII lost much of his hair due to illness and his wearing of a wig helped to popularise the fashion. But it was slow to take on, apart from its obvious attractions for older men. Louis XIV had a fine head of curly hair so was reluctant to take to a wig but, by the 1670s, the fashion was such a

---

* Originated from the Spanish *sombrero*.

rage, he capitulated. From 1670 until after the end of the century, the full-bottomed *periwig* was ubiquitous. The fine quality wig, made of human hair, was the status symbol of the well-to-do. Men who could not afford these very costly items wore wigs made of horse or goat hair or of wool. In the 1670s the periwig was dressed in a similar manner to the natural hair styles, curled and flowing. By 1680 it had become very large. It was then arranged with a centre parting and in a mass of curls and ringlets which rose to a peak on each side of the parting. These then cascaded over the shoulders and down the back nearly to the waist. The wig was of the natural hair colours, from blonde to black according to taste. With these large wig styles men were generally clean-shaven (**576B, C, 577A, C, E, 578**). The French were the chief European wig makers. They imported the hair and made up the wigs in France, then exported them to all countries.

The great wigs made both collars and hats superfluous. Men always carried a *hat*, usually under the arm but, unlike hitherto, rarely wore them. The style of hat in the 1660s and 1670s was round and either ostrich or ribbon trimmed. The crown was now lower and the brim narrower (**576A, 577C**). By the end of the century, the hat

598 English Costume, 1690–1710. Sir Christopher Wren's Library, Trinity College, Cambridge

599 *Philip IV, 1525–30*   **600** *c.1665*   **601** *c.1656*   **602** *c.1642*   **603** *1692*

was either the three-pointed tricorne or the two-pointed bicorne. It was of black felt, trimmed with gold braid and/or white ostrich tips (**577A, E**).

In the 1620s and 1630s *women* dressed their *hair* flat on top and with a short curly fringe on the forehead. The sides were fluffed and crimped out in puffs over the ears and the long back hair was swept up and twisted or plaited into a knot worn high on the crown (**567, 573**). By the late 1630s, the side hair was dressed in ringlets; a style made familiar by the portrait of Queen Henrietta Maria. As time passed, the ringlets grew longer and were wired to stand out from the face, making a wider coiffure (**570, 576C**). Its decoration was restrained and generally limited to large pearls, jewels, ribbon bows and pearl ropes. Scarves and hoods were used as outdoor head-covering. Masks often accompanied these hoods.

It was towards the latter part of the century that the tall coiffure and headdress developed. This was fashionable from 1688–90 until the end of the century and was worn contemporaneously with the tall peaked masculine periwig. Towards 1680 the feminine coiffure began to grow in height instead of, as previously, in width. The hair was curled on top and given height by being tied back with a ribbon bow. By the late 1680s it had developed into the *fontange headdress* or, as it was termed in France, *coiffure* or *bonnet à la Fontanges*. It took its name from the Duchess of Fontanges and was a coiffure piled high with curls and ringlets, surmounted by a lace cap in fluted and pleated ruffles, one row behind and above another, like organ piping. The whole was decorated by ribbon bows and pearls and a lace scarf, its lappets hanging on each side of the neck and over the bosom. Individual, long ringlets were arranged on the shoulders also. Especially tall creations had wire frames or pads inside (**577B, D, 579**).

Footwear

In the first half of the century *men's shoes* were long and narrow, with tapering square-ended toes. They had fairly high heels which were often red. They were decorated by ribbon rosettes on top (**568**). Very fashionable from 1625 to 1650 were the soft, elegant *boots*. The French learnt the art of tanning these soft leathers from the Hungarians and boots were worn on all occasions. They were high, with a funnel top which covered the knee for riding. For town wear this funnel was turned down, giving the open bucket top so typical of Cavalier dress. The weight of this top caused the boot to sag and gave creases across the calf and ankle. The silk stockings inside the boot were protected by heavier boot hose which had the lace tops visible inside the open boot top. On the instep the leather flap, called a *surpied*, was cut into the familiar butterfly form. It and the spur were held in place by the leather strap fastened under the boot. The boots had heels and often platform soles as well (**566, 569, 571, 575**).

After 1650, with the introduction of petticoat breeches, boots would have appeared incongru-ous. By 1655, shoes were fashionable and remained so until the end of the century. The ribbon rosette was replaced, first by a ribbon bow, later by a neat, metal buckle. These later styles of 1680–90 were often cut high, up to or above the ankle. The toes were more pointed and were shorter and daintier (**576A, B, D, 577A, C, E**).

Ladies' shoes were like the men's styles but had higher heels. Some were made of leather also but more often were of brocade, silk or velvet and were embroidered. Later in the century heels were very high. *Pantoffles* or slippers were also worn. These had a heel but no back; the foot was slipped into them (**585, 589, 637, 639**).

Linen and *neckwear* was of fine quality all through the seventeenth century and was an important part of the costume for both men and women. In the 1620s the ruff had become a *falling ruff*, wherein the layers of fabric were unstiffened and fell over the shoulders. Alternatively, especially in feminine dress, an open, wired, lace-edged collar was worn (**567, 573**). In the later 1630s, the *falling band* became fashionable for both sexes. This large, lawn, white collar was lace-trimmed. It covered the shoulders

604 *Spanish, 1690–5*   **605** *Italian, 1689*   **606** *Italian, 1665*   **607** *Italian, 1670–80*

Italy and Spain

A   B   C   D   E   F   G   H

completely and was tied in place at the throat by little cords with tasselled ends (**566, 568, 569, 570, 571, 574, 575**).

The *cravat* took the place of the falling band for men's wear from about 1645–50. At first it was simply a length of white linen or lawn, lace-edged, folded and tied loosely round the throat (**576A**). The name is derived from the Croatian word *crabate* and the fashion from Croat soldiers, serving at the time in the French army, who wore scarves tied round their throats for protection.

With the advent of the *justaucorps* the cravat style became more sophisticated and was tied round the throat in a bow, its ends hanging formally in folds over the chest. These were decorated with lace or fringe (**577A, C, E, 578**). A later version of the cravat, worn in the 1690s, was termed the *steinkirk*, its name being derived from the Battle of Steenkirk in Belgium in 1692.

In this style the loosely twisted ends of the cravat were tucked into the shirt front or drawn through a coat buttonhole. The idea was suggested by an opera singer who appeared for a performance with the lace cravat worn in this way suggesting an officer whose clothing has been disarranged in the heat of battle.

Accessories

By the seventeenth century these were more important and numerous. Both men and women wore beautiful leather *gloves,* embroidered and fringed. Most styles had gauntlets and some were perfumed. The best gloves were imported from Spain (**571, 577E, 586**). Ladies' gloves were usually elbow-length and of kid or silk. Men and women carried long *canes,* be-ribboned and fringed (**566, 571, 576B, 577A, C**). Both sexes carried large be-ribboned fur *muffs* (**574, 591B, 620**). Ladies carried *parasols* and both sexes had fine, lace-edged handkerchiefs. Men arranged them nonchalantly to dangle from their coat pockets. Towards the end of the century, the vogue for ladies' *aprons* grew with the aristocracy.* These aprons, large or small, white or coloured, were beautifully embroidered and trimmed with lace (**620, 627, 632**).

Both sexes used cosmetics heavily. Beauty spots,† made of black silk, were worn; they were adhesive on one side and were cut into shapes of stars, moons, hearts etc. and were carried in exquisite, dainty *patch boxes*, each with a tiny mirror in the lid.‡ The spots drew attention away from the smallpox scars which marred the faces of the majority of people (**579, 618**). Beautiful *snuff boxes* were also carried. These were jewelled or enamelled and some were painted with miniature pictures. Both sexes, in France, took snuff. Ladies and gentlemen carried *fans*, which

---

* Traditionally a garment for the bourgeoisie.
† These were termed *mouches* by the French.
‡ Forerunner of the powder compact.

were now often painted with figure compositions and landscapes. Others were made of fine lace. *Combs* were carried everywhere and spectacles were now being worn. *Jewellery* of all types decorated the costume but its use was much more restrained than it had been in the sixteenth century (**634, 636**). Ladies liked to wear a small posy of fresh flowers. To keep them fresh, they were inserted in a tiny bottle full of water and worn tucked into the front of the neckline.

England

Although English dress traditionally showed affinity with Dutch and German styles, in the seventeenth century, it was closely allied to French fashions. Partly, in the dress of the aristocracy, this was a continuation of the richness of the attire of the late Elizabethan era, partly it was due to the close connections between the English and French monarchies from 1625 onwards. Charles I, who acceded to the English throne in that year, married Henriette Marie of France, daughter of Henry IV and Marie de

609 *c.1630*   **610, 611** *1629–32*   **612, 613** *1625–30*

Germany

Medici. Queen Henrietta Maria, as she became known in England, retained her taste for French fashions and employed French tailors. Charles too was elegantly dressed à la mode. Both of them, their family and notable Cavaliers and their wives have been immortalised in the paintings of Sir Anthony Van Dyck. The painter's influence in England was so great that items of clothing were named after him. The falling band in England was called a 'Van Dyck collar' and its lace trimming 'Van Dyck edging' (**591, 592, 594, 595, 596, 634, 636, 643**).

Under the Protectorate, from 1649–60, the *Puritan* influence on dress was considerable and this made the clothes worn in these years in England much plainer than their French counterparts. There was no discernible difference in the styles of dress, simply there were several levels and variations in the sobriety or frivolity of the whole costume, according to the political and religious affiliations of the wearer. The excessively plain dress, actually inspired by the middle class version of the costume of the day, was only worn by Puritans of extreme views. In this men wore their hair cut short and uncurled, a tall black hard hat set upon it, collars and cuffs were plain white and untrimmed. There was no lace or ribbon in the costume. Fabrics were of wool or linen. Colours were sombre – black, mauve, brown, grey. The majority of people dressed less severely than this but also less flamboyantly than they had done before 1649. The traditional English penchant for compromise was the general rule. There were, however, still many people who continued to dress elegantly and fashionably and these were not all royalists; some were Cromwellian followers. Fig. **593** shows the typical compromise made by the majority of women. The lady is wearing a Puritan hat over a white cap but her falling band, cap and cuffs are all lace-trimmed. Her dress is plain but the underskirt patterned. She indulges herself with a fashionable muff.

With the *restoration* of the monarchy in 1660, French high fashion returned to England and from then until the end of the century, English dress was as à la mode as the French. Charles II, the new king, had spent part of his exile in France during the years of Commonwealth government in England. A further contact with the French court was through his sister Henrietta Stuart who married Louis XIV's brother. Close contacts between the two courts continued all the century.

Soon after Charles II came back to his throne he attempted to support British textile industries by setting a fashion for an English style of dress simpler than that current in France and using home-produced fabrics. Such a venture, like all the sumptuary laws of the past attempted by all European countries, failed completely. In the event, the reverse process was set in train. In reaction against restrictions in the years of Puritanism under Cromwell, the English aristocracy adopted even richer, more be-ribboned and lace-ornamented fashions than those worn by the French court (**597, 598**).

Southern Europe
Spain and Portugal

Time seemed to stand still in the fashions of the years 1620–60. There were changes but they were minor and Spain, after leading European modes during the sixteenth century now seemed in a backwater, unwilling to move forwards, and clinging to the hieratic dress of the court with its corsetry, rigidity, heavy use of cosmetics and jewellery, its rich, be-jewelled fabrics.

Men continued to wear trunk hose, corseted, skirted doublets, short capes and ruffs until the

615 c.*1665*   **616** *1693–5*   **617** *1690*   **618** *1695–1700*

619 *1657* 620 *1700* 621 *Emperor Leopold I* 622 *Eleonore of Austria* 623 *1700*

1620s. In 1623, Philip IV ordered the ruffs to be abandoned and replaced by the *valona*. This was the simple, white collar favoured by Philip. A card or stiffened material, faced with silk or taffeta, encircled the neck. It was open in front and rested upon and was set into the high doublet neckline; it was called a *golilla*. The valona was worn on top of this support; it was a white gauze, starched collar, plain and untrimmed (**599**). Other nations adopted this type of upstanding collar but usually wore larger versions of lace or with lace-edging. The English called it a whisk, the French, the *col rotonde*. In these other countries the fashion died out soon after 1620 but in Spain it lasted till after mid-century and the falling band was seen here more rarely than elsewhere.

By 1630 the trunk hose had been replaced by knee-length breeches, though the doublet was still unaltered; the only concession to modernity was that it was looser and less rigidly boned than hitherto. Cloaks were now knee-length (**599**).

Ladies continued to wear the farthingale with hip bolster. They retained their stiff corsetry and tight lacing. For many years they also retained

their ruffs and high, curled hair styles. By 1630 the ruff was replaced by a lower neckline and the hair was allowed to fall in long tresses over the shoulders. The whole costume continued to be richly decorated with embroidery and jewels (**600**).

Towards 1645 the last phase of the Spanish farthingale evolved. This was an immense size but, instead of a bell shape, it was flatter at front and back but extended at the sides at hip level; this was the ancestor to mid-eighteenth century *paniers* in Europe. These immense Spanish skirts are pictured in the many Velasquez portraits painted in the mid-century. Even the little children had to be encased in these monstrous frames, with corseted bodice and padded sleeves (**581, 601**).

Though court styles remained rigidly old-fashioned, military units came into contact with the styles worn by other nations and slowly Cavalier fashions spread into Spain, introducing long hair, the falling band, jacket, breeches and boots (**602**).

It was in 1660, on the occasion of the marriage

of Maria Theresa, daughter of Philip IV of Spain, to Louis XIV of France that the two courts met and the contrast between the be-ribboned, petticoat-breeched French and the corseted, farthingaled Spanish became so apparent. It was after this meeting that Spanish dress gradually came into line and followed French fashions for the rest of the century (**583, 586, 589, 603, 604**).

Italy

It had only been reluctantly that the Italians had adopted Spanish dress in the later sixteenth century, later than most other countries. It was with equal reluctance, so it seemed, that they abandoned Spanish fashion in the seventeenth. Spain, of course, dominated large areas of Italy and there was great variation in dress still in the peninsula because of the fragmented nature of its states system.

The Italians continued to produce the most beautiful and luxurious materials, silk and brocades of all kinds, velvets and satins and, above all, lace (**590**). The Spanish traditional dress was suited to display these fabrics and the

Italians may have clung to it partly for this reason. The family in **608A, B, C, D, E** illustrate the typical style of dress of the 1620s and 1630s. The hair styles are shorter than in France or England and lace, wired collars, based on the Spanish valona, are worn instead of falling bands. The figures are corseted and the ladies still wear a farthingale and, over this, very richly patterned gowns.

After mid-century, Italian dress also began to model itself on French fashions (**584, 605, 606, 607, 608F, G, H, 642**).

Central Europe
Germany, Austria, Switzerland

In the first half of the century dress was based chiefly on Dutch costume. In the 1620s men wore the doublet, with large tassets, or knee-length breeches, stockings and shoes with ribbon rosettes. A typically German hat was that with tall crown, small brim and ostrich plume decoration. The upstanding Spanish-type collar was usual but with lace-edging as in Italy (**612**). After 1630 Cavalier modes began to come in (**609**). Ladies

624, 625 *Hungarian, 1630–50*   **626** *Czech, 1650*   **627, 628** *Hungarian, 1652–72*

Hungary and Czechoslovakia

629 *Hungarian, 1690* **630** *Czech, 1670–80* **631, 632** *Hungarian, 1685–90*

also were behind the fashions for some years. They retained the farthingale and hip bolster till into the 1630s as well as a corseted bodice. They also wore a wired, lace-edged collar and a cap to match (**610**). The high-waisted gown, with sash and lower neckline and falling band, followed after 1630 (**587**).

In the second half of the century French fashions were followed. These were adopted later than in France and the length of delay involved was proportionate to the distance of the area from Paris (**614A, B, C**). There were also variations on the original theme, depending upon the quality of tailoring in the district and whether the people there had Catholic or Puritan views. In northern Germany, in particular, there was affinity, in mid-century, with Puritan styles in England and in Holland. Here, collars and cuffs were of plain white linen and ribbon trimming was limited. Also, the tall Puritan hat was in evidence (**614D, E**).

Later in the century French fashions were followed more closely. French fashion plates were published widely and the styles copied. In general, though, German versions were more sombre and less elegant (**615, 616, 617, 618**). In Austria and Switzerland they were more nearly patterned on the prototype (**620, 621, 622, 623, 638**).

Czechoslovakia, Poland and Hungary

Czechoslovakia was strongly influenced by western European modes. The country continued to adopt Spanish fashions till after 1620, but then adhered to Dutch styles and, later still, to the Cavalier dress of England and France, where lace was used widely on the costume. From 1660 onwards the French mode was followed and French fabrics as well as fashions were imported. Lace and ribbons were imported in great quantity, especially from Switzerland, France and Germany, while broadcloth came from Holland and England. The luxury accessories like fans, handkerchiefs, scarves, corsets and buttons came from abroad (**626, 630, 641**).

Details, 1620–1700

633 *Hungarian, 1671*

634 *Jewelled, gold locket, English, c.1630–40*

635 *Flemish portrait, 1620–30*

636 *Silver perfume case, English, c.1630*

637 *Hungarian shoe*

638 *Austrian, 1648*

639 *German slipper*

640 *Flemish, 1663*

641 *Polish portrait*

642 *Italian portait, 1680*

644 *Chopine*

645 *Yugoslav portrait, 1688*

643 *Queen Henrietta Maria of England, 1634*

646 c.1655 647 1635 648 c.1645 649 1635

Further east, *Hungary* was still for most of the century under Turkish control and its costume, especially that of the men, reflected this. *Masculine dress* was composed of the dolman and mente, both coat-like tunics, the latter worn on top of the former, a little longer, with fuller sleeves, a collar and with frogged decorative fastenings on the chest. These garments were accompanied by trousers or loose hose, with boots, a fur or fur-trimmed hat – the *kucsma* – and a cape. The shirt was richly embroidered at neck and sleeves but was shorter than its western counterpart, only extending to the waist. The earlier seventeenth century style of dress is shown in **624**; **628** illustrates the later mode, where the dolman and mente were cut at an angle below the waist and the whole skirt was flared. By this time fabrics for these garments, (which were imported from Italy), were luxurious, of brocade or embroidered silks and were in rich colours. Gold and silver embroidery and frogging were also used. Late seventeenth century styles are shown in **629, 631** and **633**.

Dress for *women* in the first half of the century

followed Spanish and Italian modes. This is seen in the stand-up, lace collar, tight corseting and farthingale skirt (**625**). A more national style was also currently in fashion and this had a blouse or chemise with full white sleeves and a traditional embroidered bodice/jacket open in front and laced across to the waist. The chemise finished in a neck frill and was embroidered below this. The skirt was also heavily embroidered and a decorative apron was worn over it (**627**). In the second half of the century, French fashions were emulated though some years later than the current mode (**630, 632, 637**).

Northern Europe

The general trend in *Scandinavia* was to follow Spanish styles till about 1625, then Dutch fashions till about 1670 and, after this, the French. *Danish* costume was closely allied all the century to Dutch and German styles especially in the Cavalier modes and when rhinegrave breeches were fashionable. The Rosenborg Castle collection of costumes in Copenhagen illustrates this

(646, 647, 648, 649). *Swedish* dress gained influence from England, especially in the Cavalier
styles of the 1630s and 1640s (582, 588, 650, 652,
653). The Puritan influence had effect in the
1650s (656, 657). In general, after 1660, Scandinavian dress followed the French pattern (654,
655) though, further east, in Finland, a longer
time-lag was experienced and there was also a
noticeable influence from more eastern, Russian
styles. Throughout Scandinavia in the seventeenth century all quality materials were imported,
from Italy, France, England, Holland and
Germany.

Notes on the Illustrations

544 and 545   Painting by Thomas de Keyser of Con-
stantijn Huygens and his clerk, National Gallery, London. Huygens wears a doublet, cloak and breeches of
purple-brown broadcloth with gilt frogged decoration.
His hat is black, he wears a white falling ruff. The costume
is completed by light brown gloves, white hose and light
fawn boots. The clerk's costume is in greyish-purple
with crimson sleeves, lining to cloak and shoe ties. He
wears a lace-edged collar and cuffs, grey hat and black
shoes.

546, 547, 548 and 549   A portrait by Cornelis de Vos of
himself and his family. Musées Royaux des Beaux Arts,
Brussels. De Vos is dressed all in black except for a
white, lace-edged collar. His wife wears a gown of black
with black and brown striped sleeves. Her ruff is plain
white, her cuffs white lace and her stomacher ivory
satin with a floral pattern in gold and red. Her underskirt is in brown and gold. The child standing wears a
white cap and lace-edged collar and cuffs. The dress is of
white self-coloured pattern and there is a grey-green
apron and cross-over on the bodice. The underskirt is
light brown and shoes are brown. The child seated on
the chair has a white cap, ruff and cuffs. The dress is
black with gold stripes. A double bead necklace in red
is fastened round the chest. The underskirt is gold and
brown, the shoes fawn with red ties.

550 and 551   Painting by Willem Duyster, National
Gallery, London. The woman wears a plain white
ruff and lace-edged cuffs. Her cap is brown with white
lace edge. Her dress is black with crimson sleeves, the
skirt is brown and the apron white. The man wears a
peacock blue doublet slashed to show the white shirt.
He wears a white scarf and cuffs. His breeches are grey,
stockings white and shoes brown. His hat is fawn with a
dark green plume.

552   Portrait of Anna Wake by Sir Anthony Van
Dyck, Mauritshuis, The Hague, Holland. The gown is
all black. The collar, cuffs and undersleeves are white,

650 c.1640   651 1626   652 1643   653 1644

edged with white lace. The girdle is gold and necklace and bracelet of pearls. She holds an ostrich plume fan.

553 Portrait of Cornelia Vekemans by Cornelis de Vos. Musée Mayer van der Bergh, Antwerp, Belgium. The child wears a green-gold satin dress with red ribbon bows and embroidered edging. Her sleeves and underskirt are scarlet with black banding. She has a white, lace-edged collar and cuffs. She holds a fan. Her cap is jewelled.

554 Painting by Dirk Hals also one by Jacob van Elsen, National Gallery, London. Black hat, white falling ruff and cuffs. The doublet is light yellow slashed to show the white shirt. Gloves are white leather. His breeches are golden brown and stockings yellow. The shoes have pink bows and are brown.

555 and 556 Painting by Frans Hals, Rijksmuseum, Amsterdam, Holland. 555 wears a pale blue silk doublet with gold points. His breeches are dark grey and the sash golden silk. He wears a white, lace-edged falling band, cuffs and boot hose. The ribbons at the knee are blue. His boots are of white leather and his hat black. 556 wears a buff leather jacket with scarlet sash. He has a white, lace-edged falling band, cuffs and boot hose. His breeches are golden and his boots light brown leather.

557 Painting by Bartholomeus van der Helst of 'Banquet of the Civic Guard', Rijksmuseum, Amsterdam, Holland. He wears a jacket and breeches of dark grey silk decorated with gold braid and embroidery. His baldric is pale blue, his hat black with gold band and brown ostrich plumes. He wears a white, lace-edged collar, cuffs and boot hose. His stockings are brown silk and his boots brown leather with gold edging.

558 Portrait by Van der Helst of Princess Henrietta Maria Stuart, Rijksmuseum, Amsterdam, Holland.

559–565 A family portrait by Coques, National Gallery, London. The father (559) is dressed entirely in black except for the white, lace-edged collar and cuffs and gold braid fastenings on his jacket. His wife (560) wears a black gown with white lace collar and white undersleeves. Her underskirt is red with gold lace decoration. She has a pearl necklace. The child (561) is dressed entirely in white. The eldest daughter (564), at the rear, wears a dress of gold with a white lace collar, white undersleeves and a white apron. The ribbon bows are blue and she wears flowers in her hair. The baby, in the walking cage (562) is all in white. Her sister, aged about five years (563) wears a blue gown with white apron and sleeves and white lace collar. She has flowers and lace in her hair. The sister (565) wears a red dress

654 *Swedish, 1653*

655 *Danish, 1695*

656, 657 *Swedish, c.1665*

Scandinavia

with white apron and sleeves and white lace collar and cap.

566, 567 and 568 Engraving by Abraham Bosse of 'Ladies and Cavaliers in a Ballroom'. Bibliothèque Nationale, Paris.

569 and 570 Engraving of the Gallery of the Palais Royale, Paris by Abraham Bosse.

571 Portrait of the Duke of Lorraine, Museum, Reims, France. Pale blue doublet and breeches. Grey gloves. White leather boots with white lace boot hose and white, lace-edged falling band.

572 Little daughter of Hubert de Montmor. Painting by Philippe de Champaigne, Musée Saint-Denis, Reims, France. White, lace-edged apron, cuffs, collar and cap. Blue dress with gold embroidery. Gold shoes.

573 Henrietta, Duchess of Lorraine. Portrait by Sir Anthony Van Dyck. Kenwood House, London. Black gown. Silver and white patterned undergown. White, lace-edged collar and cuffs. Pearl necklace and earrings.

574 and 575 Engravings by Abraham Bosse.

576A Painting by Le Brun, c.1660, Louvre, Paris. Blue silk jacket and petticoat breeches, decorated by gold embroidered bands. White lace cravat. Black hat with coloured plumes. Blue stockings, light fawn shoes with red heels and white ribbon bows. White shirt.

B and D Tapestry, Versailles Palace, 1660s. B is wearing a red coat with silver embroidered decoration. He has a powdered wig, white breeches with gold ribbon sashes, white stockings and shoes with gold ribbon bows. D wears a dark cloak with gold decoration and be-ribboned petticoat breeches.

C Painting, artist unknown, c.1675. Museum, Versailles. The lady wears a red dress with gold embroidered banding. She has a gold embroidered stomacher, a white lace collar, white sleeves and a white patterned underskirt.

577A Tapestry, Palace of Versailles. Late seventeenth century. Brocade justaucorps with gold frogging. White lace cravat, white shirt sleeves. Gold, decorative baldric. Black tricorne hat with gold braid. Periwig. White breeches and stockings. Black shoes.

B and E Painting, Museum, Versailles. B is wearing a red dress with gold all-over pattern. White lace collar and white lace sleeve ruffles. Fontange headdress. E is Louis XIV in a brown justaucorps with gold decoration and buttons. He wears a brown periwig, a white cravat with fringed ends, white shirt and gold embroidered wrist ruffles, brown stockings and black shoes with red lining. He carries a black tricorne hat with gold braid and white ostrich frond trimming, also brown gloves.

C Tapestry, Palace of Versailles, 1680s. Blue justaucorps with silver brocade decoration. Red hat with white plumes over periwig. White shirt sleeves and cravat. Red breeches and stockings. Black shoes.

D Engraving. The Court of Louis XIV, 1690s. Fontange headdress with lace and jewels. Pearl necklace. Jewelled, brocaded stomacher. Gown with ruched, flounced and fringed decoration. Elbow-length gloves.

578 Bust of Louis XIV by Coysevox. Wallace Collection, London.

579 as 577 D.

580 Victoria and Albert Museum, London. Late seventeenth century.

581 Infanta Margarita of Austria. Portrait by Velazquez, Louvre, Paris.

582 Portrait. Lace falling ruff.

583 Fawn suède shoe with crimson ribbon bow and brown suède shoe with red bow. Actual shoes, Rocamora Costume Museum, Barcelona, Spain.

584 Portrait of the Marchesa Ardizzone by an unknown artist. Palazzo d'Arco, Mantua, Italy. Curled coiffure with headdress of striped ribbons. Black lappets. Lace collar, black gown.

585 Red velvet shoe embroidered in gold. Silver buckle. Actual shoe, Rocamora Costume Museum, Barcelona, Spain.

586 Yellow leather glove with red and silver ribbons. Cuff of blue and silver brocade. Actual glove. Dresden State Museum, E. Germany.

587 Portrait of unknown lady. Pearl cap and necklace. White, lace-edged collar. Red and silver embroidery on black gown. Bayerische Nationalmuseum, Munich, W. Germany.

588 Portrait. Pearl and jewelled necklaces. Lace, wired collar. Plain white and white lace neckbands. Figured satin gown with pearl rope decoration and double lace cuffs. Embroidered gloves and stomacher.

589 Embroidered lady's shoe. Rocamora Costume Museum, Barcelona, Spain.

590 Milanese lace. Victoria and Albert Museum, London.

591A Cavalier dress. Portrait. Falling band over jacket. Breeches with ribbon loops at knee. Lace topped boot hose, boots, hat and gloves.

B and G From engravings by Hollar.

H Portrait of Charles I (1631), by Daniel Mytens. National Portrait Gallery, London. Grey-blue doublet and breeches, gold braid trimming. White shirt shows through slashes. Blue baldric. Buff leather boots and gloves, white stockings with lace points. Cane.

592 Actual costume, Victoria and Albert Museum, London. Doublet, breeches and cloak of yellow braided satin. Black hat with white plume. Buff leather boots. Lace-edged boot hose.

593 Portrait of the artist's wife by John Tradescant. Ashmolean Museum, Oxford, England. Grey-green silk dress over white underskirt patterned in red. White, lace-edged falling band cuffs, and cap. Black hat with white band. Dark fur muff. (not in painting).

594 King Charles I. Portrait by Sir Anthony Van Dyck, Louvre, Paris. White satin jacket with pale blue baldric and golden sword holder. White lace-edged falling band and cuffs. Scarlet breeches. White stockings. Buff leather boots and gloves. Cane. Black hat.

595 Queen Henrietta Maria. Portrait by unknown artist, National Portrait Gallery, London. Dark green satin gown decorated by ropes of pearls. White lace neck and sleeve trimming. Pearl cap. Fan.

596 Prince Charles as a small boy. Portrait by Sir Anthony Van Dyck. Musée Royal des Beaux Arts, Antwerp, Belgium. He wears a scarlet jacket and breeches with decoration in gold. White shirt sleeves. A falling band in white with lace-edging. Brown boots with red bow ties. White lace boot hose. Fawn gloves. Black hat with white ribbons.

597 and 598 From portraits mainly in the National Portrait Gallery, London.

599 Portrait of King Philip IV by Diego Velazquez. National Gallery, London. He wears a doublet and breeches of brown ornamented all over in silver. His cloak is darker, also silver embroidered. The sleeves are white and silver. At the neck he wears a valona over the golilla. His stockings are white, shoes plain black, gloves brown.

600 Portrait of the Duchess del Infantado by an unknown artist. Hispanic Society of America, New York. The gown, over a farthingale, is gold and brown, embroidered all over. The sleeves are white with red ribbons. The underskirt is striped red and gold. She wears a red ribbon and jewel in her hair, gold earrings and jewelled-edged white neckband. She holds a white silk handkerchief.

601 Painting by Velazquez 'Las Meninas'. Prado Museum, Madrid. The child wears a white gown over a farthingale. There is a red flower on her chest and the gown has black edging at neckline and sleeves.

602 Painting by artist of the Madrid School. Prado, Madrid. Brown jacket and breeches, black belt. Darker brown cloak. Light fawn leather boots with lace boot-hose. White, lace-edged falling band. Black hat.

603 Louis I of Spain as a boy. Portrait, Prado, Madrid. He wears a pale-blue silk jacket and matching petticoat breeches and stockings. White shirt, white lace cravat. Blue cape. Black shoes with red heels. Periwig powdered white.

604 Painting, Prado, Madrid. Scarlet coat with silver braid and frogging. Brown periwig. White silk and lace cravat. White lace wrist ruffles. Black stockings and shoes, red heels. Cane, with ribbon.

605 Fashion drawing. Engraving by Giovanni Giacomo de Rossi, Rome. Dark overgown bordered with tassels. White sleeves and ruffles. Black net gloves. Light undergown over striped petticoat. Fontange headdress with lace scarf. Parasol.

606 Portrait of a gentleman by Carlo Ceresa. Collezione Vincenzo Polli, Milan. Dark justaucorps with braid decoration and patterned cuffs. Breeches to match. Dark stockings, light coloured shoes with metal buckles. White lace-edged shirt and cravat. Black periwig. Black hat.

607 Portrait of Donna Olimpia Aldobrandini by an unknown artist. Galleria Doria, Rome. Gown of dark brown with orange and white with lace decoration. White lace neckband, collar and white sleeves with silver ribbons. Underskirt of cream with brown pattern. Pearl necklace and bracelets.

608A Portrait of a boy by Carlo Ceresa, 1633. Museo Civici, Milan. Dark doublet and breeches and black hat. Black shoes.

B, C, D, E The Duke and Duchess of Forano with their two children, 1626. Florentine School of Painting, Strozzi Palace, Florence, Italy. The Duchess (B) wears an ornately jewelled, embroidered gown over a farthingale. It is dark with light coloured pattern. The undergown, visible at sleeves, stomacher and underskirt is of a light coloured material, with a zig-zag design. She has a lace, wired collar and cuffs, a pearl rope necklace and bracelets and pearls in her hair. She holds a fan. The little boy (C) wears a dark doublet and embroidered light trunk hose. He has a lace-edged collar and cuffs. The daughter (D) wears a gown over a farthingale. The gown has hanging sleeves and is decorated in a sprig design. She has a lace falling band. The duke (E) is dressed in black apart from a white lace collar, cuffs and knee sashes and gold decoration on the sleeves, which are slashed to display the white shirt.

F Portrait of Lucia Valcarenghi by an unknown artist, 1670. Palazzo Marino, Milan, Italy. Dark coloured gown with all sprig floral pattern in light colours. White lace collar and wrist ruffles. Gold necklace. Jewelled brooch. Jewelled hair-band.

G Portrait of the young daughter of Vittorio Amedeo by an unknown artist, 1640–50. Galleria Sabauda, Turin, Italy. Gown decorated in gold with white lace collar. White sleeves. Pearl necklace. Hair ribbon.

H Portrait by Giovanni Bernardo Carbone, 1660. Palazzo Bianco, Genoa, Italy. Chocolate brown satin gown with gold edging. White collar and sleeves. Underskirt of pale blue satin with black lace appliqué decoration. Gold embroidered shoes.

609 Drawing by Hollar of a Cavalier, Kupferstichkabinet, Munich, Germany. Typical Cavalier dress with doublet and breeches, boots and hose, falling band and ostrich plumed hat.

610 Actual costume, Historisches Museum, Dresden, E. Germany. Yellow satin gown with silver and gold lace decoration. Red tassels on shoulders. Undersleeves of red satin with gold embroidery. White lace-edged collar, cuffs and cap.

611 and 613 Actual children's garments. Bayerische Nationalmuseum, Munich, W. Germany. 611 wears a doublet and breeches of gold brocade with gold satin sleeves. The costume belonged to Prince Philipp Ludwig at the age of about five years. 613 was the dress of Princess Maria Magdalena at the age of about two years. It is a white silk dress decorated with blue piping.

612 Actual costume, Dresden State Museum, E.

Germany. Green velvet doublet and breeches decorated with gold banding and embroidery in colours. Sleeves of lighter green satin with gold embroidery.

614A, B Engraving by Aubry, c.1650, Nuremberg Germanisches Museum. A wears a jacket with three-quarter sleeves slashed to show the white shirt which is also visible on the chest. He wears light coloured petticoat breeches over darker ones. His hair is long and natural. His black hat has white ostrich plumes. B wears a dark overgown with embroidered silk collar. She has a lighter undergown and white silk sleeves and lace cuffs. Pearl necklace.

C, D, E Coloured glass by Johann Schaper of Nürnberg, 1659–61. Bayerische Nationalmuseum, Munich, W. Germany. C wears a gold jacket over a white shirt. White, lace-edged collar and wrist ruffles. Red-brown petticoat breeches. He has blue stockings with white lining falling downwards. Above are white frills. D wears a scarlet cloak with black border over a yellow jacket, white shirt and plain collar and brown petticoat breeches. His stockings are white over red, his shoes white with red bows. His hat is grey. E wears an orange cloak turned back at the edges to show the brocade lining. His collar, jacket and petticoat breeches are white and his hat black with gold banding. His stockings are red over yellow, his shoes black with red ties. All three young men have natural long hair.

615 Actual costume, Dresden State Museum, E. Germany. Suit of cape, jacket and rhinegrave breeches in blue decorated in silver embroidery and lace and with red and silver ribbon loops. The cape has a silver lining.

616 Actual costume, Dresden State Museum, E. Germany. Dark red velvet justaucorps with high relief gold embroidery with breeches to match. Red satin lining. Belonged to Elector Johann Georg IV.

617 Actual costume, National Museum, Nuremberg, W. Germany. Justaucorps of red-brown silk with gold braid decoration. Waistcoat of blue brocade. Periwig.

618 Contemporary engraving, 1695–1700. Princess of Bavaria. A gold brocade dress with sprig all-over pattern. Deep red overgown with gold braid edging. White, lace sleeve ruffles, neck bows and fontange headdress with scarf. Beauty spots.

619 Portrait of Joseph von Orelli as a very young child by Conrad Meyer of Zürich, Switzerland. Landesmuseum, Zürich. Dress with ribbon bows. Embroidered white apron. White ruff. Gold banded cap.

620 A lady from Zürich, Switzerland. Contemporary engraving. Dark blue dress with red cuffs. White apron, sleeve ruffles, neck frill and fontange headdress. Black fur muff.

621 Emperor Leopold I of Austria, c.1670–80. Contemporary engraving. Black periwig. Black hat with white plumes. White lace cravat and sleeve ruffles. Dark jacket and breeches with braid and ruched decoration. Long cloak. White gloves. White stockings, black shoes.

622 Eleonore of Austria, c.1690. Third queen of Leopold I. Contemporary engraving. Dark gown with all-over floral pattern. Light coloured underskirt with all-over pattern in small motif. Brooches hold back the overskirt. Jewelled brooch and pendant at corsage. White neckfrill and sleeves. Jewels in the coiffure. Earrings and pearl necklace. Fan.

623 Viennese gentleman. Contemporary engraving. Black tricorne hat with gold braided edge and white ostrich frond decoration. White cravat and lace sleeve ruffles. Gold banded justaucorps. Breeches to match. White stockings, black shoes with metal buckles. Cane with tassels. Gloves. Periwig.

624 Portrait of Lászlo Esterházy, killed 1652 fighting the Turks. Hungarian. Dolman and mente. Trousers and long boots. Fur hat (kucsma) with plume.

625 Portrait, Hungarian. White lace wired collar, lace cuffs. Dark overgown with rich embroidery. Slashed sleeve, buttoned, showing white chemise. Red brocade underskirt.

626 Prague noblewoman, Czechoslovakia. Drawing by Hollar. Fur cloak. Dark fur outside, lighter fur inside shows in turned back edges. Masculine type jacket. Below, plain gown skirt is held up at the sides to show striped underskirt. White, lace-edged collar. Fur hat.

627 Actual dress, Hungarian Museum of Decorative Arts, Budapest. 1672. Black velvet embroidered in coloured silks. Open in front of bodice and laced across white chemise which has high embroidered neckline and full sleeves. Embroidered white apron – see portrait 1662, Hungarian.

628 Hungarian dolman, actual costume. Hungarian Museum of Decorative Arts, Budapest. Richly embroidered silk. Worn with trousers and boots.

629 Portrait of Daniel Esterházy, Hungarian. Mente with frogged fastenings worn over dolman which has a sash belt. Velvet hat with fur brim. Hose and boots.

630 Czech portrait. Plain satin gown with white neck edge, ribbons and jewels.

631 Portrait of Kristof Batthyány, Hungarian. Royal red mente with fur collar and frogged fastenings draped over shoulders. Under this is a belted dolman. Dark red cloth hose, leather boots. Hat with plumes.

632 Portrait, Hungarian. Brocade dress with white lace collar and ribbon bows. White chemise sleeve ruffles and white, lace-edged apron. Handkerchief and fan. Pearl necklace.

633 Engraving of Hungarian Count. Historiches Museum der Stadt Wien, Austria. Fur hat and fur-collared mente with braid and cord button loops. Worn over buttoned dolman. White collar.

634 Gold locket with portrait inside. Enamelled and jewelled decoration. English. British Museum, London.

635 Portrait of Jacqueline van Caestre by Rubens. Musées Royaux des Beaux Arts, Brussels. Lace-edged white, wired collar. Black gown with white satin decoration. Heavy gold, jewelled brooch and necklace. Pearl necklace and dainty gold necklace.

636 Enamelled silver perfume case, English. Victoria

and Albert Museum, London.

637 Hungarian shoe with gold decoration. Late seventeenth century.

638 Engraved portrait of Anton Georg Faber. Historisches Museum der Stadt Wien, Austria. Felt hat with ribbons and feathers. White cambric falling band with lace edge. Lace decorated baldric. Fur cuffs.

639 Lady's slipper. Red velvet with gold bands. Actual item. Dresden State Museum, E. Germany.

640 Detail of painting 'Officer on Horseback' by Rembrandt Van Rijn. National Gallery, London. Black hat with white plumes. Long natural hair. White cravat and waist sash. Buff leather coat. Sleeves of rich striped fabric. Embroidered leather gloves.

641 Portrait of King Wladyslawa IV, Polish. Narodowe Museum, Cracow, Poland. Natural hair with lovelock. Lace-edged falling band. *c.*1640.

642 Portrait of Italian lady. Galleria Doria, Rome. Coiffure decorated by flowers and ribbon loops. Lace-edged gown. Brocade bows. Gold ruching on stomacher.

643 Portrait of Queen Henrietta Maria. National Portrait Gallery, London. Light-coloured silk gown with lace falling band and cuffs. Pearl necklace. Dark ribbon sash. Pearl rope decoration and brooch.

644 White leather chopine. Victoria and Albert Museum, London.

645 Portrait. Miniature of Yugoslav gentleman.

646 Danish portrait. Silver brocade and embroidered jacket and rhinegrave breeches. Ribbon rosettes and loops. White shirt, laced edged collar and cuffs. Black hat with jewelled band and coloured plumes. White stockings. Buff leather boots with lace boot hose. Natural hair.

647 Actual costume, Rosenborg Castle Costume Collection, Copenhagen, Denmark. Circular cape, jacket and breeches of light brown cloth lined with golden velvet and embroidered in silver. Combined with contemporary Danish engraving. This shows long hair with love-lock, falling band, knee sashes, stockings and shoes.

648 Actual costume, Rosenborg Castle. Doublet, breeches and cape of light blue satin decorated with silver banding. Sleeves slit to show white shirt.

649 Portrait of Princess Magdalena Sybilla by unknown artist. Rosenborg Castle, Copenhagen, Danish. Black gown patterned in brown. Gold and black underskirt. Sleeves gold with white chemise showing through slashes, red rosettes. Jewelled collar and stomacher. White lace collar. Jewelled headdress. Feather fan.

650 Portrait, Swedish. Buff leather coat. Decorative baldric, leather belt. Lace-edged falling band and cuffs. Breeches buttoned up outer side. Leather boots, lace boot hose, ribbon decoration. Cane. Natural hair.

651 Portrait of young boy, Sweden. Lace-edged falling ruff and cuffs. Leather gloves. Baldric. Doublet decorated with braid. Striped breeches. Ribbon loops at knee. Shoes with ribbon rosettes.

652 Portrait of Sophie de la Gardie, by unknown artist. Nordiska Museet, Stockholm. Black gown with silver embroidery and braid. White, lace-edged collar and cuffs. Pearl necklace and bracelets. Jewelled hair band. Feather fan.

653 Portrait, Finland (Swedish). Lace falling band and cuffs. Doublet and breeches of sprigged satin. Gloves with embroidered, fringed, gauntlets. Baldric. Boots with lace-banded boot hose. Cane. Natural hair.

654 Portrait, Finland (Swedish). Gown decorated by braid banding. Ribbon bows at waist. Chemise shows at sleeves. Feather fan. Lace-edged collar. Jewelled cap. Gloves.

655 Actual costume, Danish. Rosenborg Castle, Copenhagen. Red velvet coat and breeches with silver embroidery. Blue and silver brocade waistcoat. Black tricorne hat with white fronds. Gloves. Black shoes with jewelled metal buckles. Periwig.

656 and 657 Painting, Swedish. Nordiska Museet, Stockholm. 656 wears a red dress with white collar and sleeve puffs. Jewelled necklace on top of collar. Jewelled cap. 657 wears a black jacket and rhine grave breeches with ribbon decoration. White collar, shirt and stockings. Black shoes with red heels. Black hat over natural hair.

Chapter Seven

The Eighteenth Century: Rococo Grace

For the first three-quarters of the eighteenth century France remained the undisputed cultural leader of Europe. In western Europe society was becoming liberalised and freer. The middle classes were establishing themselves and increasing their numbers; their influence waxed greatly. The arbiter of dress was less the individual Court than the larger unit of Society; still aristocratically led but with a wider base. Eastern Europe remained feudal, with a restricted ruling class and an immense population of illiterate, uncultured poor. The overriding cultural influence came from the west, from France. The French language was that of the ruling class. French customs and dress were those of the cultured leaders.

The balance of power had shifted once more. During the eighteenth century England became the supreme power at sea and, from this, her influence in trade and colonisation grew immensely. France slid to second place in this realm and consequently lost her previous important position in international affairs. Despite this she retained her overall cultural, and thus fashion, supremacy. These two countries were the major European powers in the eighteenth century and their influence and spread of their civilisation accordingly important. Other nations, for instance, Holland, Spain and Sweden, became less wealthy and influential.

The first signs of egalitarianism in dress began to develop in this century. The movement was slow and, for decades, barely perceptible, but it was from this time that the concept of high quality and privilege, for so long maintained only for the benefit of the few, the ruling class, came under attack. The concept was eroded and the quality diluted to become an acceptance of quantity. In eighteenth century dress this was evidenced by a closer adherence to prevailing fashion by most classes of the community, not only the aristocracy, as before. The richness of fabrics used and the quality of the ornamentation varied according to the wealth of the wearer, but the actual styles were similar. Inevitably the egalitarian move-ment spread into other cultural and artistic fields. It has continued and accelerated since the later eighteenth century until our own times to affect the whole quality of life. With it has come a dilution of the superb standards of the eighteenth century, the inevitable price for bringing the sharing of the beauty, talent and wealth of life – which, of course, includes costume – to an increasing proportion of peoples.

Together with a general egalitarianism in the eighteenth century came a gradual change in the position of women in society. Their importance increased as did their influence. In fashion, the outward sign of this was in the exchange of places between men and women. For centuries, especially during the Middle Ages and in the seventeenth century, the man had been the more gloriously attired of the sexes. His were the most brilliant colours, the richest ornamentation, the most elegant line and the most beautiful fabrics. From 1700 onwards men began slowly to take second place as the more splendidly dressed sex. This movement continued steadily throughout the century, and the following one, with men wearing less ornamentation, darker and duller fabrics and more severe designs of garments. It was a process which culminated in the Victorian male dressed entirely in black and grey, relieved only by touches of white at neck and cuff.

Until the 1770s, under French leadership, eighteenth century dress was noted for its exquisite fabrics in silks and satins, in delicate colours, painted, embroidered or printed in dainty floral patterns. For men, these fabrics were beautifully embroidered on the edges of garments and for women they were decorated by quantities of ribbon, ruching and flouncing. The silhouette was an artificial one with coiffures distended into immense wigs, the waistline restrictively corseted and the feminine skirt extended over enormous hoops.

The artificiality and extremity of these excesses reached their peak in France in the 1770s but, at this time, there developed in England an al-

658 *1714–15*   **659, 660** *Robes battantes, 1728–31*   **661** *c.1738*

ternative mode. Worn by both sexes, this was a more practical, comfortable version of the current fashions. It was from England that the hooped skirts and tall wigs vanished first. The more egalitarian democratic society obtaining in England was reflected in this *mode à l'anglaise* which was elegant but not artificial. Various reasons were put forward by foreigners to account for the fact that England alone challenged French supremacy of fashion in the years 1770–1800 and produced these simpler, graceful styles which were emulated by several European countries, notably Germany, Scandinavia and, eventually, France, where 'Anglomania' in dress became enthusiastically accepted as *la mode*. The reasons propounded vary from the cold, damp English climate, the English devotion to sport and to a foreign conception of an England peopled solely by the landed gentry, spending their whole lives hunting, shooting and fishing, to whom such attire would be suited. These views seem on a par with the fallacy still widely entertained on the Continent of Europe that England, and especially London, lives permanently in a damp fog. It seems more credible that these more natural styles

evolved due to the typical English characteristics of common sense and refusal to indulge in extremism, whether in politics or dress.

With the outbreak of the French Revolution in 1789 and the subsequent brief, quickly changing régimes from monarchy to republic to empire, the consequent economic and social upheavals brought total change to fashion with new modes rapidly succeeding one another. The simplicity of the English designs of the years 1770–90 had only foreshadowed the excessive plainness and décolleté lines of the 1790s. The effects of the French Revolution shocked and galvanised society all over Europe. With the later French wars and conquests, French fashions once more became influential. Only England, apart and protected by her navy, continued her own way, her fashions reflecting but complementing the French. It was in these latter years of the century that English masculine tailoring became supreme. While Paris continued to be the centre of feminine fashion, London was established as the centre for men's dress. Masculine clothes consisting of tail coat, vest and breeches now required fine tailoring and English tailors were the best in the world.

Textiles and the Industrial Revolution

The textile industry developed rapidly during the eighteenth century. This was so in many countries but England led the world in the production of fabrics. This was partly due to the establishment of her supremacy at sea, which greatly increased her trading capabilities, partly to the influx of the Huguenot workers at the end of the previous century and, most important, her role as leading exponent of the industrial revolution. The great majority of inventions in the textile industry in this century stemmed from Englishmen and Scotsmen. New mechanical processes adopted for use in weaving, spinning and knitting, added to the development in power from James Watt's work on the steam engine, had revolutionised the British textile industry by 1800. These included such milestones as Kay's flying shuttle (1733), Hargreaves' spinning jenny (1765), Arkwright's water frame (1768), Crompton's spinning mule (1779) and Strutt's knitting machine (1758). New textile centres grew up; factories were established. English textiles sold all over the world at new low prices made possible by industrialisation.

Silk was produced now in quantity in England, given an impetus by the Huguenots in Spitalfields and in the mills built at Coventry. Early in the century woollen broadcloth was still the staple English textile, made in quantity for the home market as well as the rapidly expanding colonial trade. The traditional cloth areas (Norwich and the west country) were declining by the later eighteenth century, but in Yorkshire (Leeds and Bradford) an important centre developed.

Cotton was being made and worn more and more; by 1800 the industry had surpassed the woollen trade. The British cotton industry was established in Lancashire, west of the Pennines. It expanded enormously from mid-century when the foundations of the British Empire in India were being laid down under the genius of Clive. Cotton was also grown in the Southern states of North America and this accelerated the already flourishing slave trade. Trading of negroes to the New World had been in operation since the

666   667
Robes à la Française, c.1750

662 *c.1760*   663 *1751–61*   664 *1763*   665 *1752*

France   179

A   B   C   D   E

early sixteenth century and the British had gradually acquired a larger share of this. By 1700 the so-called 'triangular trade' was well established. In this, the merchants (based in Bristol) sailed to Africa to exchange their manufactured goods of arms, hardwear, jewellery, spirits and tobacco with the African chieftains for negro labour. The second leg of the journey took the slaves to America where they were sold at great profit to work in the plantations. The ships then returned to England laden with raw materials. The development of the cotton industry caused the centre of this trade in England to move to Liverpool and rapidly accelerated the quantity. In 1791 the British transported 38,000 negroes to America, more than half the total European trading for that year. In fashion, cotton completely changed styles, colours and decoration worn in the later eighteenth century. Silks and satins were

slowly abandoned in ladies' clothes in favour of the then almost transparent, clinging lawns, batistes and gauzes. The resulting modes were simple and sparingly ornamented. White became the most fashionable shade.

The French textile industry grew apace also but it suffered a set-back from the British blockade in the War of the Spanish Succession early in the century and again, after 1789, when disorganisation and even chaos set in in French industry during the years of the Revolution and re-establishment of order. François Boucher* refers to a cartoon of these years, which shows a picture of a thin textile craftsman wearing threadbare clothes, captioned 'I'm free'!

Between these two problem periods, French textiles flourished, especially in the years 1730–50,

---

* *A History of Costume in the West* by François Boucher, Thames and Hudson, 1967.

when manufacture of silk expanded greatly. The French produced quality fabrics which sold all over Europe to make the French style of garments for both sexes. In the second half of the century they also manufactured cottons, developed printed cotton systems and perfected techniques for dyeing.

Textile production and export also flourished in some other European countries. Switzerland produced cottons, silks and quantities of ribbon. German manufactured woollen cloth and silks. Belgium also exported its textiles, as did Spain. In contrast, the industry in other countries declined: these included Italy, Austria and Holland.

Fashion Journals

The fashion journal appeared in the second half of the eighteenth century. It was a publication which gave news and illustrations of fashions which were being worn and those which were new and likely to become very fashionable. It was not a pattern book or a fashion plate; it was a magazine to inform both sexes of what was popular in Society.*

Although French fashion was supreme, and the French still issued fashion dolls and began issuing such journals as *Le Cabinet des Modes*, it was the English who seriously promoted, at this time, the production of journals for the fashion world. The *Lady's Magazine* was the chief of these, dating from 1770 and published at first in black and white and, later in the century, in colour. Between 1770 and 1800 a number of such journals appeared, illustrated by good artists and giving reliable drawings of the leading fashions of the time. They appeared in France, England, Germany, Holland and Italy. These should not be confused with the publications which featured caricatures of fashion and were for amusement only. The outstanding publication of the end of the century was the *Gallery of Fashion*, begun by Niklaus Wilhelm von Heideloff in 1794, a German

---

* The more important fashion journals of the later eighteenth century are given in *Hand-Coloured Fashion Plates* by Vyvyan Holland, Batsford, 1955 and *Fashion Through Fashion Plates* by Doris Langley Moore, Ward Lock, 1971.

669 c.1789   **670** 1788   **671** 1785–7   **672** 1789–90

673 c.*1797* **674, 675** *1795* **676** c.*1797* **677** *1790–5*

from Stuttgart who had worked for Ackermann, the bookseller and publisher of quality prints. The *Gallery of Fashion* was a superb production on fine quarto-sized paper; its annual subscription was three guineas though it only issued some twenty plates a year. The plates, issued monthly, had two or three figures and accessories on each, with descriptions of the garments. Though in plate form, they were still a record of existing modes, not future designs.

France

French fashions were worn all over Europe during most of the eighteenth century. Even countries and principalities which, hitherto, had shown especially independent and indigenous trends, succumbed to the French mode. From Spain to Russia, from Sweden to Italy, all fashionable men and women followed the French expression of taste in dress. There were a number of reasons for this spread of French influence. The trends in costume were only part of the universality of French culture abroad. The cultured classes spoke French, emulated French art and architecture and were spellbound by the court and aristocracy of France. Undoubtedly also, French silks, embroideries, coiffures and dressmaking were the finest in Europe. The trades and professions essential to *la mode* were built up in France and outstanding names began to become famous outside the borders of France in such work as millinery, dressmaking, tailoring, textile designing, haberdashery and wig making. The quality of craftsmanship produced by these leaders of fashion professions was superb and was emulated everywhere.

In the years before 1789 beautiful luxury textiles were made and worn – satins, silks, taffetas, velvets – embroidered, painted, printed and enriched by gold and silver thread and lace, plumes, ribbons, ruffles and fur. Fabrics could

Details, 18th century

678 *French, 1778*

679 *Madame Sériziat, 1795*

680 *Spanish Calèche*

681 *Italian, c.1740*

682 *French, 1750*

683 *French, 1780*

684 *French, 1785*

685, 686, 687 *Spanish footwear*

688 *Italian*

689 *Italian, 1770*

690 *French, 1776*

691 *French*

692 *Italian*

be plain or striped; they were often patterned in floral motifs, either in dainty sprigs or larger flowered designs. It was, by now, the women who wore the most elegant, beautiful clothes and, in France, it was the women in Court and Society life who had most influence. From Madame de Pompadour downwards the great courtesans of the day led the mode. Designers and craftsmen worked especially for them so that they would display, and so popularise, their designs.

There were four main phases in French eighteenth century dress, seen clearly in feminine fashions. The last years of Louis XIV up to 1715 and those of the Regency which followed saw a relaxation in the Baroque boldness and formality of the Versailles Court which Louis XIV had held in the later seventeenth century. Styles became gentler, softer, delicate and in light shades. Oriental influences were introduced in Chinese fabric designs. From 1725–50 the Rococo fashions of Louis XV were paramount. As in furniture and interior decoration, the motifs of shells, flowers, ribbons and plumes were dominant. The ensemble worn by both sexes displayed elegant curves and curls.

The years after 1750 led to more extreme styles,

artificial silhouettes and dignified, more solemn modes. Towards 1785 there was a simplification and divergence towards English fashions which presaged the total reversal of the mode after 1789.

Fashion was led in France now by a wealthy aristocracy, rather than the numerically smaller Court. Clothes and whole outfits were changed many times a day, as different ensembles were worn for different functions and hours. There were toilettes for riding, walking, dining, relaxing at home, entertaining, theatre, parties, balls and, simply, morning, afternoon and evening. Ladies relaxed in a comfortable negligée in the privacy of their homes, shedding gratefully their petticoats, corsets and hoops.

During the century egalitarianism in dress illustrated the rising importance of the professional and middle class in France. The bourgeoisie now adopted the mode to their own tastes and pockets so that two styles evolved: the Court and the aristocracy on the one hand and the bourgeoisie on the other. By the 1780s the latter were becoming the more important faction. Their dress reflected their increasing stature and it began, in its turn, to influence that of the Court.

Men's Dress 1700–1789

By 1700 the *habit à la française* had become the accepted attire for gentlemen all over Europe. This was a suit comprising coat, waistcoat and breeches. The same three garments were worn till the end of the century and, though the silhouette changed slowly, almost imperceptibly, the process was continuous. The trend was towards a slenderer, plainer, dignified streamlined effect. Fabrics became darker and less richly ornamented and there was a tendency towards making the coat and breeches of one fabric.

The *coat*, the *justaucorps* of the previous century, kept its flared skirts until about 1720. After this the skirt was arranged in a fan of pleats radiating from each hip seam. This fan-like spreading at the hip was the masculine interpretation of the feminine panier skirt. To maintain the desired shape, whalebone was inserted in the coat seam and buckram in the lining for stiffening. The coat was still collarless to accommodate the full wig; sleeves were fairly full and ended in enormous cuffs. These buttoned cuffs, the pocket flaps and the front buttoned edges were beautifully embroidered in coloured silks. The garment itself was made from velvet, silk or satin in gay, rich colours. Gold frogging and passementerie were common forms of coat decoration. The coat was knee-length and worn open or buttoned only at the waist. The centre back of the coat skirt was always slit, originally for ease in riding (**661, 693B, H, 694A, D, 701, 704, 707, 712A, D, 715A, 722, 726, 732D, F, 735**).

Towards 1760 the coat skirt lost its fullness; it was always worn open and the front skirt edges sloped to the rear. Sleeves became narrow and cuffs and pockets diminished. The front edge buttoning, formerly extending the full length of the coat, now finished at hip-level (**662, 713B, 714E, 715B, 721B, E, 734**). By the later 1770s, the garment had become still slenderer. A small collar and revers had developed, since the wig was now neatly tied back away from the neck. Ornamentation was restrained and fabrics more often of wool rather than silk and satin, though velvet was still popular. Striped materials were fashionable (**669**). The simpler English styles strongly influenced French male fashion in the 1780s. An example is the *frac* (fraque), the French version of the frock coat. This was a less formal garment than the *habit** and was quite plain; it had no pockets or cuffs but a flat collar.

The undercoat or *waistcoat* (*gilet* in France) was the most decorative garment of the suit. For

---

* This term, at the beginning of the century, was used to describe the whole suit of three garments. Later it was applied to the coat only.

694 The Palladian Bridge in the Garden. English Costume, 1730–50

the first half of the century it was made of brocade or other rich fabric, patterned all over with coloured silk embroidery or gold or silver thread; the unseen back was of more plebeian material. It followed the same design as the coat but was about six inches shorter and had long, fitting sleeves (**661, 701, 703, 713B, 722, 726, 732D, 734**). After the mid-century it became sleeveless (in conjunction with the more fitting sleeves of the coat), and gradually grew shorter (**662, 668B, E, 695A, 697, 703, 708, 713D, 715B, D, 721B**). After 1785 waistcoats were cut straight across at waist-level and sometimes had revers. The material was now plainer (**669**).

Breeches changed little in style all century. They were fitting and, in the early decades, were closed vertically with buttons. After 1730 the closure was by a panel with horizontal buttoning, similar to the Alpine trousers still worn today. In France these were called *culottes à la Bavaroise*. The garment reached to below the knee and was fastened there by a buckle or buttons. In the later eighteenth century, when waistcoats became short, the breeches reached higher and were supported by braces over the shoulder. Silk or cotton *stockings* were worn with the breeches; these were white or in light colours (**661, 662, 668B, E, 669**).

For outdoor wear in cold weather various capes and coats were worn. Early in the century long capes were fashionable but after mid-century the *redingote* was more usual. This was adapted from the English 'riding coat', which had been in common use there from the 1720s.* By 1750, in France, it was a fitted, double-breasted long coat with collar and shoulder capes. As the century advanced the redingote became shorter and less voluminous and was fashionable at all seasons; single-breasted versions appeared.

Women's Dress 1700–1750

For much of the eighteenth century feminine fashion was dictated by the hoop skirt and the corset. The silhouette was, as in the sixteenth century, an unnatural one. It must have been constricting and uncomfortable to wear but this,

---

* A similar coat had been worn in France by coachmen in the seventeenth century.

as in the sixteenth and, later, in the nineteenth century, did not deter the ladies from wearing it. The silhouette was an attractive one, it was feminine and, the more beautiful the natural figure, the better would appear the ensemble. This was sufficient to ensure the continuity of the style.

The construction and design of the corsets and hoops employed in the costume of these years is described on pages 191, 192. The *gowns* worn on top of these frameworks, changed considerably during the first fifty years of the century. For the first decade styles remained much as they had been in the late seventeenth century. The neckline was low and square, edged with a frill. The bodice was fitting, pointed in front, constricted and a decorative stomacher covered the centre front. Sleeves were three-quarter length, ending in lace flounces. The overskirt was looped back and up at the sides to display the elegant underskirt (**658, 723**). Such a style was worn over a hoop, circular in section. This fashion had developed in England early in the century and

there the framework had a greater circumference (**693A, C**).

In France the hoop came in about 1718. The style of gown worn over it was then quite different. It was the *contouche* or *sacque* (sack) *gown*, which had evolved from the house dress worn at home for relaxation a few years earlier. This had a fitted waist in front but flowed loosely over an immense hoop at back and sides. The neckline was low and wide with ribbon bows down the centre front. Such hooped skirts in France were called *paniers*. Sleeves were elbow-length in pagoda style (**659, 693G**). From this, about 1720–30, evolved the *robe à la française* or the so-called Watteau gown.* In this, the front of the bodice was still fitting, over a stomacher or *échelle* of ribbon bows, while the back was designed in large box pleats (Watteau pleats), which extended from neckline to hem (**660, 694C, H, 714D**). The sleeves ended in a cuff at the elbow,

---

* This appears to be a mis-nomer because the gowns depicted by the painter Watteau are not of this type and are, in general, fashions of the earlier years of the century.

696 *1788–90*   **697** c.*1775*   **698** *1783*   **699** *1792*

700 *English, 1764–7*   **701** *English, c.1755*   **702** *Dutch, 1750–60*   **703** *Dutch, c.1770*

below which depended the lace flounces of the chemise. These gowns went by various names: *robes volantes, robes battantes* etc.

Towards mid-century the silhouette changed and the circular hoop form developed into an elliptical one, flatter at front and back and wider at the sides. The *robe à la française,* with its 'Watteau pleats', continued to be worn (**666, 667**), though also fashionable, especially outside France, was the English mode for fitted waist with panier skirt (**694B, G, 732A, E**).

Differing styled garments for times of day and specific functions were available and ladies changed their clothes many times a day. Negligées of various types evolved for 'comfort' use when women could lay aside corsets and hoops and relax. Jackets and capes accompanied such gowns.

Fabrics were varied, mostly light and dainty. Popular were taffeta, satin, damask, corded silk, lawn and lace. Materials were striped or plain or with dainty floral patterns, mostly in pastel shades. Decoration was by lace, ribbons, flowers and flounces.

A vital characteristic of eighteenth century feminine dress is the movement and method of wearing which was dictated by the panier skirt. The earlier styles of large circumference circular hoops lent a lilting, gentle motion to the skirt as the lady walked. It was a flowing movement, feminine and provocative. The mid-century panier with its extreme width instilled a different motion. Here the lady had to turn sideways to negotiate a doorway or enter a sedan chair. With the later articulated panier she would sweep up the skirt with her elbows or hands. Her arms were restricted to her sides and she could only move the forearm over the width of the panier. A whole etiquette evolved from the deployment of the fan within these limitations. The results were coquettishly feminine.

Women's Dress 1750–1780

During these years the *robe à la française* became more constricted by the corset and side paniers. The waist was acutely slenderised, and the gown designed to accentuate this with a curving full bosom above. The waist line was higher and less pointed in front. The décolleté neckline was edged by lace flouncing or a soft fichu. Often the overskirt was looped up and back to fall in a train; the shorter underskirt displayed a dainty toe. The gown was made of satin, silk, taffeta, velvet or brocade. Motifs were small and dainty, colours were pastel. In the 1770s decoration was lavish, in the form of festoons of flowers, flounces, ribbon bows and loops and quantities of lace and tulle (**668D, 695C, D, 702, 706, 713A, C, 720B, D, 721C, D, 737F, G, 740**).

By 1775 the *robe à la française*, with its pleated back, was reserved for Court dress and formal wear. The side paniers extended widely and the corseting was strict. Other forms of gown took its place for more normal wear. In France in the 1770s there were several alternative styles. Most of these were due to Oriental or eastern European influences and were French derivations based on what was thought to have been worn in these

regions. The most popular was the *robe à la polonaise*,* worn from about 1773–85. It was tight-bodiced and very waisted, while the overskirt was drawn up by inside cords to make three draped swags of material worn over three paniers. The swags were edged with pleating or flouncing and decorated by ribbon bows, the back one being longer than the side drapes. The underskirt was also flounced and ruffled and was short enough to clear the ground all round and display the shoes (**668A**). Other styles included the *robe à la circassienne, à la levité, à la levantine* and *à la turque*. These were variations on the theme, with differing sleeve styles, overskirts drawn up in several loops all round the underskirt, back pleated designs and those with jacket tops ending in a peplum (**713E, 737E**).

Also in the 1770s the English gown styles were being worn more and more in Europe. These were much simpler and less restrictive than the French fashions and by 1775 French ladies also

* Not worn in Poland.

704 *1720–30*   **705** *c.1775*   **706** *1750*   **707** *1740–5*

Holland

708, 709 *1780–90*   **710** c.*1790*   **711** *1785–95*

were succumbing to their attraction. By 1780 the elegance and beauty of these classic styles become so attractive that the desire to wear them developed into an Anglomania in France, where English men's fashions had been the mode for some years already. The *robe à l'anglaise* had a fitted bodice but with a higher, less restricted waist than French gowns. It had a full, long skirt, sometimes open in front to show the underskirt but both were fairly plain with only a hem flounce. Sleeves were fitting and the décolleté neckline was edged by a soft, white fichu. In the 1780s this was very full, to accentuate a high breast line. This was the pouter pigeon silhouette (**696, 700, 721A, F**).

Women's Dress 1780–1789

In France these years were a transitional time between the lavish ornamentation and extreme, artificial styles of the 1770s and the no less cataclysmic upheaval in fashion which resulted from the Revolution. The trend accelerated rapidly away from constriction, artificial silhouettes and over-decoration towards simpler,

yet elegantly feminine modes. The English fashions were the prime influence. Variations upon the *robe à l'anglaise* were worn, their wearers sensing these fashions to be in tune with the Rousseau inspired 'naturalism' now prevalent in France. There were several styles of gown, all fairly high-waisted and décolleté, with bouffant fichus at the neckline and with long, fitted sleeves. Some designs had a waist-length jacket and others were coat dresses on redingote pattern. The skirts were full, more slender than previously and often had trains (**670, 671, 698, 711**).

With the trend towards simpler gowns, the selection of fabrics in fashion changed also. The heavy satins and velvets gave place to lighter materials such as muslin, gauze, cambric and linen. White or light colours were fashionable and patterns were sprig or spot type or restricted to a border hem. These lighter fabrics were given an added popularity by the 'naturalist cult'. Queen Marie Antoinette's enjoyment at 'playing milkmaid' led to further simulated bucolic pleasures by the aristocracy. Such fabrics were considered suitable for 'peasantry' attire and were used also for caps and aprons to complete the ensemble. A specific style called the *chemise à la reine* was based on a gown worn by the queen. This had a low neck edged by a ruffle, a sash at the waist and a simple, full skirt with hem flounce.

Underwear, Hoops and Corsetry

Underwear had hardly altered: the chemise, drawers and fine linen petticoats were still worn. The linen was barely visible for much of the eighteenth century; only a frill or ruffle at the neckline and ruffles at the sleeve could be seen. From the late 1770s the soft linen or cambric white fichu decorated the neckline. This grew larger and fuller in the 1780s in bouffant styles.

The eighteenth century *corset* evolved from the seventeenth century bodice. Its aim was to slenderise the waist and give a concave silhouette to the chest, raising the breasts to fullness. It was open at the back and laced across. It was made from two layers of heavy linen, stiffened with paste or glue and reinforced by whalebone in the seams. Tabs at the waistline spread out over the hips. The corset was covered with the gown

bodice material and sleeves were attached. The centre front of this, with the separate stomacher attached on top, was worn outside the skirt. The underskirt was then connected by hooks to loops in the corset waist. Towards mid-century the corset became slenderer and with a greater number of whalebone strips inserted into it. The extensive demand for whalebone at this time led to a boom in the industry. New companies were formed to satisfy fashion needs. The corset was worn until the 1780s (**973**).

With the fuller skirts of the early years of the century, heavy petticoats were needed to give a rounded shape. These were stiffened with paste and, in France, called *criardes* (screaming, clamorous) because of the noisy rustling which they emitted in movement. Soon whaleboned petticoats became necessary to support the immense skirt fabric weight. The mode came from England where such petticoats had been worn from 1709–10. They were circular in section, like a dome and, despite masculine mocking and caricaturisation, grew steadily in dimension until about 1750. In

A   B   C   D   E

England this hoop petticoat was called an 'improver', in France it was a *panier* (basket). Several hoops of whalebone were inserted in a petticoat of rich, heavy fabric and vertical whalebones were added to maintain the shape (**975**).

From about 1730 in France the circular section changed to an oval, with the greater width at the sides. By 1750 the sides were excessively wide and the front and back considerably flattened (**977**). It was then necessary to turn sideways to pass through a doorway and was difficult to sit in a chair despite furniture designed with extra width for the purpose. A new type of panier was evolved which consisted of several cane or whalebone hoops, not inserted in a petticoat but strung together by tapes. It was tied on at the waist in similar manner and was thus an articulated panier (**976**). In order to negotiate an entrance a lady

need only lift the skirt upwards by placing her elbows under the paniers and this would reduce the width sufficiently for passage. The system was equally useful for seating oneself in a chair or entering a sedan. Soon pockets and slits in the skirt enabled the wearer to slip her hands inside to raise the paniers.

In the 1770s polonaise and similar gowns had three or more small paniers. By 1780 the fullness of the skirt was concentrated at the back and a bustle was worn. This was a pad, which rested on the buttocks, tied on round the waist.

Ladies' Outdoor Wear

For most of the century ladies wore *scarves* and *capes* according to season, since these were best suited to covering panier skirts. In summer they were made of lace, silk or tulle and were shoulder or waist-length. Warmer winter wear would be of velvet, fur-edged and lined and would be three-quarter or full-length and having front fastenings. From 1770 the *pelisse* became fashionable. Probably of eastern origin, it was of velvet or satin and was lined and edged with fur. Neither a scarf nor cape, it had a large square collar and slits for the arms (**668C**). After 1775 waist-length *jackets* of various styles were fashionable with the *robe à l'anglaise* (**696, 713E**).

Men's Dress: Linen, Coiffure, Hats

The seventeenth century *cravat* was replaced towards 1720 by the folded *stock*. Made of white silk or muslin, this was a pleated band of material worn round the neck and fastened at the back. A finely pleated or lace-edged jabot was attached which frothed on the chest in the opening of the waistcoat. The *solitaire*, a black ribbon attached to the wig bow, often encircled the neck on top of the stock. It could be knotted or finished in a bow in front (**661, 662, 681, 692, 746, 751**).

Men wore *wigs* for most of the eighteenth century and for much of this time wigs were powdered white or grey. The long, full-bottomed *periwig* continued in fashion for about a decade after 1700 (**704, 715A, 722, 726, 745**). As always, the younger men adopted the new style first and the older generation clung to earlier fashions. So, after about 1710, younger men were tying back the curls of the periwig with a black ribbon into a bow. At the same time the wig itself was worn much smaller and the peaks on each side of the parting had gone. Soon the parting was abandoned and the wig combed back in soft waves on top and on the temples. These waves or soft curls at the temples were called 'pigeon's

A   B   C   D   E

A   B   C   D   E

wings' and the style of wig a *tie wig* (**661, 692, 693H, 694A, 712A**). Towards mid-century the back hair was dressed in a black silk bag, the *bag wig* (**707, 713B, 721E, 732D, 734, 735**), and soon the 'pigeon's wings' were replaced by horizontal curls. At first there were three curls, one above the other, then two and finally only one (**662, 668B, 669, 697, 701, 708, 713D, 714A, 715B, 721B, 746**).

In the 1750s the *catogan* (cadogan) *wig* became popular. In this the back hair was looped under and tied with black ribbon (**720E**). With both this style and the bag wig the solitaire was worn. Alternative ways of depressing the back hair were in different types of pig-tail, in one, two or three, either encased in black silk or merely tied in a ribbon bow at either end of the tail. In the 1770s, when women were wearing excessively high coiffures, men also, for a short time, wore their wigs combed up high in front (**695A**). The last phase in the fashion for wigs was the hedgehog (*à l'hérisson*), which was worn in the 1780s.

In this the hair was cut raggedly all over so that the ends stuck out like hedgehog quills. The back hair was dressed as before (**672**). After 1760 men had more and more reverted to wearing their own hair, powdered, in wig styles. After 1785 most men returned to natural hair, unpowdered, and worn fairly short and simply coiffured (**674, 728**).

The wearing of wigs, which had been continuous since the 1660s, had permanently changed the custom of wearing *hats*. Previous to 1660, men had worn hats all the time, indoors and even at table. The large periwigs had rendered the wearing of a hat superfluous and men usually carried their hat under their arm except in inclement weather. With the smaller wigs of the eighteenth century this custom still continued because of the wig powder and because the wearing of a hat would disarrange the side curls. Until the 1770s the eighteenth century hat was still the *tricorne*, made of black felt and trimmed with gold braid and/or white ostrich tips. It continued to be large while large wigs were worn (**681, 704, 722, 726**), but as the wigs became smaller, so did the tricorne (**693H, 713B, D, 714E, 715D, 721E, 732D, 734**).

In the last third of the century several styles of hat became fashionable. First to appear was the *bicorne*, the two-pointed felt hat, based on the Swiss military style (**669, 699**). In the 1780s, with the return to natural hair styles or smaller hedgehog wigs, hats were worn much more commonly again, though men never returned to the universal wearing of hats on all occasions as before. Certainly never again did they keep their heads covered indoors in the presence of a lady. The late century hats were generally round, tall-crowned styles which originated in England. They were made of felt, beaver or fur and had ribbon and buckle decoration. Alternative styles were lower, with rolling brims (**672, 674, 710**).

Women's Dress: Hair and Hats

Coiffure fashions for women moved in the reverse direction from those of the men. While men had worn the large periwigs in the later seventeenth century and early eighteenth and their wig styles had gradually diminished until they returned to natural hair in the 1780s, women did not wear artificial hair at all until mid-century but gradually adopted larger coiffures after this to reach a climax of absurdity in size and overdecoration in the 1770s, returning to natural hair at the same time as the men.

The high *coiffure* with natural curls and the lace fontange continued in fashion for a few years in the eighteenth century (**723, 724, 752**). Soon the fontange vanished and for nearly 50 years women wore their hair simply and neatly. In the 1720s and 1730s it was fairly short and dressed plainly back from the forehead and in simple curls at the back. Flowers, ribbon bows and dainty, white, be-ribboned caps with lappets were perched on top of the head (**659, 660, 693A, G, 694G, H**). Towards mid-century the hair was dressed in side curls and was swept up off the forehead, sometimes over a pad to lift it higher. For evening or formal wear false ringlets were

716 *French Swiss, 1770–80*   **717, 718** *Czech, 1748*   **719** *French Swiss, 1770–80*

Switzerland and Czechoslovakia

195

A   B   C   D   E   F

added and flowers and plumes decorated the coiffure (**666, 667**).

From 1750 onwards the small neat coiffure disappeared. The hair was dressed with pomatum and powdered white.* The coiffure grew larger and from 1760 increased in height, either by means of wearing a wig or by placing pads under the natural hair and dressing it over them. In the 1770s coiffure styles reached extremes. A tremendous height was achieved with pads and false hair. The coiffure was decorated by pearl ropes, ribbons, plumes and flowers. Ringlets fell over the shoulders and bosom and the back hair was dressed in a chignon or cadogan; at the sides were enormous sausage curls. Extremes of style were reached by the aristocracy especially for formal balls and functions. Such complex coiffures could not be dressed by the wearer or even the ladies' maids. A competent hairdresser was needed in attendance and the profession became a valued one, its members well-to-do with high salaries. Such hairdressers would spend several hours on a single head. Before an important function a day or more of work were needed and the wearer could not sleep properly until the ball was over for fear of damaging the costly erection. Coiffures reached absurd heights and decorative means as each wearer tried to outdo her rivals with baskets of fruit and models of windmills or battleships included in the coiffure. Such 'heads' were left untouched for several weeks between hairdressers' visits. The constant application of pomatum and rice or wheat powder led to their becoming verminous with consequent discomfort. How our ancestors of 200 years ago would

---

* The sticky pomatum and the powder on top held the coiffure in place. This was the eighteenth century equivalent of hair lacquer.

have appreciated the invention of hair lacquer sprays (**668A, C, D, 688, 690, 695B, 742, 754**).

After 1780 feminine hair styles followed the same pattern as the men's. Hedgehog wigs were fashionable (**670, 671, 744**) and then in the 1790s neat small heads with natural curls returned (**673, 676**).

Women wore *caps* during the whole of the eighteenth century. In the early decades these were tiny, only covering the top of the head but they became larger by mid-century. They were generally white, had a flounced or lace edge and were decorated by ribbons and flowers (**659, 660, 712B, E, 732A, E**). After 1750, as the coiffure

grew larger, so did the caps. By 1770 these were as varied in style as the coiffures and equally vast. They were complex and extravagant, being finished with pleating and ruching, flounces, plumes, flowers and large ribbon bows (**668C, 670, 684, 691, 743**).

Also in the 1770s *hats* became fashionable. These were introduced from England where many styles were available. Some were small and dainty, of straw or silk, perched at an extreme angle on the coiffure and decorated by plumes and ribbons (**668A, 678, 690, 700, 721A**). In the 1780s very large hats were worn, also of English origin. These had a wealth of ribbon, plume and

A   B   C   D   E   F

721 Palace of La Granja. Spanish Costume, 1750–70

722 *Italian, 1718–20*   **723** *Italian, 1700–10* **724** *Italian, 1700–5*

725 *Spanish, c.1720*

726 *Spanish, c.1710*

flower trimming (**671, 694B, 713E, 744**). Most useful as outdoor protection for the high coiffure styles of the years 1773–83 was the calèche or cabriolet (in England, calash). This was a large, articulated hood made as a hooped frame covered in ruched and padded silk. This could be pulled up or folded down, as required, over the coiffure in the manner of a carriage or perambulator hood. It was tied with a ribbon bow under the chin (**680, 747**).

Footwear

For much of the eighteenth century, *men* preferred to wear *shoes* rather than boots. These were generally of black leather with fairly low heels. The square toes of the seventeenth century soon gave way to a natural rounded shape and upstanding tongues and buckles became much smaller (**661, 668B, E, 669, 693B, H, 695A, E, 697, 701, 703, 704, 708, 712A, D, 713B, D, 748, 749**). In the later eighteenth century *boots* became fashionable again. These were in varied

styles but, in general, were in leather, well fitting and with neat turned down cuffs. Like the hats, boot styles came from England (**674, 707**). Shoe styles of the last 20 years of the century were cut lower and were almost heel-less. They resembled slippers and were decorated only by a neat bow. (**672, 677, 710, 728**).

Until 1775 *women's shoes* were high heeled with curving elegant heels; the toe was pointed. Shoes were made of many different materials: kid, satin, brocade, velvet. They were richly embroidered and decorated by gold and silver braid, ribbon ties, lace, ruching and jewelled buckles. High heeled mules and slippers were also worn. Shoes were often made to match or blend with the gown and, in the 1760s and 1770s, were frequently visible, with the wearing of the shorter skirts of the time. *Stockings* were coloured, either to match the gown or in red, pastel shades or white (**659, 668C, 682, 683, 686, 687, 713E, 732E, 753**). After the Revolution heel-less slippers, tied on with ribbons, were fashionable.

Accessories

These were numerous and similar to those described for the seventeenth century. *Men* carried *canes*, wore *swords* (at least until 1780) and carried lace-edged *handkerchiefs, gloves* and *fur muffs* (**672, 674, 677, 693B, 694A, 704, 708, 741**). The *snuff box* was a prized eighteenth century article and some were of beautiful workmanship in gold, enamelwork and ceramic (**699**). Many museums have fine collections. *Watches*, still costly, were now more frequently owned. Late in the century they were worn in pairs as fobs below the waistcoat. Sometimes one was real, the pair a dummy. Alternatively they were set into buttons in the waistcoat. In the 1790s steel became more fashionable than precious metals. Buttons and buckles were often of this material and were set with jewels. A German jeweller invented a paste to reproduce genuine jewellery. Quantities of paste jewellery were made. In France the reigns of Louis XV and XVI were the 'golden age of paste'. Both men and women wore such jewellery. They also wore tiny bouquets of artificial flowers.

Women used *cosmetics* freely. They applied paint and powder but more knowledgeably than before. Face patches were still used widely. Perfume was generously applied. Clothes and personal articles were scented. Ladies carried exquisite perfume cases and even wore rings which held scent. In an age when clothes were costly, dry cleaning not available and their coiffures 'opened up' too infrequently, such aids were more than necessary. The eighteenth century was not, like the sixteenth, an age of jewellery. Decoration was by lace, ruching, ribbons and flounces. The décolleté necklines demanded ornamentation and this was provided by the collarette of ribbons and lace encircling the throat (**667, 715E, 720B, D, 737G, 743**). Later in the century a black ribbon with central locket or jewel was popular (**689, 698, 702, 709, 714C, 744**).

The most typical feminine eighteenth century accessory was the folding *fan*. Many of these were exquisitely made and very costly. Sticks could be of ivory, tortoiseshell, mother-of-pearl, gold or

727 *Spanish, 1799* **728** *Spanish, 1795* **729** *Italian, 1790* **730** *Italian, 1798* **731** *Spanish, 1798*

Italy and Spain

199

A   B   C   D   E   F

silver. Stretched over these, the fan could be made from painted vellum, kid or satin. The art of the fan was important to every lady; it was carried and used coquettishly, provocatively, admonishingly, invitingly as required (**659, 660, 668A, 673, 688, 694B, 695D, 705, 714C, D, 715E, 720D, F, 721C, D, 727, 737C, F**). Women also carried beautiful *handkerchiefs*, be-ribboned *canes*, *muffs* and *parasols*, which did not close (**668C, 671, 696, 698, 702, 706, 711, 732E**). Long *gloves* were worn throughout the eighteenth century but more especially after 1785 when sleeves were short and ruffles had been abandoned. They were in light colours, of kid or silk (**670, 733**). Small *bags* and purses were also carried but, again, these were more fashionable at the end of the century

when skirts were less full and pockets not so suitable. Such purses or reticules had handles to be hung over the arm. They were made of silk or velvet and richly embroidered. Some were beaded or fringed (**673, 676, 694H, 695B, 713C**). Posies of real *flowers* were still fashionable. These were kept fresh by being worn at the corsage in a tiny flask full of water. A pocket was designed especially to hold this in the top of the corset.

French Costume 1789–1800

The dress of these few years is discussed separately because the cataclysmic events of the French Revolution of 1789, the Reign of Terror, the succeeding Directoire and Empire were naturally reflected in the styles of clothes which people wore. This resulted in quickly changing fashions as one influence succeeded another and as the French people attempted to adapt themselves to fast moving events. Outside France costume developed more slowly. Fashions moved steadily away from the artificial silhouette and over-decoration of the 1770s to a freer, more natural mode. The Revolution in France affected dress elsewhere too but less so than in its country of origin. The general trend towards a social equality expressed in dress, a diminution of privilege and a greater severity in masculine attire continued uninterruptedly, but it was around 1800 before Paris fully reasserted itself as the centre of the fashion world. In the meantime, England was the central influence on dress.

In France itself, the changes of style were abrupt and acute. In the early years of the Revolution people dared not wear items of dress associated with the former aristocracy: powdered wigs, paniers or bustles, breeches or any rich decorative fabrics and ornamentation. In men's attire, breeches and stockings were automatically linked

to Court dress and a longer pantaloon or trouser was worn in conjunction with a long sock. The aristocracy contemptuously referred to the wearers of such garments as *sans-culottes*, literally, without breeches. The name stuck but most people deemed it safer, at least for a while, to go along with the theme.

The early years of the 1790s had a permanent effect on men's dress in Europe. The influence of Society on dress was replaced by the political assembly. Its members wore black; austere and plain. After a few years, colours returned and, under Napoleon, luxury and culottes returned to Court, but men's dress never again (until the young of the present day) was to be seen in bright colours, rich fabrics and with jewellery, lace, ribbon and embroidered decoration. Certainly the effect of the Revolution was greater on men's dress than women's. Women are always greater individualists and less likely to follow a cause. For them, femininity, their attractiveness to men is more important than the movement towards social equality or freedom for political action and loyalty to husband and family stronger than that

733 c.*1797*   **734** *1750*   **735** *1743*   **736** *1750*

A B C D E F G

towards the nation. They joyfully abandoned the shackles of corset and panier and wore diaphanous, décolleté garments, freed of layers of petticoats at last. Their only contribution towards the political themes of the day was to adopt what the French of 1790 thought to be the costume of the Ancient Greeks. This, the original 'democracy' was thought to represent the political ideal. This cult of the antique led especially to Greek decoration on garment hems, for instance, the key or fret design, and to classical hair styles. Apart from this, it is difficult to discern any other similarities with the dress of the Ancient Greeks.

In the early years of the Revolution it was considered fashionable to dress in accord with the new democratic movement of liberty. One's clothes should be simple, unadorned and, in the case of women, so few and of such thin material as to be almost transparent. Such styles were patently unsuited to either the climate of northern and central France or the figures of most of the population. The vogue faded quickly in favour of a generally simplified costume.

After the execution of the king in January 1793

there were several attempts to design a costume suitable for everyone. These styles were designed by the intelligentsia, chiefly painters such as David and were based upon a labourer's normal attire or upon classical dress. They were neither genuine in the sense of being a practical worker's outfit, nor attractive or sensible costumes for wear by the average man or woman. There was a musical comedy air of unreality about them. One style had loose trousers and a short jacket called a carmagnole,* a red cap and sabots. Another was a long Greek chiton with himation and a soft woollen cap with decorative band. A third had had a knee-length belted chiton, fitted trousers tucked inside short boots, a round cap and a cloak. The feminine design was totally unfeminine and guaranteed to make most women look unattractive. It goes without saying that all attempts to make everybody dress alike were doomed to failure. The ideals of the designers were not in question; it was their understanding of human nature which was inadequate.

* Named after a garment worn by workers in Carmagnola, near Turin.

It was clear that such a dreary levelling down in dress could not be long maintained in a country so noted for the individuality of its people and one with an upper class so accustomed to a high standard of living. After the end of the Reign of Terror, in 1794, people wanted to forget, to relax and to enjoy stability of life once more. In the years of the Directoire (1795–99) fashion journals began to be published again and the various forms of patriotic dress were forgotten. The *sans-culottes* returned to normal men's fashions and only the young enthusiasts, the '*incroyables*', continued to assert their ideals by their mode of dress.

In general, the average *masculine attire* over the years 1789–1800 was for elegant, restrained garments, slenderly cut, fitting and without ostentatious decoration or colouring. The coat did not close but had steel buttons and frog fastenings. It had neat cut away tails. The waistcoat, cut straight across at waist level, contrasted in material with the coat; one of these was often

striped. Breeches or pantaloons were tight, stockings plain. Low-cut shoes or slippers or soft, fitting leather boots were worn. The hair was short and hats of bicorne or tall-crowned design (**669, 728**). An alternative coat style more common after 1790, was the double-breasted redingote with deep lapels and high collar. It was cut away square in front to show the waistcoat or was more of frock coat style with skirts (**674, 699, 710**). The dandy or elegant young man verging upon the '*incroyable*' cut his hair short and raggedly and wore his collar higher and lapels larger (**672, 677**).

In the late 1780s the *feminine* silhouette had already abandoned paniers and tight corseting, retaining only a soft belt and a small bustle. The gown was simple with full skirt and low neckline (**670, 671**). From 1789 fashions changed quickly in France. Cotton, muslin, tulle and gauze replaced velvet, silk and satin. Few garments were worn. The belt and bustle were abandoned. The gown waistline rose sharply to a line im-

738 *1796–7*　　　**739** *1780–5*　　　**740** *1750–60*　　　**741** *1710–20*

Russia

Details, 18th century

742 *Swedish, 1780*

743 *German, 1780*

744 *Mrs. Siddons, English, 1784*

745 *William Congreve, English, 1709*

746 *Dutch, c.1775*

747 *English Calèche*

748, 749 *Men's shoes, Danish, c.1700*

750 *Hungarian*

751 *German Prince, c.1760*

752 *German, c.1700*

753 *German, 1725–50*

754 *Queen Sophia Magdalena, Swedish, 1782*

mediately under the breasts. Simultaneously the neckline sank so that the gown bodice was only three to four inches deep, barely covering the breasts. These were delineated by ribbons or bands tied round just below them. Sometimes a jewelled metal band was worn here. The skirt fell long and loose from the high waistline without gathers or pleats in soft folds, generally to a train. The skirt itself was often slit up to the knee. Sleeves were usually short. Until 1797 garments became fewer and materials thinner and more transparent. Only one thin petticoat was worn (or none at all), a simple chemise, stockings sometimes or, more commonly, tights, as total underwear. Women shivered. To try to keep warm they wore a thin negligée-type overgown or a three-quarter length tunic on top of the gown and draped themselves with elegant cashmere or silk, narrow stoles. These varied greatly in colour, size and shape. Most were fringed or tasselled.

The thin fabrics were most often in white or very pale colours. They were plain or patterned with spots or tiny sprigs of embroidery. Gown hems were decorated only by fringe, embroidery or a narrow flounce. There were no pockets in such a limited costume so a *reticule* was carried. *Fans* were still in vogue and long *gloves* fashionable. *Jewellery* was worn in abundance but its designs were elegant and unostentatious. Classical themes were the vogue. Ballet type low-cut *slippers* covered the feet. These were often tied on round the ankle with ribbons. *Sandals*, of Greek design, were also fashionable and rings decorated the bare toes.

The *hair* was fairly short and simply and beautifully dressed in classical manner. The Greek chignon style was most fashionable. This had a fringe on the forehead and the hair was bound by ribbons or a metal fillet on the brow. The short, shaggy 'Titus' cut (Roman) was also popular. *Caps* and *hats* were fashionable. These changed styles with bewildering rapidity. There were toques with tall plumes, lofty-crowned hats like those of the men, straw hats tied on with ribbon bows and dainty, white caps. In winter, *muffs* were carried and *cloaks* with hoods worn or, alternatively, *redingotes* of cloth covered the scanty dresses (673, 676, 696, 711, 715E, 727, 730, 731, 733, 738).

As with masculine dress, 1789 was a watershed. In feminine fashion, designs looked backwards for the first time to an earlier mode, in this case,

to classical Greece, and, from this time onwards, fashions changed with much greater rapidity than ever before.

For most of the eighteenth century *children's costume* reflected that of their elders (658, 663, 664, 665, 693D, E, 694E, F, 712F, 724, 729, 732B, C, 737B). In the last 20 years of the century simpler designs of dress for children, originating from England, began to be made. Little boys wore sailor suits, comprised of short, open jackets over a shirt and long, loose trousers. Their hair was short and loose under straw hats. Little girls had muslin or cotton dresses over taffeta underskirts, tied with a sash at a high waistline. Their hair was combed naturally and tied with a ribbon or covered by a cap (675).

England

English fashions were closely modelled on the French until after 1775. There were minor differences before this, due partly to the high quality of the woollen cloth and cottons produced in England, which led to a greater use of these materials. Men's coats and breeches were sometimes of cloth at a time when a Frenchman would be dressed in velvet or satin. Also, in England, it was not unusual for a gentleman's coat, waistcoat and breeches to be of one material; this was rare in France. Similarly, in ladies' attire, cottons were seen often, much earlier in the century than they would be in France, where silk was in general use. All through the century English dress was a little less artificial and elaborate than the French equivalent style. In the 1760s and 1770s, when French ladies wore such vast wigs and caps to cover them, the English versions were less obtrusive (693, 694, 701, 745).

From about 1765–70 English fashions began to influence *masculine dress* all over Europe and English tailoring became de rigueur for wealthy men in all countries, France included. There was a group of young men who formed a club in London on their return from the Grand Tour and who dressed extravagantly. This was the Macaroni Club and the Macaronis, as they called themselves, wore a more extreme form of the masculine style of this period, which was from the late 1760s to about 1775. Their coats were slender and cut away in front to sloping tails, displaying an elegant, striped, short waistcoat and elaborate white linen. Their breeches were skin tight, with ribbon loops at the knee. They wore very high wigs with a tiny tricorne hat perched on top.

Such exaggerated dress was untypical. The average English gentleman of these years differed from his French colleague only in having a superbly cut suit, which was plainer, in less bright colours and most attractively slim. He chose from a greater variety of wigs but wore particularly the cadogan, the ramillie or pig-tail and he was seen in one of several different styles of overcoat. The ramillie wig, named after the Duke of Marlborough's battle of Ramillies, had hanging plaits, tied top and bottom with black ribbon; the pig-tail was similar, but the plaits were encased in black silk. The frock coat, the *frac* in France, was commonly worn in the 1780s and 1790s, while the most usual top coat was that with collar, shoulder capes and cuffs. This was fairly long and was made, alternatively, in cape form (**695A, E, F, 697, 699**).

Ladies' fashions followed closely upon the French mode until about 1775 (**693A, C, G, 694B, C, G, H, 695B, C, D, 747**). After this English dress became much simpler than its French equivalent. The *robe à l'anglaise* was much plainer than a French gown of 1775 (**700**) and, after 1780, became a specific style, not just a simpler version of the French. This style had a low neckline finished with a full, white fichu. The fichu was edged with flouncing or lace and gave the full bosom line known as the 'pouter pigeon' silhouette. The sleeves were fitting, as was also the bodice, though this was less rigidly corseted than in France. The skirt was gathered into the bodice and was full but not worn over paniers, only flounced petticoats and a small bustle. The fabrics from which these gowns were made were decorated with stripes or spots or just dainty sprig designs. Some had a simple hem flounce but many had no added ornamentation at all.

Ladies (like their menfolk) returned at a much earlier date than their French counterparts to natural hair styles. Hedgehog wigs were fashionable in the 1780s but many women wore their own hair powdered and in soft ringlets and curls. The most characteristic English feature was the hat. In the 1780s this had a very large brim, often sweeping, and the hat was decorated by tall plumes, flowers, lace and immense ribbon loops and bows. These hats were given different names; some were called Gainsborough, after the portrait

painter, some Marlborough, after one of his sitters (**696, 744**).

With the simpler gown styles of the 1780s, ladies often wore a fitted, waist-length jacket, double or single-breasted, with revers and a collar. A feminine version of the redingote was also worn. This had a similar bodice but was long and open in front to show the gown skirt.

Western and Central Europe

Well-to-do society closely followed French fashions except in the years 1780–95, when the English mode was dominant. The separate, national characteristics were noticeable in the wearing of the mode, the quantity of elaboration and luxury of materials as well as preferences for certain of the eighteenth century fashions.

In the *Low Countries* the traditional bourgeois mercantile population adopted French elegance like other countries (**702, 703, 704, 705, 706, 707, 708, 709, 710, 711, 746**).

In *Germany* the French fashion was pursued in a rich, luxurious manner. Ladies loved panier skirts and German hoops were larger than elsewhere, the gowns being more elaborately ornamented than even those of the French Court of the 1770s. Court etiquette was strict, on Spanish lines, and detailed regulations laid down which fabrics, colours and forms of decoration were permitted to be worn, according to the wearer's rank and station. The mode was always, however, French. Only in the north, in Prussia, was a different line taken. Here, Frederick the Great attempted to build up Prussia's textile industry and enforce the wearing of home produced fabrics. Foreign imports of luxury materials were forbidden. He was partially successful but, inevitably, French modes were followed by the wealthy (**712, 713, 743, 751, 752, 753**).

The same adherence to French fashion obtained in Switzerland and Austria. This was only in the chief towns of *Switzerland* and styles varied somewhat between the French and German speaking areas, with a natural close affiliation to Paris in French Switzerland. In such a mountainous country, outside the larger towns, local dress was retained (**714, 716, 719**). The *Viennese* Court also followed French fashion but Spanish influence was still strong. Under the Empress Maria Theresa, Austrian dress was more Baroque and less elegant than that of Paris. Panier skirts were especially large and wigs and embroidered *habits* more luxurious and formal (**715**). As in Germany, specific luxury in dress was permitted and regulated according to class and position. A closer affinity with French dress was noticeable after the marriage of the Empress' daughter, Marie Antoinette, to Louis XVI of France.

Central and Eastern Europe

Costume in *Czechoslovakia* closely followed the French mode (**717, 718**). In *Poland*, despite the feudality of the country, Society had whole-heartedly adopted the French culture. After 1750 French fashions were more widely worn than before, though in smaller, provincial towns, the aristocracy was still influenced by more eastern modes akin to those worn in Hungary.

Eighteenth century *Hungarian dress* was more influenced by western Europe than before. In *men's clothes*, where the Turkish styles had been worn for centuries, the French mode began to break through. In the first half of the century stylish men still wore the dolman and mente but the cut of these garments slowly changed. The dolman was fitting on the torso, longer waisted and had flaring skirts – a parallel to the French coat of the time (**720A**). The mente also became slenderer fitting and was shorter (**720C**). After this the dolman became sleeveless, influenced by the French waistcoat designs and, in the second half of the century, fashionable men abandoned these Hungarian garments, which they had kept to for so long, and adopted the *habit à la française* in its entirety. They wore satin, silk or velvet embroidered coats, brocade waistcoats, and silk breeches and stockings replaced their cloth trousers. At the same time they turned to wigs and tricorne hats instead of natural hair and fur-edged Hungarian hats (**720C**), as well as French styled shoes to replace Hungarian boots (**720E, 750**).

Feminine dress had been influenced by French fashion in the seventeenth century and the trend continued. Until about 1750–60 the Hungarian mode of laced-across bodice and bouffant, natural sleeves was still seen, the full skirt beautifully embroidered (**720F**). After this, the Hungarian nobility followed the current vogue (**720B, D**).

Southern Europe

In Spain, Portugal and Italy the French mode was followed by Society though national, and in Italy regional, differences were to be seen. *Spanish men* wore especially decorative large cravats and stocks and their garments were fitting, the coats tending to be shorter than in France. *Ladies* loved their Spanish shawls and mantillas; they wore beautiful, large, tortoiseshell combs in their dark hair and carried parasols against the hot sunshine (**680, 685, 686, 687, 721, 725, 726, 727, 728, 731**).

The climate also influenced the *Italian* version of French modes, particularly in Rome and Naples where temperatures were higher. Both men and women wore thinner fabrics than in France and in especially brilliant colours. Ornamentation was more elaborate and embroidery richer. Cotton materials were widely employed in the Venetian Republic; black was fashionable for many garments in the north-west part of the country. It was used for outer wear and for ladies' gowns (**681, 688, 689, 722, 723, 724, 729, 730, 732**).

Northern Europe

Despite the distance from Paris, *Scandinavia* enthusiastically adopted French culture and dress. Court dress showed a little Spanish influence in its especially wide paniers but, in general, French modes were worn by Society (**734, 735, 736, 737F, G, 742, 754**).

In the 1770s King Gustav III of Sweden introduced a *national style of dress* which he decreed should be worn by the Court, the nobility and the professional classes. This was an attempt to curtail, in Scandinavia, the excesses and luxury of the French modes of the time, to introduce a fashion suited to the northern climate and one which would patronise the home textile industry. The masculine style was to be based on early seventeenth century dress, but it became something of a mixture of past styles adapted to the later eighteenth century. It was, however, a specific mode which consisted of a straight jacket with a broad sash on top at the waist. Fitting breeches and stockings were worn, with ribbon rosettes at the knee. The shoes were of seventeenth century design but French types of current wig were worn. The cloak was simple and straight (**737A, D**).

The *ladies'* version of the *national dress* was, as can be imagined, closer to the current French modes. The most typical were polonaise or circassienne styles, though an early seventeenth century design of ruff or whisk was sometimes worn with the high, be-feathered coiffure (**737C, E**).

Denmark also introduced the Gustavian style and it was published in illustrated journals in other countries in western Europe. Though not an unqualified success, it was worn extensively during the lifetime of the king and achieved its purpose in curtailing the excessive extravagancies of the French dress of the 1770s, to be seen elsewhere. It also led to increased consumption of home-produced fabrics. Towards the end of the century Scandinavia reverted to the current European modes (**733**).

Russia was slower to adopt French fashion. In the first half of the century beautiful fabrics were worn by the nobility, silks of all kinds, finely embroidered and jewelled, but the styles of garments were influenced more by the east than by Paris. The fabrics themselves were imported from China, Persia and Turkey. From about 1730 fine silks were made in Russia and the Empress Elizabeth, who reigned 1741–62, began to import French clothes for herself and her Court. She had a passion for beautiful attire and, like England's Queen Elizabeth of the sixteenth century, left a wardrobe, when she died, full of thousands of luxurious gowns and accessories.

From mid-century the Russian nobility more and more adopted the French culture, its language, customs and dress. The Empress Catherine II tried more than once to introduce a simpler, national form of dress but, unlike King Gustav, she was unsuccessful. The Russian aristocracy, having at last been introduced to the elegance of western attire, were not going to abandon it so quickly (**738, 739, 740, 741**).

Notes on the Illustrations

658   Portrait of Mlle. de Béthisy by Alexis Belle, Palace of Versailles. Bright blue gown with floral pattern in orange, red, brown and black. Apron of white embroidered transparent gauze. Lace neck frill and sleeve ruffles. Hair powdered white, flower decoration, fan.

659 and 660   Painting by de Troy 'The Declaration of Love'. Staatliche Schlösser und Garten, West Berlin. 659 wears a sacque gown of ivory satin embroidered in cream silk. She wears a white lace collarette and sleeve ruffles and a white cap, lace-edged and trimmed with flowers and ribbon. 660 wears a similar gown, with pleated back in a deep blue brocade decorated with red and white flowers. Her tiny white cap has a pink ribbon bow.

661   Actual Costume, Musée du Costume de la Ville de Paris. Brown velvet coat and breeches with gold embroidery. Salmon coloured silk waistcoat embroidered all over in soft colours. White powdered tie wig with pigeon's wings. Black bow and solitaire. White stockings, black shoes.

662   Actual Costume. Musée du Costume de la Ville de Paris. Deep rose velvet coat and breeches embroidered in coloured silks in a floral design. Brocade waistcoat. White powdered bag wig and solitaire. White stock and jabot. White stockings, black shoes.

663   Duke of Burgundy as a small boy. Painting, Palace of Versailles painting gallery. Blue dress and hat with black fur trimming. White cap and sleeve ruffles. White hat plumes.

664   Portrait of the Count d'Artois by François Drouais, Louvre, Paris. The boy wears a grey silk coat with blue ribbon. He has dark breeches and black boots. His wig is powdered white.

665   Portrait by Nattier, Palace of Versailles. A cream satin gown with gold lace decoration. Cream lace apron, stomacher and sleeve ruffles. Natural hair with a flower.

666   Actual Costume, Boston Museum of Fine Arts, U.S.A. Robe à la Française of ribbed silk in cream, patterned in gold and crimson. White powdered hair with plumes, flowers and ribbons.

667   Actual Costume, Musée du Costume de la Ville de Paris. Cream faille gown in robe à la française style. Embroidered in strawberry design in coloured silks. Collarette. White powdered hair.

668A   Bibliothèque Nationale, Paris. Polonaise gown Decorative hat over cadogan style wig. 1781.

B   Actual Costume, Musée du Costume de la Ville de Paris. Plum coloured satin coat, waistcoat and breeches. Embroidered in colours in silk, floral design. Powdered wig. White stockings, black shoes, c.1781.

C   Drawing. Galerie des Modes et Costumes Français. Dark satin pelisse with fur edging and lining. White decorative cap, baigneuse style. Powdered wig. Satin shoes. 1778.

D   Portrait of Queen Marie Antoinette by Mme. Vigée-Lebrun. Palace of Versailles. White satin gown with gold decoration and tassels. White coiffure and plumes. c.1775.

E   Actual Costume, Musée du Costume de la Ville de Paris. Beige patterned velvet suit with coloured silk embroidered panel edging. White powdered wig. White stockings and black shoes. c.1770.

669   Actual Costume, Musée du Costume de la Ville de Paris. Striped faille coat in light and dark green. Steel buttons. Cadogan style white wig. Plain white breeches and stockings. Fawn waistcoat. Black shoes. Black bicorne hat with gold braid and lace.

670 Actual Costume, Victoria and Albert Museum, London. Cream silk gown embroidered in sprig and grass pattern with flowers. White fichu and sleeve ruffles. Powdered hedgehog wig. White lace and ribbon cap.

671 Actual Costume, Boston Museum of Fine Arts, U.S.A. Robe à l'Anglaise in striped satin in yellow and cerise. Decorative embroidered skirt border. White fichu. White hedgehog wig. Pink silk hat lined with cream silk. Decoration by white crown fabric and blue and yellow striped ribbon. Cane with tassels.

672 Actual Costume, Victoria and Albert Museum, London. Grey silk coat with buttons covered in material. White waistcoat embroidered in sprig pattern in colours. Fawn stockinette breeches. Striped stockings, black slippers. Powdered hedgehog wig. Cane. Fawn felt hat.

673 Actual Costume, Musée Historique des Tissus, Lyons, France. Mauve tulle dress with silk embroidery. White satin undergown with green silk chenille decoration. Reticule. Fan. Long white gloves. Silk turban with coloured plumes.

674 Portrait of Monsieur Sériziat by Jacques Louis David. Louvre, Paris. Black cloth coat with black silk collar and cuffs. White waistcoat and stock. Fawn breeches. Brown leather boots and gloves. Black felt hat with ribbon and metal buckle.

675 The painter's daughter by Gerard. Louvre, Paris. Dressed all in white.

676 Actual Costume, Musée Historique des Tissus, Lyons, France. Silk dress with appliqué embroidery in self-colour. Reticule. Long gloves. Turban with feather.

677 Actual Costume, Victoria and Albert Museum, London. Gold striped coat in silk. Striped waistcoat. Fawn stockinette breeches. White stockings. Black slippers. Cane. Natural hair cut 'en brosse'.

678 Drawing from 'La Gallerie des Modes'. Hat of silk decorated by plumes, pearl ropes, tassels and ribbons.

679 Portrait of Mme. Sériziat by Jacques Louis David. Louvre, Paris. White gown and fichu. White lace cap under natural straw hat. Dark green ribbons. Natural hair.

680 Silk Calèche. Rocamora Costume Museum, Barcelona, Spain.

681 Portrait. Istituto Gazzola di Belle Arti, Piacenza, Italy. Black tricorne hat with white ostrich tip ornamentation. White powdered periwig.

682 and 683 French footwear, Musée du Costume de la Ville de Paris. 682 is a white kid mule embroidered in coloured silk and silver. Leather heel. 683 is a pink satin shoe with coloured silk embroidery.

684 Drawing from 'Galerie des Modes'. White cap and fichu. Natural hair.

685, 686 and 687 Spanish footwear. Rocamora Costume Museum, Barcelona, Spain. 685 is a man's slipper in white silk embroidered in silver. 686 is a lady's shoe in black silk with diamanté buckle. 687 is a lady's shoe in striped silk.

688 Portrait of Ludovica Battaglia Belloni by Pietro Bini. Accademia Gallery, Venice. Pale blue silk overgown. White lace neck edging. Mauve échelle on stomacher. Gown of green patterned in darker green in sprig pattern. White lace headdress. Fan.

689 Portrait of the Grand Duchess of Tuscany by Mengs. Prado, Madrid. Jewelled hair ornament. White coiffure. Pale blue gown with dark blue decoration. White neck edging.

690 Engraving from 'Galeries des Modes'. Silk hat with flowers and ribbons perched on top of tall white coiffure.

691 Engraving from 'Galeries des Modes'. White cap.

692 Portrait of a gentleman by Rosalba Carriera. National Gallery, London. White powdered tie wig. Pale blue coat with silver embroidery. White stock.

693 All from portraits in galleries in England.
A Cobalt blue taffeta gown. Pale blue silk underskirt embroidered in sprig pattern in colours of pink and green. White silk hem flounce, sleeve ruffles, neck edging and cap 1714–20.

B Pale green velvet coat with silver embroidery. Brocade waistcoat. Powdered periwig. White cravat. Dark red breeches, white stockings, black shoes. Cane, gloves. 1715–18.

C Young girl dressed similarly to A.

D, E Small boys dressed similarly to H.

F Pale green taffeta sacque gown with coloured embroidery in floral design. White cap with lappets. 1725.

G Lavender silk sacque gown with dark green velvet bows. Cream satin petticoat. White cap and lappets. 1720–4.

H Blue grey velvet coat with brocade cuffs. White tie wig. White stockings, black shoes. 1730.

694A Portrait painting. Dark red silk coat with brocade cuffs. White tie wig. Gloves, cane. White stockings, black shoes. 1732.

B Painting. Pale blue silk gown, English style. Satin bows. White fichu and sleeve ruffles. Cane. Straw hat with striped ribbon, 1745–50.

C Actual Costume, Victoria and Albert Museum, London. Pink gown with embroidered silk pattern in colours. Watteau pleats. White cap. 1750.

D Portrait of Frederick, Prince of Wales. National Portrait Gallery, London. Red velvet coat, waistcoat and breeches. Gold decoration and buttons. White pig-tail wig. Black tricorne hat with white ostrich tips. 1745–50.

E, F Children dressed like A and B.

G Actual Costume, Museum of Costume, Bath. Brocade gown in green, crimson and white on a gold ground. White lace sleeve ruffles and neck frill. White cap. 1735–40.

H Painting. Cream silk gown with embroidery in coloured silks. Echelle bodice. White cap with lappets and ribbons. Reticule. 1750.

695A Painting. English style frock coat in green velvet with gold edge. Striped breeches in two shades of green. White and red striped waistcoat. White powdered wig, cadogan style. White stockings, black shoes. 1770.

B Actual Costume, Museum of Costume, Bath. Gown and undergown of white silk with white ribbon decoration and embroidered pink roses. Darker bodice and train. White wig. Reticule. 1777.

C Actual Costume, Museum of Costume, Bath. Olive green satin dress decorated in embroidered white flowers. White wig. c.1763.

D Actual Costume, Museum of Costume, Bath. Cream dress embroidered all over in a floral design in coloured silks. White lace sleeve ruffles. White coiffure. 1760

E, F Paintings. Plain dark coats with embroidered front edges. Striped stockings. Black shoes. White pig-tail wigs. 1765–75.

696 Actual Costume, Museum of Costume, Bath. Brown silk gown, white fichu, white muslin underskirt in self-colour design of lover's knots on zig-zags. Dark green velvet hat with brown ribbons and white plumes. Natural hair. Gloves. Cane.

697 Actual Costume, Museum of Costume, Bath. Dark green coat with embroidered edges in white and pinks. White powdered wig. Red silk cloak. White stockings, black shoes.

698 Actual Costume, Museum of Costume, Bath. Striped muslin gown in white with pink decoration. White fichu. Dark green satin petticoat. White powdered coiffure. Gold locket necklace. White satin muff embroidered with tiny roses.

699 Actual Costume, Museum of Costume, Bath. Red cloth coat with brass buttons. White waistcoat and breeches. Striped stockings. Black shoes. Black bicorne hat. Powdered hedgehog wig.

700 Actual Costume, Museum of Costume, Bath. Pale blue watered silk gown. Black lace fichu. White lace sleeve ruffles. White hat over white lace pleated cap. Black ribbons.

701 Actual Costume, Museum of Costume, Bath. Patterned velvet coat. White stockings, black shoes. White powdered bag wig.

702 Actual Costume, Rijksmuseum, Amsterdam. White satin gown with self colour ruching decoration. White lace sleeve ruffles and handkerchief. Natural hair.

703 Actual Costume, Rijksmuseum, Amsterdam. Strawberry pink wool coat and waistcoat. Breeches striped in green and grey. White stockings and stock. Black shoes. White powdered wig.

704 Actual Costume, Rijksmuseum, Amsterdam. Brown and fawn brocade coat, waistcoat and breeches. White stockings, black shoes. Cream lace cravat. Brown felt tricorne hat with gold braid edging. Cane.

705 Actual Costume, Rijksmuseum, Amsterdam. Striped damask gown in fawn and brown with tiny embroidered flowers on fawn stripes. Cream lace sleeve ruffles and apron. Fan. Brown hair.

706 Actual Costume, Rijksmuseum, Amsterdam. Gold and green brocade gown with Watteau pleats. brown hair.

707 Painting by Van Loo, Louvre, Paris. Red coat with gold braid trimming. Black boots. White wig.

708 Actual Costume, Rijksmuseum, Amsterdam. Grey velvet coat with silver stripe. Rich embroidery on pockets and edges. White satin lining. Waistcoat embroidered all over. Breeches to match coat. White stockings, black shoes. Cane. White tie wig.

709 Actual Costume, Central Museum, Utrecht, Holland. Light cotton gown with sprig pattern. Dark caraco on top in French style. White lace-edged fichu and sleeve ruffles. White coiffure.

710 Painting, Musée Communal, Brussels. Red coat. White and gold striped waistcoat. Gold breeches. Stockings striped gold and white. Black slippers. Black hat over grey powdered hedgehog wig.

711 Actual Costume. Rijkmuseum, Amsterdam. Yellow-green taffeta dress. White neck ruffles. White coiffure with cadogan style finish. Cane.

712 A–E Engraving, Nuremburg City Library.

F Actual Costume, Bayerische Nationalmuseum, Munich. Coat of brown wool and navy braid. Waistcoat of navy silk and gold braid. Silver buttons.

713A Actual Costume, Bayerische Nationalmuseum, Munich. Blue brocade robe à la française decorated in pink, white and green floral design. 1750.

B Engraving by Tanjé. Print Room, Munich. Dark coat, light waistcoat with gold borders. Breeches to match coat. White stockings, black shoes. White bag wig. c.1750.

C Actual Costume, Bayerische Nationalmuseum, Munich. White silk gown with coloured embroidered sprig pattern. White Alençon lace fichu. Brown silk reticule with coloured silk embroidery. 1750.

D, E Engraving by Chodowiecki, Dresden Print Room. 1770.

714A Actual Costume, Bernisches Historisches Museum, Berne, Switzerland. Brown velvet coat. Brocade waistcoat in green and brown. Black velvet breeches. White stockings, black shoes. Grey powdered wig.

B Actual Costume, Schweizerisches Landesmuseum, Zürich, Switzerland. Brown dress embroidered with sprig roses in red and green. White neck and sleeve frills. Brown hair. 1750.

C Actual Costume, Bernisches Historiches Museum, Berne, Switzerland. Cream dress, embroidered in flowers in yellow, red and blue. Cream lace at neck and sleeves. Cream ribbon cross-over stomacher. White coiffure with flowers. Fan. 1750.

D Actual Costume, Schweizerisches Landesmuseum, Zürich, Switzerland. Rust-red dress with white all-over pattern in floral motif. White wig with blue ribbons and white plumes. 1770–80.

E Actual Costume, Schweizerisches Landesmuseum, Zürich, Switzerland. Navy blue coat. Black breeches. White stockings, black shoes. Grey wig, red velvet waistcoat. Black tricorne hat with silver braid and button decoration. 1745.

715A Portrait of Kaiser Karl VI by Johann Kupezky. Historisches Museum der Stadt Wien, Vienna. Brown coat with gold lace decoration and red ribbons. Grey powdered periwig. Breeches to match coat. White stockings, black shoes with red heels. 1716.

B Portrait of Joseph II by Pompeo Battoni. Kunsthistorisches Museum, Vienna. White coat with red cuffs and gold buttons. Red waistcoat with gold decoration. Grey breeches. White stockings, black shoes. Powdered white wig. c.1770.

C Empress Maria Theresa, portrait in Kunsthistorisches Museum der Stadt Wien, Vienna. Pink dress with white embroidery and white lace ornamentation. White powdered hair c.1750.

D Engraving of Joseph II. Historisches Museum der Stadt Wien, Vienna. 1790.

E Portrait of the painter's wife by Füger. Osterreichische Galerie in Wien, Vienna. Black satin gown with white ruff, fichu and stole. Red ribbon in natural coiffure. c.1797.

716 Actual Costume, Schweizerisches Landesmuseum, Zürich, Switzerland. Cream cotton dress embroidered in brown, red and green. Green ribbon bows. Natural hair with coronet of small pink flowers and green leaves. Black neck ribbon with silver jewel.

717 Sculptured figure of nobleman. Coat with frogged decoration. Patterned waistcoat. Cloak with decorative border. Lace cravat. Periwig.

718 Sculptured figure, Rococo style gown over paniers with looped back overskirt, with jewels and pearl ropes clasping the material back. Lace headdress.

719 Actual Costume, Schweizerisches Landesmuseum, Zürich, Switzerland. Apple green silk coat and breeches. Deep red silk waistcoat embroidered in gold. White lace jabot and sleeve ruffles. Natural brown hair.

720A Actual Costume, Hungarian Museum of Decorative Art, Budapest. Silk dolman embroidered with gold fastenings and patterned all over in woven design. Trousers, boots, 1741.

B Actual Costume, Hungarian Museum of Decorative Arts, Budapest. Robe à la Française in floral patterned silk. Ribbon and ruched decoration. Natural hair. 1750.

C Actual Costume, Hungarian National Museum, Budapest. Originally the property of Duke Samuel Teleki. Golden brown silk mente with brown fur worn over fitted dolman. Narrow trousers, boots decorated in silver. Cap to match mente. c.1780.

D Actual Costume, Hungarian National Museum, Budapest. Rococo dress in green silk damask in floral design. Ruching decoration.

E Actual Costume, Hungarian Museum of Decorative Arts, Budapest. French style of coat, striped in silver. Embroidered in pastel shades of coloured silks. Cadogan style powdered wig.

F Actual Costume, Hungarian National Museum, Budapest. Hungarian style ball dress in embroidered silk. White chemise with full sleeves. White lace sleeve ruffles and neck edging. Powdered coiffure with ribbon and flower decoration. Fan. c.1775.

721A Actual Costume, Museo del Pueblo Espanol, Madrid. Dark purple ribbed silk gown with silver braid edging. White petticoat and fichu. Silk hat with plumes and flowers over powdered coiffure, 1770.

B Actual Costume, Museo del Pueblo Español, Madrid. Plum coloured silk coat with floral embroidery at edges White silk waistcoat also embroidered. Dark grey silk breeches. White stockings, black shoes. White lace jabot. Powdered wig.

C Actual Costume, Museo del Pueblo Español, Madrid. Robe à la francaise in striped material of cream and red. Powdered coiffure, 1750.

D Actual Costume, Rocamora Costume Museum, Barcelona. Panier silk dress, striped and in sprig pattern. Fawn with silver and coloured embroidery. Fan. Powdered coiffure. c.1760.

E Actual Costume, Museo del Pueblo Español, Madrid. French style coat of blue silk with silver braid and buttons. White stockings, black shoes. Tricorne hat over powdered bag wig, c.1750.

F Actual Costume, Museo del Pueblo Español, Madrid. Olive green satin dress embroidered in silver thread in floral design. White fichu. Pale green satin petticoat. Cream lace flouncing. Powdered coiffure, 1765.

722 Portrait of Paravicini by an unknown artist. Quadreria dell' Ospedale Maggiore, Milan. Plain coat, brocade waistcoat. Dark breeches and stockings. Black shoes and tricorne hat. Powdered periwig.

723 Portrait of Paola Arconati by unknown artist. Marchese Crivelli Milan. Jewelled, embroidered stomacher. Plain gown over patterned undergown with lace ornamentation. White lace sleeve ruffles and neck frill. Lace fontange headdress.

724 Painting of a little girl. Galleria Nazionale, Parma. Dress and apron in silver grey with orange bands and sprig pattern. White lace sleeve ruffles, neck frill and fontange headdress. Gold embroidered shoes. Pearl rope bracelets.

725 Portrait of the Infanta Ana Victoria, Prado, Madrid. Blue satin gown with gold, jewelled stomacher. White lace undersleeves and neck frill. Jewel set in powdered hair.

726 Portrait, Prado, Madrid. Red velvet coat with silver decoration and yellow lining. Yellow silk waistcoat with silver ornamentation. Red breeches and stockings. Black shoes and tricorne hat. Powdered periwig.

727 Actual Costume, Rocamora Costume Museum, Barcelona. White silk dress decorated by silver fringe and sequins. Overdress of olive green decorated by embroidery in a spot pattern.

728 Actual Costume, Rocamora Costume Museum, Barcelona. Grey silk coat with steel buttons. Breeches to match. Lace jabot and sleeve ruffles. Black slippers, white stockings. Natural hair.

729 Portrait of Francesco di Borbone as a boy by Mme. Vigée-Lebrun. Galleria Nazionale di Capodimonte, Naples. Plain light coloured coat over striped waistcoat. Dark breeches. White stockings, black shoes. White, lace-edged collar. Natural hair.

730 Portrait of Duchess Maria Valcarzel by Giosué Sala. Quadreria dell' Ospedale Maggiore, Milan. Plain jade green dress. Bead necklace and pearl ropes. Gold jewelled hair ornaments.

731 Actual Costume, Rocamora Costume Museum, Barcelona. White muslin dress embroidered in coloured silks. Border hem in classical pattern. Stole of stripes of yellow and tan with tan fringe.

732A Painting by Antonio Guardi, Ca' Rezzonico, Venice. White satin gown over hoop. Brown fur. Red échelle bows. White cap with flowers. Gold embroidered cuffs, white sleeve ruffles.

B and C Painting by Pietro Longhi, Ca' Rezzonico, Venice. B, the little boy, wears a pale blue coat with silver embroidery and buttons, darker blue breeches and light brown boots. His hair is powdered white. C, the little girl, wears a pale pink dress and apron with white decoration and ruffles. Her hair is powdered white and she wears a pink bow. 1752.

D Painting, Ca' Rezzonico, Venice. Red coat with gold decoration and buttons. Gold brocade waistcoat. Black breeches. White stockings, black shoes. White stock and wrist ruffles. White powdered wig. Black tricorne hat.

E Painting by Pietro Longhi, Galleria Accademia, Venice. White satin dress with white lace-edged sleeve ruffles and handkerchief. Pink ruffles on bodice and pale blue échelle bows. White cap with flowers and pink ribbons. White shoes.

F From same painting as E. Brown coat with gold buttons. White stock and wrist ruffles. Fawn stockings, black shoes. Grey powdered wig. 1745–50.

733 Actual Costume, Nordiska Museet, Stockholm. White cotton dress, printed. Stole. Turban with plumes. Swedish.

734 Actual Costume, Rosenborg Castle, Copenhagen. Scarlet cloth coat with gold ribbon decoration. Beige silk lining. White, embroidered waistcoat. Danish.

735 Actual Costume, Rosenborg Castle, Copenhagen. Silver brocade coat and breeches. Powdered bag wig. Danish.

736 Actual Costume, Nordiska Museet, Stockholm. Striped satin dress. White lace fontange headdress. Swedish.

737A Actual Costume, Nordiska Museet, Stockholm. Swedish National dress, c.1780. For Royal household

staff. Black coat and breeches. Red sash and rosette. Black cloak with red lining.

B Actual Costume, Nordiska Museet, Stockholm. Green cloth suit, 1762.

C Swedish National dress, 1778. Polonaise type gown but with a train. Powdered coiffure with plumes and jewel.

D Portrait of Gustav III in National dress. c.1778. Dark coat and breeches. White stockings, black shoes. Dark cloak with light lining.

E Fashion plate, Swedish National dress, 1778. Polonaise style gown with ruff. Powdered coiffure decorated by plumes.

F Actual Costume, Nordiska Museet, Stockholm. Robe à la française in striped velvet with lace and fringe ornamentation. c.1760.

G Actual Costume, Nordiska Museet, Stockholm, c.1770.

738 Actual Costume, Hermitage Museum, Leningrad. Plain white dress with light coloured stole decorated in dark embroidery in paisley-type pattern.

739 Actual Costume, Hermitage Museum, Leningrad. Dark coat and breeches with light spot all-over pattern. Brocade waistcoat. White stockings, black shoes. Powdered bag wig.

740 Actual Costume, Hermitage Museum, Leningrad. Plain silk gown à la française. Powdered hair.

741 Actual Costume, Hermitage Museum, Leningrad. Dark coat decorated by gold braid and buttons. Breeches to match. Brocade waistcoat. White stockings, black shoes. Powdered periwig. Cane.

742 Portrait. Swedish National dress with white lace neck open ruff and dark slashed puff sleeves. Powdered coiffure with ribbons and plumes.

743 Portrait of Crown Princess of Bavaria. Bayerisches Nationalmuseum, Munich. Powdered hair with white cap decorated by ruching and ribbon bows. Green dress with white ruched decoration and collarette. White ribbon bows.

744 Portrait by Gainsborough, National Gallery, London. Black hat, ribbons and plumes. Powdered hedgehog wig. Gown striped blue and white with blue neck scarf and white fichu. Gold stole. Black velvet neck ribbon.

745 Portrait by Kneller, National Portrait Gallery, London. Brown periwig and brown velvet coat.

746 Rijksmuseum, Amsterdam. White powdered bag wig.

747 Black silk calash, Museum of Costume, Bath.

748 Black, man's shoe, Danish. Rosenborg Castle, Copenhagen.

749 Black, man's shoe, Dutch. Rijksmuseum, Amsterdam.

750 Leather boot, 1730. Hungarian Museum of Decorative Arts, Budapest.

751 Portrait miniature of Prince Max III Joseph of Bavaria. Bayerische Nationalmuseum, Munich. Powdered wig.

752 Portrait miniature of a German princess. Bayerische Nationalmuseum, Munich. Hair piled high in style of fontange headdress. Pearl ropes wound round ringlets.

753 Lady's shoe in pink silk decorated with silver lace. Bayerische Nationalmuseum, Munich.

754 Portrait of Queen Sophia Magdalena, Nordiska Museet, Stockholm. Powdered coiffure with jewels and flowers.

Chapter Eight

The Nineteenth Century: Internationalism

National influence upon the fashionable world in Europe had been diminishing since the later seventeenth century. By 1815, an international style had become established: ladies wore clothes based upon French fashions, gentlemen on those set in England. Among the bourgeoisie, and also the peasantry, local variations were infinite and marked but, at fashionable level, mutations were rarer. At certain times during the century, nationalist movements led to short-term rebellions from the set pattern but these were local and limited.

In Hungary, for instance, the dolman and mente, together with trousers worn with boots, continued fashionable wear for men in the early years of the century, but soon English tailoring was supreme here as elsewhere. In the 1820s and 1830s, ladies' dress closely followed the German pattern which, in itself, was less svelte than the French and behind the times. During the 1848 struggles for independence, the Hungarian national colours of red, white and green were fashionable; again, in the 1860s, with the resurgence of national feeling and aspirations, there was a reversion, especially by men, to the national, earlier forms of dress. The 'Attila' style of coat and vest of this time was more like the dolman and mente than an English gentleman's attire, but these trends were ephemeral. The masculine, national garments, together with the feminine white blouse worn under a gown whose bodice was laced across it, survived until the end of the century for formal and evening wear but for general, day use the international mode was followed.

During the first seven or eight years of the new century certain countries suffered economic problems in their textile industries, due to the blockading of ports during the Napoleonic Wars. England was one of these, also Holland. After this time, the textile industries of all European countries began to flourish and expand. Mechanisation increased output immensely, especially in linen and cotton. England was the most pros-

perous country in this field and London became the economic centre of the world. Trade overseas to the Americas, the Indies, the Far East and Australasia expanded explosively. British fabrics had a world-wide sale and dominance. In Europe, a road and canal network was established and sea routes for trade served distant lands.

It is sometimes thought that the unification of Europe (England excepted) under the dominance of Napoleonic France was responsible for the establishment of French fashion as the international mode. Strangely this is not precisely true. There were, moreover, in the years 1805–15, several versions of the French mode which included that of the emigré aristocrats, who tended to adhere to pre-1789 fashions in their host countries, and the administrative French official staffs who preferred more advanced Revolutionary vogues. Neither was fully acceptable to the other European countries, who sought the elegance of the latest French fashions.

The chief contribution towards French fashion dominance in feminine dress was made by English tourists who flocked to Paris just before and after Waterloo. The enthusiasm of these, together with that of the Allied armies of occupation in 1814–15, led to an overwhelming adoption of French feminine fashion which lasted for the whole century in Europe.

In contrast, the well-dressed Englishman, with his immaculately tailored attire, took Europe by storm. No other nation produced such elegant, even dandified, gentlemen. For the remainder of the century, English tailoring and fashion was *de rigueur* for the well-dressed man.

The French textile industry also began to flourish again during the Napoleonic wars. English fabrics were then restricted from entry into France and French cottons and silks were produced and sold in fine quality and great quantity in Europe. An important landmark in the textile world was the development of the new loom by *Joseph Marie Jacquard*. This revolutionised the production of brocaded fabrics

755 *French, 1800* **756** *Swiss, 1805* **757** *French, 1810* **758** *French, 1800–5*   **759** *Dutch, 1805*

by its ability to weave patterned textiles. Jacquard introduced his loom in 1801 and, by 1806, it had been taken over for development by the French government, with a royalty and pension paid to the inventor.

Napoleon Bonaparte, like Louis XIV, actively interested himself in French industry. He re-introduced a court apparel of a richness of quality, style and decoration not seen since before the Revolution. Such garments were made of velvets, silks, brocades and gold and silver cloth; ladies were adorned with diamond necklaces and lace, they wore trains and nodding plumes.

In the years between 1815 and 1850 costume was influenced strongly by the taste of the middle classes. Bonaparte had re-introduced richness and luxury, leading the fashions by his court styles of dress. After 1815, under the French Restoration and in the prevailing Romantic climate, the classical themes of the years up to 1820 gave place to the ideas stemming from the new, literary revival of Medievalism. In women's dress, the waist was re-discovered and delineated; ladies dressed in a feminine manner with bell-shaped skirts, dainty ankles tentatively displayed

and there was a return to heavier and more varied materials and a greater quantity of ornamentation. Medieval coiffures and style of footwear were introduced.

English modes and manners were fashionable, especially so in men's attire, which was modelled on such elegants as Beau Brummell and Lord Byron. This was particularly so in the 1830s.

Though the French mode was followed throughout Europe by fashionable women and the English mode by men, each country still imprinted something of its national character upon the styles. The dress was international but there were greater national variations than appertains in the twentieth century, because mass production of garments had not yet fully standardised costume. The Austrian, German and Italian dress, for this period of the nineteenth century was old-fashioned when set against French or English styles. It also displayed greater formality and a certain heaviness of form.

The 1850s, 1860s and 1870s were decades of prosperity and luxury; upper class dress evidenced this. Despite the European wars and upheavals of these years, the principal nations were wealthy and prominent citizens continued to dress elegantly in quality fabrics and in fashions which were now changing more rapidly. The Second Empire in France, under Napoleon III and his beautiful Empress Eugénie, led the world in these fashions. These were the years of the fantastic crinoline and bustle skirts, requiring vast quantities of material and decoration to make them up. During the same period, dress for men became stereotyped and excessively formal, its fabrics heavy, its colours sombre. The dress of the two sexes acted as a foil, one to the other. Never can costume have been so overweighted and uncomfortable; yet, elegant and impressive, it certainly was.

Two factors greatly influenced the production of such luxurious garments which were being made available to far greater numbers of people than hitherto. One was the mechanisation process and consequent marketing of ready-made clothes which lowered the prices and brought such fashions within the range of so many more people; the other was the development of *haute couture* in France, where the great couturiers established their salons with designs made

especially for the trend-setting, fashionable wealthy. Such designs then percolated through to the general public in amended form.

The most important event in mechanised dressmaking was the introduction of the *sewing machine*, which gave relief at last to the drudgery of handstitching by seamstresses, who, for so long, had worked incredible hours for a pittance. The first patent was obtained by the Englishman *Thomas Saint* in 1790 for a machine which sewed leather. It was the Frenchman *Barthelemy Thimmonier* who developed a sewing machine in 1829 which produced a chain stitch by means of a hooked needle. By 1831 his machines were being used to make French army uniforms but, as previously in the eighteenth century, opposition to these new mechanical means of production was so violent that workers, afraid for the possible consequent loss of their employment, destroyed the machines. The set-back was only temporary and Thimmonier developed his machine further to work faster and on a greater variety of fabrics.

Other machines were then produced elsewhere, notably in the U.S.A. It was *Isaac Merrit Singer* who perfected the sewing machine, patenting his

760 *German*, c.*1800* **761** *Spanish*, c.*1800* **762** *Swiss*, c.*1805* **763** *Swedish*, *1802* **764** *French*, c.*1808*

design in 1851, and bringing it into general use in America and England. This machine had a straight needle and was able to work continuously. Its use revolutionised the garment making industry and, by the 1860s, quantities of ready made clothes were available. As yet the quality was not good but the garments were cheap and provided a range of wear for a great number of people. Germany was the country which first took advantage of this industrial potential. With the aid of sewing machines, the immense crinoline skirts could be made and ornamented in a minimum of time, so encouraging this fashion throughout the population. France, too, realised the potentialities of the mass production market in clothes. Mass retail outlets were needed. In Paris, the department stores were initiated: the Ville de France in 1844, leading to the Grand-Halles in 1853 and the Bon Marché in 1876.

At the same time, all over Europe and in the Americas and Australasia, development was fast changing the methods of production of textiles. In spinning, weaving and dyeing industrialisation was increasing fast as also was the production of the raw materials. Here, for example, the raising of sheep for wool in Australia had expanded at a tremendous pace from the 29 sheep imported in

1788 to a flock of 20 million animals in 1860. The new synthetic dyes developed by industry resulted in a vogue for garments in vivid shades of purples, reds, blues and greens in the 1860s and 1870s.

Until the mid-nineteenth century dressmakers had controlled the design and production of ladies' garments. In France, a new era began in 1858 when Princess Metternich introduced the designs of a certain Mr. Worth to the royal family in Paris. *Charles Frederick Worth*, an Englishman, left London (where he had been working at Swan and Edgar, the drapers) at the age of 20, for Paris. In Paris, in 1846, he began work in a wholesale silk house and later went into partnership with Dobergh. His wife encouraged him to design model gowns which he displayed as a collection to an interested, enthusiastic clientele. Success came quickly. He established his business in the Rue de la Paix and soon made a reputation as a couturier. A seal was set upon this reputation when he received the patronage of the Empress Eugénie.

From this time onwards *haute couture* established itself in France and became world famous. Worth employed elegant, attractive girls to display his creations. Other designers followed suit and employed these mannequins who presented their designs to wealthy clients and to foreign buyers who spread the fashions all over the world. The establishment of such quality designers went hand in hand with the equally speedy development of the ready-to-wear trade. Both ends of the fashion spectrum were important to one another, the one to set the tone and taste with the provision of rapidly changing and evolving designs, and the other to provide the outlet which published them to the world and made them popular. As each fashion reached the general public through the ready-to-wear market so the couturiers evolved a new one for their clients. It was the establishment of *haute couture* which finalised the acceptance of French fashions throughout the world at all levels of society.

Improvements in communication and transport spread these designs more and more quickly and this led to new fashions following upon one another at greater speed. At the same time, especially from 1880–90 onwards, clothes were designed for a greater variety of activities, for sport, for holidays, for work. These were more practical and simple than before. The Paris example of setting up department stores to market and display fashionable clothes had now been followed by all great cities; Liberty's in London's Regent Street was one famous example. Such stores not only sold the Paris modes from the great houses of fashion, they also popularised the simpler, practical gowns for ordinary wear.

The nineteenth century was the most important time for the publication of engraved *fashion plates* and *journals*. These were hand-coloured until the last quarter of the century when printed colour work began to be published. That was then a period of decline for such journals. Until about 1830–40 most journals were published in France and England. Some famous publications were produced in the years 1800–40 such as the French *La Belle Assemblée*, *Le Petit Courrier des Dames*, *La Mode*, and *Le Bon Ton* and the English *The Ladies' Cabinet* and *The Ladies' Gazette of Fashions*. Some publications were illustrated by first class artists, for instance, *Sulpice Guillaume Chevalier*, who worked for some time for *La Mode*. He signed himself 'Gavarni'; a practice which stemmed from a printing error early in his career when, on one occasion, his name was con-

766 *Italian, 1818*   **767** *Italian, 1815*   **768** *German, 1811*   **769** *Swedish, c.1800*

A B C D E F G

fused with that of the subject of his feature – Gavarnie, a French Pyrenean village near the frontier.

After 1830 there was a tremendous increase in the number of publications and nearly all European countries produced one or more. From 1860 Germany's *Die Modenwelt*, published in Berlin, was an important journal. It had a wide circulation and was published in 14 languages under different titles; the English version was *The Season*. In the 1870s Vienna, until now not an important fashion centre, became so at a time when France and Prussia were engaged in war. *Wiener Mode* and *Wiener Chic* were outstanding publications of the 1880s and 1890s. In the second half of the century the Americans entered the fashion journal field and several, later world

famous papers were launched – *Harper's Bazaar* and *Vogue*, for example. Also in this period were published some famous English journals such as the *Queen* and the *Englishwoman's Domestic Magazine*. Both of these were started by Samuel Beeton, husband of the Mrs Beeton of *Book of Household Management* fame.

Fashion journals and plates together with actual costumes held in museum collections provide a generous, detailed record of every facet of dress in the nineteenth century although, in all sources, men's costume is less well represented than women's.

Men's Costume 1800–1850

During this half of the nineteenth century men were dressed principally in three garments – a tail coat, a waistcoat and pantaloons or trousers. Changes in masculine style were slow and limited but these were sufficient to make it simple to differentiate between a coat of, say 1820, and one of 1850. Colours, in general, became more sombre from 1800 to 1850, fabrics became heavier and decoration more restrained. The years 1800–30 were those which established the English gentleman as the best dressed, most elegant man in Europe. The dandy, with his imperturbability, his grace and ironic elegance, enunciated a long-lasting vogue. The best known of these dandies was *George (Beau) Brummell* who, patronised by the Prince Regent, set the stage for the aristocratic gentleman's bearing and manner. He dressed simply and plainly in subtle colours with unobtrusive ornamentation. Typical of his attire was the blue tail coat with brass buttons worn over a fawn waistcoat and accompanied by white or light-coloured buckskin pantaloons and black Hessian boots. His evening dress had a white waistcoat and blue stockinet pantaloons strapped over black slippers.

For the first decade of the century, the *tail coat*

with high collar boned up to the ears, cut square across in front at the waist and falling to long tails at the back, was worn with pantaloons or knee breeches. The lapels of the coat were large, its sleeves fitting. It was worn over one or two waistcoats, one generally striped and extending below the other but both were cut away straight in front.

By 1820 two chief tail coat styles had evolved, one double-breasted and cut away straight in front and with knee-length tails, the other single-breasted and cut away in a sloping line on the hips and with rounded tails. Between 1810 and 1830 all coats became more waisted, fuller on the chest and lapels became smaller or were formed into a rounded, shawl collar, standing away from the neck at the back. Sleeves became fuller, especially at the top, and were pleated or gathered into the armhole. Materials tended to become heavier, generally in wool, cloth or velvet and colours darker – navy, brown, tobacco colour or dark green.

The *waistcoat* followed the same trend as the coat, becoming waisted and fuller on the chest. One was still sometimes worn on top of another

771 *French, 1820–5*   772 *Spanish,* c.1820   773 *Polish, 1825–8*   775 *French,* c.1820

774 *1825*

1820–30

776 *Austrian, 1826*   **777** *German, 1823*   **778** *Russian, 1827*   **779** *Austrian, 1826*

but both were waist length by 1830. The garment was generally white or light in colour, striped, embroidered or spotted and was often made from piqué.

From 1800 onwards breeches lengthened into *pantaloons*. Till 1840 they generally opened with a broad front flap. They were fitting and made from an elastic type of material like stockinet or soft doeskin in grey, beige, lemon or white. Some were of finely striped cotton and, especially fashionable, was the buff or yellow nankeen fabric, a strong cotton imported from Nanking in China. There was great opposition to the wearing of long pantaloons in England, where breeches and stockings were considered more dignified. Also, in France, Napoleon's court dress insisted upon knee breeches. By 1820, however, the popularity of pantaloons was general and they were either tucked into tall boots or strapped under the instep of the shoe. The pantaloons were supported by shoulder braces. Towards 1830 they were cut more fully at the waist and over the hips and were

less tightly fitting over the legs also (**757, 760, 764, 765A, F, 767, 769, 770A**).

In the years from *1825–40* the waisted appearance of the coat was accentuated and the chest and hips were padded to make this more marked. Corsets were worn by many men. The tails were cut separately from the coat and seamed on, enabling this corseted look to be more clearly delineated. The collars were rolling but many had pointed lapels also. The coat was generally worn open and tails were fairly short. Sleeves were full at the shoulder, then fitting below. The coats were of cloth, popularly in blue, claret or fawn. They had velvet collars and metal or pearl buttons. Waistcoats followed the line of coats. Trousers were full on the hips but tight on the legs and still strapped under the instep. From about 1835–40 the fly opening began to replace the horizontal flap. Materials were more varied now, corduroy and twill became alternatives to stockinet and buckskin (**776, 779, 781, 791F**).

By the years *1840–50* alternative styles of coat

had appeared. Tail coats were still fashionable but the skirted frock coat worn open or the closed redingote style had been seen for some time. The general cut of coats was now less waisted and hip and chest padding had disappeared. Pantaloons, now trousers, were fuller and had lost the instep strap. It was in these years that the colour began to disappear from men's dress. Coats were generally black or dark grey, waistcoats white or light grey and trousers matched the coat or were plain, striped or checked grey (**780G, 785, 791A, 796**).

Men's Dress 1850–1900

There were four types of *coat* for men in these years, suitable for different occasions. Three of these had tails; the tail coat, the frock coat and the cutaway; the fourth was a jacket which, in the 1870s, was designed as part of a three-piece suit. All these, except the frock coat, still exist in present day equivalents, though the coats with tails are now only worn on formal occasions.

The *tail coat* continued to be worn until about 1860, for use in town but it was seen less often after 1855. Like the other formal coats, it was in black or very dark cloth and had a collar and revers buttoned higher on the chest than hitherto. The tails were knee-length or shorter (**797A, E, 814**). The style has survived in evening attire. It was in black, worn open in front with black or white waistcoat and black trousers. The outfit was completed by a white shirt, black socks, slippers and crush hat. It was not only the origin of today's evening dress formal 'tails' but differed from these only in detail.

The *frock coat* was worn until the end of the century as formal city day wear. Its skirts were knee-length and level all round. This double-breasted garment was worn unbuttoned. It was the most characteristic wear of the second half of the century. It was made of black cloth for much of this time though lighter grey versions were fashionable in the 1890s (**807C, F, 832E**).

The *cutaway coat* was also formal wear and had tails. First introduced earlier in the century, it

780 Regent Street, London. English Dress, 1830–40

781 *German, 1839*

782 *Swedish, 1830*

783 *Spanish, 1830–40*

784 *Spanish, 1839–40*

785 *Russian, 1832*

largely replaced the tail coat in the 1850s and was preferred for less formal occasions to the frock coat and by younger men. It was black or grey, single-breasted and was cut away in front to rounded, short tails. The edges were often finished with braid. It was the prototype of our formal day dress of today, the morning coat (**806, 818B**).

In the 1850s a *jacket* was introduced for informal wear and was worn with trousers of a different material. The coat was plain, black or dark, and the trousers were check, plaid or striped. At first such jackets, which were known as *sack coats*, being shapeless and ill-cut, were only worn indoors informally. By the 1860s they were regarded as suitable for street wear for informal occasions. The style had a high buttoned small collar and revers and generally only the top button was fastened. It was a single-breasted garment, its rounded front edges finished with braid. Some designs had velvet collars.

After 1870, complete *suits* of jacket, waistcoat and trousers of all one material were introduced. These were still ill-fitting, loose and sack-like.

They were made of patterned tweed or dark, plain material. As time passed, the cut improved and the suit was worn more often but, until the end of the century, it was never worn by gentlemen for any but morning attire, travel or country wear (**807A, 812, 813A, 823F**). A jacket for evening dress, the *dinner jacket*, was introduced in 1880. It was never, in this century, worn at any function where ladies were present.

From 1885–90 the three-piece *lounge suit* was everyday attire for many men though not considered suitable for formal town wear. The cut had improved, though the revers were still high and the jacket single-breasted. The rounded front edges became square cut in the 1890s. A dress, black or dark blue sack coat was introduced at this time for wear with a black waistcoat and striped trousers. In the early twentieth century this developed into the classic 'city attire'. It was in 1895 that vertical creases were introduced into trouser legs and it became fashionable to turn up the hems. This was an English idea which quickly spread to France.

The 1890s also saw the introduction of a

variety of dress suited to informal, country and holiday wear. Tweed jackets with knickerbockers were made for cycling, shooting or walking. These were in check or plaid patterns. Called *Norfolk jackets* they had waist-belts, vertical pleats back and front and large patch, hip pockets. Matching knickerbockers were worn with woollen socks, gaiters and boots or shoes.

Men's Dress. Outdoor Wear

There were three chief styles of *overcoat* in the early decades of the century. The dress style was the *redingote*, a double-breasted coat, waisted and with knee-length flared skirt. The collar and sleeve patterns followed those of other coats (**791A**). The travelling and cold weather coat was the Garrick (carrick), which was long and voluminous; it had collar and cuffs as well as several, tiered shoulder capes. Whereas the redingote was generally made in plain dark cloth, the Garrick was in grey, fawn, blue or green tweed

and was usually check or plaid patterned (**769, 780E**).

The researches of *Charles Macintosh*, the Scottish chemist, into the use of naphtha, led to his invention of a waterproof fabric. In this, two thicknesses of rubber were cemented together with naphtha. By 1830 this material was being used to make travelling coats, usually on the Garrick pattern, with shoulder capes.

A third style of overcoat was strongly influenced by the Polish, Russian and Hungarian styles of military coat. These had stand-up or high collars and braided and frogged fastenings arranged in rows across the chest (**787**).

A joke, which led to a current fashion, is told of the wager by the Earl of Spencer in 1792. When the tails of his coat were wrenched off in an accident on the hunting field, he wagered that he could make the remaining waist-length coat into a popular fashion. He did, but it became a feminine not a masculine one.

From 1840 there was great variety in overcoat

786 *French*, c.*1830*   **787** *Polish*, c.*1830*   **788** *Russian, 1833*   **789** *Austrian, 1835*   **790** *Dutch, 1834–5*

1830–40

A   B   E   F

styles. Indeed, it is commented that, in a sombre age for masculine wear, overcoats supplied the brightest note of interest. Styles of Garrick continued to be fashionable all the century (**823A**), long, fitted dress coats for winter, in dark materials, with or without capes, were also commonly seen (**825, 828C**), while for more formal, city wear, a straight well-cut, black coat was usual (**816, 818G**). Short coats, reaching only to the hips, were fashionable. These had fur collars and, often, patch pockets on the hips (**813E**). Cloaks and capes were also worn, especially for evening. These had coloured silk, quilted or fur linings.

Men's Dress. Hair and Hats

Hair was cut fairly short and was worn in natural curls and waves. At first it was combed forwards over the forehead and ears (**834**). After 1820 it was longer and bushier. In the 1830s a left

side parting was fashionable and curls were arranged over the ears. Sidewhiskers were grown longer (**757, 760, 764, 765A, E, 767, 769, 770A, 776, 785, 787**).

The mid-century years from about 1845–70 were the time of varied short hair styles and an incredible choice in *whiskers*. Sidewhiskers were in fashion, also long whiskers on the cheek bones and jaw line which left the chin free. These were called Dundreary whiskers or Piccadilly Weepers in England; in France they were cutlets.* Alternatively, full beards of varied lengths were fashionable, worn with or without moustaches. 1860–65 was the zenith of the 'age of whiskers' (**779, 781, 791A, F, 796, 797A, E, 806, 807A, C, F, 812, 813A, E, 814, 818B, G**).

In the last two decades of the century whiskers

---

* In the late 1960s and early 1970s this facial decoration has been revised as a fashion chiefly for the young, who seem unaware that they are resuscitating the modes of their despised Victorian ancestors.

and beards were cut shorter but moustaches were generally worn. The hair was often parted and was also short (**823A, F, 825, 828C, 832E**). It was in the second half of the century that macassar oil was widely used to flatten and keep the hair in place. Since it badly stained upholstery, the crocheted, embroidered anti-macassars draped over the backs of chairs and sofas became an essential item in interior décor of the average parlour.

The *bicorne hat* was still to be seen early in the century but its use was confined more and more to the military (**760**). The most usual style until 1815 was the *English round hat* with tall, conical crown and small, rolled brim. This was usually made of felt or beaver in grey, beige or black. It had a cord and buckle trimming (**769**). From 1820 onwards the nineteenth century headcovering was the *top hat*. The shape evolved during the century from the curved-sided version in the early years to the tall, straight-sided 'stovepipe' design of the mid-century to a lower crown in the later

decades. At first it was made from beaver in grey, fawn or white. By the 1840s it was a black silk or polished beaver hat with narrower brim. A collapsible opera hat was also introduced (**757, 770A, 779, 780G, 781, 785, 787, 791A, F, 796, 807F, 812, 813E, 814, 816, 818B, G, 825, 828C, 832E**).

The top hat continued to be the formal, fashionable wear till after 1900, but in the last 40 years of the century, alternative styles of head covering appeared for casual, summer or sporting wear. The *bowler hat* was the most fashionable of these. At first only adopted for casual wear, it soon became established for everyday use. Also known as the derby or billycock, this round, felt hat with rolling brim, in black or brown, had first been worn in the 1850s, named after its original hatter (**807A, 813A, 823A, F**). In the 1880s, soft, felt hats were introduced and, in summer, *straw boaters*. *Caps* of plaid or check wool, some with ear flaps in Sherlock Holmes' manner, were usual for sport or travelling.

792 *Russian, 1843–4*   **793** *French, 1840–5*   **795** *Austrian, c.1840*

794 *Austrian, c.1840*   **796** *Spanish*

1840–50

Men's Dress. Footwear

Until 1925–30 *boots* were more generally worn than shoes. There were several styles and the most elegant and well-fitting were British made. There was the English *jockey boot*, with turned down cuffs in grey or buff and the *hussar boot* of hard, black leather, cut with a lower back and tall front decorated with a tassel. In England this was called the Hessian boot. There was also a high leather boot reaching to above the knee in front, though lower at the back. This was generally called the *Wellington boot* though it was worn by Napoleon also (**760, 769, 770A**). For evening and indoor wear, low cut *slippers* were usual which were heel-less, generally black and had ribbon tie decoration (**764, 765A, F, 776, 779**).

After 1820 soft boots were usually worn inside the trousers; they had narrow, square toes. From the 1830s boots were shorter and *spats, gaiters* or *spatterdashes* were worn on top (**767, 781, 785, 787, 796, 812, 813A, E, 814, 816, 818B, G, 823A**). In the 1850s boots were laced but a decade later were more commonly buttoned. Laced or buttoned *shoes* were also worn later in the century. Heel-less slippers were worn in the evenings.

Men's Dress. Neckwear and Linen

Until about 1830 white *collars* were unstiffened and attached to the shirt. They were turned upwards and, in the first decade of the century, were especially large and covered the cheekbone. There were varied ways of tying the *cravat*, which was generally of white linen. Often a black satin cravat was worn on top and the neckwear was then bulky and high under the chin (**834**). The *shirt* still had small ruffles but these tended to disappear by 1830 (**757, 760, 764, 765A, F, 767, 769, 770A, 776, 779, 781, 785, 787, 796, 797A, E**).

By mid-century collars were detached from the shirt and were starched. Later the points were turned down. The cravat tie gradually became smaller and less obtrusive; by 1850 it was replaced by a necktie. This was made up as a flat scarf, its two ends crossed over in front and fastened by a decorative pin. By the later 1860s knotted and bow ties were worn. The last 20 years of the century saw great variations in neckwear. A deep, turned-down softer collar was usual with lounge suits and sports attire while the white stiff collars, upstanding or winged, were worn with more formal dress. Silk striped or plain neckcloths, knotted or bow ties were equally in favour. White shirts had stiff or pleated fronts. Detachable stiff cuffs were general (**791A, 806, 807C, F, 812, 813A, E, 814, 818B, G, 823A, F, 825**).

Men's Dress. Accessories and Etiquette

Accessories were less numerous and obtrusive than in the eighteenth century. In the early decades, with the tail coat cut away square in front at the waist and the tightly fitted pantaloons, a pair of *fob watches* was fashionable, depending on ribbons or straps just below the waist one on each side. Later, custom restricted this to one only. *Snuff* was still taken and elegant boxes were carried in waistcoat pockets. *Cigar* smoking became the custom about 1830, after the introduction of wooden matches. By 1860 *cigarette* smoking had become common and ladies also began to adopt the habit, usually only in secret. However, the majority of ladies professed to abhor the smell of stale tobacco smoke and their husbands had to wear special smoking jackets to indulge and then only in the smoking room of the house or hotel.

By mid-century the *gold watch* with chain suspended across the waistcoat front had become the symbol of success. *Gloves* were worn at all times and *sticks* carried. There was a vogue for a monocle, attached to a black ribbon, held in the eye.

Etiquette in the wearing of jewellery and accessories was as strict for gentlemen as it was for ladies. By the 1880s and 1890s gentlemen wore only discreet forms of jewellery and any ostentation here was not tolerated. Only one watch chain should grace the waistcoat, only one ring should be worn, cuff links and tie pins should be restrained in design. White gloves must be worn at a dance and must not be removed. Light grey gloves were permitted to the theatre. Canes could be carried to evening functions but must be of malacca with simple knobs. A gentleman must always take his hat with him; there were specific rules as to where he should place it when being entertained or at a ball.

Women's Dress 1800–1820

The history of women's fashions in the nineteenth

798 *Hungarian, 1857*

799 *Spanish, c.1850*

800 *French, 1858*

801 *Spanish*

1850–60

802 *Dutch, 1855*   **803, 804** *French, 1855*   **805** *Russian, 1853*   **806** *French, 1850*

century is totally different from that of the men. Where men's styles changed slowly and became steadily more sombre and, towards the end of the century, more informal, ladies' changed even more rapidly as the years passed, displaying the utmost variety possible in style, fabrics and ornamentation. It would be difficult to imagine a greater contrast between the white, diaphanous draperies of the early century, the romanticism of the 1830s, the prim femininity of the 1840s, the immensity of the over-flounced crinolines, the elegance of the draped bustles and the final, slender-waisted, full-busted tea gowns of the *fin de siècle*.

Unlike the other expressions of art in the nineteenth century, costume was not fully eclectic. Some ideas were inspired by the past, the classical draperies, the crinoline skirts, for example, but the fashions of the century could only have been produced in this era; they were a mirror of this age, each decade different in silhouette and mode, each reflecting the social, political and economic life of its time. The development of style was continuous, constantly changing, but in a forward direction. There was no recapitulation, no repetition. Each few years produced a different form and every student of costume will readily recognise and identify that of any decade in the nineteenth century simply by being confronted with a black silhouette; no further detail should be necessary.

In order to present this development clearly, the illustrations of this chapter are grouped in decades (the nationalities being given in the notes at the end of the chapter) and two pages show the designs for each decade. Similarly the text deals with each period in turn, chronologically, discussing accessories and detail together with the main fashion.

In the first decade of the century *gown styles* continued in the same type of modes as those of the late 1790s. Fabrics were white or light coloured and were thin: muslin, batiste, lawn, tulle, gauze and taffeta. They were plain or spotted or had a little coloured embroidery at hem, sleeves and neck. The style was still for a very high waistline, immediately under the breasts, which was marked by a sash or ribbon tie. The bodice had a very low round or square neckline so that it was only a few inches deep in front. Sleeves were very short, generally puff. Skirts were full, gathered into the high waistline and falling to the ground with a train at the back (**765B, D, 770C**).

The suggestions, often quoted, that the fabric of these dresses was kept damp so that they would cling to the figure and that nothing was worn underneath them are both apocryphal. When a little thought is given to the former idea, it is realised that damp muslin would simply appear creased and droopy. It could only cling if kept perpetually wet and it is difficult to credit the most stupid of females with wishing to remain in a dripping condition all the time.* Equally it was only the fanatic few who wore almost nothing underneath such gowns.

The derivation of this style of dress of the early 1800s was classical or, at least, what the French thought to be classical. A glance at classical statuary or frescoes will show that these dresses bore little relationship to the draped classical chiton and the latter had more often been richly coloured, not just white. The idea behind the mode of the 1800s was possibly to represent the white marble of the statuary.

---

* The legend derives from a comment made many years ago by the Frenchman Henri Bouchot that women *looked as if* their garments were kept damp.

Even in the years 1800–10, when winters, fortunately, were fairly mild, it was necessary to wear other garments on top of the diaphanous gown. There were several possibilities: spencers, shawls and stoles, tunics and overdresses or tabliers. The *spencer* was very fashionable. A waist-length jacket, it was dark in colour, popularly of velvet and had a stand-up collar and long, fitting sleeves which came down low over the hand as far as the first row of knuckles. It could be worn open or fastened with frogging, braid or buttons (**761, 766**).

Shawls and stoles were ubiquitous and varied greatly in size and shape. Some were square, others rectangular; most were richly patterned and coloured to contrast with the gown. Fringe, tassel or lace edging was fashionable. They were made of cashmere, velvet, silk, muslin or gauze according to season (**755, 765C, E, 768, 770D**). Feather boas were also often worn (**759**).

Tunics and *overdresses* took many forms. Some were three-quarter length and were of the same style as the gown underneath with low neckline and high waist. The tunic was made from velvet, silk or satin in colours; it had a patterned hem, often in Greek fret design, and fringed edges (**765E**). Overdresses usually hung from the shoulders, incorporating sleeves, then fell to a long train at the rear (**758**). Some designs were made with the mameluke sleeve which was designed in several puffs, slashed, separated by

807 The Crystal Palace. English Dress, 1850–60

ribbon ties. It resembled the early seventeenth century mode (**763**).

After 1810 there were several cold winters and ladies decided that they had had enough of wearing Mediterranean-type clothing in Paris, London or Berlin. Warmer measures were needed. Slowly, between 1810 and 1820, changes came. The gown neckline rose, for day wear* and round the neck-edge was worn a 'Betsie', a little ruff or ruffle.† Waistlines were still very high but long, fuller sleeves came into vogue; the train disappeared and the skirt rose to display the feet, its hem finished by a flounce or fringing (**766, 770B, D, F**). Fabrics also became warmer and more varied; to muslin and gauze were added silks, brocades, velvets and wool. Colours were still light but more variety was seen here than previously.

---

* The evening gown was still décolleté. It was from this decade that the distinction in neckline between day and evening dress dates.

† This was of English origin, referring to the fashions under Queen Elizabeth I.

Long *coats* became fashionable. These had high waistlines also, long sleeves with puff tops and fitting bodices with collars. They reached to just below the ankle, just covering the dress (**770E, G**). A fur or fur-lined version was introduced about 1808 for winter wear. (The former had a silk lining and the latter a cloth exterior.) They were based on Russian and Polish designs and the name was taken from the prototypes – witzschoura or witchoura.

In the last years of the eighteenth century and the first two or three of the nineteenth a minimum of *underwear* was usual. The ideal was the natural figure. The extremely fashion conscious more elegant figures cast aside corsets, bodices, petticoats and wore flesh-coloured tights made of stockinet. The majority of women found this fashion too chilly also not especially favourable to making the gown hang well so retained a simple petticoat, a chemise and stockings. They also wore a body band or belt about six inches deep round the abdomen and a narrow breast band designed to lift the bosom. Drawers or pantalettes were

808 *French, 1863*

809 *Austrian, 1863*

810 *French, 1863*

811 *Dutch, 1865*

812 *1864*

A   B   C   D   E

worn by most women. They reached down to mid-calf level and were usually lace-edged.

This type of minimum underwear was ideal for the young or slim but less so for the not-so-young or not-so-slim who had been conditioned all their lives to wearing a rigid corset. By 1807-08 a *corset* was being worn once more by many women. It had bones and lacing but was designed only to flatten the abdomen and buttocks, not to slenderise the waist which was still unaccentuated and at a high line. In 1816 a divorce corset was introduced. This did not refer to the breakdown of marriage but to the separation of the breasts. The top of the corset rose in the centre to a triangular point, made of padded metal, which separated one breast from the other. It was a short-lived mode.

Classical *hair* styles were fashionable until 1807-08. Hair was curly and fairly short. Wigs were popular also, as were false switches which could be added, especially for evening coiffures. The Greek chignon style was still favoured for some years; it was held in place by nets, ribbons and combs (**765B, C, D, E**). *Turbans* and *scarves* of all kinds were popular as headcovering until 1810. These had ostrich plume and ribbon decoration and were made in all materials and colours (**755, 758, 759, 761, 763**).

From *1810-20* the hair was longer and often arranged in curls in front and over the ears. Some styles had centre partings. *Bonnets* became fashionable, decorated by ostrich plumes, ruching and lace; they were tied under the chin with wide ribbons. Shapes of bonnet varied from the tall crowned type to a wide brimmed shape framing the face, also a small, close-fitting design. They were made of straw or gauze in the summer; velvet or satin in winter (**766, 770B, E, G, 846**).

Footwear, from 1800-20, was a light slipper

814 *German, 1874* **815** *Swiss, c.1879* **816** *German, 1873* **817** *Hungarian, 1875*

made of kid or silk. It was heel-less and low cut and generally fastened by ribbons crossed over the instep and round the ankle (**766, 768, 770B, D, F, G, 835**).

Because of the thin, loose dresses, ladies now had to carry reticules or bags instead of, as hitherto, being able to put their personal necessaries in capacious pockets concealed in hoop skirts. These reticules were dainty; they had handles and were generally drawn up at the top by cords. Most designs were of velvet, silk or brocade and were embroidered, beaded, fringed or tasselled (**762, 763, 765B, 770G**). Other accessories included *parasols* (**761, 770G**), *fur muffs* (**758**), *fans* (**768**) and *gloves*. These were very long with the early, short-sleeved dresses, either white or strongly coloured, then became short with the later, long-sleeved gowns (**755, 756, 759, 766, 770F**).

Women's Dress 1820–1850

Between 1820 and 1825 the waistline gradually dropped from its high line under the breasts to the natural level. As soon as this position had been

reached, the natural instinct to slenderise the waist was re-asserted. Tight-lacing returned and the smallness of the waist was accentuated once more by a wide belt pulled tightly. At the same time the skirt became fuller, the straight long form of the 1810s evolving into a bell shape which reached the ankles. This larger area of fabric needed ornamentation; the lower part was scallopped, flounced and decorated by rows of braid, embroidery, ribbon bows and flowers.

The day neckline was either a square or cut across in a boat shape. The square form was often filled in by white silk or lace and with a collar. Evening styles retained the low, wide décolletage. Sleeves became fuller at the top. Evening styles were short puffs; day wear was in leg-of-mutton style, full at the top, fitting on the forearm. Shoulders were sloping and their width accentuated by the full top of the sleeve (**771, 772, 773, 775, 777, 778**).

Colours were still predominantly white or light, though the fuller skirts led to an increase in patterned fabrics in stripes, spots and checks as well as dainty floral patterns. Muslin, batiste and silk were fashionable for summer, velvets and wool for winter. Evening wear was made in gauze, tulle and silk in pale colours.

During the years 1800–20 white had become established as the normal wear for wedding dresses. At first this was simply because white was the most fashionable colour. Over the years white came to represent purity and virginity in the bride so, after 1820, when coloured dresses were worn more often than previously, white remained correct for a wedding gown.

Shawls were still popular for extra warmth in all seasons. In silk, cashmere and velvet they were of brilliant colours, embroidered or made from striped or plaid material. Long scarves were draped round the shoulders in summer, made of tulle, silk or lace (**778**). *Cloaks* were fashionable, especially for evening wear (**775**), feather boas were still slung round the shoulders and fur tippets worn. In winter long *coats* were of cloth or velvet and many were fur trimmed or lined. They followed the form of the gowns.

The trend towards a slenderer waist, sloping shoulder line and fuller skirt continued in the years *1830–40*. The previous decade had been a transitional one; in the 1830s the new fashion was established. It was a feminine romantic theme reflecting the Romantic age in literature, painting and the decorative arts.

The development of the trend can be perceived in comparing the illustrations in figs. **782** and **786** of the costume of 1830 with fig. **790** (1835) and **784** (1839). The evening gown neckline is now lower and partly off the shoulders. There are still puff sleeves, often very large, the waist is a little high but slender, and the skirt fairly full, pleated in at the waist and reaching to the ankles (**786**, **850**). Fig. **782** shows the equivalent day dress with high neckline with collar and leg-of-mutton sleeves.

This leg-of-mutton sleeve (*gigot* in France) was especially fashionable in the early 1830s (**782**). It reached its largest dimensions about 1833–35 when it was padded and fitted with metal springs to keep the desired shape. After 1835–36 the fullness moved lower down the arm and the sleeve was gathered tightly at the shoulder and finished with a fitted cuff. This accentuated the

818 London's Riverside, the Palace of Westminster. English Dress, 1870–80

sloping shoulder line further (**784**). It was fashionable now to wear a cape of the same material as the gown over the shoulders (**790**).

An alternative shoulder covering was provided by the *canezou*. This was a white shawl-like blouse covering the shoulders and descending in two lappets which were tucked into the belt in front. It had been worn in many forms since 1800 and continued well after mid-century but it was especially typical of the 1830s. It was wide on the shoulders, accentuating both the slope and the width. It was generally lace, ruffle or pleating trimmed (**788, 833**). A similar styled fichu was also fashionable (**780H, 784**). Evening gown necklines could be softened by a fichu or berthe of lace, worn on top.

The fuller skirts of the later 1830s were now gathered and pleated into the waistline, which had become slenderer, lower and was shaped round at the back and slightly pointed in front. Materials were a little heavier and the fullness of the fabric precluded the quantity of skirt trimming of the previous decade. Colours were stronger. Fabrics included brocade, silk, velvet, wool and gingham.

For *outdoor wear* ladies in the 1830s still wore shawls and scarves but these were less fashionable than before (**780F**). Long coats were fitted at the waist and had the same designs of sleeve, bodice and skirt as the gowns. They were in strong colours in cloth or velvet (**780D**). Also fashionable were cloaks, capes and mantelets worn in various lengths and often fur trimmed (**780C**).

As the waistline dropped to its normal level and a slender figure was desired so corset lacing became tighter and the *corset* itself longer. In the 1820s it had been simply shaped to control the stomach and lift the breasts slightly. By 1835 it was more elaborately shaped to slenderise the waist and it extended downwards to hip level. It was laced up the centre back and whalebone strips were inset. A broad metal busk was inserted up the centre front. The fuller skirt also required support and shaping. At first hip and bustle pads, tied round the waist were adequate. Soon they had to be replaced by stiffened petticoats. Starched and flounced ones were worn on top of a quilted petticoat. The chemise, pantalettes and petticoats were lavishly decorated with lace.

Stockings were white or flesh coloured. For evening, a black net stocking over a flesh coloured one was much in vogue. *Footwear* was still

819 *Dutch, 1879*

820 *French, c.1875*

821 *Swiss, c.1876*

822 *Russian, 1872*

heel-less until about 1838–39 when a low heel was introduced. Low cut slippers continued in fashion in black, white or colours. Higher cut shoes also ankle boots were now worn. These were of kid, silk or velvet and were laced. Toes were narrow and square ended. Grey or fawn gaiters could be worn on top of the shoes (**771, 772, 773, 775, 782, 784, 786, 793, 836**).

The general trend continued in the *1840s*, but by this time the heavier, fuller skirts, the plainer sleeves, the sloping shoulders and the ringleted hair styles combined to give a drooping, more serious air. The romantic feminism was giving place to the mid-century prim and proper lady. The lightness and gaiety had disappeared and ladies were beginning to be weighed down by the sheer quantity of clothes. Except for the décolleté evening gowns (**792, 793**), every part of the female form (save for the face) was decorously covered from high neckline to long sleeves, heavy skirts sweeping the ground and enveloping bonnets. The lady of the 1840s still managed, despite all this, to look feminine and dainty. She had a tightly fitting bodice, a very slender waist extending to a deep point in front and a very full

skirt gathered in at the waist (**791E**). The skirt was often decorated by flounces set horizontally at intervals (**791C**). This was an especially favoured style for evening gowns (**797F**).

Colours in the 1840s were stronger and darker. Striped and plaid materials were fashionable also shot taffeta and watered silks. There was a wide selection of *fabrics* including cashmere, alpaca, silks, tulle, muslin, cotton, velvet, merino and crêpe. Some fabrics were plain but patterns were becoming more the vogue in all-over sprig designs and checks.

Outdoor wear was at its most varied from fitted long coats with full skirts to all kinds of shawls and scarves, which had returned to fashion with the immense skirts (**795, 797**). It was the top part of the body which needed the extra warmth, the lower part being already encased in six or seven underskirts from a red flannel one on the inside to a corded calico one, a horsehair one* and, over this, three or four starched calico or muslin ones, flounced to support the weight of the gown

* The crinoline of the early 1850s took its name from these horsehair petticoats. *Crinis*, Latin for hair, also the French *crin*, and *linum*, Latin for thread.

824 *Austrian, c.1880* **825** *German, 1882*   **826** *German, 1880*   **827** *French, 1885*

skirt on top. Also fashionable were capes and cloaks and the mantelets, visites and pélerines (**791D**). These were of varied length from a shoulder covering to a garment extending to the waist, hips or ankles. Mostly they had part sleeves or were slit to allow the hands to pass through.

The *hair styles* of the 1820s began to change in tune with the rest of the costume. The Grecian coiffures disappeared and hair was grown longer; slowly the design became more elaborate. Hair was combed in loops and swirls and piled higher on the top of the head. It was decorated with flowers and plumes (**771, 772, 773, 775, 777, 778, 844**). In the 1830s the coiffures rose higher to elaborate arrangements on top of the head in plaits and switches. Evening coiffures were especially ornate (**782, 786, 793, 833, 850**). The 1840s brought a different style of coiffure, more demure and decorous. The hair was parted in the centre and pulled back sleekly to side ringlets. At the back a ring of plaits was set with curls depending from it. Evening coiffures were decorated with plumes and lace (**792, 797B, D, F, 837**).

In the 1820s and 1830s either *bonnets* or *hats*

were worn. Both of these grew larger in design in these years and were profusely decorated by ribbons, plumes and flowers. Both hats and bonnets had wide ribbons depending from them; the bonnets were always tied under the chin, the hats sometimes (**773, 777, 778, 780C, D, F, H, 782, 784, 788, 790, 842**). By the 1840s the bonnet was *de rigueur*. The coal scuttle design with the wide brim had been fashionable but now the poke bonnet took over. This projected considerably in front of the face and largely hid it from view. By 1845 this front had shortened and the bonnet was smaller. It was made of varied fabrics: silk, gauze, crêpe and straw according to season. It was decorated, inside and out, by flowers and ribbons and was always tied under the chin by a large ribbon bow. Veils were worn with many bonnets (**791C, D, E, 795, 847**). Indoors, white caps, lace-edged and ribbon trimmed, were often worn.

Accessories were similar to those of the years 1800–20. *Reticules* were carried until the 1840s when fuller skirts made them less necessary (**777, 782, 791D**). *Parasols* were in use (**777, 778, 780F**), *gloves* were long for evening, short for day-time wear (**771, 772, 786, 792, 793, 797B, D, 850**). Black silk mittens were also worn. Lace handkerchiefs were carried and jewellery included cameos and sets of earrings, brooch and bracelet. Fresh flowers in jewelled holders were attached by a chain to a finger ring. *Fans* were becoming more important again as an item of etiquette. They were carried especially in the evenings (**771, 773, 786, 792, 793, 797B**). Fur *muffs* were fashionable in winter (**780C, D**).

Women's Dress 1850–1870

The history of feminine fashion in these years is dominated by the *crinoline*. The immense skirt was the focal centre of the design, the rest of the ensemble being adapted to show it to advantage. The circular form of the skirt remained fashionable for the whole decade of the 1850s, while its circumference grew steadily all the while.

By 1850 even the half dozen stiffened petticoats became inadequate to support the weight of the gown skirt in its desired form, so the crinoline appeared. At first this was like its predecessors, the sixteenth century farthingale and the eighteenth century hoop, an underskirt of stiff (horsehair) material with whale-bone hoops inserted at intervals to maintain the shape (**980**). But, unlike its predecessors, the crinoline did not stop at its proportions of 1850. Despite all criticism and ribaldry from the medical profession, men in general and humorous illustrated magazines, the crinoline skirt grew larger and larger and its popularity with all classes increased. It was the feminine status symbol of the 1850s.

Opposition was greatest in England and the USA. Indeed, in America, the anti-crinoline movement (progenitor perhaps of today's women's lib movement) endeavoured to point out by propaganda to the mass of silly women the indignities that they suffered by succumbing to the domination of the crinoline. This proposed reform was bolstered by a suggested alternative attire. The leader and champion was *Mrs Amelia Bloomer* who travelled to both London and Dublin in 1851, dressed in the new mode to hold mass

A   B   C   D   E

828 Costume 1880–90. Paris Riverside

829 *French, 1891*

830 *Swedish, 1892*

831 *Russian, 1890–5*

meetings to popularise it. The reform dress consisted of long, full trousers, belted at the waist, to replace the scorned crinoline, worn with a bodice or jacket. The exercise was a total failure though a number of women joined in the crusade and wore the new dress in the streets. They were ridiculed and had to give up. All that survives of this episode is the name 'bloomers', which was given to these trousers. Mrs Bloomer's failure was because the experiment was far ahead of its time and also her costume was so inelegant and unattractive.

Meanwhile, in 1856, the *cage-crinoline* was patented. This was a wired metal structure which provided the requisite shape without the weight and avoided the necessity for wearing quite so

many layers of petticoats. It was taken up with enthusiasm by all classes of women. It was cheap and a great success. The skirt circumference grew greater. 1859–60 was the zenith of the style of the circular crinoline. In the 1860s its shape gradually changed from a circle to an oval. Then the front was flattened, also the sides and the fullness concentrated at the back (**982**). The crinoline was still worn until the later 1860s (though its shape had altered), but then it took the form of a bustle (*tournure* in France) with additional metal strengthening at the back to support the immense weight of the material draped there.

With the crinoline skirts women continued to wear a quantity of *underwear* including the white, lace-trimmed chemise, ankle-length pantalettes and some flounced petticoats. The waistline was now very slender, in contrast to the immense bell-shape of the skirt. The *corset* was laced tightly to achieve this despite protests and warnings issued from time to time by the medical profession. As the crinoline grew larger the corset was more tightly laced but it left the bosom free, rising high in front under the breasts, lifting them slightly. The corset was made of boned silk and ribbon. Like all underwear it was lavishly decorated by ribbons and lace (**978**).

Though the crinoline skirt remained in fashion for about 20 years, so long that it seemed as though it had always been in fashion, *gown* styles altered between the 1850s and 1860s. The *day gown* of the 1850s had a fitted bodice generally fastened up the centre front and a small collar at the throat. Pagoda sleeves, full at the bottom and often only three-quarter length, were fashionable. The skirt was popularly decorated by flounces. Ornamentation was lavish, most commonly by braid, frogging, fringing, tasselling, ribbon ruching, bows and embroidery. *Fabrics* were varied with wool, alpaca, mohair, velveteen and brocades in winter and linen, cambrics, muslin, lace, silk, satin and taffeta in summer. *Colours* were strong and dark; especially fashionable were the new aniline dyes in strident tones of purple, magenta, crimson, green and royal blue, as well as softer tones in plum, blue, brown and cream. Plaids, checks and stripes were especially favoured (**798, 799, 802, 807B, E, H**).

Evening gowns were similar in style but had low, wide, off-the-shoulder necklines and tiny puff sleeves. Their skirts were popularly designed in a large number of tiny flounces* and often the overskirt was tied back by ribbon bows to display an even more flounced underskirt (**797B, 801, 805**). Evening gowns were generally made in white or pale colours in satin, silk, gauze, tulle, lace or tarlatan. They were even more lavishly decorated than day gowns with artificial flowers, ribbon bows and ruching.

The *gown styles* of the *1860s* slowly changed to a concentration of the material and interest at the back. The high neckline was worn for most of the decade but towards 1868 a square neckline became fashionable. The tight bodice was buttoned down the centre then extended, princess style, to a

plain skirt front or to a tablier (apron) front. Sleeves were still three-quarter with flounces or lace ruffles below them. All the fullness of the skirt was concentrated at the back and, by 1868–69, the material was drawn up and back in flounces and decorated by large ribbon bows. Sashes, if worn, also were tied at the back with wide ribbons which accentuated this line. Decoration increased especially in the form of fringing, tasselling, braid and flounces. Fabrics were especially varied and commonly one or more contrasting materials, colours and designs were used in one gown. Stripes were especially fashionable (**811, 813B, C, D**).

There were many alternative forms of *outdoor wear*, but all of these concentrated on keeping the top part of the body warm; the lower part was still so be-wrapped by petticoats to make further layers superfluous. Long coats were rare and heavy winter coats extended only to three-quarter length. These had wide sleeves and immense cuffs and collars. They were generally on princess line with full skirts to cover the crinoline. Velvet or braid band decoration was popular (**807D**). More common were half-length coats or cloaks trimmed with braid, fringe, tassels or fur. These could be waisted or hung loose in turkey-back style (**798, 807E, 809**). All kinds of shawls, scarves, mantelets and berthes were still worn in a variety of colours and materials and with a quantity of decoration (**805, 813B**).

Hair was grown very long. It was parted in the centre and drawn back loosely to a round bun or chignon at the nape; often this was held in place by a chenille net. In the 1860s the chignon was larger and set higher on the head; the round form was twisted into a more complex style. For evening wear flowers, lace, pearls, combs, gold and silver nets and ribbon bows were used for decoration and control (**797B, 801, 802, 805, 811, 813C, D**).

The *bonnet* was the predominant headcovering of the 1850s. It was smaller than the style of the 1840s and was worn further back on the head to show the face and front hair. It was decorated with flowers and bows inside the brim as well as outside and was still tied under the chin with a wide ribbon bow (**798, 799, 807B, D, E, H, 847**). In the 1860s either bonnets or hats were worn. Towards the end of the decade, the small *hat* perched forward on the forehead became fashionable; this displayed the curls and swirls of the

---

* In 1859 the Empress Eugénie appeared at a ball in a white satin gown with over a hundred flounces on the skirt.

back chignon. *Toques* were also fashionable at this time. *Caps* were worn indoors (**809, 813B, D**).

Stockings were usually white in the 1850s while coloured ones were re-introduced in the 1860s. Evening stockings generally matched the gown. *Slippers* were worn with ball gowns but for day wear *boots* were the usual footwear. Both designs had heels and the boots were laced or buttoned. Satin, silk, kid or leather was used (**838, 840**).

Important accessories still included the *parasol* (**799, 807B, H, 813B**), fur *muffs* (**798, 799, 807B, E, 809**) and *handkerchiefs* (**801**). *Gloves* were worn always, even at home, often with a bracelet on top (**797B, 798, 799, 801, 805, 807D, E, 813B, D**). This was an age of the *fan*. With evening dress especially it was an essential item of expression, just as it had been in the eighteenth century (**797B, 801, 843**). Particularly fashionable in the field of *jewellery* were shell cameos and gold lockets hung on a gold chain or a black ribbon round the neck. Small perfume boxes or bottles made of gold or silver were carried, which contained a tiny sponge soaked in perfume.

Women's Dress 1870–1890

Whereas the 1850s and 1860s had been dominated by the crinoline, the two succeeding decades were those of the *bustle*. Fashions were changing now more quickly. *Haute couture* was launching new designs each year, developing the style; at the other end of the fashion scale mass production was increasing and the opportunity given by the ready-to-wear trade was being taken up by more women all the time. The bustle enjoyed two distinct decades of popularity, once in the 1870s and once in the 1880s. In each case, the rise and fall of the fashion from its inception to its demise, occupied about 10 years.

In the *bustle gowns* the interest of the design was centred at the back, especially in the skirt. It was in this part of the costume that the changes in silhouette were subtle, yet continuous. By 1870 the crinoline form had become that of a bustle; by 1875, this reached a crescendo when the skirt draperies were swept up to form almost a horizontal shelf below the waist at the rear from which they descended in a torrent of ruffles, pleats and bows to a long train sweeping the floor. Between 1878 and 1880 the bustle declined to a sleek hip-line, the draperies swathed and tied back at a lower level around the knees. From *1880–85* a new bustle crescendo arose, a slightly different line, and, by 1890, had vanished again. Each year's high fashion was a little different from the one before or after, the process continuing steadily in crescendo or diminuendo as appropriate to the date.

As with the crinoline, the bustle gown styles demanded a structure under them to support the immense quantity of material used, also to provide the fashionable figure to show off the design. The bustle shape was at first formed by a crinoline skirt with the fullness concentrated at the rear, whalebone or metal bands being inserted into a shortened petticoat. Later, the bustle or *tournure* became simply a metal wire basket or horsehair and gauze pad which rested on the buttocks and was tied on round the waist (**985**). Alternative *tournures* were incorporated into a complex petticoat which included many stiffened ruffles and pleats at the back, set in rows between waist and ground (**981**). At the hem were sewn pleated, stiffened 'sweepers' (*balayeuses*), which acted as dusters to absorb the dirt, and keep clean the gown train on top (**986**). In the years 1878–82 usually no bustle was worn, the hips being sleek and the fullness of the skirt draped lower down. After this the bustle returned, reaching its greatest size about 1885 then diminishing once more.

An important item of wear needed to complement the bustle skirt was the restrictive *corset*. This had been tightly laced to produce a tiny waist with the full crinoline skirts, but it had been short, since the size of the skirt made it unnecessary to flatten the stomach or hips, which were hidden. The bustle gowns needed not only a very slender waist but a full bosom and hip line to stress this. The corset was required to mould the figure from a high, uplifted bosom to low on the hips (**979**). Such long corsets tended to ride up and wrinkle and whalebones would break at the waist as the lady seated herself. As the curve between breasts and waist and waist and hips became more pronounced, this was a frequent occurrence, so steel replaced whalebone more and more. The centre front of the corset was fitted with a metal busk called a *buse en poire* (spoon busk, in English), because of its form which was narrow at the top and widening below the curving waist into a pear shape. It was in these years that the storm of protest arose from the

A   B   C   D   E   F

medical profession. Doctors tried to inform parents of the damage being done to the young girls' bodies by encasing them into such an extreme form of corset, but the criticisms made little difference. Ladies young and old, followed, or tried to follow, the fashionable silhouette accepting, as a natural unpleasantness of life, the fainting fits or the 'vapours'.

The *gowns of the 1870s* were, like the drawing rooms of the time, over-decorated and extravagantly cluttered. The square or high neckline was edged with ruffles and lace and sleeves ended in a cuff with a bow and more ruffles. The waistline was fitting, generally in princess style but, below this, the skirt fabric was swept up and back to a riot of gargantuan ribbon bows, ruffles and flounces to fall in stages to a long train. The front was often draped in apron fashion (*en tablier*) and also ruffled. Generally, two or three different fabrics and colours were to be seen in the skirt: the overskirt of one colour; its lining, visible as it was folded or swept back, of another and the underskirt, which showed in front and below, different again. Knife-edge pleats were fashionable, also fringe, lace and tassels. Stiff, rustling fabrics were popular, especially taffeta and heavy satin and silks. Colours were strong and patterned fabrics contrasted in one garment with plain ones (**817, 818C, E, F, 820, 822**).

By *1877–78* the bustle was diminishing and the draped skirt was arranged lower, giving a sleek, fitting hip-line and causing ladies to walk with small steps as the material was pulled tightly round the knees. Internal tapes directed the fullness towards the rear (**815, 818A, H, 819**). By *1880* the skirt, though still long and ornamented, was quite slender (**818D, 824, 826, 828B**). By *1884* the bustle had returned and full, draped-up, complex gown styles were prevalent in the years 1885–86 (**823C, 828D, E**).

In the 1880s there was an increase of different types of costume for differing functions, seasons and times of day; the rules of etiquette for wearing these were strict and definitive. The formal gown, with its quantity of material and excessive ornamentation, was reserved more for afternoon and evening wear, while simpler clothes began to appear for morning use or office wear. One style had a pleated skirt without a train and a jacket fitted to the waist with a short flared skirt or peplum below to accommodate the bustle. The material at the front of the skirt was swept up and back to the bustle draperies (**828D**). Tweeds and check and plaid wools were popular for such suits, which were in general use also for travel; they became more strictly tailored after 1885 and were worn with blouses by 1890.

There was great variety in *coats, jackets*, wraps and *cloaks*. Most designs of coat or jacket were fitted at the waist. Coats were long or three-quarter length, while jackets were short to accommodate the bustle skirts. In winter sealskin coats were fashionable also fur-trimmed wool or tweed ones. Check and plaid fabrics were often seen. Silk was used for warmer weather, decorated by lace or fringe (**818A, D, F, 823C**).

Ladies wore high *boots* rather than shoes now. These were buttoned or laced; they had heels and pointed toes. They were made of fabric or kid, often with patent leather heels and toe-caps (**848**). *Shoes*, when worn, had similar heels. *Evening slippers* were of brocade, velvet or silk and were frequently embroidered. *Stockings* matched the gown or the petticoat.

The *coiffure* was very feminine and dressed elaborately. Hair was drawn up and back to show the ears. It was dressed in curls on the forehead and in complex ringlets and sweeps at the sides and back (**815, 817, 820, 822, 826, 827, 828B**). The closed *bonnet* had disappeared but small bonnet and *hat* styles were perched on top of the head or worn at an angle. Both were tiny and decorated by ribbons and plumes. Many were tied under the chin with ribbon bows (**818A, C, D, E, F, H, 819, 823C, 824, 828D, E, 849**).

Fans were still carried with evening dress (**817, 822, 826, 841**). *Parasols* were usually long-handled, of walking length (**818F, H, 819, 824, 828E**). Small fur *muffs*, often decorated by sprays of violets, were very fashionable in autumn and winter (**823C, 828D**).

Women's Dress 1890–1900

The fashionable silhouette of this decade was completely different. Gone were the framework petticoats, bustles and draperies. In their place was a simpler, most elegant form. The interest had moved from the bustle to the sleeves. The 1890s were the years of the return of the leg-of-mutton or balloon sleeve, a fashion which reached its peak in 1895, then slowly diminished. The characteristics of the silhouette, apart from the sleeves, were a very high neckline, a full bosom, a wasp waist, sleek hips and a bell-shaped skirt. To achieve the desired effect a tightly-laced, boned, long *corset* was essential (**983**), also a full flounced or jabot bust line, then a silk or taffeta *petticoat*, fitted to the knee then, below this, flared, flounced and lace-trimmed. This, together with a taffeta skirt-lining, produced the coveted frou-frou sound with movement. The hour-glass silhouette needed only one petticoat and this, together with the skirt and underskirt, were held up daintily while walking in the street. Comparable in feminine coquetry to the earlier use of the fan, this complex art was especially characteristic of the age.

Clothes were more varied now, designed for the function whether it be a formal reception, a theatre evening, a ball, sport, an office, the country, travel or sea-bathing. *Fabrics* were equally varied comprising especially beautiful furs like Persian lamb, Russian sable, chinchilla and seal to delicate materials such as lace, tulle, muslin, satin, velvet and damask and heavier ones like tweed and poplin. Lace and fur were lavishly used for trimming and decoration.

Tailoring was by now of the highest standard and tailored suits, worn with softly feminine or shirt blouses were very popular. In all garments, whether suit or tea gown, the same characteristics of silhouette were maintained. Only *evening* and *ball gowns* differed in that their sleeves were elbow-length, their décolletage notable and their skirts very long with trains. The day-time bell-shaped skirt was cut in many gores then lined and stiffened to retain its slender shape. Jackets and tiered capes with high collars were particularly fashionable (**823B, D, E, 829, 830, 831, 832A, B, C, D, F**).

Ladies still wore *boots* of elegant, high buttoned or laced design and made in beautiful colours in kid or leather (**845**). Low cut *slippers* for evening wear were generally black or bronze in kid and *stockings* were fashionably of black net. *Shoes*, like the boots, were high-heeled and had pointed toes. Coloured leather was fashionable for these also.

Hairstyles were simple, in curls on the forehead, then swept up at the sides and back to a chignon or bun fairly high on the head. Evening decoration was by plumes, jewels and aigrettes (**829, 830, 831**). *Hats* varied from small toques, perched on top of the head, decorated with plumes, bird's wings and flowers (**823B, 832A, C, F**), to large-brimmed hats, profusely decorated with ribbon bows, flowers and birds' wings and, popularly, both hat and face were covered by a spotted net veil (**823D, E, 832B, D, 851**). Large hat pins (useful also in self-defence) were essential for these large hats.

Nineteenth Century Children's Costume

It was during this century that tentative attempts were first made to design clothes especially for children, rather than insisting on them wearing a miniature form of adult dress. Certainly there was a considerable easing of the restrictions on movement which had been in force in previous centuries. That this relaxation was in large part only a reflection of adult modes is borne out by the fact that the simpler, freer styles were prevalent especially in the first forty years of the century, at a time when adult dress was also freer and lighter while, by the 1870s and 1880s, once more, children, especially girls, were encased in whalebone and yards of material. Certain designs were made especially for children, such as the sailor suits and hussar jackets but there was, as yet, only a limited movement towards designing clothes suitable specifically for children.

Nineteenth century *babies' clothes* were a little less restrictive and cumbersome than previously. Long clothes were usual until about eight months, after which shorter garments were worn. The baby was still encumbered with many layers and there was excessive anxiety about leaving off items of clothing, especially woollen ones, in case the child caught cold. A baby's outfit generally consisted of a chemise, stays or a flannel stomach band, flannel petticoat, further petticoats, a dress and coat. Two caps were worn night and day. White was the usual colour in materials of cambric, muslin, linen and lace, with ribbon trimming. After 1850 fabrics were heavier and more layers of clothes worn. Indeed, babies wore more garments in 1900 than they had in 1800.

In the first half of the century *boys* wore long trousers and short, loose jackets or belted three-quarter ones. The trousers were supported by braces over a blouse which had a large collar and a bow finish. They had peaked caps or straw hats (**780A, 783, 789, 797C**). Towards mid-century boys' clothes tended more to the effeminate and they were kept in skirts as long as possible. These skirts were worn over flounced petticoats and showed lace-trimmed pantalettes beneath (**804**).

From mid-century plaid and tartan materials were popular for children and Scottish style kilts were worn. *Boys* wore hussar jackets and these, made in black, were called Eton jackets. Indeed, the public schools adopted, in general, such jackets worn with black trousers for younger boys, while older ones had tail coats. By the 1870s boys wore knickerbocker suits and Norfolk jackets or sailor suits. Young boys wore a sailor blouse with square collar and knickerbockers and a straw sailor hat. The version for older boys was more severely naval. Such suits were popular winter and summer, navy blue serge with cloth cap being worn in winter and white drill with straw hat in summer. Boys of 12–14 began to wear the same styles of clothes as their fathers.

Girls were dressed more freely and comfortably in the first 30 years of the nineteenth century than ever before. They wore soft, dainty dresses, long or three-quarter length according to age, and tied with a sash at the currently fashionable waist level. They had spencer jackets, capes and cloaks and, in winter, coats or pelisses. Under the dresses girls wore ankle-length pantalettes of white cambric with lace trimming. Their styles of shoes, stockings and bonnets were like those of their mothers (**756, 762, 774, 780B**).

In the 1840s dresses for *girls*, like the adult ones, began to have fuller skirts and flounced petticoats were worn underneath, generally displaying lace-edging below the dress hem (**791B, 794**). In the 1850s girls were put into boned corsets from the age of about 11 and crinoline petticoats were worn under the increasingly full skirts. The length of these varied according to the age of the child. In little girls these skirts were just below knee-level and the petticoats showed below. The styles of dresses, boots, hair and bonnets were miniature versions of the adult ones (**800, 803, 807G, 810**).

Girls' clothes in the 1870s and 1880s were at their most restrictive in this century. They wore tightly laced, boned corsets, despite ever increasing warnings from doctors of the dangers of constricting the bodies of growing children into these cages. The damage which could be caused by impeding circulation and breathing, by restricting the development of the muscles of chest and abdomen and even of displacement of vital organs was described and publicised but most mothers continued to dress their daughters in the fashions of the day: the wasp waist, emerging from its swathes of bustle draperies, continued supreme (**821, 823, 828A**).

Notes on the Illustrations

755 French actual costume. Boston Museum of Fine Arts, U.S.A. White cotton gauze dress with wool embroidery in red of laurel leaves and Greek key pattern. White bonnet hat. Dark green scarf with border in red and black.

756 Swiss actual costume. Bernisches Historisches Museum, Berne, Switzerland. Pale green dress with black and white stripe. Black velvet sash.

757 French. Fashion Plate 'Costume Parisien'. Brown coat and buttons. Sage green trousers strapped under instep. Black top hat. Brown gloves and stick. White cravat. Black boots.

758 French actual costume. Boston Museum of Fine Arts, U.S.A. Promenade dress of white India muslin with cotton embroidery. Brown overdress. Fur muff. Silk hat.

759 Dutch actual costume. Costume Museum, The Hague, Holland. Cream silk dress with silver embroidery. Velvet turban and plume. Feather boa. Long gloves.

760 German actual costume. Museum für Geschichte, Hamburg, Germany. Red coat, white self-coloured striped waistcoat, white trousers. Black leather boots. Black bicorne hat with gold braid decoration. White cravat. Brown gloves.

761 Spanish actual costume. Museo del Pueblo Español, Madrid, Spain. White batiste dress with sprig embroidered pattern. Mauve spencer with silver frogging. Silk hat and plume. Parasol, gloves.

762 Swiss actual costume. Bernisches Historisches Museum, Berne, Switzerland. White cotton dress with white stitched embroidery. White ruffles and pantalettes. Embroidered velvet reticule.

763 Swedish fashion plate. National dress influence still in sleeve design. Overdress with ruched edging. Scarf in chignon pattern. Reticule.

764 French actual costume. Musée du Costume de la Ville de Paris. Marine blue cloth coat with gold buttons. White breeches and stockings. Black slippers.

765A English fashion plate. Dark blue cloth tail coat with velvet collar. White breeches and stockings. Black slippers. White cravat and collar, 1800.

B English actual costume. Museum of Costume, Bath, England. White muslin dress with white spot. Velvet reticule, 1802.

C English actual costume. Museum of Costume, Bath, England. Deep blue tunic with gold decorated hem and neckline. White muslin spotted dress with gold hem. Transparent stole with fringed ends, 1808.

D English actual costume. Museum of Costume, Bath, England. White and gold dress. White gloves, 1800.

Details: 19th Century

833 French, c.1830

834 George IV, English

835 Spanish, c.1820

836 French, c.1830

837 Austrian, 1845

838 Austrian, c.1840

839 French, 1895

840 Polish, 1860

841 Folding fan, English, 1870–80

842 French, 1830

843 Spanish fan, c.1850

844 Polish, 1820

845 Spanish, c.1890

846 Spanish, 1814

847 English, c.1850

848 Spanish, 1880–90

849 French, 1872

850 Austrian, 1834

851 English, 1895

247

E English fashion plate, 1810. Dark red tunic with key pattern border hem and fringing. White gown. Transparent gauze stole. Ribbons and plumes in the hair.

F English fashion plate, 1802. Claret velvet tail coat with silk collar. White breeches and stockings. Black slippers.

766 Italian fashion plate. Corriere delle Dame, Milan. Dark spencer with piped decoration. White, spotted dress with lace flounce. Bonnet to match spencer. Lace and plume decoration.

767 Italian fashion plate. Corriere delle Dame, Milan. Dark cloth tail coat. Fawn trousers with instep strap. White waistcoat. Black top hat.

768 German actual costume. Museum für Geschichte, Hamburg, Germany. Oyster satin dress. White tulle stole with embroidered edge. Fan.

769 Swedish actual costume. Nordiska Museet, Stockholm, Sweden. Blue tail coat. White pantaloons with black leather boots. Dark Garrick overcoat. Brown felt hat and brown gloves.

770A French costume. Painting, Louvre, Paris, 1819. Grey tail coat. Fawn pantaloons and black boots. Black top hat.

B French actual costume. Musée du Costume de la Ville de Paris. Bright green satin redingote with spot pattern in darker green. Tulle betsie. Silk hat with ribbons and flowers. Gloves, c.1815.

C Dutch actual costume. Kostuum Museum, The Hague, Holland. Off white dress in heavy cotton with hand embroidered decoration in reds and greens. Bands of coloured flowered braid on bodice, 1811–15.

D Russian actual costume. Hermitage Museum, Leningrad, U.S.S.R. White dress with spotted muslin flounces and coloured embroidery. Light wool stole with coloured borders and fringing, 1818–20.

E Polish actual costume. Narodowe Museum, Cracow, Poland. Plum-coloured taffeta coat. Flowered bonnet, 1811–15.

F French actual costume. Musée du Costume de la Ville de Paris. Bright green dress. Green cords and fringing. White tulle betsie. Gloves, c.1815.

G Polish actual costume. Front view of coat in E. Flowered silk hat. Reticule. Parasol, 1811–15.

771 French actual costume. Boston Museum of Fine Arts, U.S.A. White satin ball dress with gold metal embroidery. White slippers and gloves. Circular white lace fan. Deep red leaves as hair decoration.

772 Spanish actual costume. Rocamora Costume Museum, Barcelona, Spain. Cream dress with open lace-work overlay. Self-coloured ribbon ornamentation on bodice and on skirt. White gloves. Flowers in hair.

773 Polish actual costume. Narodowe Museum, Cracow, Poland. Cream silk gauze dress. Hat to match with plumes. Fan. Cream silk slippers.

774 Fashion plate, Ackermann's Repository. White dress and pantalettes. Blue sash.

775 French actual costume. Musée du Costume de la Ville de Paris. White percale dress embroidered in cotton. Green taffeta manteau lined with pink taffeta.

776 Austrian fashion plate, Wiener Moden. Dark blue tail coat with black collar. White waistcoat, cravat and collar. Grey pantaloons, mauve striped socks and black shoes. Cream gloves. Black top hat.

777 German actual costume. Historisches Museum, Frankfurt-am-Main, Germany. Dark silk dress with white inset and wrist ruffles. Silk hat with ribbons and plumes. Gloves, reticule, parasol.

778 Russian actual costume. Hermitage Museum, Leningrad, U.S.S.R. Dark satin dress with light coloured ribbon decoration. White lace-edged stole. Silk hat with ribbons and flowers. Parasol.

779 Austrian fashion plate. Wiener Moden. Brown cutaway coat. Fawn waistcoat. Spotted fawn cravat, white collar. Black top hat. White trousers, pink striped socks, black shoes. Brown gloves, cane.

780A English fashion plate, 1830. Dark coat and cap. Light trousers, Collar and bow.

B English actual costume. Museum of Costume, Bath, England. Gold embroidered dress. White muslin and lace pantalettes. Bonnet with ribbons, c.1829.

C English fashion plate, 1840. Dark blue velvet cloak with open sleeves, grey fur collar, edging and muff. Pale blue satin dress, bonnet and ribbons. Spotted veil. White gloves.

D English fashion plate, 1835. Dull purple cloth redingote with shoulder capes. Silk bonnet with ribbons and plumes. Black fur muff.

E English fashion plate, 1830. Grey Garrick overcoat, light grey trousers.

F English fashion plate, 1838. Red cotton shawl with white muslin flounces. Spotted pink dress with white flounces. Parasol. Silk bonnet with plumes and ribbons.

G English fashion plate, 1830. Grey cloth overcoat with black velvet collar. Grey beaver top hat. White buckskin trousers, black boots.

H English actual costume. Museum of Costume, Bath, England. White dress decorated with embroidered flowers in red and blue. Black velvet shoulder cape, embroidered in colours and edged with black lace. Dark brown silk bonnet with brown and white lace and flowers, 1837.

781 German costume. Portrait by Krüger of Baron von Arnim. Till 1945 in the Royal Palace, Berlin, Germany. Dark maroon coat. Fawn waistcoat. Black and white stock and white collar. Fawn trousers, white spats, black boots. Black top hat.

782 Swedish actual costume. Nordiska Museet, Stockholm, Sweden. Promenade dress of blue wool decorated with satin. White collar. Embroidered reticule. Bonnet with striped ribbons and flowers. Gloves.

783 Spanish costume. Painting, Museum for Nineteenth Century Painting, Madrid, Spain. Black jacket. Grey trousers with coloured braces. White shirt and collar, red bow. Black boots and hat.

784 Spanish actual costume. Rocamora Costume Museum, Barcelona, Spain. Cream cotton dress printed in a flower design in brown and yellow. White fichu. Cream silk bonnet with ribbons and flowers. Gloves.

785 Russian costume. Portrait by Tschernelow of Schukovska. Black frock coat with dark grey trousers and light grey waistcoat. Black stock. Black top hat and boots.

786 French actual costume. Musée du Costume de la Ville de Paris. Ball dress in pink taffeta embroidered in green and brown silks. White gloves. Black ribbon at throat and wrists. Fan. Pink slippers.

787 Polish actual costume. Narodowe Museum, Cracow, Poland. Sea-blue cloth redingote with black braid and tassel fastenings. Black top hat. Black and white stock and white collar. Grey trousers, black boots. Light grey gloves. Cane.

788 Russian actual costume. Hermitage Museum, Leningrad, U.S.S.R. Dark blue taffeta dress with white berthe. Light silk bonnet with ribbons and flowers.

789 Austrian costume. Painting of the Eltz family by Ferdinand Georg Waldmüller, Österreichische Galerie in Wien (Vienna). Golden-brown coat with black belt. White trousers, black boots.

790 Dutch actual costume. Kostuum Museum, The Hague, Holland. White figured dress. White bonnet with tulle, ribbon and plume decoration.

791A German fashion plate. Berliner Modenspiegel. 1845. Black coat and top hat. Dark grey trousers, black boots. White collar, dark grey cravat. Gloves, cane.

B Swedish actual costume. Nordiska Museet, Stockholm, Sweden. Embroidered white wool dress. White pantalettes. Bonnet, c.1840.

C Hungarian actual costume. Hungarian National Museum, Budapest, Hungary. White wool dress with striped decoration in the Hungarian national colours—red, white and green. Bonnet to match, c.1848–50.

D Swiss actual costume. Bernisches Historiches Museum, Berne, Switzerland. Brown satin mantle and dress with ruched decoration. Brown silk bonnet and ribbons. Fawn parasol. Embroidered handbag.

E Polish actual costume. Narodowe Museum, Cracow, Poland. Golden moiré silk dress. Fringed decoration. Silk bonnet, c.1840.

F German fashion plate. Berliner Modenspiegel, 1845. Dark cutaway coat, light trousers, black shoes. Black top hat, gloves, cane.

792 Russian actual costume. Hermitage Museum, Leningrad, U.S.S.R. Self-coloured brocade dress for evening. White gloves, fan.

793 French actual costume. Boston Museum of Fine Arts, U.S.A. Ball dress in silver gauze shot with pink silk bodice and Indian white muslin overskirt embroidered in silk sprays. White gloves, fan. White slippers, 1840–5.

794 Austrian costume. Painting of his daughter by Franz Alt, Österreichisches Museum der Stadt Wien, Vienna. Costume all in white.

795 Austrian actual costume. Österreichisches Museum der Stadt Wien, Vienna. Dress is pink silk striped in black and light green. Self-coloured fringe decoration. Bonnet to match, c.1840.

796 Spanish costume. Portrait, Museum for Nineteenth Century Painting, Madrid, Spain. Navy tail coat, fawn waistcoat. Black cravat, white collar. Grey-blue trousers, black boots. Black top hat. Gloves, cane.

797A English fashion plate. Black tail coat, dark grey trousers, striped gold and white waistcoat. White shirt collar and cravat. Black boots, 1850.

B English fashion plate. Evening gown of pink satin over an underskirt of white silk. Decoration by lace, ruching, flounces and flowers, 1855.

C English actual costume. Museum of Costume, Bath, England. Light brown wool suit with waistcoat to match. Coat hangs loose without buttons. White collar. c.1856.

D English actual costume. Gallery of Costume, Platt Hall, Manchester. Evening gown in white poplin with woven sprig pattern in self-colour. Crimson cord decoration on sleeves, cream lace frills, c.1845.

E English fashion plate. Dark grey coat with lighter grey check trousers. White collar and cravat, 1847.

F English actual costume. Bethnal Green Museum, London. Tiered skirt in white muslin spotted in pale blue. Cobalt blue bodice, sleeves and flounce edging. Blue silk fringed shawl, 1845–50.

798 Hungarian actual costume. Hungarian National Museum, Budapest, Hungary. Dark green silk dress and coat. Grey decoration and fringing. Pale grey fur muff. Gloves, Bonnet of green silk with white lace ornamentation.

799 Spanish actual costume. Rocamora Costume Museum, Barcelona, Spain. Deep green silk day dress with green fringing and ruching and black edging. Pale green bonnet. White and black bows. Pink silk parasol. Black fur muff.

800 French fashion plate. Journal des Demoiselles, Paris. Electric blue silk dress with white lace at neck, wrists and hem. White stockings, blue boots. Fawn gloves.

801 Spanish costume. Painting, Gallery of Nineteenth Century Painting, Madrid, Spain. Evening gown in red. Skirt flounces, sleeves and décolletage with black lace overlay. White gloves. Pearl necklaces and bracelets. White lace handkerchief. Fan. Ribbons and pearl ropes in hair.

802 Dutch actual costume. Kostuum Museum, The Hague, Holland. Grey-green taffeta dress with self-colour ruching and fringing. White lace collar. Flowers and lace in the hair.

803 and 804 French fashion plate. Les Modes Parisiennes. The little girl wears a pale grey dress striped in deep pink. Her sleeves, collar, and petticoats are white. She has white stockings and shoes. The little boy wears a light grey dress with dark brown velvet banding. His cap is to match. He wears white pantalettes, white stockings and brown boots. His sleeves are white.

805 Russian actual costume. Hermitage Museum, Leningrad, U.S.S.R. A white silk evening dress with pink roses. White spotted muslin stole with lace edging. Ribbons and flowers in the hair.

806 French fashion plate. Les Modes Parisiennes. Evening dress. Black coat and trousers. White waistcoat, shirt, cravat, collar and gloves. Black shoes.

807A English fashion plate, 1860. Bowler hat. Short, plain coat. Check trousers.

B English fashion plate. Yellow taffeta dress with cerise stripes on flounces. Black fur muff. Lace covered parasol. Bonnet, 1860.

C English fashion plate. Light-coloured coat and trousers. Plaid waistcoat. Felt hat, 1855.

D English fashion plate. Tweed brown coat with dark green velvet banding. Cream silk dress. Silk bonnet. Gloves, 1859.

E English fashion plate. Blue silk dress. Darker blue velvet cloak trimmed with ermine to match muff, 1857.

F English fashion plate. Black coat and top hat.

G Fashion plate. Dark grey silk jacket. White and blue dress with lace showing under hem. White stockings and boots. Black patent toes. White bonnet with blue bows, 1855.

H English actual costume. Museum of Costume, Bath, England. Brown muslin dress patterned all over in colours. Straw bonnet with pink ribbons. Pale brown parasol, 1851.

808 French fashion plate. Le Follet. Brown jacket and trousers. White blouse and stockings. Brown boots.

809 Austrian actual costume. Modesammlung des Historischen Museums der Stadt Wien, Vienna. Grey-blue silk dress decorated with black lace. Dark red velvet coat with gold braid. Pale blue silk bonnet. Gloves. Fur muff.

810 French fashion plate. Le Follet. Grey blue taffeta dress. White stockings, brown boots. Dark hat with plume.

811 Dutch actual costume. Kostuum Museum, The Hague, Holland. Olive green taffeta dress with stripes of black and green.

812 Dark wool coat with fur edging. Tweed trousers. Black silk hat.

813A French fashion plate. Tweed suit with bowler hat, 1863.

B German actual costume. Museum für Geschichte, Hamburg, Germany. Light green dress with dark green pattern and stripes. White lawn and lace berthe. Dark green parasol. White bonnet with flowers and cream ribbons. Gloves, 1860.

C Spanish actual costume. Rocamora Costume Museum, Barcelona, Spain. Pale grey silk day dress. Caerulean blue stripes and fringing, 1863.

D Austrian actual costume. Modesammlung des Historischen Museums der Stadt Wien, Vienna. Brown silk dress with tassels and flounces. Hat to match, 1868–70.

E Fashion Plate. Dark grey cloth coat with black silk collar. Dark grey trousers. Black hat. Fawn gloves. Cane, c.1865.

814 German fashion plate. Deutschen Herrenmoden, Dresden. Business suit. Black tail coat with dark grey trousers. White waistcoat and shirt. Black hat and boots.

815 Swiss actual costume. Bernisches Historisches Museum, Berne, Switzerland. Brownish-mauve taffeta dress with self-colour accordion pleating and ruching and brown lace.

816 German fashion plate. Europäische Modenzeitung für Herrengarderobe, Dresden, Germany. Black frock coat with light grey trousers. Black hat and boots.

817 Hungarian actual costume. Hungarian National Museum, Budapest, Hungary. Wine red velvet ball gown. White lace decoration. Underskirt of champagne-coloured silk.

818A English fashion plate. Cream coloured wool dress with plaid skirt draperies. Plum-coloured velvet jacket with grey fur trimming. Silk hat and plumes, gloves, 1877–8.

B English fashion plate. Dark grey cutaway coat with lighter grey trousers. White waistcoat. Black stock, white collar. Black hat and shoes. White gloves and spats. Cane, 1874.

C English actual costume. Gallery of Costume, Platt Hall, Manchester, England. Black silk day dress with white lace neck and waist frills. Hat to match, 1872.

D English fashion plate. Blue-grey coat with shoulder capes. Dark blue velvet hat with plumes, 1879–80.

E English actual costume. Gallery of English Costume, Platt Hall, Manchester, England. Deep magenta cashmere day dress with black braid edging and black velvet trimming. Hat to match, 1870.

F English fashion plate. Fawn cloth coat with braid edging. Yellow ribbon bow at back. Cream dress with brown accordion pleating. Brown hat with cream ribbons and plumes. Umbrella, 1875.

G English fashion plate. Black cloth coat. Grey trousers. White spats, black boots. Grey hat, 1875.

H English fashion plate. Grey poplin promenade dress in princess style. Ultramarine blue velvet bows and accordion pleating. Cream straw hat with white plume. Gloves. Umbrella. 1876–7.

819 Dutch actual costume. Kostuum Museum, The Hague, Holland. Grey silk rep dress with cream lace ruffles at neck and sleeves. Umbrella. Cream hat with dark grey velvet decoration with flowers.

820 French actual costume. Musée du Costume de la Ville de Paris. Beige and brown faille dress. Decoration in fringe and passementerie.

821 Swiss actual costume. Schweizerisches Landesmuseum, Zürich, Switzerland. White piqué dress with white lace ornamentation. Pink belt. Dark blue bows. White boots and gloves. Straw hat with cherries and ribbons.

822 Russian actual costume. Hermitage Museum, Leningrad, U.S.S.R. Ivory satin evening dress with tulle flounces. Fan.

823A English fashion plate, 1892. Inverness overcoat. Tweed trousers. Bowler hat. Gloves.

B English actual costume. Museum of Costume, Bath, England. Deep purple velvet dress with leg-of-mutton sleeves in paler mauve brocade. Purple velvet hat with ostrich plumes and black spotted veil. Grey gloves. Purple umbrella, c.1893.

C English actual costume. Gallery of Costume, Platt Hall, Manchester, England. Red satin dress with cream lace flounce and darker red hem and ribbons. Green jacket with white fur. Felt hat with ribbons and plume. Fur muff, 1886.

D English fashion plate, 1893. Sealskin coat trimmed with lighter-coloured fur. Velvet hat with ribbons, plumes and veil. Gloves, umbrella.

E English actual costume. Costume Museum, Bethnal Green, London. Pink walking costume with lace trimming. Hat with ribbons, plumes and face veil. Gloves, 1895.

F English fashion plate, 1889. Short fawn cloth coat, tweed trousers. Brown bowler hat. Lemon gloves.

824 Austrian actual costume. Modesammlung des Historischen Museums der Stadt Wien, Vienna. Brown silk costume with brown spotted velvet trimming, also brown cord ornamentation and cream lace ruffles. Brown velvet hat and cream plume. Umbrella, gloves.

825 German fashion plate. Universal-Modenzeitung für Herren-Garderobe, Dresden. Dark cloth overcoat and trousers. Black hat. Overcoat has muff pockets.

826 German actual costume. Hessisches Museum, Kassel, Germany. Wine red silk dress with beige lace ornamentation. Fan.

827 French actual costume. Boston Museum of Fine Arts, U.S.A. Worth evening gown. Pale green taffeta. Skirt in three colours: train in green taffeta, overskirt in green velvet patterned in gold and centre panel of green with gold fringe at hem. Cream net ruching at hem of train and on sleeves.

828A French/American fashion plate, 1878. Dark wool dress with silk sash and accordion pleating. Black boots.

B Russian actual costume. Hermitage Museum, Leningrad, U.S.S.R. Dark brown dress with white spot. Train in cream and brown silk. Black tulle flouncing down centre front, 1880.

C German fashion plate. Universal-Modenzeitung für Herren-Garderobe, Dresden, 1882. Dark tweed overcoat with shoulder cape. Lighter tweed trousers. Black hat and boots. Gloves, cane.

D German actual costume. Historisches Museum, Frankfurt-am-Main, Germany. Tweed costume. Dark velvet hat and fur muff, 1885-7.

E Swedish actual costume. Nordiska Museet, Stockholm, Sweden. Plain taffeta dress with spotted drapery. Velvet hat and plume. Gloves, umbrella, 1882-4.

829 French actual costume. Victoria and Albert Museum, London. Worth evening dress. Dark green velvet bodice, cream brocade skirt, striped with pink sprays. White tulle overskirt and flouncing. Cream silk 'sweepers'. Fan.

830 Swedish actual costume. Nordiska Museet, Stockholm, Sweden. Cream satin ball dress embroidered in metal thread. Pearl necklace. Plumes in hair. Fan.

831 Russian actual costume. Hermitage Museum, Leningrad, U.S.S.R. White silk evening dress with silver decoration. Dark velvet cloak with light silk lining.

832A Dutch actual costume. Kostuum Museum, The Hague, Holland. Dark blue velvet and grey-blue silk rep suit. White gloves. Umbrella. Straw hat with flowers and lace, 1896.

B Russian actual costume. Hermitage Museum, Leningrad, U.S.S.R. Worth dress of plain velvet. Straw hat, gloves. Lace and velvet parasol, c.1893.

C Austrian actual costume. Modesammlung des Historischen Museums der Stadt Wien, Vienna. Grey wool coat with grey piping. Velvet hat with bird's wing ornamentation, 1897.

D Austrian actual costume. Modesammlung des Historischen Museums der Stadt Wien, Vienna. Light grey dress with grey wool cape decorated by black and white braiding. Hat with veil and ribbons, 1895-1900.

E English fashion plate, 1899. Grey tweed overcoat with trousers to match. White hat, black boots. Fawn gloves, cane.

F French actual costume. Musée du Costume de la Ville de Paris. Pink taffeta dress with green squares decoration. Cream lace jabot. Velvet hat with plume, 1895.

833 French actual costume. White muslin berthe over dark floral dress. Musée du Costume de la Ville de Paris.

834 Portrait of King George IV by Sir Thomas Lawrence. National Portrait Gallery, London. Black stock, white collar.

835 Blue satin slipper. Rocamora Costume Museum,

Barcelona, Spain.

836 Black boot embroidered in coloured silks. Musée du Costume de la Ville de Paris.

837 Painting by J. B. Reiter. Österreichisches Museum der Stadt Wien, Vienna. Ribbon hair decoration. Red dress.

838 White satin boot, Viennese. Österreichisches Museum der Stadt Wien, Vienna.

839 Cream satin evening shoe with pearl embroidery. Musée du Costume de la Ville de Paris.

840 White satin boot. Narodowe Museum, Cracow, Poland.

841 Circular folding fan in green silk, wooden handle. Gallery of Costume, Platt Hall, Manchester, England.

842 Fashion plate. La Mode. White silk hat with white lace trimming and flowers.

843 Pleated white silk fan decorated with lace and flowers, ivory handle. Rocamora Costume Museum, Barcelona, Spain.

844 Portrait of Celiny Stadnickiej. Narodowe Museum, Cracow, Poland.

845 Crimson velvet boot with gold braid decoration. White satin lining. Rocamora Costume Museum, Barcelona, Spain.

846 Natural straw hat with white ribbons and flowers. Rocamora Costume Museum, Barcelona, Spain.

847 Split straw bonnet with flowers on the exterior and ribbons inside. Gallery of Costume, Platt Hall, Manchester, England.

848 Crimson satin boot. Rocamora Costume Museum, Barcelona, Spain.

849 Fashion plate. La Saison. Purple silk bonnet, ribbons and plumes.

850 Portrait of Amalie Klein by Friedrich von Amerling. Obere Belvedere, Vienna. Deep crimson gown. White gloves. Gold bracelets. Pearl necklace, earrings and brooch.

851 Black velvet hat, black lace veil, pale blue ribbons with black pattern and pink roses. Gallery of Costume, Platt Hall, Manchester, England.

Chapter Nine

The Modern World: 1900–1975

More than any other form of human expression, fashion has mirrored accurately the events and developments experienced by twentieth century society in Europe. The two world wars represent divisive barriers set at intervals during these 75 years. Life before and after these upheavals was different; in each case there could be no return to the life that had gone before, though there has been a certain continuity in the general social trend. So it has been with fashion. All the important happenings, with their consequent reactions, have imprinted themselves on the dress of our time: the wars themselves, the emancipation and consequent employment of women outside the home, the erosion of privilege, the re-distribution of wealth, the emergence of an urban society from the earlier agricultural one.

Because the two world wars each speeded up the development of twentieth century society, giving tremendous impetus to the changes which were to come, they present natural dividing lines for the fashions of the century. In discussing the evolution of these modes, it is natural to do so in three periods, each quite different from that preceding or post-dating it. These are 1900–20, 1920–45 and 1945–75.

1900–1920

Even within the first two decades of the century, harbingers of the changes to come in dress were evident by 1911–12. It is often suggested that 1914 was the watershed, the time when the old life ended and a new era began. But change, evidenced in fashion, showed itself a few years before this; the war simply caused an acceleration in the pace of change, bringing about in four years what might have taken thirty in times of peace.

In the years 1900–20 the fashion in *men's clothes* changed only imperceptibly with an immeasurably slow trend towards informality. Formal day dress comprised the cutaway morning coat or the frock coat in grey or black, worn with striped trousers. For evening, gentlemen were dressed in black 'tails' or dinner jacket – white tie for the former, black tie for the latter. The greater informality showed in the pre-eminence for everyday town wear of the three-piece lounge suit, while the Norfolk jacket worn with knickerbockers or trousers was usual for country or travel. Colours were still conservative, worsted or tweed the usual materials. Style had changed very slightly towards a looser fit and trouser creases and turn-ups were more common. London remained the fashion centre for men (**852A, 855, 861E, I, 865, 926, 928**).

The predominant interest, in the whole of the twentieth century, is in feminine dress. There were three distinct modes here during the first two decades: the clothes of 1900–10, the pre-war years of 1910–14 and those of the war and immediately after. The first decade was, indeed, the end of an era, a continuation of nineteenth century social life. Wealth and privilege remained and the class of society to which they pertained continued to set the fashion. Their dress was elegant and graceful, made of flimsy materials with fussy trimming at neck and hem on a tall, full-bosomed, wasp-waisted figure. Femininity, gracious manners and behaviour marked the lady. The ankles were not to be seen; gloves must always be worn, the pompadour coiffure was surmounted by a sweeping hat with a garden of ornament. These years represented the final appearance of the lady of leisure, displaying her feminine charm and graceful mien and a knowledge of her 'correct' place in the world of men.

The shape of the costume until about *1908* was still an artificial one, calling for tight lacing and boning to fulfil fashion needs. This was a different shape from the late nineteenth century one, which had demanded an excessively slender waist, full bosom and sleek hips. The early years of the twentieth century saw a new line: the *S-bend*. This evolved from the straight busk-fronted *corset* of about 1902, which was designed

to support the abdomen but not to restrict the thorax with inward pressure on the diaphragm, as had been the case with the late nineteenth century waisted corsets. But, although the new straight-busked front had the recommendation of medical authorities, who had been campaigning for years to abolish the concave corset front, the advice of these gentlemen was still unheeded in the feminine search for a tiny waist. The ladies laced up the new corset as tightly as the old and created a new figure distortion. Due to the intractability of the straight-front busk, the bosom above it was pushed forward and the hips, below it only at the rear, backwards (**984**). The new fashionable ideal was thus achieved: a full, forward bosom, a tiny waist and generous, backward-slanting hips. If nature was inadequate to conform to these requirements, bust bodices and petticoats were suitable padded or lined with starched flounces. The bosom line was not uplifted, but was worn low to overhang the tightly encircling waist belt. The fashionably tall woman dressed in this S-bend line sailed into a room carrying all before her. The style was immortalised in the drawings of the American, Charles Dana Gibson and it became that of the 'Gibson girl'.

1905 was the zenith of the Gibson line and, by 1908, the waistline rose and a more natural figure was allowed to be followed. A corset was still worn but it was longer, less waisted and there were fewer bones inserted in it (**987**). The desired figure was more natural but it was also very slim so that the tall, full-busted, full-hipped women, who had looked so impressive a year or so earlier, were now out of fashion. In fact, such figures have not so far returned to fashion at all.

Underwear was less cumbersome than in the late nineteenth century; fewer layers were worn. For fashionable ladies it had become much more expensive. The 'set' of knickers, bust bodice, chemise and petticoats was now called lingerie. Taffeta or silk were widely used, with lace trimming, and the frou-frou sound was essential. Two petticoats were worn: a shorter one of wool (for winter) or percale (for summer), then a taffeta or silk long, outer one. This used a great deal of material and was costly. Its design included tiers of flounces, pleats, ruching and ribbons. The gown skirt was a slim bell-shape, opening out like a flower at the hem. The hem of the petticoat, which was accordion pleated or flounced, was seven yards round and swept the ground or it was elegantly lifted at one corner in the street.

Gowns, for town, afternoon and evening wear were elaborately decorated with lace, embroidery, fringe and fur. Except for evening, they had very high necklines, boned at the sides up to the ears and often encircled by pearl dog-collar necklaces. The bodice was full in front, drooping over a tight waist sash. Sleeves were long and full with tight wrist cuff or three-quarter ending in a cuff and ruffle. Trains were worn on all such gowns (**852B, C, D, E, 853, 854, 856, 857, 858, 860**). Clothes for travel and informal wear were now more varied. The *tailored suit* was fashionable; by 1905 it was the accepted street wear. Jackets could be waisted or straight, like masculine ones. Skirts just cleared the ground and were cut in gores or box pleats. Navy, brown and black broadcloth and serge were fashionable with white in summer. Blouses were

masculine and severe or soft and fussy. The former had starched collars and ties.

Hair was fashionably in the pompadour style, back-combed and piled up on top of the head over pads and with a chignon at the nape. Large combs of tortoiseshell or amber held the hair in place. *Hats* became larger between 1900 and 1906 and were excessively so by 1909. They were perched on top of the coiffure, heavily ornamented with plumes, flowers and ribbons (**852B, C, D, E, 853, 854, 856, 857, 858, 860, 925, 927, 929**).

In the second decade of the century fashions began to change more quickly. Paris was still the centre of the European mode and there were now many famous names in the world of *haute couture* here, who were bringing out new ideas. Eastern influences were important especially those from Russia. The Russo-Japanese war was in the news and introduced Oriental features such as the kimono sleeve. It was *Paul Poiret* especially who created designs incorporating an oriental manner and introducing a new, vivid colour range. These included flame red, orange, cerise, violet, royal

853 *Swedish, 1906*   **854** *French, c.1900*   **855** *French, 1905*   **856** *French, c.1900*

857 *French, c.1905*

858 *Spanish,*
c. 1900

859 *French, 1904*

860 *French (Russia), 1904*

blue and emerald green. His dresses were derivative, from the Orient and from the past, but had an original, new look in the years 1908–12 when he introduced them. He designed Empire high waistline gowns, sumptuous tunics worn over sultana trouser skirts with oriental turbans, the heavy be-furred cape top over the slender, ankle-tight skirt, as well as a kimono gown.

The choreography of Diaghilev's Ballets Russes, appearing from 1909, inspired both Poiret and other designers at this time. Art Nouveau textiles provided a further exotic theme for costume use. Among the other outstanding couturiers of this time were *Madeleine Vionnet, Jeanne Lanvin, Mme. Pacquin* and *Mme. Gerber*. Mme. Vionnet was especially known for the bias cut which she introduced, while Mme. Lanvin used a beautiful range of colours and designed in rich materials such as gold and silver fabric and brocades.

By 1910 a few women had begun to challenge the accepted view of their status; suffragettism

was under way and more women were working for a living and earning independence; some professions were attacked and successfully entered. A reflection of this is to be seen in dress. The frills and lace had gone, also the wasp-waist corset, trailing gowns and flower garden hats. The years *1910–14* illustrate in dress a period of transition and a desire to throw off unsuitable, over-feminine clothing. New, alternative designs followed one another thick and fast, not yet practical for working women but with a natural, unrestricted figure. At first the waistline was high but this soon returned to normal. A whole range of skirt designs evolved, many of them patently absurd. The hobble skirt was introduced in 1911. This had a wide band encircling it just below the knees. It was only marginally popular but was adapted a year or so later to a more convenient style, draped and tapered towards the ankle. Tunic skirts of varied design appeared; some had two or three tiers of tunic over a draped, narrow skirt. Evening dress tiers were flared and wired out like lampshades. Others were draped under and pulled up unevenly around the figure. The peg-top skirt was the mode in 1912–13. This had a full draped, panier effect on the hips, diminishing in width towards the ankle. The high neckline of the first decade of the century had given way first to a square, then a round and finally a low V neck. This might have a collar or be plain with lace-edging or an insertion (**861A, B, D, F, G, H, 862, 863, 864, 868, 870, 931**).

New *materials* were entering the fashion world; Chanel was using art silk in 1915 for her designs and, in 1918, introduced jersey fabrics for dresses and suits. These materials lent themselves to garments falling in simple, soft folds. The chemise gown, first worn in 1914, became fashionable in 1917 for this reason. It was a straight dress with long, fitting sleeves and a straight tunic on top. Evening versions were made of georgette, gold and silver cloth or crêpe lamé. They began to be designed with an uneven hemline by 1917, with a small 'tail' train at the back, while the front and sides varied from six to twelve inches from the ground. These dresses

were sleeveless and had low V necklines and full bodices draped over a sash at the waist.

It was the war which established the fact that women were capable of skilled work in addition to or instead of domesticity and, in the same way, it was the war which necessitated more practical clothing for the job. Some women wore uniform but these were a minority; a greater effect was apparent in civilian dress. The absurdities of the hobble or lampshade skirts were outmoded and women began to express their emancipation in what they wore. A skirt above the ankle (eight inches above the ground) appeared for the first time and it was one of sensible width for movement (**866, 867, 869**). Hats became small, pulled more firmly on to the head and hairstyles were neater and close to the head in waves and curls; underwear was comfortable. The girl of today would judge these clothes to be dowdy and restrictive but they were the beginning of a revolution in feminine dress which accompanied the social and economic emancipation.

As the ladies' ankles became visible in public for the first time, their feet could be seen to be

861 English Dress, Street Scene, 1914–21

862 *English, 1912*   863 *French, 1911*   864 *English, 1913*   865 *English, 1910*

clad in high, laced or buttoned *shoes*, made of kid, suède or gabardine and with high, slim heels and long, pointed toes. They were in beige, grey or black for day wear but evening slippers matched the gowns. *Stockings* followed a similar colour range.

1920–1945

Men's dress advanced with slow, hesitating steps towards informality and greater variety in garments, colour and materials. The *lounge suit*, single or double-breasted, was the usual wear for most occasions. In style, the slim trousers gave way in the 1920s to the 'Oxford bags', which were very wide – up to 24 inches – at the turn-up. After 1929 the width was reduced but, all this period, men's trousers were far wider than they are today. The suit was of one material, which varied according to occasion and season from worsted to tweed. A more formal version comprised the black or dark jacket, black waistcoat and black and grey striped trousers (**871D, 887, 892**).

By 1925 grey *flannel trousers* were being worn

for holidays and travel, with a tweed jacket and a woollen pullover. Alternatively, the Norfolk jacket and knickerbockers with heavy woollen stockings evolved into 'plus fours'.* In these the knickerbockers were fuller with an overhang below the band at the knee (**881**). Coloured sports *shirts*, with attached collars, became popular; aertex, silk and rayon were used for these as well as cotton. Ties became brighter and gayer.

Raincoats, mackintoshes and *overcoats* existed in many styles, single or double-breasted, belted or loose. They were all less fitting and much longer than modern ones. Water-repellant fabrics had now been perfected and British rainwear was renowned (**882**).

Fewer men wore a *hat* in the 1930s, but the bowler, felt trilby and homburg styles were still the vogue for those who did, while the top hat was reserved for formal morning or evening dress (**944, 946**). This type of *formal dress* was now worn less often. The frock coat had disappeared while the cutaway, now a morning coat,

---

* So-named because, to produce the overhang, the length was originally increased by four inches.

was retained only for very formal day-time occasions. Evening dress, 'tails' and dinner jacket, were worn more often than they are today. Men of all ages and class wore dinner jackets for all dances, dinners and parties, while 'tails' were reserved for more special functions.

In the 1930s especially, the cult of sunbathing, as well as that of country walking (hiking) had taken hold. People were now accustomed to the idea that exposing the skin to sun and air was a good thing and that the wearing of too many layers of clothes, so essential a century earlier, were not necessarily conducive to good health. Designs of masculine *underwear* illustrated this trend. Younger men especially adopted short, elastic topped pants and sleeveless vests in interlock and rayon.

After the war many *women* continued their quest for interesting careers outside the home. A majority still spent their lives as wives and mothers, giving all of their time to home life, but the break had been made and, as time passed, more and more, younger women especially, entered professions and varied fields of work previously only open to men. Many such women

learned to combine successfully a career and homemaking.

In the 1920s this emancipation went to their heads and the reaction against Victorianism was acute. Women demanded functional, comfortable clothes, a freedom to do as men did – smoking, free love, equality of opportunity and, therefore, freedom of attire. Many women, mistakenly, felt that to work as successfully at a job as a man had done, they must appear to be masculine or, at least, unfeminine. For ten years women hid the attributes of femininity given to them by nature: breasts, sloping shoulders, small waist, ample hips and flowing hair. To assert their new-found freedom, they emulated masculinity with flattened breasts, tubular, unwaisted dresses, and shingled hair; they exposed their legs instead. A specific carriage was adopted; the pelvis was thrust forward to accentuate the flatness of the bosom and hips and arms were set akimbo, low on the hips (a most unladylike gesture by nineteenth century standards), and eyes peered out mysteriously under a hat pulled down well over the eyebrows.

The boyish look was 'in'. Pyjamas were worn as well as nightdresses, trousers appeared on the

866 *English, c.1919*   **867** *French, 1916*   **868** *Austrian, 1914*   **869** *English, 1918*   **870** *French, 1912–13*

1910–20

beach, called lido pyjamas (**885**). The fashionable figure was thin rather than slim. One must have a slender neck, no bosom, no hips and twiggy legs. It was the age of the flapper. If one's figure did not conform, one must diet. Skirts rose nearly to the knee (never above, in these years), and waist-line, or rather its suggestion, was low on the hips. Trimming and decoration was at a minimum.

This revolution in feminine dress was not at first accepted by Parisian *haute couture*. The rank and file of ladies had run away from their leaders and were dictating their terms. The couturiers attempted to win them back with eclectic designs, recreating styles from the past. They had to accept, as designers have several times had to accept later in the twentieth century, that a fashion which is not in tune with public demand will not 'go', no matter how good the publicity and marketing.

All efforts to put the clock back having failed, the couturiers followed the tide and designed for it. They produced clothes for all occasions, in-formal and holiday as well as evening and dress attire and the quality of dress improved. The negative ugliness of the line of the 1920s dress could not be obscured but it could be given a little elegance and quality. Unless its wearer had chic and was slim and beautiful, the results would be unfortunate at best and hideous at worst, but a good designer with a feeling for colour and fabric can work wonders.

The famous names of the pre-1920 years were joined by new ones and the years 1920–45 were great years for *haute couture*. The return to a vestige of femininity was helped immensely by the bias cutting of Mme. Vionnet, the easy-to-wear suits and dresses in jersey materials by Mme. Chanel and the formal evening dresses in lovely fabrics by Mme. Lanvin. Other famous names include Mme. Pacquin, Mlle. Carven and Edward Molyneux while, in the 1930s, Balenciaga and Mme. Schiaparelli initiated a tentative return to the breasts and the waist.

Although the clothes during the 1920s were straight and tubular and similar for everyone, fashions changed quickly and each year was a little different. The middle classes now led the mode; only price and quality of fabric and cut varied. The cult of simplicity was supreme for the whole decade. The most notable variation was in the *hem-line* which was the same for all garments whether day dress or evening, suit or coat. In 1920–21 the skirt was ankle-length (**876, 877**), but from 1922 the hem-line steadily rose, reaching its shortest level, just covering the knee, in 1927 (**871A, C, F, 873, 875, 878, 879**). As it shortened it was cut straighter and narrower so that, in the mid-1920s, it was like a tube. In 1927 designers tried to lower the line in order to give variety by introducing longer panels of draped fabric at the sides and back. This was especially characteristic of evening gowns of 1928 and 1929, but the actual hem-line did not begin its descent until 1929–30 (**871E, 872, 874, 880**).

The natural *waistline* was unmarked and ignored between 1921–22 and 1930. The bodice was tubular and loose, with a belt or sash worn low on the hips. It was decorated by a cockade or jewel. Sleeves were long and fitting or very short, but most commonly dresses were quite sleeveless, with perhaps a floating panel of material hanging behind the arm. Necklines were completely plain and either in a very low V, bateau or square shape. Some evening gowns had low V backs also (**871B**).

Suits were especially fashionable in the 1920s. The blouse, generally of crêpe de chine or knitted wool or silk, was worn outside the skirt and ended on the hips. Skirts were often pleated all round. Fur was popular on suits and coats, both as a trimming and for the whole garment (**878**).

The ideal figure for the *1930s* was still slim and clothes were cut to cling to the figure, especially over the hips. Styles were quite different from those of the 1920s; femininity had returned, the breasts were no longer flattened and, by 1937, the uplift bra had begun to define them. The waistline was at its normal level again and accentuated by a belt or shaping. The hem-line had fallen abruptly to about eight inches above the ground and skirts were pleated or gored. The material was often cut on the bias to ensure a clinging fit over the hips. Designs had become fussier with decorative sleeves gathered, pleated and puffed and cowl or jabot necklines (**883, 884, 886**).

Evening gowns were long and the backless and halter necklines fashionable. The classic draped gown in crêpe or rayon jersey fabrics was most usual, though a bouffant skirt was also popular. The bodice was fitting or tightly draped. In 1938–39 the strapless evening gown with boned bodice was introduced, also the off the shoulder mode with a straight across, turned down cuff décolletage (**888, 889, 890, 891**).

872 *French, 1926–8* **873** *Spanish, 1922–3* **874** *French, 1928* **875** *French, c.1925* **876** *French (Holland), 1922*

War-time styles were influenced by the large number of women in uniform. Civilian dress too acquired a shorter skirt, to just below the knee, and padded shoulders, especially in tailored suits and coats. This gave the square box silhouette characteristic of the years up till 1946. There was no particular accentuation of breast or hips but a belt generally confined the waist at the normal level. Most outfits had an efficient and practical appearance. In summer, though, dresses tended to the 'little girl' effect with their full, fairly short skirts and draped bodices. Suits were especially fashionable, also jumpers and skirts. These were years of austerity and privation in Europe. *Haute couture* was at a standstill, especially in occupied France while, in England, clothing coupons limited the replenishment of the wardrobe. These were the years of marking time in fashion, of practicability and keeping warm (**893, 894, 895, 896**).

It would be difficult to imagine a greater contrast than that between the *ideal feminine figure* of 1900–10 and that of the 1920s. Yet, since only a few women possessed either of these naturally, some form of constriction was necessary for the remainder. The 1920s demanded a tube-shaped figure, of equal width from shoulder to pubis and with no curves or protuberances. The immature, slender figure needed no assistance for this and such girls and women wore little or no corsetry. For the rest of the feminine population a bra and corset were required.

The word *brassière* had been introduced into England from the USA in 1912; its origins there are obscure. In French the word means a baby's vest, a shoulder strap or leading strings: perhaps, there is a connection? The French word for brassière in the English sense is *soutien-gorge*. Later the word brassière became bra as it is today. In the 1920s the garment was a flattener not an uplifter. It was of strong, white cotton and covered the body to the waist, with straps over the shoulders.

The *corset* was a belt to the waist, made of a boned fabric. Not-so-slim ladies soon found a spare tyre protruding between the two garments so the one-piece corselette was introduced. This encased the torso and was guaranteed by the manufacturers 'to provide a flat form from shoulder to hem'. Apart from the corselette, *underwear* was scanty; a chemise and cami-knickers, with a thin petticoat, were the sum total.

877 *Dutch, 1922*   **878** *Dutch, 1925*   **879** *French, 1923*   **880** *English, c.1929*   **881** *English, 1930*

1920–30

882 *English, 1933* 883 *Molyneux, 1938* 884 *English, 1935–5* 885 *French, 1931* 886 *English, 1936*

Elastic was beginning to be widely used in corsetry. It had been employed in footwear in the nineteenth century but, due to problems in producing adequate lengths of latex strip, it had not been possible to incorporate the material into corsetry. By 1930 a method was established to transport the latex emulsion in tankers, direct from the plantation source to the factories, which could then make fine thread elastic in long lengths. From this time onwards calico and whalebone were outmoded and adequate support could be given by elastic belts and corsets (989). Slide fasteners were also used in these and, from 1933, the zip fastener became general. Pantee girdles were also worn.

In the 1930s appeared the proper *bra*, made to uplift and delineate the breasts. Typical designs were of rayon or cotton, the elastic straps crossed over the back to fasten on buttons at the front. The back, elastic hook and eye closure came later. Underwear was now prettier, longer and decorated with lace.

Hairstyles in the 1920s were no less revolutionary than the rest of the costume. The hair was cut short, at first just to a bob but, by 1922, to a shingle. It was a severe style, developing into the 'Eton crop', which made girls look just like young boys (871A, B, C, E, F, 872, 873, 874, 875, 876, 877, 937). Slightly longer styles came in at the end of the 1920s then, in the 1930s, the feminine coiffure reappeared, but long hair, dressed in a bun or chignon, did not return. First the marcel wave made the hair easier to control and, in the 1930s, permanent waving took over. The coiffure was set in waves close to the head and arranged in curls at the nape. Longer hair was fashionable in the war years, on the shoulders in waves and curls or a gleaming page-boy bob (941). With the short hair styles, the metal pins, kirbigrips, as well as slides, were used for holding the hair in place (883, 884, 888, 889, 890, 891, 893, 894, 895, 938, 942, 943).

Hats in the 1920s were small and fitted the head. By 1923 the *cloche hat* appeared. This was of felt, generally undecorated, and had a small brim. It encased the head like a helmet from eye-level in front to low on the back of the head behind. This was an unattractive style even on such beautiful women as Greta Garbo (878, 879, 880). In the 1930s different and very varied

887 *English, 1939*   888 *English, 1937*   889 *French, 1935–6*   890 *English, 1933*   891 *French, c.1932*

designs took its place. There were Tyrolean hats, halo hats, turbans, sailor hats, berets, pillbox shapes and cartwheels. Veils and chenille nets (called snoods) were fashionable. Many designs were worn perched on the front of the head, often over one eye; a strap at the back held such hats in place. Some women began to wear gay scarves, tied under the chin, in place of a hat. This was especially typical of the war years (**883, 884, 885, 886, 894, 895, 896, 930, 938, 940, 942, 943, 947**).

With short skirts, *stockings* became more important. Flesh tones were worn in silk, wool and lisle. During the war silk stockings were in short supply and many women went bare-legged for as much of the year as possible.

Ladies wore *shoes* or *slippers* all this period. In the 1920s styles had high, curved heels and low fronts. Some were court designs, others had straps and buttons, with upstanding tongues. Patent leather, kid or suède were fashionable materials for day wear. Evening styles were in satin, brocade or gold or silver (**871E ,F, 872, 873, 874, 875, 876, 877, 878, 879, 880, 933, 935**). In the 1930s high-heeled shoes with slimmer heels were usual for town or formal wear. Many informal styles appeared, varying from low-heeled brogues for

country walking to sandals without backs or toes (**883, 884, 886, 889, 945**). Wedge and platform soles or cuban heels were fashionable in the 1940s. Materials were varied but especially popular were two-colour shoes in white buckskin with brown, blue or black leather at toe and heel (**894, 895, 896, 948, 949, 951**).

During these years there was a rapid development in clothes to wear for different occasions. Informality was the keynote for sport, holidays, the beach, country walking etc. and suits, short jackets, jumpers, skirts and trousers became popular. Long gowns were always worn for evening functions, to the ankle or to the ground, while tailored suits, dresses and coats remained the fashion for day wear in town or at work.

Costume jewellery was introduced and was fashionable, especially in the 1930s. Ornamentation of this type was rarer in the 1920s, when the usual decoration was in the form of long, dangling earrings and very long necklaces reaching to below the waist. Pearls were worn with jumpers and blouses; in the 1930s the twin set with pearl necklace was the hallmark of the well brought-up middle class girl.

Cosmetics were used more widely, in natural

tones, and were more skilfully applied than previously. Lipstick was introduced. Cosmetics were carried in the handbag; lipstick and powder (from the powder compact, then called a flapjack) were applied in public. This was not, though, a practice indulged in by well-mannered girls.

As with hats, gloves were worn less often now. Parasols had disappeared and umbrellas were short (**939**). Handbags were large, except for evenings, when they were made of brocade, silk or gilt leather.

1945–1975

European fashion since the Second World War has become completely international. Fashion journals and television bring to men and women up-to-date information on what is the latest trend. In the 1960s and 1970s, in particular, the accent is on youth; advertising and production in the clothing industry are trained to bear upon this new market. Teenagers have money to spend and enjoy trying out the latest ideas. In these years two sets of fashion have developed side by side: clothes for the young and clothes for everyone

else. In Europe the only exception to this internationalism in dress is in the eastern bloc where the populations discover what is being worn in the west less quickly and easily. In the Soviet Union, especially, news is slow to percolate and, even when people know what is in fashion, they cannot obtain it. The shortage of man-made fibres and any form of corsetry and support make it impossible for any but the privileged few to achieve the elegance and comfort in dress available to Western Europe. Anyone who has travelled independently in Eastern Europe will have been the repeated recipient of wistful requests to act as a purchasing agent in one of the foreign tourist shops where only foreign currency will buy the longed-for bra or crimplene suit.

Men's Dress

Though not subject to the rapid changes of fashion which have overtaken feminine dress in these years, men's clothes have altered dramatically. The trend has been towards more variety in garments for different occasions, less formality and greater casualness. The introduction and

892 *English, 1941*　　**893** *English, 1946*　**894** *English, 1941*　　**895** *Spanish, 1945*　　**896** *English, 1943*

1940–6

897 *Dior, French, 1947*   **898** *English, 1948*   **899** *English, 1948*   **900** *English, 1948*

increased use of man-made fibres, with consequent easy-care garments, has completely altered the pre-war picture of worsted lounge suit or sports jacket with flannel trousers to cover all day-time wear. Lightweight summer suits in a variety of fabrics, many drip-dry and non-iron, have become increasingly popular, even with the more conservative, older man. This is probably due to the great increase in overseas tourist travel since the English climate does not appear to have changed. Equally, as men have learned to appreciate the comfort of wearing a lightweight suit instead of sweltering in worsted on a hot summer's day, they have largely abandoned heavy, long overcoats in winter (**909, 910B, K**). Instead, they turn on the car heater and make the short trip to office or factory in raincoat, short overcoat or suède, sheepskin lined jacket (**904**).

For business and *town wear* worsted and tweed are still used for men's suiting but many of these fabrics are now mixtures, part natural, part man-made fibre, blending the advantages of warmth and quality appearance of the former with the creaselessness, easy care and hardwearing factors of the latter. Weaves, patterns and colours

all show far more variety since 1945 while, for casual and holiday wear, patterns and colours are as diverse as in feminine dress (**910G**).

The *cut and line* in men's clothes has also changed markedly. In the 1950s, jackets were cut more loosely with longer lapels while trousers became narrower and lost their cuffs (**904**). In the 1960s, several jacket styles were worn, some waisted and long, others brief. Some longer styles were derived from abbreviated versions of the frock and cutaway coats of the nineteenth century (**918**). Trousers became very narrow and were cut tighter and lower and lower on the hips (**912**). Teenage styles were extreme and young men looked as if they had been poured into their trousers. Chunky hip belts became popular. In the 1970s, though the low-cut, snug-fitting hipline has continued, the narrow trouser has become a wide bell bottom style and cuffs have been re-introduced (**924**).

Uni-sex clothes have had a limited following. This generally means the girl wearing her boy friend's designs rather than the other way around, but young men have adopted brilliant colours in their shirts and trousers as well as in beach and sportswear.

Men rarely wear hats nowadays except fur hats in winter. Since the late 1960s, the fashion for longer *hairstyles* has become more prevalent. At first it was only young men, particularly students, who adopted the shoulder length coiffure. By the early 1970s, almost all men, of whatever age, were wearing their hair longer than they had before and younger men, in all walks of life, adopted quite long hair. This is often beautifully coiffured, probably permanently waved or kept attractive by a blow wave. The old-fashioned barber, dispensing his 'short back and sides' has almost disappeared, but young men spend as much, and probably more, than their girl friends on the care of their coiffure. From the rear, the heads of both sexes are of similar appearance and most often it is the girl who wears the shorter hair though, in the mid-1970s, there are signs of shorter styles for men again. Viewed from the front the difference is clearer as the young man, especially in the late 1960s and early 1970s, sported sideburns, beard, moustache or long sidewhiskers. The variety of facial hair was extensive but by 1974 cleanshaveness was returning.

Like the rest of the costume, men's *footwear* has become more varied. Different materials are used and plastic has become more common as the price of leather has soared. The extremely pointed toes of the 1950s (winkle-pickers) gave place in the 1960s to more elegant, natural shoes and boots, but the 1970s have seen a protracted period of fashion for the high platform soles. At first a vogue for ladies' footwear, the fashion spread to men's and, with the long, bell-bottomed trouser, the soles and heels have become higher and higher. Despite the difficulty of walking in such footwear and warnings from the chiropodist profession, the popularity of these styles shows little sign of abatement yet among the fashionable young.

All kinds of *man-made fibres* are now, in the 1970s, used for men's clothes as for women's. For both sexes the range of drip-dry clothes has brought greater comfort, variety and ease of care than ever before in the history of costume. The development of synthetic textile fibres has revolutionised the clothing industry and made possible an easy-care wardrobe not dreamed of in 1939. It has not, however, as was forecast in the 1950s, meant the abandonment of natural textiles – wool, cotton, linen and silk – often mixtures are used,

901 *French (Holland), 1952*   **902** *English, 1958–9*   **903** *English, 1960*   **904** *English, 1960*

1949–60

905 *French, 1950* **906** *English, 1950*   **907** *French, 1950*   **908** *French, 1950*   **909** *English, 1950*

especially in western Europe. In general, natural fibres are produced in poorer countries and artificial ones in the richer, industrialised ones. Cotton and wool especially, now treated for crease resistance and easy washing, have increased their production greatly since 1945.

Though it has been largely since 1940 that synthetic fibres have been developed, the concept is not new. Elizabeth Ewing* gives a full and interesting account of the history of the subject. She tells us that Robert Hooke (English) in 1664 suggests in his *Micrographia* that threads could be spun from an 'artificial glutinous composition' following the principle of the silkworm, also that in 1734, René de Réamur (French) thought that gums or resins could be drawn out into fibres from which an artificial textile might be produced. In 1855 George Audemars (Swiss) took out a patent for a process in which he had produced artificial fibres by using the inner bark of a mulberry tree and combining it with a rubber solution after he had nitrated and dissolved it in a mixture of ether and alcohol. In 1883 Sir Joseph Swan

(English), while working on carbon filaments for electric light bulbs, developed a process whereby a nitro-cellulose solution was squeezed in a coagulating medium to produce a filament.

Neither of these nor other ideas were followed up and it was not until the French chemist de Chardonnet (father of the rayon industry) produced his acetate rayon in the late 1880s that artificial textiles appeared to be possible. Viscose rayon was produced in the 1890s and, in 1911, acetate rayon was developed by British Celanese. It was in the 1920s that rayon began to be used for clothing, especially for underwear. Until the Second World War, however, rayon was always considered to be inferior and a cheap substitute for silk or satin.

The man-made fibre revolution is essentially post-war. It was the introduction of nylon which successfully initiated the challenge to silk. The firm of Du Pont (USA) developed the process and gave it the name nylon. The research programme had been begun by Du Pont in 1927 and they announced the discovery of nylon in 1938 when they produced the first nylon stocking. The research over these eleven years had cost 27

* *Fashion in Underwear* by Elizabeth Ewing, published by B. T. Batsford, 1971.

million dollars: an investment which was to prove a sound one. Nylon stockings went on sale in the USA in 1939 but the war slowed up the development programme. In Britain, ICI obtained nylon rights from Du Pont and, with Courtaulds, combined to form the new company of British Nylon Spinners Ltd. After the war production began and the silk stocking gave place, permanently, to nylon stockings and, later, nylon tights.

Women's Dress

Austerity clothes, coupons and the severe, straight lines of war-time dress continued for a couple of years after the end of the Second World War, then came the bombshell. Sensitive to the yearning of women all over Europe for a return to pretty, feminine clothes, Christian Dior launched his 'New Look' in his first Paris collection in February 1947. His designs could not have presented a greater contrast to the clothes which women had been wearing for seven years. The new line was feminine and unpadded, shoulders were rounded and sloping, the waist closely defined,

also the uplifted bosom, while skirts were full and long, extending to twelve inches above ground level. Under these swinging skirts were to be worn rustling, flounced taffeta petticoats; once again the frou-frou sound of the *fin de siècle* was to be heard (**897, 898, 899, 900**).

Dior's 'New Look' made it impossible for women to adjust their existing clothes to his styles. One can raise a hem, insert padding, take in a waist, but one cannot make a long, bouffant skirt out of a tight, short, straight one. A new wardrobe was necessary and most women acquired one between 1947 and 1948. Dior had aimed at the mature women who loved his designs, but young people acclaimed them even more and, with their slender waists and shapely bodies, displayed them to perfection.

Why then, since women greeted the 'New Look' with such affection, did it not endure? By 1949, styles were already changing. Skirts slowly became shorter, a trend which continued steadily into the mini-skirts of the 1960s. They also became straighter and the short evening dress replaced the previous long styles as well as the ballet

910 English Dress, 1966–7

911 *1967*　　　912 *1968*　　　913 *1967*　　　914 *1968*　　　915 *1965*

length of the later 1940s (**901, 902, 903, 905, 906, 907, 908**). The severe, padded shouldered and straight jacket did not return nor did the military austerity. Shoulders remained sloping and feminine, waists were still defined and busts curved but Dior's line was short lived. Why was this? It is a question which does not seem to have been answered satisfactorily by fashion historians. It is true that the feminine public will not for long accept a style which they do not care for. An example of this is the later midi-skirt length where the trade endeavoured to re-impose the 1930s skirt length without its elegant bias cut and within nine months it was dead. Dior's 'New Look' does not come into this category. It was, of course, a mode looking to the past, but it was welcomed and women loved it. I would suggest that the reason for its short life was its impracticability for women who, by now, in large numbers were going out to work at all kinds of jobs. A tiny, fitted waist and a full skirt reaching nearly to the ankles is not practical wear in the office, classroom or laboratory. Women soon reverted to a more sensible skirt and a more comfortable, looser line.

It was in the late 1960s that fashion enabled women to have the best of both worlds. Having passed from the feminine, impractical 'New Look' to the abbreviated mini, hot pants and undefined waistline, by 1968 bosom, waist and hemline had become a free option. A metamorphosis had taken place in that there has been since that time no accepted definitive fashion line, hem-line or suitability of one type of garment over another for specific wear. Only by fabrics and colours are occasions noted. Women of all ages can be attractively, comfortably and femininely attired in trouser suits, knee-length dresses, mini- (though not too abbreviated) skirts and maxi-length coats and dresses. Party and cocktail clothes have never been so varied and so feminine. Women can wear comfortable clothes for work and look pretty in the evening. Easy care fabrics make the changeover simple (**910, 911, 913, 914, 915, 916, 917, 919, 920, 921, 922, 923**). The tendency to 'cash-in' on the *teen-age market* had been growing since 1945. This trend could be seen in many forms – gramophone records, transistor radios, soft drink packaging.

Advertising has been directed more and more towards this potentially profitable market. The world of teenage fashion has seen, perhaps, the strongest movement and, in the 1960s, it developed to a marked extent. A complete wardrobe for young people, girls and boys, was evolved, unsuitable and almost impossible to wear for many adults. Such clothes were not expensive for young people like to change their wardrobe often (916, 917, 918, 919). This desire has always characterised youth but only now one which it has become possible to gratify. Teenagers in the USA, Holland, Scandinavia and England took most wholeheartedly to mini-skirts and skin-tight pants (the influence of the Roman Catholic Church in Latin countries certainly acted as a deterrent here) and the young people clearly delighted in wearing clothing styles which were specifically their own and which the majority of the adult world just could not wear without looking slightly ridiculous.

It is a tribute to the commonsense and innate elegance of most women, young and old, that they have resisted successfully commercial pressures put upon them to abandon the mini-skirt and take up the midi. The mini-skirt lives on, now sensibly not too short and largely confined to summer wear for the fairly young and shapely-legged. The midi was never an attractive easy-to-wear length; it was dowdy and suited few.* Equally, the hot pants commercial venture was short-lived. However alluringly described and presented as the 'latest mode', hot pants were never anything but short shorts, unsuited to the climate of northern Europe, most of the feminine sex and not very comfortable except on a beach.

With the development of nylon, *underwear* became easy care, comfortable, pretty and inexpensive. It became entirely mass-produced and hand-stitching had disappeared. The natural underwear of the present day has made possible the wearing of comfortable yet elegant trousers and mini-skirts. With the synthetic elastics, such as Lycra, the modern stretch girdles and bras have made it possible for all figures of women to wear trouser suits and, without tights and pantee girdles, most could not wear mini-skirts (988).

The 1950s were the years of the uplift bra and the 'sweater girl' form. A circular stitching was

* Fashion designers have still not given up the attempt to re-impose this skirt length as, witness the late 1974/Spring 1975 Paris collections (920).

916 *1967*　　　**917** *1971*　　　**918** *1967*　　　**919** *1970*

Clothes for the Young, 1965–72

used to make the high, pointed breast line (**990**). The strapless bra was worn with backless evening gowns and beach wear. In the 1960s and 1970s the bra is still worn by most women, though the young tend to abandon it, but the uplift line is less prominent. The accent is on natural form without specific delineation and each woman can interpret the fashion as she wishes.

The tight, permanently waved *hairstyles* of the pre-war years gave place in the 1950s to more natural lines. The hair was softly curled or worn nearly straight and often quite long. This could be dressed in a chignon, plait or knot at the nape or on the crown. By 1959 the high bouffant beehive look was fashionable, with excessive backcombing to produce the height. The mid-nineteenth century coiffure with centre parting and side sweeps was also popular.

Since 1960 hair styles have varied greatly. In general, they are soft and natural; tight curls and waves are 'out'. Many young girls wear their hair very long and loosely flowing. Some teenagers, in particular, drape their tresses curtainwise over their faces, leaving the eyes to peer through, rather like those of an Old English sheepdog. Apart from the young, women follow their own bent, wearing what suits them; there is no set style. Many wear their hair straight, others take advantage of the softer perms to give their coiffure a bouffant or carelessly windswept appearance (**913, 914, 916, 917, 919, 921, 922, 923, 963, 964**). *Hats* are worn less often now, apart from a range of fur designs for winter and plastic rain hats in bright colours and gay designs (**911, 915, 919, 920, 954**).

Footwear has changed constantly in design since 1945. Shoes, sandals and low or high boots have all been fashionable in these years. The cuban heels and wedge soles of the 1940s gave place to elegant higher heels with 'New Look' dresses. The ankle-strap and sling-back shoes were fashionable (**953, 955, 958**). Then followed the stiletto heels and very pointed toes in the late 1950s, when heels could be four inches high with tips only three-eighths of an inch in diameter and fatal to wood floor surfacing (**960**). The low-cut front with pointed toe was also worn with flat heels and casual shoes of this type were comfortable and very popular (**961**). The 1960s (**952**) were noted for the extreme fashionableness of high boots in coloured suèdes, leathers and plastic (**914, 917, 919, 966**). Coloured, patterned stock-ings were also in vogue. The 1970s are characterised by the chunky, broad toes and high platform soles. The more extreme versions of this style are generally only worn by the young, while more normal and comfortable designs are available for everyone else (**965**).

Notes on the Illustrations

852A English actual costume. Museum of Costume, Bath, England. Black cloth overcoat with black astrakhan collar and lining. Black hat. Grey waistcoat. Grey check trousers. Grey spats over black boots, *c*.1897.

B English actual costume. Museum of Costume, Bath, England. Oatmeal coloured twill promenade dress. Striped muslin undersleeves. White feather boa. Navy straw hat decorated with ostrich plumes, flowers and stuffed birds, *c*.1908.

C English actual costume. Museum of Costume, Bath, England. Pale blue muslin dress with black lace trimming and decoration. Long white gloves. Biscuit coloured straw hat decorated with black velvet ribbons and with flowers. Parasol covered in rows of white lace inside and black lace on the exterior, 1904.

D English actual costume. Museum of Costume, Bath, England. Grey silk promenade dress with matching lace trimming and fringe at hem. Mauve silk sash. Cream coloured kid gloves. Red velvet shoes with metal buckle. Red silk umbrella. Mauve velvet hat decorated by feathers and stuffed birds, 1911.

E English actual costume. Museum of Costume, Bath, England. Navy blue dress and cape. Silver braid decoration. Black umbrella. Blue ribbon hat with feathers, *c*. 1897.

853 Swedish actual costume. Nordiska Museet, Stockholm. Check black and white wool promenade dress (bought in Nice). White sash belt. White lace blouse with black bow at throat. Silk umbrella. Black hat with white lace bows. Black gloves.

854 French actual costume. Musée du Costume de la Ville de Paris. Midnight blue silk velvet dress with white spot pattern and white lace decoration. Velvet hat with birds' wings and flowers.

855 French fashion plate, La Mode Artistique. Black frock coat. White waistcoat. Grey and black striped trousers. Black hat. White gloves. Cane.

856 French actual costume. Musée du Costume de la Ville de Paris. White silk formal gown with white silk muslin undersleeves and skirt decoration.

857 French actual costume. Musée du Costume de la Ville de Paris. Evening gown designed by Ernest Raudnitz. Princess style in cream tulle over pink silk taffeta. Cream lace sleeves and skirt decoration. Ivory satin neckband. White plume fan.

858 Spanish actual costume. Rocamora Costume Museum, Barcelona, Spain. Evening gown in cream and black lace with pink chiffon at neck and wrists. Fan.

859 French actual costume. Musée du Costume de la Ville de Paris. Little girl's party dress in cream silk with cream guipure decoration.

860 French actual costume. Hermitage Museum, Leningrad, U.S.S.R. Evening gown designed by Worth. Pale blue brocade with plain sash. Long gloves.

861A English fashion plate, 1914. Silk dress with double tiered skirt over peg-top design. Fur muff. Felt hat with plumes.

B English department store catalogue, 1917. Beige woollen winter coat with collar, cuffs and hem of skunk fur. Black fur and beige felt hat. Umbrella.

C English department store catalogue, 1920. Pale blue wool coat and hat with white fur collar, cuffs and muff. White gaiters.

D English actual costume. Museum of Costume, Bath, England. Twill oatmeal coat with self-coloured pattern and embroidery. Black silk umbrella and black velvet hat, 1918.

E English newspaper photograph. Grey worsted suit. Light grey trilby felt hat with black band. Grey spats over black shoes, 1914.

F English actual costume. Museum of Costume, Bath, England. Brown satin suit with darker brown embroidery. Peg-top skirt. White lace blouse. Purple straw hat with white plumes, 1914.

G English fashion plate, 1916. Brown serge suit with black fur trimming. Brown gaiters over black shoes. Cream felt hat. Brown umbrella.

H English actual costume. Museum of Costume, Bath, England. Grey satin dress with brown fur edging. Pink lining to scarf. Straw hat with plume. Fur muff, *c.*1921.

I English fashion plate, 1920. Fawn wool overcoat. Brown worsted trousers. Spats over brown shoes. Black bowler hat. Gloves, cane.

862 English actual costume. Museum of Costume, Bath, England. Evening gown of purple georgette with silver embroidered hem. Evening cape of velvet, striped in red and purple with decoration in gold thread and pearls. Black fur collar and hem.

863 French actual costume. Boston Museum of Fine Arts, U.S.A. Evening dress of black satin underskirt, with train, also sash. Overdress of black net decorated with gold and black sequins, jet and rhinestones. Grey net bodice similarly decorated. White chiffon stole with grey and black ornamentation.

864 English actual costume. Museum of Costume, Bath, England. Evening gown of coffee-coloured brocade with cabbage rose design over underskirt of black georgette. Plume and jewel headdress.

865 English tailor's brochure. Evening dress of black

920 *1974–5*   **921** *1971*   **922** *1972*   **923** *1974*   **924** *1971*

1970–5

Details, 20th Century

925 c.1905
926 1914–16
927 c.1907
928 1915
929 c.1902
930 1929
931 1914
932 1926
933 1924
934 1927
935 1925
936 1916
937 1928
938 1937
939 1925
940 1942
941 1944
942 1935
943 1936
944 1933
945 1935
946 1934
947 1945
948 1946
949 1944
950 1948
951 1945
952 1964
953 1950
954 1965
955 1948
956 1960
957 1949
958 1950
959 1948
960 1960
961 1958
962 1949
963 1965
964 1965
965 1973
966 1960
967 1950

274

tail coat and trousers. Black silk lapels and braid trouser side seams. White shirt, collar, tie, waistcoat and gloves. Black socks, slippers and hat.

866 English actual costume. Museum of Costume, Bath, England. Navy silk dress with white dot pattern and inset and neckline of light blue velvet. Black hat with black net veil and white ostrich plumes. Shoes with gaiters.

867 Paris fashion. Museum of Costume, Bath, England. Satin dress with white collar. Hat with plume. Black silk handbag. Gaiters and shoes.

868 Austrian fashion plate, Wiener Chic. Dark blue tunic dress with hobble skirt. Grey hat with blue bow and plumes. Blue umbrella. White gloves and collar. Black shoes.

869 English fashion design, The Lady. Plain suit with dark velvet collar. Hat and umbrella. Gaiters and shoes.

870 French actual costume. Victoria and Albert Museum, London. Nigger brown figured velvet dress with overdress in brown crêpe decorated in self-coloured ribbon. White neckline. Black fur edging and muff. Dark brown felt hat with white plume.

871A Department store advertisement. Black lace evening dress over black silk underdress, 1928–9.

B Cream crêpe-de-chine dress.

C English actual costume. Museum of Costume, Bath, England. Flame-coloured georgette evening dress in darker shades towards hem. Pink ostrich plume fan with tortoiseshell handle. Gold shoes, c.1928.

D Tailor's design. English. Dark grey worsted three-piece suit. White collar, dark tie. Black shoes, grey spats, 1926.

E English department store advertisement. Green lace evening dress. Flesh-coloured stockings. Green silk shoes, 1928.

F English fashion plate. Yellow muslin and silk evening dress with sequin embroidery. Pale flesh-tint stockings and yellow velvet shoes, 1926.

872 French actual costume. Boston Museum of Fine Arts, U.S.A. Paris evening dress and cape by Molyneux. Black silk crêpe with gold embroidered decoration. Pink silk cape lining and dress decoration.

873 Spanish actual costume. Rocamora Costume Museum, Barcelona, Spain. Underdress of cream chiffon, overdress of beads in white and grey.

874 French actual costume. Boston Museum of Fine Arts, U.S.A. Evening dress in silk encrusted in sequins in black, mauve and green. Red plume fan.

875 French actual costume. Musée du Costume de la Ville de Paris. Evening gown in grey-mauve satin covered by overdress in pearled, orange tulle. Orange satin sash.

876 French actual costume. Kostuum Museum, The Hague, Holland. White crêpe georgette dress with glass embroidered decoration. Pink ostrich feather fan, Victoria and Albert Museum, London.

877 Dutch actual costume. Kostuum Museum, The Hague, Holland. Saffron silk crêpe dress with decoration in white and silver beads and spangles.

878 Dutch actual costume. Centraal Museum, Utrecht, Holland. Crêpe de chine suit with darker embroidery. Fur stole. Felt hat with fur pom-pom.

879 French design, Vogue. Cloth coat with fur collar and trimming. Shoes with gaiters. Felt hat with silk ribbon.

880 English actual costume. Museum of Costume, Bath, England. Black velvet dress with orange spot pattern. Orange velvet jacket. Black hat, shoes and handbag.

881 English manufacturer's advertisement. 'Plus fours' in brown herringbone tweed. Green woollen pullover and socks. Brown leather shoes. Brown striped shirt and collar. Brown tweed cap.

882 English actual costume (author). Dark fawn waterproof trenchcoat with leather buttons. Brown striped worsted trousers. Brown shirt, coloured tie. Brown leather shoes and gloves. Brown felt hat.

883 Molyneux design in Harper's Bazaar. Light wool jacket and dark pleated skirt. Halo hat.

884 English manufacturer's advertisement. Rust-coloured cloth coat with pale grey fur collar. Hat to match coat. Black suède handbag and shoes. Fawn gloves.

885 Fashion drawing. Beach pyjamas in dark green and patterned yellow cotton. Linen hat.

886 English actual costume (author). Printed georgette dress in brown, orange and yellow with brown sash. Pale grey gloves and fur. Brown hat and veil. Brown suède handbag and brown leather shoes.

887 English actual costume (author). Evening dress. Dinner jacket and trousers of black worsted with black corded silk lapels and braid trouser side seams. Black silk tie. White wing collar and pleated shirt front. Black patent leather shoes.

888 English actual costume. Museum of Costume, Platt Hall, Manchester, England. Formal gown of gold lamé worn at the Coronation in 1937. Shoes to match.

889 French actual costume designed by Jeanne Lanvin. Boston Museum of Fine Arts, U.S.A. Emerald green crêpe dress based on oriental harem style. Gold leather shoulder straps, belt and shoes.

890 English actual costume. Museum of Costume, Bath, England. Evening gown of pale green lace decorated with bands of silver lamé. Jewelled shoulder straps.

891 French actual costume designed by Chanel. Victoria and Albert Museum, London. Deep blue sequined evening dress.

892 English actual costume (author). Formal evening dress. Black tail coat and trousers. Corded silk lapels, braid trouser side seams. Semi-stiff white shirt, pearl and gold studs. White stiff wing collar, white piqué tie and waistcoat. Black socks and black patent leather shoes.

Corsets and Underwear, AD 300–1975

968 *Roman underwear, 4th century*

969 *Metal corset, early 16th century*

970 *Spanish farthingale, 16th century*

971 *French farthingale, late 16th century*

972 *Waist bolster, c.1600*

973 *Brocade corset, 18th century*

974 *Boned bodice, c.1660*

975 *Panier skirt, 18th century*

976 *Whalebone and tape folding panier, 18th century*

977 *Side paniers*

978 *Corset, 1868*

979 *Corset, 1878*

980 *Horsehair crinoline, 1858*

981 *Bustle petticoat, 1875*

982 *Cage crinoline, 1862*

983 *Corset, 1898*

984 *Corset, 1903*

985 *Bustle, 1887*

986 *Petticoat, 1878*

987 *Long corset, 1909*

988 *Nylon and Lycra bra and pantee girdle, 1970*

989 *Suspender belt, 1925*

990 *Corselette, 1950*

893 Fashion drawing in Vogue. Ice blue satin evening gown with black satin cuffed décolletage. Black suède gloves. Silver sandals.

894 The utility suit. Prototype designed by Hardy Amies in check tweed. Actual costume, Victoria and Albert Museum, London. Black felt hat with brooch. Black patent leather handbag. Leather shoes.

895 Fashion designs, Croquis de Mode, Madrid. Cloth coat with hat to match. Sling handbag. Sling-back platform soled shoes.

896 English actual costume (author). Pale blue rayon dress with white spot pattern. Navy suède handbag, gloves and shoes. Navy hat of velvet leaves with veil.

897 Christian Dior's New Look. Actual Costume, Victoria and Albert Museum, London. Black hat and skirt. Cream linen jacket. Black shoes.

898 Fashion drawing, Vogue. Dark brown coat with astrakhan collar. Red felt hat with brown pom-poms. Red leather shoes and gloves.

899 Fashion photograph, Vogue. Lavender crêpe dress with dolman sleeves. Navy suède ankle-strap shoes.

900 Fashion drawing, Vogue. Dull red and black herringbone tweed coat. Black velvet collar and cuffs. Red hat with black feathers. Red gloves. Black suède ankle-strap shoes.

901 French actual costume designed by Pierre Balmain. Kostuum Museum, The Hague, Holland. White silk evening dress with black polka dot pattern. Long black gloves. Jewelled white satin handbag and shoes.

902 Fashion drawing, Vogue. Short evening dress of silver grey nylon net. Gold kid sandals and bag.

903 Fashion drawing, Vogue. Lilac wool day dress. Black trimming and shoes.

904 English actual costume (author). Short soft tweed overcoat with fleece lining. Striped worsted trousers. Black leather shoes. Felt hat. Suède gloves.

905 French costume, fashion drawing, News Chronicle. Suit and hat to match. Black gloves and shoes.

906 English design, Vogue. Red, white and black jacket in wool, lined with red wool. Black worsted suit. Red felt hat and red fabric gloves. Black suède handbag and shoes.

907 French fashion, Christian Dior. Model photograph, the Daily Mail. Three-quarter wool coat over dark skirt. Velvet beret. Black shoes and belt.

908 French fashion designed by Jeanne Lafaurie. Fashion photograph, Union Française des Arts du Costume. Black straw hat with dark satin cocktail dress. Black gloves and shoes.

909 English actual costume (author). Brown tweed herringbone overcoat with raglan sleeve. Fawn gabardine trousers. Brown leather shoes with crêpe soles. Brown felt hat. Brown striped shirt and collar with red tie.

910 All actual costumes photographed by the author.

A Nylon fur coat in light brown over dark brown skirt. White fur hat. Black patent leather shoes. Patterned mauve stockings.

B Light grey raincoat over grey lounge suit. Grey felt hat. Brown gloves. Light brown boots.

C Dark brown nylon fur coat. Black and white check wool trousers. Light coloured boots.

D Three-quarter coat and skirt of red wool. Flesh-coloured stockings. Brown shoes and handbag.

E Nylon fur coat dyed cerise with white fur lining. Black lace patterned stockings. Black plastic shoes.

F Green cloth coat with grey fur trimming. Hat to match. Dark brown stockings. Green plastic shoes.

G Light grey worsted lounge suit.

H Dark red tweed coat with black fur collar and hem. Brown check trousers. Brown slip-on shoes. Red felt hat.

I Cobalt blue wool suit. White stockings. Black suède boots.

J Primrose wool suit with hat to match.

K Grey tweed overcoat. Light grey gabardine trousers.

911 Magazine advertisement. Lilac coloured coat with hat to match. Gold and white silk blouse. Flesh-coloured stockings with lilac patent leather buckled shoes.

912 Aquascutum check worsted suit in brown. White shirt, patterned silk cravat. Brown suède boots.

913 Butterick design of top striped in cerise and navy with white leather belt. White pleated skirt. White plastic shoes and handbag. Light stockings.

914 Emcar design of bitter chocolate wool flannel dress. Black boots.

915 Design for cobalt blue alpaca suit (Vogue). White fur collar and hat. Black gloves and shoes.

916 Striped nylon summer dress in black, white and cerise (Vogue). White lacy stockings. Cerise hat, bag and shoes.

917 Party outfit (Vogue) in red and black flowered cotton. Black suède boots.

918 Men's outfitters advertisement. Grey worsted suit on cutaway pattern. Black leather shoes.

919 Woman's magazine. Black wool skirt and black leather boots. Turquoise top with suède jacket in squares of fawn, rust, brown and dark brown with blue edging. Black felt hat. Brown leather belt with metal buckle.

920 Town dress by Christian Dior. Black and white fleck wool coat and skirt with silver fox collar. Black velvet jacket and hat. White jabot blouse. Black stockings and shoes.

921 Magazine advertisement. Nylon jersey maxi dress in white, green and orange. White shoes.

922 Manufacturer's advertisement. Trouser suit in red, black and fawn patterned wool over red wool tunic with black belt.

923 Advertisement, C and A. Golden coloured polyester/wool French cut slacks with rayon blouse in dark brown and gold. Brown buttons and shoes. Throat band to match blouse.

924 Party suit, men's outfitter's advertisement. Deep rose-coloured velvet jacket and trousers. Toning shirt and patterned tie. Grey leather shoes.

925 French actual costume. Musée du Costume de la Ville de Paris. Straw hat decorated by muslin and white lace. Hat for automobile driving tied on with taffeta scarf.

926 Manufacturer's advertisement, English. Straw boater with ribbon band.

927 French actual costume, Musée du Costume de la Ville de Paris. Black taffeta hat with white plumes. Jewelled neck collar.

928 Newspaper photograph. White wing collar, black bow tie.

929 French actual costume, Musée du Costume de la Ville de Paris. Pale coloured straw hat with black straw border. Black velvet ribbon bows. Black lace yoke, white neck ruffles.

930 Fashion drawing, Vogue. Beige velvet turban.

931 Austrian fashion plate, Wiener Chic. Maroon silk hat and collar. Grey plumes.

932 Fashion drawing, Vogue. Cloche hat designed by Rose Descat (French).

933 Actual shoe, English. Platt Hall, Manchester. Leather.

934 Fashion drawing, French. Embroidered silk handbag with beads. Metal mount, leather handle.

935 Fashion drawing, French. Gold kid evening shoe.

936 Actual boot, Platt Hall, Manchester, England. Fawn suède laced boot with black leather toe and heel.

937 English, fashion drawing, magazine. The Eton crop.

938 English magazine photograph. Brown felt hat and ribbons.

939 Actual umbrella (author). Striped silk in blue, pink and white. Cream coloured handle.

940 English magazine photograph. White felt hat and ribbon.

941 English magazine photograph. Page-boy bob hairstyle.

942 Newspaper photograph, English. White woven fibre hat with navy ribbons.

943 Actual hat (author). Red Tyrolean-style with cord and feather.

944 Men's outfitter's advertisement, English. Black bowler hat.

945 Magazine advertisement, English. Blue leather shoe with natural leather heel.

946 Men's outfitter's advertisement, English. Light fawn felt hat, brown ribbon.

947 Actual hat (author). Navy straw with veil. Flowers and snood.

948 Actual shoe (author). Tan leather and white buckskin. Wedge sole.

949 Magazine advertisement, English. Blue leather and white buckskin.

950 Magazine advertisement, English. Brown leather shoe.

951 Actual shoe (author). Brown leather, wedge sole.

952 Magazine advertisement, English. Buffalo suède shoe.

953 Actual shoe (author). Black suède shoe in ankle-strap design with platform sole.

954 Wolsey advertisement, English magazine. Blue felt hat.

955 Magazine advertisement, English. Square-backed leather shoe.

956 Magazine advertisement, French. Deep purple wool handbag.

957 Fashion drawing, French magazine. Powder blue felt hat and ribbons.

958 Newspaper advertisement. Jay's Ltd. for Huskees boot. Suède boot with crêpe sole and sheepskin lining.

959 Fashion drawing, English magazine. Grey felt hat with pink ribbon.

960 Newspaper advertisement, English. Shoe with stiletto heel in black patent leather.

961 Magazine drawing, English. Apple green suède shoe.

962 Man's leather sandal (author).

963 Hair shampoo advertisement, English magazine.

964 Beauty competition, English magazine.

965 Newspaper advertisement, English. Black patent leather shoe, platform sole style.

966 Magazine advertisement. White leather 'cossack' boot.

967 Dolcis advertisement. Red leather handbag with zip fastener.

968 Breast band and pants. Mosaic, Villa, Piazza Amerini, Sicily, about fourth century A.D.

969 Metal corset designed possibly to support a weak figure. Wallace Collection, England.

970 Canvas skirt with pliant wood hoops. Contemporary drawing c.1570–80.

971 Similar structure with fabric gathered and tied on at the waist under the bodice busk.

972 From Dutch caricature drawing.

973 Actual corset. French, Brooklyn Museum, U.S.A.

974 Actual corset bodice. Victoria and Albert Museum, London. White satin with lace and embroidery.

975 Contemporary engraving. English c.1748.

Glossary

Glossary

The figures in brackets refer to appropriate illustrations.

Abolla A Roman military cloak similar to the Greek chlamys.

Aigrette Feathery plume used in hair and headdress decoration (**676**).

Alpaca Fabric woven from wool and hair of the llama.

Balayeuse see Sweeper.

Baldric A silk sash or leather band slung over one shoulder and round the opposite hip. In Medieval times it was decorated by silver or gold bells. Later it was fastened on the left hip and carried the sword holder (**278A, 556**).

Band The name given to the sixteenth century ruff (**516**). Applied in the following century to the decorative collars worn outside the doublet (**569**).

Bandbox Round boxes made to contain the bands.

Barbette Worn by women in the thirteenth and fourteenth centuries. A piece of white linen pinned to the hair at each side of the head above the ears and draped around the chin and in front of the neck (**205**). Survives in nun's attire.

Basquina A wide underskirt worn with a farthingale in sixteenth century Spain.

Batiste A finely woven linen fabric. Named after the thirteenth century French weaver Baptiste Chambrai.

Berthe A garment popular in the 1830s especially. Made of white fabric with lace or pleated edging, it covered the shoulders and terminated in lappets tucked into the waistbelt in front (**833**).

Bicorne A flat black man's hat, with point at front and rear, fashionable in the late eighteenth century and early nineteenth (**699**).

Bliaud An over-tunic worn by both sexes in the early Middle Ages. It was fairly long and belted at the waist while the skirt was often slit at the sides or in front to allow easier movement. A knee-length bliaud was worn by peasants and soldiers (**176, 197**).

Bombast Padding made of cotton and rags used to stuff in the linings of sixteenth century garments.

Bracco, braccae A rough covering wrapped round the hips and legs worn in northern Europe in the early centuries AD (**141**).

Braguette French word for cod-piece.

Braies Loose drawers or breeches belted or tied with cord at the waist. The lower end was tucked into the chausses or hose below the knee. Worn from pre-Roman days until the early Middle Ages. After the thirteenth century the braies became shorter in the leg as the hose grew longer and, by the later fifteenth century, were short underpants (**142**).

Broadcloth Fine quality woollen cloth, woven in widths of thirty inches and over.

Buskin A thick-soled boot worn by Greeks and Romans. In drama, a deeper cork sole was inserted to add height to the actor's stature (**18**).

Bustle A framework worn under the skirt in the 1870s and 1880s to support the heavy draperies swept up and back. At first a whalebone or metal and canvas half-cage with fullness at the rear, later a pad or wire basket tied on round the waist with tapes and resting on the buttocks (**981, 985**).

Cabriolet see Calash

Cadogan A wig style of the 1770s worn by men and women wherein the back hair was looped up and tied, generally with black ribbon. In the later eighteenth century the name referred to the club-shaped termination to the tied pig-tail (**695A**).

Caftan (Kaftan) A coat-like garment of Oriental origin. Worn in Turkey, the Middle East and Russia especially. It generally had long sleeves and could be held round the waist by a broad sash (**525**).

Calash (*Calèche*) A silk cage covering for the immense wigs worn by ladies in the later eighteenth century. It was made of silk which covered a whalebone framework which could be raised and lowered like a carriage hood (**747**).

Calceus A Roman shoe covering the foot generally as far as the ankle (**77**).

Canezou A shoulder covering worn chiefly in the years 1820–50 and resembling a berthe.

Carmagnole A short jacket worn by French revolutionaries in the 1790s. Originally worn by workers who came to France from Carmagnola in Italy.

Carrick A gentleman's overcoat of the later eighteenth and of the nineteenth centuries. Originally a coachman's overcoat it was heavy, double-breasted and with one or more shoulder capes (**769**).

Caul A metal or cord net in gold or silver, jewelled

at the intersections and worn in differing designs of Medieval headdresses for ladies (**211, 278D, 302**). (Also crispine, crespinette.)

Chainse A white undertunic of fine linen worn in the early Middle Ages. It had long sleeves and was visible below the bliaud at wrists and hem. In feminine costume it was ground-length. Later it developed into the shirt and the chemise (**173**).

Chamarre A rich fabric, fur-lined and trimmed coat. Fashionable in the fifteenth and early sixteenth centuries, it was wide with full sleeves and was usually worn open (**467**). Its prototype was the Spanish sheepskin coat, the *samarra*.

Chaperon Medieval style of hood, with shoulder cape and liripipe (**280**).

Chausses A hose made of shaped, seamed pieces of cloth covering the foot and leg and pulled up over the lower part of the braies. In the early centuries AD these were often held to the legs by cross-gartering. In the Middle Ages they gradually became longer, developing into long stockings and, finally, tights (**142, 258, 321**).

Chignon Feminine hairstyle where the hair is twisted into a knot at the nape or on top of the head. Fashionable in Greek costume and in many succeeding ages (**29, 763**).

Chiton Ancient Greek tunic worn by both sexes (**18, 29**).

Chlamys A light woollen cloak worn by the men of Ancient Greece (**17**).

Chopine Pattens to slip on over the hose or shoes for ladies to walk in the streets. Chopines, which were especially fashionable in Italy and Spain in the sixteenth century, had exceptionally high soles. Venetian designs, of wood, were generally called *zoccolo* (*zoccoli*) and extended up to two feet or two feet six inches in height (**339, 342**).

Clavus (clavi) Purple stripes to denote rank and position in Roman dress. These stripes or bands were sewn or woven vertically on tunics and togas (**77, 106**).

Cloisonné Enamel inlay on metal jewellery.

Codpiece A small bag to conceal the front opening of masculine hose in the fifteenth century. Made of the same fabric as the hose it was attached by points and lacings. Sixteenth century codpieces were padded to protrude excessively and were also used as a pocket to hold money, handkerchief, etc. (**321, 362D**).

Coif A linen cap covering the head. Generally white, it could be worn alone indoors in the Middle Ages or then, (and later) under a hood or helmet (**208**).

Collet monté The later sixteenth century standing collar, edged with lace and wired to stand up behind the head, worn by ladies (**471C**).

Col rotonde see whisk.

Cotehardie A term used extensively for both feminine gowns and masculine tunics in the Middle Ages between about 1300 until 1430. It is generally applied to fitting garments, buttoned part- or full-length and having long or half sleeves (**220, 225**).

Cothurnes A high boot worn by Greeks then Romans. It was laced up the front, often fur-lined and had an animal's paw or head decorating the top.

Counterchange design A form of decoration especially fashionable in the fourteenth century when the design on one half of a garment was counterchanged so that, on the other half, the colours of the ground and pattern are reversed (**280**).

Couvrechef A Medieval term for a veil or kerchief covering the head (**205**).

Crackow see Poulaine.

Cravat Decorative neckwear for men made of white silk, linen and lace. The name is thought to have been derived from linen neckwear worn by a Croatian regiment in the 1660s. Differing forms of cravat evolved over the years, particularly in the seventeenth and nineteenth centuries (**576A, 577A, 578**).

Crespinette see Caul.

Criarde Petticoats of gummed linen worn in the eighteenth century before paniers were in use. The name derives from the noise made when the wearer moved. *Criard* = clamorous.

Crinoline Nineteenth century boned petticoat. The name derives from the horsehair fabric from which they were made. *Crinis,* Latin for hair, also the French *crin,* and *linum,* Latin for thread (**980**).

Crispine see Caul.

Cross-gartering Strips of linen wound round the braies to hold them in position. (Northern Europe, fifth to eleventh centuries) (**148**).

Cucullus Hood attached to a cloak. Ancient Rome.

Culottes French term for breeches, seventeenth to early nineteenth century.

Dagges Ornamentally cut edging to Medieval and early Renaissance garments (**257**).

Dalmatic (dalmatica) A long, wide-sleeved tunic from Dalmatia. Worn in late Roman and in Byzantine costume. Later became part of Christian liturgical dress.

Damask A rich silk or linen fabric with a pattern of flowers and animals. The design has a satin, shiny finish contrasting with a dull, rougher ground. Originated in Damascus.

Dolman An oriental garment of Turkish origin. Worn in Hungary for many centuries in the form of a coat. Made from rich ornamental fabric

(720A). Also a late nineteenth century loose, long coat for ladies.

Doublet A masculine tunic worn especially from the fifteenth to the seventeenth century. Originally of quilted manufacture, its style changed over the years but it remained a fundamental outer body garment (**445, 489**).

Dundreary whiskers Nineteenth century facial hair with sidewhiskers separated by a shaven chin (**812**).

Échelle Derives from the French word for ladder. The front of the bodice or stomacher decorated in the seventeenth and eighteenth centuries by graduated ribbon bows (**632**).

Falling band Lace or linen collar worn in the seventeenth century, see band (**571**).

Falling ruff An unstarched, soft ruff (**545**).

Farthingale The canvas or linen petticoat containing whalebone hoops worn in the sixteenth century to provide the required skirt shape (**970, 971**).

Femoralia Roman underwear drawers.

Fibula(e) A pin or brooch used chiefly in classical dress to fasten draped garments (**48**).

Fichu Worn by ladies, a white silk or cotton neckcloth draped round the throat and shoulders. Especially fashionable in the late eighteenth century (**696**). Originally of lace, often black.

Fontange A tall headdress initiated for ladies in the late seventeenth century. Made of white lace in tiers, decorated with ribbons and jewels (**577B, D**).

Frogging Looped braid button fastenings, often in gold and silver, used on men's coats especially in the eighteenth century (**707**).

Frontlet The loop on the forehead under late fifteenth century feminine headdresses. Also the jewelled metal edge of their sixteenth century hoods (**425, 429**).

Galerus A Roman round cap usually made of fur or skin.

Gamurra A sixteenth century feminine gown worn in Italy.

Garde-corps A fourteenth century garment which evolved from the surcoat. Either sleeveless or with elbow-length wide sleeves (**195**).

Garrick see Carrick.

Gipon Prototype of the doublet, worn in the Middle Ages. At first the name usually refers to the undertunic.

Goffering The use of a goffering iron which, when heated, was used to set the convolutions of the white, starched, sixteenth century ruff (**462**).

Golilla Card or stiffened fabric support for the Spanish white collar of the 1620s. Popularised by Philip IV (**599**).

Gonelle Long gown or tunic worn by both sexes in Merovingian and Carolingian dress. The English word 'gown' derives from this (**149**).

Gorget The Medieval white throat covering worn with the wimple. See also barbette.

Habit à la française Term used to describe the gentleman's suit of coat, waistcoat and breeches in the early eighteenth century. Later the term was applied to the coat only (**661**).

Hedgehog wig Late eighteenth century style worn by both sexes where the hair was cut raggedly short (**744**).

Himation A Greek cloak, rectangular in shape, large and worn draped by both sexes (**20**).

Hose Medieval, leg coverings. At first they were stockings, later they lengthened to the waist to become tights. Made of seamed material often striped or parti-coloured (**321**).

Houppelande A full overgown worn by both sexes in the Middle Ages, chiefly in the years 1375–1425. Earlier examples had high collars and were ground-length; they had very wide sleeves (**223, 234**).

Jerkin A garment similar to the doublet, generally sleeveless, and worn on top of it (**440**).

Justaucorps Originally a military garment it became the masculine coat when this replaced the jacket in the later seventeenth century (**577E, 604**). It finally evolved into the habit à la française.

Kandys A Persian style of caftan or coat. Seen in Byzantine dress.

Kucsma A Hungarian fur or fur-trimmed hat (**624**).

Lacerna A Roman cloak, hooded and full.

Lamé A rich fabric with gold or silver threads.

Liripipe The lengthened peak of the Medieval hood (**253**).

Love-lock A seventeenth century style of hairdressing when men grew a lock of hair very long and tied the end with a ribbon bow (**592**).

Mamillare A linen or wool breast band worn by Roman women.

Maniakis (maniakes) The decorative, jewelled collar worn by Byzantine emperors (**108**).

Mente Longer coat worn by Hungarian men over the dolman (**720C**).

Merino Wool woven from the Spanish sheep of that name.

Mohair Wool woven from the Angora goat from Asia Minor.

Paenula Worn by men, a Roman garment like a blouse or poncho. It had a hood and was slipped on over the head on top of the tunica.

Pagoda sleeve A term applied especially to ladies' gowns of the eighteenth century when the fitting sleeve flared out at the elbow (**666**).

Palla Roman equivalent of the Greek peplos, draped and usually open at one side (**82A**).

Pallium Like the himation, worn in classical Greece and Rome as a draped outer garment. In the later days of the Roman Empire it was folded lengthwise to resemble a long scarf which was hung round the shoulders. Eventually it became a Church vestment.

Paludamentum The Roman military cloak of purple wool worn by senior officers.

Panier The term applied to the several varieties of whalebone-reinforced petticoats and structures worn under eighteenth century skirts – the eighteenth century equivalent of the farthingale. It derives from the French *panier* = basket (**976, 977**).

Pantalettes Worn by little girls in the nineteenth century. This underwear was later lace-trimmed and showed below the dress hem (**794**).

Pantaloons Women's undergarment in the nineteenth century. The word was also used for early nineteenth century men's trousers which fastened with a front panel buttoned to the waistcoat with three buttons. The term trousers was then applied when the fly fastening replaced this.

Pantoffle In the sixteenth century this was an overshoe which was slipped on top of the shoe or hose; it had no back. Later the word was used for slippers (**451**).

Particolouring A Medieval system of decoration wherein one half or one quarter of a garment was in one colour and design and the other(s) of a different one (**259**).

Partlet A collar or yoke which was detachable from the tunic or gown. It was usually white, embroidered and jewelled (**441**).

Passementerie A form of appliqué decoration embroidered or woven, in silk, cotton or metal thread and incorporating beads, cord and fringe.

Patten A wood, leather or cork undersole which was worn in the Middle Ages, out-of-doors, to protect the hose and soft shoes. The patten was fastened on to the foot by straps and buckles (**313**). (See Chopine.)

Peasecod-belly The unusual masculine silhouette produced in the second half of the sixteenth century by padding the doublet front to give a paunch shape. The fashion spread from Spain and was especially extreme in form in France (**473, 507**).

Pelisse A loose cloak, often of velvet, fur-edged and having a large collar and slits for the arms. Worn over the full hoop skirts. Some designs had attached hoods (**668C**).

Peplos The Greek garment worn by women which was a rectangle of material folded over and pinned on each shoulder. One side was generally left open. The fabric was draped in varied ways and the corners were often weighted (**25**).

Peplum In Ancient classical dress this is the Roman equivalent of peplos. In more modern times the word is used to describe the short flounce or full skirt attached to a fitting bodice (**828D**).

Periwig A word commonly applied to the full-bottomed wig of the seventeenth century. In fact periwig simply means wig, any type of wig, and is derived from the French *perruque* via peruke, then perwyke in English.

Petasos (petasus) A broad-brimmed Greek hat as seen in the Tanagra statuettes. The hat was tied on by strings under the chin (**30, 31**).

Petticoat breeches see Rhinegrave breeches.

Picadils The scalloped or tabbed edge at neck and armhole fashionable in late sixteenth and early seventeenth century dress. The name Piccadilly was given to this London thoroughfare because of a tailor there who specialised in making picadils at this time (**476**).

Piccadilly weepers Alternative name, see Dundreary whiskers.

Pigeon's wings The fluffed-out side portions of a man's wig in the second quarter of the eighteenth century (**661**).

Pileus see Pilos.

Pilos The round felt cap worn by Greek men. The pileus was the Roman equivalent (**19**).

Plastron A metal breastplate in armour. In costume the word was applied to the fur front of the sideless surcoat worn by Medieval ladies, also to later decorative stomachers (**229, 238**).

Pluderhosen German word for the loose, knee-length breeches worn by men in the early seventeenth century. In England these were termed Venetians (**532A**).

Points Metal-tagged laces used widely in costume from the thirteenth to the sixteenth century to attach the edge of one garment to another (**346**).

Pomander A gold or silver filigree hollow sphere containing ambergris or other perfume. This depended from a lady's girdle or a necklace or was carried by men. Especially fashionable in the sixteenth century. The name derives from the French *pomme d'ambre* (**438**).

Poplin A ribbed fabric made from linen or cotton with wool.

Poulaine Style of footwear fashionable from the later fourteenth century till about 1465. This had an extended length at the toes which became exaggerated about 1385. The vogue was said to be most extreme in Poland so that English versions were termed crackows after the Polish city of that name (**314**).

Pourpoint The Medieval body garment or tunic

which later became the doublet (**347**).

Rebato The metal supporting frame worn at the back of the neck under large sixteenth century ruffs. Of Spanish origin.

Redingote 1. In men's dress the French word for the heavy travelling coat worn in England in the early eighteenth century. The coat was full and long with large collar and revers. The term redingote derives from riding coat. During the eighteenth and nineteenth century it changed considerably in style being worn first as an overcoat and later replacing the coat (**791A**). 2. In women's dress it was fashionable in the late eighteenth century as a double-breasted, high-waisted coat-gown with revers and collar but open in front below the waist.

Reticule The dainty handbag of the Directoire and First Empire years. Also called a ridicule (**676**).

Rhinegrave breeches (rhinegraves) A masculine fashion of the years 1650–1675 when breeches were like wide shorts or kilts and decorated excessively with ribbon loops, ruffles and lace. An apron of ribbon loops hid the front closure. Also called petticoat breeches, the fashion is thought to have been introduced to France by Rheingrafen Karl (**615**).

Ropa An outer garment worn by women in the years 1560–1720. Of Spanish origin, it was also fashionable in England and in Holland especially; here it was called a *vlieger*. Often of velvet with fur or jewelled trimming it had puff sleeves and a high collar. It was fastened at the throat then hung open in front over the gown (**527D**).

Sagum The rough, rectangular cloak of wool or fur worn by Celts and Gauls and adopted for military use by Rome. Fastened on the right shoulder by a thorn and later a fibula (**145**).

Sans-culottes The name given to French revolutionaries who adopted trousers for wear instead of breeches and stockings to distinguish themselves from the aristocrats. Literally the term translates as 'without breeches'.

Sideless surcoat (surcote) A full gown, with fur-edged arm-holes extending to the hips, worn by ladies in the fourteenth century (**243**).

Socca (soccus) A soft shoe worn in classical times.

Solea A simple Roman sandal with wooden sole, generally worn indoors.

Solitaire The eighteenth century fashion of a black ribbon which tied the wig at the nape and was then brought forwards to be fastened in front of the neck (**746**).

Spatterdash Leather or cloth leggings to protect stockings and trousers from being splashed by mud. Worn in the eighteenth and nineteenth centuries. Later became merely spats.

Spencer A waist-length jacket with long sleeves worn by women in the Directoire period and early nineteenth century (**761**).

Steinkirk A cravat worn in the 1690s wherein the ends were tucked into a coat buttonhole. The name derives from the battle of Steenkirk in 1692.

Stock Eighteenth century neckwear for men which replaced the earlier cravat. Made of folded white linen (**776**).

Stocks Sixteenth century leg coverings. The word later developed into stockings.

Stola The chief garment of Roman women. It was ground-length and loose, the drapery being held in place by one or more girdles (**78**).

Stomacher A separate front panel of rich decorative fabric ending in a point at the waist and worn on top of the gown bodice. Of Spanish origin, it was fashionable in the sixteenth and early seventeenth century. Laced to the figure, the stomacher was often boned and was decorated with jewelled embroidery (**520**). The stomacher reappeared in the late seventeenth century when it was decorated with graduated ribbon bows, see Échelle.

Strophium Worn by Roman ladies. A long narrow strip of material wound round the body on top of the undertunic to help support and delineate the breasts.

Supportasse see Rebato.

Surpied The quatrefoil-shaped piece of leather worn on top of the instep of the seventeenth century boot (**592**).

Sweeper The pleated and ruffled edges to the hem of late nineteenth century petticoats which 'swept' the floor and kept the dress hem clean.

Tabard A sleeveless or short-sleeved tunic worn over armour in the Middle Ages. Where appropriate the arms decorated the garment, making it a coat-of-arms.

Tablier (en) Describes feminine gowns which are designed with an apron front, such as styles of the 1870s. French *tablier* = apron (**813D**).

Tablion The richly embroidered panel on the cloak worn by Byzantine sovereigns (**109A, D**).

Tasset The tabs at the waistline of the seventeenth century doublet (**612**).

Tebenna The cloak worn by Etruscan men (**57**).

Tippet Name given to the streamers hanging from the elbow-length sleeves of the Medieval tunic or gown (**280**). Also applied to small shoulder capes, usually of fur, worn especially in the nineteenth century.

Toga The Roman cloak worn by the Roman citizen. Usually made of white wool and in shape a segment of a circle. It grew larger under the Empire and its draping became a complex art (**83F**).

Torc (torque) A necklace of twisted metal made by the Celts and Gauls also, later, the Romans (**136**).

Touret A word used to describe several different parts of early Medieval feminine headdresses. It sometimes refers to the fillet, sometimes to a veil. It is generally bound round the forehead as in a nun's coif.

Tournure French word for bustle.

Tricorne The three-cornered hat worn by men in the eighteenth century (**681**).

Trunk hose The garment covering the body from waist to above the knee in the sixteenth century (**445**).

Tutulus 1. Name given to the headdress of the pagan Etruscan and Roman priest and his wife. This was composed of braids, built up into a conical shape. The word then became applied to a felt cap of this form (**27**, **63**). 2. The word is also used to refer to the bronze fastenings in Bronze Age dress.

Valona The white collar worn by Spanish men in the 1620s. Particularly favoured by Philip IV. See Golilla.

Venetians see Pluderhosen.

Verdugado The Spanish farthingale worn in Spain.

Verdugo The pliant wood bands used in the farthingale petticoat structure.

Vertugade (vertugale or the *mode vertugadin*) French terms for farthingale and the style.

Vlieger see Ropa.

Whisk English term for the stiffened lace or lace-edged white collar supported on a card or frame which followed the ruff in the early seventeenth century. The French term was *col rotonde* (**457**, **478**, **608E**).

Wimple A simple headcovering worn by women from the early Middle Ages. A piece of material, square or circular in shape, draped over the head to the shoulders and held in place by a band round the brow. Later worn with barbette or chin band so that the throat and chin were also covered (**198**).

Zoccolo see Chopine.

Sources of Information on Costume

Sources of Information on Costume

In Europe these are widespread and varied. In general, the chief sources for the centuries before AD 1600 are the churches, museums and galleries which have collections of sculpture, paintings, portraits, mosaics, relief carving, stained glass, drawings and engravings, jewellery, arms, medallions, effigies, embroidered textiles and illuminated manuscripts.

From AD 1600 onwards there exist many collections of actual garments and complete costumes. A few examples exist from before this date and these comprise particularly articles made from leather. Many costume collections are devoted to national and regional dress; only those displaying fashionable dress, as covered in this book, are listed here.

For the student who requires extensive and detailed information on all the costume museums and galleries available in Europe, it is helpful to consult the comprehensive guide, published in four languages, by the Palazzo Grassi in Venice, which is available in major libraries. This is:

> *Guida Internazionale ai Musei e alle Collezioni Pubbliche di Costumi e di Tessuti.*
> Published by the Centro Internazionale delle Arti e del Costume. Palazzo Grassi, Venezia, 1970.

A list of the larger, most useful collections of costume sources in Europe is given here, presented alphabetically, under the country concerned.

The quality and quantity of actual costumes to be seen in collections varies greatly from country to country. It bears little relationship to the importance of the country concerned in the history of costume. The majority of costume collections have been assembled over the years by individuals and have later been donated to museums and cities. Countries which possess excellent and extensive collections include Great Britain, Spain, Sweden, Switzerland and Holland. Several countries such as France and Italy possess good collections but lack buildings in which to display them. Others, such as Germany and Poland, lost much of their collections in the Second World War and are now re-establishing them.

AUSTRIA

Vienna
Kunsthistorisches Museum – Paintings.
Österreichische Galerie – for Medieval paintings, *Museum mittelalterlicher österreichischer Kunst* and for the paintings of nineteenth century dress, *Galerie des XIX und XX Jahrhunderts* in the Upper Belvedere.
Historisches Museum der Stadt Wien – Paintings and drawings and a few items of costume.
The chief costume section of this museum is on the outskirts of the city at *Hetzendorf Schloss* in the *Modesammlung*. The costumes are chiefly from the nineteenth century.

BELGIUM

Antwerp
Musée Royal des Beaux Arts – Paintings, especially Medieval and Renaissance.
Musée Mayer van den Bergh – Paintings and wood sculpture.
Bruges
Musée Groeninge (Beaux-Arts) – Paintings.
Brussels
Musées Royaux des Beaux-Arts de Belgique – Paintings of all periods but especially early Renaissance and Medieval.
Musées Royaux d'Art et d'Histoire – a small collection of costumes.

CZECHOSLOVAKIA

Prague
Národní Galerie – Collection of costumes, eighteenth to twentieth centuries.

DENMARK

Aarhus
Koebstadmuseet 'Den Gamle By' – Collection of costumes from 1770 onwards.
Copenhagen
De Danske Kongers Kronologiske Samling paa Rosenborg (Rosenborg Palace) – Costumes and accessories of the Danish royal family 1600–1940.
Nationalmuseet
Costume collections from 1690 onwards also the remarkable and unique collection of Bronze Age Danish costumes (1500–900 BC) and costumes from fourteenth century Greenland. Illustrated accounts available in large libraries.

FINLAND

Helsinki

Kansallismuseo − Nationalmuseum − Collection of costumes from 1750 onwards.

Turku

Turun Kaupungin Historiallinen Museo − Collection of costumes from 1760 onwards.

FRANCE

Angers

Musée des Tapisseries, Château d' Angers − Tapestries.

Bayeux

Musée Tapisserie de la Reine Mathilde − This remarkable tapestry is embroidered in coloured wool on a strip of linen 70 metres long. It was worked between October 14th 1066 and July 14th 1077. The finest source for eleventh century costume, it shows the clothes of men and women of different classes and occupations at the time of the Norman Conquest.

Lyons

Musée Historique des Tissus et Musée Lyonnais des Arts Decoratifs − Some costumes and silk textiles.

Paris

Musée du Louvre − Paintings, sculpture, jewellery from Ancient Greek onwards.

Musée de Cluny − Paintings and tapestries.

Musée des Arts Decoratifs − Paintings and tapestries.

Musée du Petit Palais − Paintings especially of nine-teenth century dress.

Musée du Costume de la Ville de Paris − a superb collection of several thousand costumes, unfortunately not permanently on display but exhibitions of specific periods are held regularly and the costumes photographed and published in booklet form.

Centre d'Enseignement et de Documention du Costume − Collection of 3500 costumes and accessories (also not permanently on display), textiles, books, periodicals, drawings, and photographs of costume. Help and advice given to students of costume.

Versailles

Musée National du Château de Versailles − Paintings and tapestries.

GERMANY (West)

Frankfurt-am-Main

Historisches Museum
A large collection of costumes from 1750 onwards.

Hanover

Historisches Museum am Hohen Ufer − Collection of costumes from 1760 onwards.

Kassel

Staatliche Kunstsammlungen − eighteenth and nineteenth century costumes.

Lübeck

Museum fur Kunst und Kulturgeschichte des Hansestadt, Lübeck − costumes from the eighteenth and nineteenth centuries.

Münich

Bayerisches Nationalmuseum − Collection of costumes from the eighteenth and nineteenth centuries also accessories. Only a few costumes tastefully on display. Most of the collection is stored. The museum also has a collection of paintings, sculpture and carving useful to a student of costume.

Alte Pinakothek − Paintings.

GERMANY (East)

Collections of costume in **Berlin** damaged during the Second World War still not yet fully displayed and catalogued.

Dresden

Historisches Museum
Costume collection from the sixteenth century onwards. Illustrated catalogue available in large libraries.

GREAT BRITAIN

Bath

Museum of Costume, Assembly Rooms − A fine collection of costumes from 1610 to the present day, displayed with imagination and attraction. Twentieth century dress is comprehensive for all decades − an unusual and useful feature.

Belfast, Northern Ireland

Ulster Museum − Costume collection mainly from Northern Ireland *c.* 1750−1930.

Birmingham

City Museum and Art Gallery − Large costume collection from eighteenth century onwards.

Broadway, Worcestershire

Snowshill Manor − Good collection of costumes from the late seventeenth to the nineteenth century.

Cambridge

Fitzwilliam Museum − Paintings.

Edinburgh

Royal Scottish Museum − Large collection of European costume, seventeenth to twentieth century.

National Gallery of Scotland − Paintings.

Scottish National Portrait Gallery

Glasgow

Glasgow Art Gallery and Museum − British costumes from 1760−1935.

Gloucester

City Museum and Art Gallery − Large costume collection from the mid-eighteenth century onwards.

Hereford

City Museum and Art Gallery − Large collection of costume and accessories 1750−1930.

Leicester

Museum and Art Gallery – Large costume collection from the sixteenth century onwards.

London

The Victoria and Albert Museum – A very large costume collection. Display in the Costume Court of dress from 1580 onwards. Fashion dolls, also fashion plates mounted in leaf form round the Court. The museum also contains a fine collection of portrait miniatures, textiles, stained glass, sculpture and carvings, as well as its outstanding library.

A branch of the Victoria and Albert Museum is at *Bethnal Green* in the *Museum* where there are costumes from 1750–1935 on display as well as children's costumes from 1780–1890. There is also a large collection of fashion dolls, mainly from the nineteenth century.

The British Museum – A superb collection of jewellery from Minoan, Greek, Etruscan, Roman, pre-historic, Saxon and Medieval periods. Equally fine collection of illuminated manuscripts. The library.

The London Museum – Costumes on display from 1575 to the late nineteenth century.

The National Gallery – Paintings.

The National Portrait Gallery – Painted portraits and a few sculptured busts.

Hampton Court Palace – Paintings.

Manchester

Gallery of English Costume, Platt Hall – An excellent display of costumes from the eighteenth century onwards.

Northampton

Central Museum and Art Gallery – Costume from 1700 to 1930. Specialises in footwear – Roman to the present day.

Worthing

Museum and Art Gallery – Large collection of English costumes, seventeenth century onwards.

York

Castle Museum

English costumes 1740–1930 and accessories.

HOLLAND

Amsterdam

Rijksmuseum – Paintings, tapestries, carved wood sculptures. Costume collection chiefly from the eighteenth and nineteenth centuries.

Assen

Provincial Museum van Drenthe – Prehistoric clothing and footwear from the peat bogs.

's-Gravenhage (The Hague)

Kostuummuseum – Most comprehensive and large collection of costume, mainly eighteenth century, to the present day, as well as varied range of accessories.

The Mauritshuis – Paintings.

Utrecht

Centraal Museum – Good collection of costume, well displayed, from about 1760 to the present day.

HUNGARY

Budapest

Iparművészeti Múzeum (Museum of Decorative Arts) – Costume collection from sixteenth century onwards. Illustrated catalogue available in large libraries.

Magyar Nemzeti Múzeum (Hungarian National Museum) – Very fine collection of costume and accessories from the fifteenth to the twentieth century. Illustrated catalogue available from large libraries.

IRELAND

Dublin

National Museum of Ireland – English and Irish costumes and accessories, 1750–1900.

ITALY

Florence

The Uffizi Gallery – Paintings.

Milan

Pinacoteca di Brera – Paintings.

Naples

Musei e Gallerie Nazionali di Capodimonte – Paintings, mosaics and sculpture, including Roman work from Pompeii and Herculaneum.

Rome

Musei Capitolini – Greek and Roman sculpture.

Musei e Gallerie di Pittura del Vaticano – Paintings and sculpture.

Museo Nazionale di Villa Giulia – Etruscan sculpture, painting and jewellery.

Museo Nazionale Romano (in the Baths of Diocletian). Roman sculpture.

Tarquinia

Museo Nazionale – Etruscan sculpture, painting and jewellery.

Venice

Galleria dell'Accademia – Paintings.

Museo Correr – Paintings and examples of Spanish lace and Italian velvets.

Ca' Rezzonico – Paintings and a few Venetian costumes.

La Scuola Dalmata in the Church of San Giorgio degli Schiavoni. Wall paintings by Carpaccio very useful for costume information.

NORWAY

Bergen

Vestlandske Kunstindustri Museum – Large collection of costumes in store.

Oslo
Kunstindustrimuseet i Oslo – Costumes and accessories from the eighteenth century onwards.

POLAND

Cracow (Kraków)
Muzeum Narodowe w Krakowie (National Museum) Polish dress of the aristocracy showing French influence. Seventeenth to nineteenth centuries. Illustrated catalogue available in large libraries.
Warsaw
Muzeum Narodowe w Warszawie (National Museum) Large collection of costumes, seventeenth to nineteenth century.

RUMANIA

Bucharest
Muzeul de Arta al Republicii Populare Romine – Costume collection, fifteenth to nineteenth century.
Cluj
Muzeul Etnografici al Transilvaniei – Large collection of costume, accessories and jewellery, fashionable and regional.

SPAIN

Barcelona
Museo de Indumentaria, Coleccion Rocamora – Costume museum collection. Excellent collection, finely displayed, of costumes from the seventeenth century to the present day with well displayed accessories.
Museo de Arte de Cataluña – Paintings.
Madrid
Museo del Pueblo Español – Collection of historical and regional costumes.
Museo del Prado – Paintings.
Museo Nacional, del Siglo XIX – Paintings, nineteenth century.
Museo Arqueológico Nacional – Sculpture, mosaics, paintings and jewellery of pre-historic, Roman, Medieval and Renaissance periods.
Museo de las Descalzas Reales – Paintings.

SWEDEN

Göteborg (Gothenburg).
Historiska Museet – Large collection of costumes from the eighteenth century onwards.

Malmö
Malmö Museum – Women's costumes from the eighteenth century onwards. Illustrated catalogue available in large libraries.
Stockholm
Kungl. Livrustkammaren (Royal Armoury) – Costumes of the royal family, sixteenth century onwards.
Nordiska Museet – Very large collection of costumes from 1600–1960.

SWITZERLAND

Basle
Historisches Museum – Paintings and drawings.
Berne
Bernisches Historisches Museum – Eighteenth and nineteenth century dress also a lansquenet costume. Tapestries and painted glass.
Kunstmuseum – Paintings.
Schönenwerd
Schumuseum – Footwear through the ages.
Zürich
Schweizerisches Landesmuseum – Good collection of eighteenth and nineteenth century costumes also jewellery of the Roman, Iron Age and early Medieval periods.

U.S.S.R.

Leningrad
Hermitage Museum – Fine collection of textiles and costumes from the days of Peter the Great until the nineteenth century. Illustrated books of the collection available in large libraries.
Moscow
Gosudarstviennaia Oruzheinaya Palata Moskovskovo Kremlia (The State Armoury in the Kremlin) – Costumes and accessories of tsars, clergy and famous people from the fourteenth century onwards. Also tapestries of the sixteenth and seventeenth centuries.

YUGOSLAVIA

Belgrade
Muzej Primenjene Umetnosti – Costume collection of the nineteenth century. Serbian and European.
Zagreb
Muzej za Umjetnost i Obrt – Costume collection of the years 1700–1915 of Croatian aristocratic families. Dress especially from Vienna, Paris and Budapest.

Bibliography

Bibliography

Books recommended for further study listed under the country, area or civilisation concerned.

Books are available in the English language unless stated otherwise.

European General

ASSAILLY, G. D'., *Ages of Elegance, five thousand years of fashion and frivolity*, Macmillan, 1973.

BIGELOW, M. S., *Fashion in History*, Burgess Publishing Co., Minneapolis, U.S.A., 1970.

BOEHN, M. VON, *Modes and Manners*, Vols. 1–4, Harrap, 1932–5.

BOEHN, M. VON and FISCHEL, O., *Modes and Manners of the Nineteenth Century*, 4 Vols., Dent, 1927.

BOSTON MUSEUM OF FINE ARTS, U.S.A., *She walks in Splendour. Great Costumes 1550–1950*, French, English and American costumes, 1963.

BOUCHER, F., *A History of Costume in the West*, Thames and Hudson, 1967.

BOUQUET, A. C., *European Brasses*, Batsford, 1967.

BRAUN, RONSDORF, M., *The Wheel of Fashion* (Costume since the French Revolution 1789–1929), Thames and Hudson, (English edition 1964).

BRUHN, W. and TILKE, M., *A Pictorial History of Costume*, Zwemmer, 1955.

CHASE, E. W. and I., *Always in Vogue*, Doubleday and Co. Inc., New York, 1954.

CONTINI, M., *Fashion from Ancient Egypt to the Present Day*, Hamlyn, 1967.

DAVENPORT, M., *The Book of Costume*, 2 Vols., Crown Publishers Inc., New York, 1968.

EVANS, M., *Costume Throughout the Ages*, J. B. Lippincott Co., Philadelphia, 1950.

EWING, E., *Fashion in Underwear*, Batsford, 1971.

HILL, M. H. and BUCKNELL, P. A., *The Evolution of Fashion*, Batsford, 1967.

HOLLAND, V., *Hand-Coloured Fashion Plates 1770–1899*, Batsford, 1955.

HOTTENROTH, F., *Le Costume chez les Peuples Anciens et Modernes*, 2 Vols. Almand Guerinet, 1884–91, reprinted E. Weyhe, New York, 1947.

KELLY, F. M. and SCHWABE, R., *Historic Costume 1490–1790*, Batsford, 1929; *A Short History of Costume and Armour 1066–1800*. Batsford 1931, reprinted David and Charles, 1972.

KÖHLER, C. and SICHART, E. VON, *A History of Costume*, Harrap 1928, Dover paperback, 1963.

KYBALOVÁ, L., HERBENOVÁ, O. and LAMAROVÁ, M., *A Pictorial Encyclopedia of Fashion*, Hamlyn, 1968.

LAVER, J., *Costume*, Cassell, 1963; *A Concise History of Costume*, Thames and Hudson, 1969.

LELOIR, M., *Histoire du Costume de L'Antiquité à 1914*, 5 Vols. Ernst, 1933–49. In French.

LOOMIS, R. S., *Arthurian Legends in Medieval Art*, Oxford University Press, 1938.

MOORE, D. L., *Fashion Through Fashion Plates 1771–1970*, Ward Lock, 1971.

MORYSON, F., *An Itinerary Containing His Ten Yeeres Travell through the Twelve Dominions of Germany, Bohmerland, Sweitzerland, Netherland, Denmarke, Poland, Italy, Turky, France, England, Scotland and Ireland*, James Mac Lelose and Sons, Glasgow University Press, 1907 (First printed John Beale, London, 1617).

NORRIS, H., *Costume and Fashion*, 4 Vols, Dent, 1924–38.

RACINET, M. A., *Le Costume Historique*, 6 Vols., Firmin-Didot et Cie, Paris, 1888. In French.

RUBENS, A., *A History of Jewish Costume*, Weidenfeld and Nicholson, 1973.

RUPPERT, J., *Le Costume*, 5 Vols. Les Arts Decoratifs Serics, Flammarion, 1958. In French.

SAUNDERS, E., *The Age of Worth*, Longmans Green and Co., 1954.

STOCKAR, J., *Kultur und Kleidung der Barockzeit*, Werner Classen Verlag, Zürich/Stuttgart, 1963. In German, English summary.

THIEL, E., *Geschichte des Kostüms (Europäische Mode von der Antike bis zur Gegenwart)* Henschelverlag Kunst und Gesellschaft, Berlin, 1960. In German.

THIENEN, F. VAN, *Acht Eeuwen Westeuropees Kostuum, 1100–1960*, De Haan, Antwerp, 1960. In French and Dutch.

WAFFEN UND KOSTÜMKUNDE. Journal published in Dresden and, later, Berlin. Full title Zeitschrift der Gesellschaft für historische Waffen und Kostümkunde. Articles on all European countries.

WAUGH, N., *Corsets and Crinolines*, Batsford, 1970.

WEIDITZ, C., *Das Trachtenbuch des Christoph Weiditz von seinen reisen nach Spanien (1529) und den Niederlanden (1531/2)*. Verlag von Walter de Gruyter and Co., Berlin and Leipzig, 1927.

WILCOX, R. T., *The Mode in Costume*, Scribner, New York, 1947; *The Mode in Footwear*, Scribner, New York, 1948; *The Mode in Hats and Headdresses*, Scribner, New York, 1948; *The Dictionary of Costume*, Batsford, 1970.

WORTH, J. P., *A Century of Fashion*, Little, Brown and Co., Boston, 1928.

The Ancient World

This section includes all races and civilisations up to the year AD 1000.

BROHOLM, H. C. and HALD, M., *Costumes of the Bronze Age in Denmark,* Nyt Nordisk Forlag, Copenhagen, 1940.

EVANS, M. M. and ABRAHAMS, E., *Ancient Greek Dress,* Argonaut Inc. Chicago, 1964.

HALD, M., *Olddanske Tekstiler,* Nordisk Forlag, Copenhagen, 1950. In Danish, English summary.

HOPE, T., *Costume of the Greeks and Romans,* a Dover paperback, 1962 taken from Thomas Hope's 'Costume of the Ancients' first published 1812 by William Miller.

HOUSTON, M., *Ancient Greek, Roman and Byzantine Costume and Decoration,* Black, 1947.

KIVIKOSKI, E., *Finland,* Thames and Hudson, 1967.

KLINDT-JENSEN, O., *Denmark before the Vikings,* Thames and Hudson, 1957.

LAVER, J. and KLEPPER, E., *Costume in Antiquity,* Thames and Hudson, 1964.

NEUSTUPNY, E. and J., *Czechoslovakia,* Thames and Hudson, 1961.

PIGGOTT, S., (Ed.) *The Dawn of Civilisation,* Thames and Hudson, 1961.

QUENNELL, M. and C. H. B., *Everyday Life in Prehistoric Times,* Batsford, 1968.

SAVORY, H. N., *Spain and Portugal,* Thames and Hudson, 1968.

TACITUS (Tr. H. Mattingley), *The Agricola and the Germania,* Penguin Books, 1970.

TALBOT-RICE, T., *The Scythians,* Thames and Hudson, 1957.

TRUMP, D. H., *Central and Southern Italy before Rome,* Thames and Hudson, 1966.

Austria

STUBENRAUCH, P. VON, *Wiener Moden,* 1826.

Czechoslovakia

SKROŇKOVÁ, O., *Fashions through the Centuries, Renaissance, Baroque and Rococo,* Spring Books, 1959.

Denmark

CHRISTENSEN, S. F., *Kongedragterne fra 17 og 18 aarhundrede,* 2 Vols. De Danske Kronologiske Samling paa Rosenborg, København, 1940. In Danish, English notes to plates.

Finland

PYLKÄNEN, R., *Barokin Pukumuoti Suomessa 1620–1720* (Baroque period in Finland), Suomen Muinaismuistoyhdistyksen Aikakauskirja Finska Fornminnesföreningens Tidskrift, Helsinki, 1970; *Säätyläispuku Suomessa. Vanhemmalla Vaasa-ajalla. 1550–1620.* (The Costume of the nobility, clergy and burghers in the earlier Vasa period), same publisher as above, Helsinki, 1955. In Finnish but English summary.

France

EVANS, J., *Dress in Medieval France,* Oxford University Press, 1952.

GRAND-CARTERET, J., *Les Élégances de la Toilette. Robes, chapeaux, coiffures, 1780–1825.* Michel Albin, Paris, 1911. In French.

HACHETTE, Librairie, *Encyclopédie par l'image. Histoire du Costume en France,* Hachette, 1924.

MUSÉE DU COSTUME DA LA VILLE DE PARIS, Illustrated booklets from the Museum Collection. Text in French. *Costumes Français 1725–1925,* 1962; *Élégances du XVIIIᵉ Siècle, 1730–94,* 1963; *Costumes Français du XVIᵉ au XXᵉ Siècle,* 1957; *Costumes Français de 1750 a 1900,* 1963; *Costumes de Cour et de Ville du Premier Empire,* 1958; *Modes de la Belle Époque, 1890–1910,* 1962; *Modes Romantiques, Costumes Français, 1820–45,* 1960; *Poufs et Tournures, Costumes Français de femmes et des enfants, 1869–89,* 1959.

PITON, C., *Le Costume Civil en France du XIIIᵉ au XIXᵉ Siècle,* Flammarion, 1913. In French.

SEE, R., *Le Costume de la Révolution à nos jours,* Gazette des Beaux Arts, 1929. In French.

WILHELM, J., *Histoire de la Mode,* Librairie Hachette, 1955. In French.

Germany

DIEDERICHS, E., *Deutsches Leben der Vergangenheit in Bildern,* 2 Vols. 15th to 18th century. 1760 pictures of wood cuts and engravings, 1908.

DIE MODENWELT, Collection of 19th century fashion plates, Berlin, 1890.

EBERHARDT, H., Booklet of *Deutsches Ledermuseum und Deutsches Schumuseum, Offenbach-am-Main, 1961.* In German.

FISCHEL, O., *Chronisten der Mode. Mensch and Kleid in Bildern aus drei Jahrtausenden,* Müller Verlag, Potsdam, 1923.

FRANKFURT-AM-MAIN, *Frankfurter Modenspiegel,* History Museum catalogue, 1962.

HOTTENROTH, F., *Handbuch der Deutschen Tracht,* Verlag von Gustav Weise, Stuttgart, 1895–6. In German.

MARTIN, K., *Minnesänger, Vierundzwanzig farbige Wiedergaben aus Manessischen Liederhandschrift,* 2 Vols. Verlage Woldemar Klein, Baden-Baden and Dr. Rudolf Georgi, Aachen, 1966. Notes in English. 24 colour plates of costume about 1290–1310.

MUTZEL, H., *Kostümkunde für Sammler,* Berlin, 1921.

NAUMANN, H., *Die Minnesinger in Bildern der Manessischen Handschrift,* Insel-Verlag, Leipzig, 1933. In German.

NIENHOLDT, E., *Kostümkunde,* Klinkhardt and Biermann, Brunswick, 1961.

STAATLICHE KUNSTSAMMLUNG, *Historische Prunkkleidung,* Catalogue of costume collection, Dresden, 1963.

WALDBURG-WOLFEGG, J. GRAF, *Das Mittelalterliche Hausbuch,* Prestel-Verlag, Munich, 1957.

Great Britain

BOUQUET, A. C., *Church Brasses*, Batsford, 1956.

BROOKE, I., *English Costume of the Early Middle Ages*, Black, 1964; *English Costume of the Later Middle Ages*, Black, 1964; *English Costume of the Age of Elizabeth*, Black, 1964; *English Costume of the Seventeenth Century*, Black, 1964; *English Costume of the Eighteenth Century*, Black, 1964; *English Costume of the Nineteenth Century*, Black, 1964; *English Children's Costume since 1775*, Black, 1964; *Dress and Undress, The Restoration and Eighteenth Century*, Methuen, 1958.

BUCK, A., *Victorian Costume and Costume Accessories*, Herbert Jenkins, 1961.

CLAYTON, M., *Catalogue of Rubbings of Brasses and Incised Slabs*, Victoria and Albert Museum. H.M.S.O., 1968.

CUNNINGTON, C. W. and P., *Handbook of English Costume in the Sixteenth Century*, Faber and Faber, 1954; *Handbook of English Costume in the Seventeenth Century*, Faber and Faber, 1954; *Handbook of English Costume in the Nineteenth Century*, Faber and Faber, 1954; *Handbook of English Mediaeval Costume*, Faber and Faber, 1954; *A Dictionary of English Costume, 960–1900*, Black, 1965.

CUNNINGTON, C. W., *English Women's Clothing in the Nineteenth Century*, Faber and Faber, 1952; *English Women's Clothing in the Present Century*, Faber and Faber, 1952.

CUNNINGTON, P. and BUCK, A., *Children's Costume in England, 1300–1900*, Black, 1965.

EWING, E., *History of Twentieth Century Fashion*, Batsford, 1974.

GIBBS-SMITH, C., *The Fashionable Lady of the 19th Century*, Victoria and Albert Museum, H.M.S.O., 1960.

LAVER, J., *Children's Fashions in the 19th Century*, Batsford, 1951; *Nineteenth Century Costume*, Victoria and Albert Museum, 1947; *Taste and Fashion – from the French Revolution until Today*, Harrap, 1937.

LAVER, J. and KLEPPER, E., *Costume through the Ages*, Thames and Hudson, 1964.

MAXWELL, S. and HUTCHINSON, R., *Scottish Costume, 1550–1850*, Black, 1958.

SITWELL, S., *Gallery of Fashion, 1790–1822*, Batsford, 1949.

YARWOOD, D., *English Costume from the 2nd Century BC to 1972*, Batsford, 1972; *Outline of English Costume*, Batsford, 1972.

Holland

CENTRAAL MUSEUM, UTRECHT. *De Costuum-Verzameling, 1750–1930*, Catalogue of the Museum Collection, 1947.

HAAGS GEMEENTEMUSEUM (Municipal Museum of the Hague), *Huis in Huis Uit, 1770–1970*, Exhibition catalogue of dress and furniture, 1971.

NEDERLANDS KOSTUUMMUSEUM, DEN HAAG (Dutch Costume Museum at The Hague), *Kabinet van Mode en Smaak*, (live models in dresses from the Museum Collection. Text in Dutch, English Summary, F. Van Thienen; *Vrouwenkostuum, 1800–1820* (Women's Dress). English text, 1966.

THIENEN, F. VAN, *Das Kostüm der Blutezeit Hollands, 1600–1660*, Deutscher Kunstverlag, Berlin, 1930. In German; *The Great Age of Holland, 1600–50*, Harrap, 1951.

Hungary

EGYED, E., *Három évszázad divatja* (Three centuries of fashion), Budapest, 1965. Costumes from the Hungarian Museum of Decorative Arts, Budapest. In Hungarian, summary in French.

HÖLLRIGL, J., *Catalogue of Costume Exhibition at the Hungarian Museum of Decorative Arts, Budapest*, 1938.

Italy

BENTIVEGNA, F. C., *Abbigliamento e Costume nella Pittura Italiana*, 2 Vols. 15th to 18th century. Carlo Bestetti, Rome, 1962. In Italian.

LEVI-PISETZKY, R., *Storia del Costume in Italia*, Istituto Editoriale Italiano, Milan, 1964–9. 4 Vols. in Italian.
Vol. 1. *Il Costume dopo la caduta dell' impero d'occidente* (AD 475–1300).
Vol. 2. *Il Trecento ed il Quattrocento* (14th and 15th century).
Vol. 3. *Il Cinquecento ed il Seicento* (16th and 17th century).
Vol. 4. *Il Settecento* (18th century).
Vol. 5. *L'ottocento* (19th century).

RODOCANACHI, E., *La Femme Italienne a L'Époque de la Renaissance*, Hachette et Cie, Paris, 1907. In French.

Poland

GUTKOWSKA-RYCHLEWSKA, M. and TASZYCKA, M., *Fashionable Clothes and Accessories of the 19th Century*, Narodowe Museum, Cracow, 1967. In Polish, French captions.

KOPFF, A., *Muzeum Narodowe w Krakowie*, Kraków, 1962. In Polish.

MUZEUM NARODOWE W KRAKOWIE, *L'Art à Cracovie, 1350–1550*, Published by the Museum, 1964. In French.

Spain and Portugal

BERNIS, C., *Indumentaria Española en tiempos de Carlo V (1500–60)*, Instituto Diego Velazquez de Consejo Superior de Investigaciones Cientificas, Madrid, 1962. In Spanish. Spanish Costume.

MADRAZO, C. B., *Indumentaria Medieval Española*, Instituto Diego Velazquez de Consejo Superior de Investigaciones Cientificas, Madrid, 1955. In Spanish. Spanish Medieval Costume.

ROCAMORA, M., *Museo de Indumentaria Coleccion Roca-mora*, Graficas Europeas, Barcelona, 1970. Catalogue of Museum Collection, in Spanish.

Sweden

BERGMAN, E., *Nationella Dräkten* (18th century national dress in Sweden under Gustav III), Nordiska Museets, Stockholm, 1938. In Swedish, summary in English.

EKSTRAND, G., *Karl X Gustavs dräkta*, Kungl. Livrust-kammaren (The Royal Armoury), Stockholm, 1959. In Swedish, English summary.

HAZELIUS-BERG, G., *Modedräkter fråu 1600–1900*, Nordiska Museet, 1952. In Swedish, English summary.

MALMÖ MUSEUM, *Katalog över Dräktsamlingen, Kvin-nodräkte* (Women's dress from costumes in the Museum), 1928.

NØRLAND, P., *Nordisk Kultur XV : Dragt*, Albert Bonniers Forlag, Stockholm, 1941. In Swedish.

NYLÉN, A. M., *Journal of the Royal Armoury*, Kungl. Livrustkammaren, 1967; *20th Century, The Clothing Industry and Fashion*, Stockholm, 1968.

SVÄRDSTRÖM, S., *The Royal Armoury*, Kungl. Livrust-kammaren, Stockholm, 1966.

WALLIN, S., *Kopparmattes kläder och hans samtidas* (reprint from Svenska Kulturbilder Vol. 1), Stock-holm, 1934; *Ståndsmässig Dräkt* (Reprint from Svenska Kulturbilder Vol. 4), Stockholm, 1931.

Switzerland

DAS NEUE SCHUMUSEUM BALLY, *Ausstellung Felsgarten*, Schönenwerd, 1942.

FORRER, R., *Archäologisches zur Geschichte des Schues aller zeiten*, Bally-Schumuseums in Schonenwerd, 1942.

U.S.S.R.

LEVINSON-NECIAIEVA, *Costume of the 17th Century and Costume of the 18th Century*, Booklets from the collection in the Oruzeinaia Palace in the Moscow Kremlin, 1929–30. In Russian.

MOSCOW KREMLIN, *The State Armoury Museum Collec-tion*, Oruzeinaia Palata, 1958. In four languages, including English.

RYBAKOV, B. A., *Treasures in the Kremlin*, Peter Nevill, London, 1962.

SHARAYA, N. M. and MOISCENKO, E. I., *Russian Dress from the 18th to the end of the 19th Century*, Catalogue of the Collection in The Hermitage Museum, Leningrad, 1962. In Russian.

Yugoslavia

MUSEJ ZA OMJETNOST I OBRT, Miniatures in Yugoslavia, Zagreb, 1964.

Index

The numerals in **bold** type refer to the figure
numbers of the illustrations.
Sub headings are listed chronologically.